BERLITZ®

DISCOVER
TURKEY

Edited and designed by
D & N Publishing,
Ramsbury, Wiltshire.

Cartography by
Visual Image, Street, Somerset.

Although we have made every effort to ensure the accuracy of all the information in this book, changes do occur. We cannot therefore take responsibility for facts, addresses and circumstances in general which are constantly subject to alteration.

If you have any new information, suggestions or corrections to contribute to this guide, we would like to hear from you. Please write to Berlitz Publishing at one of the above addresses.

Acknowledgements

The author would like to thank the following people for their help in the production of this guide: Simru Önhon of the Turkish Ministry of Tourism in London; Serkan Kılıç and his family, and İnayet the barber in Antakya; Taco and Murat in Izmir; Aymer Selma Güler in Istanbul; Mehmet (Hans) Turan and Ahmet Büyükzeytinci of Dervish Brothers; Ahmet Duvarcı and Naim Çalişkan in Konya; Micky and Michelle at the Seçkin Konaklar in Bodrum; Nivedita Navang and Bhupinder Sagoo at Olympos; Gökhan Temiş and Yusuf Eroğlu in Selçuk; and Necati Alaylar in Erzurum.

Photographic Acknowledgements

All photographs by the author except for the following: Colorific 317; Hulton Deutsch Collection 64; Telegraph Colour Library 318/19; Trip 118.

Photograph previous page: Rock-cut dwellings, Zelve

 The Berlitz tick is used to indicate places or events of particular interest.

Phototypeset, originated and printed by C.S. Graphics, Singapore.

BERLITZ®

DISCOVER

TURKEY

Neil Wilson

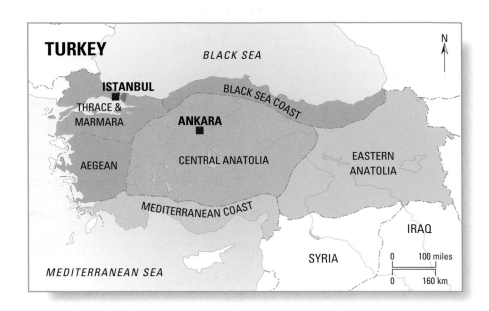

Contents

Maps: Turkey 4, 8; Ottoman Empire 55; Roman Provinces 48; Thrace and Marmara 122; Aegean Region 150; Mediterranean Coast 198; Ankara and Central Anatolia 252; Cappadocia 274; Black Sea Coast 298; Eastern Anatolia 314.

Town and Ruin Plans: Ankara 255; Ephesus 172; Istanbul 87; Konya 287; Pamukkale 186; Pergamum 152; Perge 229; Topkapi Palace 91.

Talking Turkey

Turkey is a big country. From Izmir in the west to Van in the east is 1,450km (900 miles). It covers an area of 780,000 sq km (301,000 sq miles), bigger than Great Britain and France added together – obviously, you won't be able to see it all in a single trip, unless you plan to stay for five or six months. Most visitors have their first experience of Turkey on a package holiday to Istanbul or one of the Aegean or Mediterranean resorts, and this book concentrates on the attractions found in those areas. However, on subsequent visits you may be a bit more adventurous and explore further off the beaten track, so we have included coverage of the most important sights in the rest of the country.

First of all, of course, you will want to get organized for your next holiday. The following section includes all the information you will need to plan any number of successful trips to Turkey.

When to Go

Turkey's huge size means that it spans a number of climatic zones, from the tem-

Turkey offers spectacular scenery, a colourful culture, and friendly people. Its shops abound with quality carpets and handicrafts, and its restaurants serve a range of delicious foods.

perate forests of the Black Sea coast to the semi-arid plains of southeastern Anatolia.

Istanbul enjoys a temperate climate with warm, dry summers and cool, wet winters. July and August are the hottest months. The prevailing wind, the *poyraz,* blows down the Bosphorus from the northeast, and provides a welcome cooling breeze, but when the wind drops it can become uncomfortably humid, with occasional thunderstorms. The southwest wind, called the *lodos,* usually brings storms on the Sea of Marmara. The best times to visit the city are the months of May and June, when the days are pleasantly warm, and the shores of the Bosphorus are bright with spring flowers and the blossom of Judas trees. Winter is generally cold, wet and uncomfortable. Snow is not uncommon in midwinter, though it rarely lies for more than a few days.

7

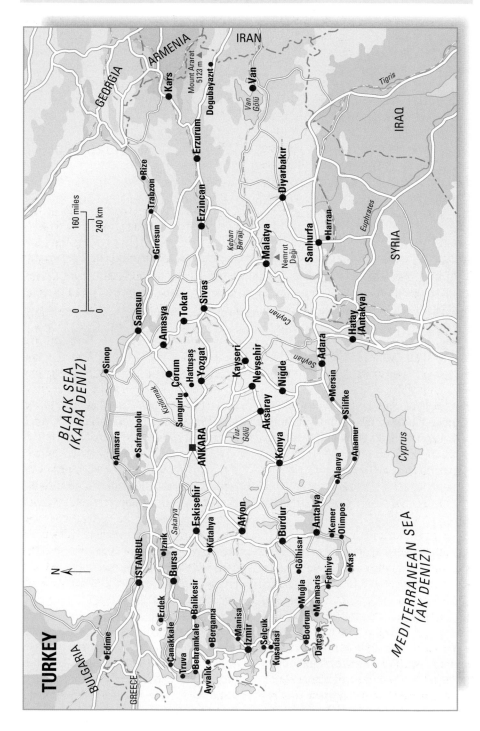

The south and west coasts, where the holiday resorts are concentrated, enjoy a typical Mediterranean climate, with hot, dry summers and mild, rainy winters. Summer days are generally hot and sunny, temperatures often reaching 29°C (84°F) and above, while the sea is warm enough for comfortable swimming from April to October. A brisk northwesterly breeze, called the *meltemi,* often sets in during the afternoon, providing good sport for experienced sailors and windsurfers. Around late September or early October, thunderstorms mark the end of the settled summer weather, though fine days often continue well into November. The package holiday season finishes at the end of October – if you visit the Mediterranean coast in November you will have the place almost to yourself, with the added advantage of cheaper hotel prices.

The Black Sea coast has warm summers and mild winters, but the sea is noticeably chillier than the Mediterranean and Aegean. This is the wettest part of Turkey, with rain falling throughout the year, especially in the east towards the Georgian border.

Extensive mountain ranges shield the interior of Turkey from rain-bearing winds, creating a semi-arid climate in central and eastern Anatolia. The high steppes that stretch from Ankara to Cappadocia see little rainfall, with hot, dry summers and cold winters. In the northeast the city of Erzurum bakes in summer temperatures as high as 30°C (86°F), but freezes under a blanket of snow from December to March. The summit of Nemrut Dağı is snowbound for most of the year – July and August are the best times to visit. The hottest part of the country is the Euphrates Basin between Gaziantep and Diyarbakır, where the summer afternoons can reach 42°C (108°F).

As with Istanbul, May and June are the best months for a trip to central Anatolia. The plains are ablaze with wildflowers, and the mountain peaks are still scenically clad in snow, while the weather is settled and sunny without being too hot.

What to Take With You

Clothing

The holiday resorts of the Aegean and Mediterranean coasts are very easy going as far as clothes are concerned – beachwear, shorts and T-shirts are the order of the day. But in cities such as Istanbul, Ankara and Izmir, a slightly more formal dress code is observed – long trousers or skirt with a shirt or blouse. Many tourists wear shorts in Istanbul, even though the practice is generally frowned upon by the locals, especially if you venture near or into a mosque. In the less tourist frequented towns and villages of central and eastern Anatolia you should dress fairly soberly to avoid offending local sensibilities.

From June to September the days are usually hot and sunny – lightweight cotton clothes are the most comfortable choice – but evenings sometimes turn cool, especially in spring and autumn, so take along a jacket or sweater. Remember also to take a long-sleeved shirt, sun hat and sunglasses to protect against the strong midday sunshine. Good walking

Much of central Anatolia is dry steppe land, but the lush green valleys of the Aladağ mountains are well watered by melting snow (overleaf).

shoes or boots are recommended if you intend to explore archaeological sites. During the winter, warm clothes and a raincoat or umbrella will be needed.

Respectable clothing should, of course, be worn when visiting mosques and other Islamic monuments – long trousers or skirt, a long-sleeved shirt or blouse, and a headscarf for women. At the Blue Mosque in Istanbul, robes are provided for unsuitably clad tourists. Remember to take off your shoes before entering a mosque.

Useful Extras

A small day pack or 'bumbag' is useful for carrying travel documents, money, camera, spare film, sunglasses, maps, reading material, your copy of *Discover Turkey*, and any other odds and ends. A Swiss Army knife and a small flashlight are worth their weight in gold on anything but the simplest package holiday trip. In summer, insect repellent will come in useful, plus a mosquito killer for your hotel room – the best kind is the small plug-in hotplate that heats a replaceable tablet of insecticide, releasing an odourless vapour for up to eight hours. If you are planning to stay in budget accommodation, soap, towel, toilet tissues and a universal sink plug are recommended. But whatever you do, don't pack too much. There is a lot to be said for the old adage – decide how much money and how much luggage you need, then take twice as much money and half as much gear.

Health and Medical Care

The main health hazards in Turkey are sunburn and travellers' diarrhoea. Take along a sun hat, sunglasses and plenty of high-factor sun-screen. Cover up or stay indoors during the middle part of the day, and limit your sunbathing sessions to half an hour or less until you begin to tan. Sunburn can seriously ruin your holiday.

Travellers' diarrhoea can be avoided by eating only freshly cooked food, and drinking only bottled water and canned or bottled drinks (without ice). Avoid restaurants that look dirty, food from street stalls, undercooked meat, salads and fruit (except fruit you can peel yourself, such

In country areas the traveller will be the object of much friendly curiosity to local school children.

as bananas, oranges and melons), dairy products and tap water. The standards of hygiene in most tourist hotels and restaurants are usually quite adequate, but you can never be sure.

If you are unfortunate enough to be laid low by a stomach bug, rest up and take plenty of fluids to avoid dehydration – soft drinks will do, but a solution of four heaped teaspoons of sugar and a half-teaspoon of salt in a litre of bottled water is best. Most cases clear up in three or four days; if diarrhoea persists for more than a week, seek medical advice – your hotel will be able to recommend a doctor.

For minor ailments, seek advice from the local **pharmacy** (*eczane*). These are usually open during normal shopping hours. After hours, at least one shop remains open all night, called the *nöbet* or *nöbetci*; its location is posted in the window of all other pharmacies.

There are no compulsory **immunization** requirements for entry into Turkey. Up-to-date vaccinations for tetanus, polio, typhoid and hepatitis A are recommended, especially for independent travellers who intend 'roughing it' in rural areas. There is a slight **malaria** risk from March until October on the Mediterranean coast between Antalya and Antakya, and along the Syrian border. If you intend to visit these areas, you should take a course of anti-malaria tablets (available from your doctor at home).

A small **first-aid kit** comes in handy, especially if you are travelling with kids. Keep it small – Band-Aids, tweezers, a wound dressing, a bandage, antiseptic cream, aspirin, and antihistamine ointment for insect bites and stings should allow you to cope effectively with minor disasters without having to seek out a doctor or pharmacist.

*O*ne of the mainstays of Turkish cuisine is the abundance of fresh fruit and vegetables.

Insurance

There is no free health care for visitors to Turkey – all medical services must be paid for, and doctors and hospitals often expect immediate cash payment. British travellers can find much useful advice in the Department of Health's free booklet *Health Advice for Travellers*, available by telephoning the Health Literature Line on 0800 555777; in the USA, call the Center for Disease Control International Travellers' Hotline on (404) 332 4559.

Medical treatment can be very expensive, so you should not leave home without adequate insurance, preferably including cover for an emergency flight home in the event of serious injury or illness. Your travel agent, bank, building society or insurance broker can provide a comprehensive policy which will cover not only medical costs, but also theft or loss of money and possessions, delayed or cancelled flights, and so on.

Tourist Information Offices

The Turkish Ministry of Tourism's overseas offices can provide information to help you plan your trip. They supply a wide range of colourful and informative brochures and maps, including lists of hotels and campsites.

UK: 170-173 Piccadilly, London W1V 9DD, tel. (0171) 734 8681; fax (0171) 491 0773.
USA: 821 United Nations Plaza, New York, NY 10017, tel. (212) 687 2194; fax (212) 599 7568.
1717 Massachusetts Avenue NW, Suite 306, Washington DC 20036, tel. (202) 429 9844; fax (202) 429 5649.

The Ministry of Tourism has tourist information offices (*Turizm Danışma Bürosu*) in cities and tourist resorts throughout the country. The staff can help with general enquiries, advise on local accommodation, and provide official guides and interpreters, but outside of Istanbul and the main resorts they rarely have much in the way of maps, literature or detailed information.

Opening hours are generally 8.30am to 12.30pm, and 1.30pm to 5.30pm, closed Saturday and Sunday; branches in major tourist areas stay open longer, including weekends. Most towns also have an information office run by the local authorities. The principal offices in Turkey are listed below:

Istanbul
Meşrutiyet Caddesi 57, Tepebaşı, Beyoğlu, tel. (212) 243 3472. Open 9am to 5pm, Monday to Friday. There are smaller offices on Divan Yolu in Sultanahmet (by the tram stop), and in the lobby of the Hilton Hotel in Taksim.

Thrace and Marmara
Edirne: Talatpaşa Caddesi 76A, tel. (284) 225 5260.
Çanakkale: Vilayet Konağı, tel. (286) 217 5012.
Bursa: Fevzi Çakmak Caddesi, Fomara İşhanı Kat 6, tel. (224) 254 2274.

Aegean Coast
Bergama: Izmir Caddesi 54, tel. (232) 633 1862.
Izmir: Gaziosmanpaşa Bulvarı (near Cumhuriyet Meydanı), tel. (232) 484 2147. Open daily 8.30am to 7pm (5pm in winter).
Kuşadası: Liman Caddesi (on corner opposite entrance to ferry and cruise ship terminal), tel. (256) 614 1103. Open daily 8am to 6pm (8pm July and August).
Bodrum: Oniki Eylül Meydanı (on quayside below St Peter's Castle), tel. (252) 316 1091. Open 8am to 8pm Monday to Friday, 9am to 7.30pm Saturday, closed Sunday.
Pamukkale: Örenyeri (near the museum), tel. (258) 272 2077.

Mediterranean Coast
Marmaris: İskele Meydanı (by the ferry harbour), tel. (252) 412 1035. Open daily 8am to 8pm in summer; 8am to noon and 1 to 5pm Monday to Friday in winter.

Fethiye: İskele Karşısı (between commercial jetty and marina), tel. (252) 614 1527. Open daily 8am to 8pm in summer; 8am to noon and 1 to 5pm Monday to Friday in winter.
Antalya: Cumhuriyet Caddesi 91, tel. (242) 241 1747. Open 8am to 5.30pm Monday to Friday, 9am to 5pm Saturday and Sunday. There is another small office near the top of the stairs on the south side of the old harbour.
Alanya: Damlataş Caddesi 1, tel. (242) 513 1240.
Silifke: Gazi Mahallesi, Veli Gürten Bozbey Caddesi 6, tel. (324) 714 1151.
Antakya: Vali Ürgen Alanı 47 (on the roundabout on the road north to İskenderun), tel. (326) 216 0610.

Central Anatolia

Ankara: Gazi Mustafa Kemal Bulvarı 121, tel. (312) 229 2631. Open daily 8.30am to 5pm.
Kayseri: Kağnı Pazarı 61 (near the castle), tel. (352) 231 1190.
Ürgüp (Cappadocia): Park İçi, Kayseri Caddesi, tel. (384) 341 4059.
Konya: Mevlana Caddesi 21, tel. (332) 351 1074. Open 8am to 5.30pm Monday to Friday.

Black Sea Coast

Safranbolu: Çeşme Mahallesi, Arasta Çarşısı 7, tel. (372) 712 3863.
Sinop: Hükümet Konağı, Kat 4, tel. (368) 261 5207.
Trabzon: Atatürk Alanı, Meydan Parkı Köşesi, tel. (462) 321 4659. Open daily 8am to 7pm in summer, 8am to 5pm Monday to Saturday in winter.

Eastern Anatolia

Erzurum: Cemal Gürsel Caddesi 9A, tel. (442) 218 5697.

Şanlıurfa: Asfalt Yol Caddesi 4D, tel. (414) 215 2467.
Diyarbakır: Kültür Sarayı, Kat 6, tel. (412) 221 7840.
Van: Cumhuriyet Caddesi 19, tel. (432) 216 2018.

Passports and Customs Regulations

Citizens of the UK and Ireland will need a full passport to enter Turkey (a Visitor's Passport is not acceptable). A visa is required, but you do not have to apply for it in advance – you buy a sticker from the visa desk at your point of entry into Turkey before going through passport control. The cost is £5; no change is given, so each person should take a £5 note with them (Bank of England only – Scottish notes are not accepted); US citizens also require a visa, costing $20, which can be obtained from a Turkish embassy or consulate, or at your point of entry. (Visa regulations change from time to time, and should be confirmed through your travel agent.) Remember that a £10 departure tax is levied on all international departures from UK airports.

Your passport stamp allows you to remain in Turkey for up to three months. If you want to stay for a longer period, you can apply for a residence permit (difficult to get – details from a Turkish Ministry of Tourism information office). Alternatively, you can leave the country for a day or two (e.g. cross into Greece or Bulgaria) then re-enter for another three months.

The purchase and export of **antiquities** is strictly forbidden. If you buy any object which might be classified as an antiquity (e.g. antiques, old coins and even old carpets), make sure that it is from a reputable dealer, who will be able to provide you with an invoice (*fatura*) stating its value. 'Roman' coins and figurines offered by boys at archaeological sites are almost always worthless fakes, and even if they were genuine you would be committing a criminal offence by buying them.

There is no limit on the amount of foreign **currency** that may be brought into Turkey, but no more than US$5,000 worth of Turkish lira can be brought into or taken out of the country. The accompanying table shows what you can take into Turkey duty free and, upon your return home, into your own country. In addition to your personal clothing, you may bring in duty free a camera, five rolls of film, a video camera with five video cassettes, a pair of binoculars, a typewriter, a radio, a tape recorder, and sporting equipment, including a sailboard, which should be declared when you enter the country.

Turkey has applied for membership of the EC. If this is granted, then obviously the customs situation will change.

How to Get to Turkey

By Air

Scheduled Flights

Major airlines fly into Istanbul and Ankara from all over the world. The national airline, THY (*Türk Hava Yolları*, or Turkish Airlines), flies twice daily from London Heathrow to Istanbul, and twice weekly to Izmir, with connecting services to Ankara and other cities throughout Turkey. For details, tel. (0171) 499 4499. British Airways also offers two flights a day from Heathrow to Istanbul. For details, contact British Airways, tel. (0181) 897 4000 (London area) or 0345 222111 (rest of UK).

By shopping around various travel agencies you will find numerous reduced fares, such as APEX and Standby. This is especially true for British and Australian travellers, but remember that discount fares have a number of restrictions. APEX tickets must be booked and paid for 7 to 28 days in advance, depending on destination,

DUTY-FREE ALLOWANCES								
Into:	Cigarettes		Cigars		Tobacco	Spirits		Wine
Turkey*	200	and	50	and	200g	0.5L	or	0.5L
Canada	200	and	50	and	900g	1.1L	or	1L
UK and Ireland	200	or	50	or	250g	1L	and	2L
USA	200	and	100	and	**	1L	and	2L

*In addition to these allowances, you may buy up to 400 cigarettes, 100 cigars and 500g of tobacco from a Turkish duty-free shop when you arrive in the country.

** A reasonable quantity.

(NB: In late 1994 Turkey and the European Union were negotiating an agreement to lift trade barriers, and may enter into a customs union from January 1996. The duty-free allowances for Turkey should then be the same as for EU countries check before you go.)

define a minimum and maximum stay, and charge penalties for cancellations or changes in departure date. Coming from North America you may not find many bargain flights direct to Turkey unless you are flying from New York – Turkish Airlines has a daily direct flight from Newark to Istanbul. For details, call (212) 986 5050. It may well be worth buying a cheap ticket to a major European city, and then travelling on to Turkey from there.

Charter Flights and Package Tours

Charter flights are usually the cheapest way to get to Turkey, but these flights are only available during the main holiday season (April-October), carry many restrictions and offer little flexibility. For instance, most tickets are for stays of multiples of seven nights, departing on a particular day of the week, and often have inconveniently late or early departure times. There is also a legal requirement that accommodation be provided, even on flight-only tickets. This usually takes the form of a hotel voucher, which you may be asked to show on arrival in Turkey. Check the conditions carefully before you buy. Charter flights are available from Dublin, Gatwick, Manchester, Glasgow, and a number of other cities in the UK to Izmir, Dalaman (on the south coast near Marmaris), and Antalya.

There are literally hundreds of package tours available, with flight and accommodation included in the price. These are worth considering if you plan to stay in the one place, though there are also 'two-centre' holidays that combine a trip to Istanbul with a week in an Aegean resort, or a week in Cappadocia followed by a week in Bodrum, or even a week in each of two different resorts. You might like to try a *gület* cruise – one or two weeks aboard a Turkish yacht, cruising the beautiful coastline between Bodrum and Antalya. Gülets are built for comfort, and can accommodate 8 to 12 people. There are also many special interest packages available, which cater to the traveller with a particular interest – hiking, learning to sail, botany, natural history, archaeology. Your travel agent can provide details.

Airports

Atatürk International Airport (*Atatürk Havalimanı*) lies 24km (15 miles) to the southwest of **Istanbul**. The international (*dışhatları*) and domestic (*içhatları*) terminals are linked by a free shuttle bus, with a journey time of about five minutes. The airport has all the facilities you would expect – currency exchange, bank, post office, car hire, tourist information desk, restaurants and duty-free shops. As yet there is no airport hotel – the nearest hotels are in Yeşilköy and Ataköy, about 8km (5 miles) away. A bus service called *Havaş* runs between the airport and the city centre, with services hourly between 6am and 11pm, half hourly from 2 until 6pm; the journey time is around 30 minutes, maybe longer if traffic is heavy. Buses depart from the far side of the car park outside the arrivals hall; setting down points are at Aksaray in the old city, and Şişhane near Taksim Square.

There is also a large and hectic taxi rank outside the arrivals hall. Taxis are faster and more convenient than the bus, taking only 20 to 30 minutes to the city centre. If the rank is very busy, attract the attention of a dispatcher and tell him your destination; he will then direct you to a cab, which may have to be shared. Drivers will usually accept payment in dollars, Deutsche Marks or sterling, but may try to rip you off – it is best to pay in Turkish lira and pay the amount on the meter. Ignore the approaches of shady characters offering cheap fares – they are crooks. Stick to the official yellow taxis. Information – international flights, tel. (212) 573 4093; domestic flights, tel. (212) 574 2443.

Izmir is served by Adnan Menderes Airport, 18km (11 miles) southeast of the city. A rail service connects the airport with Alsancak station in central Izmir; trains run hourly between 7am and midnight. The *Havaş* bus service meets Turkish Airlines flights, and deposits passengers at the THY city terminal near Cumhuriyet Meydanı. Information – international flights, tel. (232) 251 2626; domestic flights, tel. (232) 251 2525.

Many charter flights arrive at **Dalaman** Airport on the southwest coast between Marmaris and Fethiye. It has 24-hour banks, cafés, car-hire desks and tourist information, but there is no public transport service. If you have a flight-only ticket that does not include transport to your resort, then you will have to take a taxi to the bus station in Dalaman town, 6km (4 miles) away, or all the way to the resort. Dalaman is 50km (31 miles) from Fethiye, 120km (75 miles) from Marmaris, 160km (100 miles) from Kaş, and 200km (125 miles) from Bodrum. Information – tel. (252) 692 5899.

Esenboğa Airport is 33km (21 miles) north of **Ankara**, the Turkish capital. *Havaş* buses meet Turkish Airlines flights, departing around 30 minutes after touchdown, and take you to the THY terminal near the railway station in the city centre. Airport-bound buses depart from the terminal about 90 minutes before domestic flight departures, and two hours before international flights. Information – international flights, tel. (312) 312 6026; domestic flights (312) 312 1010.

By Road

From the UK, the main overland route to Turkey passes through Germany, Austria, Hungary, Romania and Bulgaria. You will need to obtain transit visas for passage through Romania and Bulgaria; apply to the appropriate consulates at least 10 days in advance. The distance from London to Istanbul is about 3,000km (1,900 miles); allow at least four days of steady driving. You can cut down on driving time by heading to Italy and using the summer car-ferry services from Venice to Izmir, or from Ancona to Kuşadası. Reservations must be made well in advance.

Motorists planning to take their own vehicle abroad need a full driver's licence, an International Motor Insurance Certificate, and a Vehicle Registration Document. You will also need a Green Card (make sure it's valid for the Asian sector if you plan to cross the Dardanelles or the Bosphorus). An official GB nationality plate must be displayed near the rear number plate, and headlamp beams must be adjusted for driving on the right. Full details are available from the AA and RAC, or from your insurance company.

By Rail

The days of the Orient Express are long gone, and the rail journey from London to Istanbul is long and slow, going via Munich, Vienna, Belgrade and Sofia. A rail ticket is no cheaper than a charter flight, but it does allow more flexibility, especially if you have a Eurail Pass. (A Eurail Pass is valued on all European and Turkish railways – details from your travel agent.) As with road travel, a transit visa is required for Bulgaria. Allow about three days for the full journey from London to Istanbul. For details, contact British Rail at London Victoria, tel. (0171) 834 2345.

By Sea

There are numerous ferry services linking the Italian ports of Venice and Ancona to Izmir, Kuşadası and Antalya. The most popular route is the Turkish Maritime Lines (TML) service from Venice to Izmir, with one departure a week from April to October. The ferry leaves Venice on Saturday night, and arrives at Izmir at midday on Tuesday; the return trip departs Izmir Wednesday afternoon, arriving in Venice on Saturday morning. Services and timetables are subject to frequent changes and cancellations, and should be checked in advance. The UK agent for TML, which runs many Turkish ferries, is Sunquest Holidays Ltd, 9 Grand Parade, Green Lanes, London N4 1JX, tel. (0181) 800 5455.

There are also numerous small ferries that ply daily in summer between the Greek islands and the Turkish coast. The main services are Lesbos–Ayvalık, Çeşme–Chios, Samos–Kuşadası, Kos–Bodrum, Rhodes–Marmaris and Symi–Datça.

Getting Around in Turkey

Istanbul

Istanbul's **bus** (*otobus*) service is cheap and frequent, but often slow and crowded. You can buy tickets in booklets of five or ten from the kiosks (*gişe*) at main bus termini, or from newsstands – look for a sign saying 'IETT bilet'. When you board a bus, place a ticket in the metal box beside the driver (one ticket, *bir* or *tek bilet*, is sufficient for most routes; some longer routes require two tickets, *iki* or *çift bilet*). All buses have a sign on the front showing their destination, and one in the side window showing the route details.

*M*any Greek islands lie *close to the Turkish coast, and can easily be visited on day trips. This ferry runs from Çeşme, near Izmir, to Chios.*

Istanbul has a new **light rail** service (*tramvay*) which runs from Sirkeci out to the Topkapı bus station at the city walls, and on into the suburbs. The section of line between Aksaray and Sirkeci will probably be of most interest to tourists, with stops at Sultanahmet (Ayasofya, Topkapı and the Blue Mosque), Çemberlitaş (Grand Bazaar) and Laleli (hotels). You must first buy a ticket (*bilet*) from a booth near the tram stop, then give it to the attendant as you enter the platform. Trams run every five minutes or so, but can still be very crowded during rush hours. A restored 19th-century tram runs along İstiklal Caddesi, from the top station of the Tünel to Taksim Square.

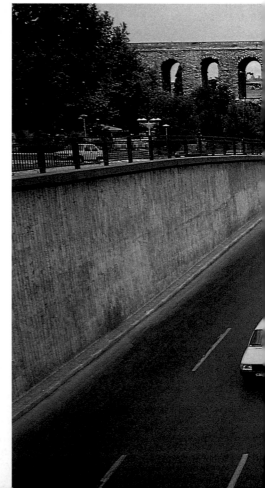

*I*stanbul's new tram line provides a useful link between the hotel district of Laleli and sights such as Hagia Sophia and the Grand Bazaar.

*I*n Istanbul, a car is more of a hindrance than a help. Traffic jams are common, and parking is a problem. Here, traffic thunders beneath a 4th-century aqueduct.

A tiny underground train called the **Tünel** climbs the steep hill from the Galata Bridge up to Pera. To find the bottom station, bear right from the bridge and enter a pedestrian underpass full of shops; at its far end, go up the left-hand stairs, and head for the newsstand straight ahead. The rather inconspicuous entrance is first on the right by the newsstand. Buy a tiny token (*jeton*) and place it in the turnstile slot. Trains leave every few minutes, and take only 90 seconds to reach the top.

The main point of departure for Istanbul's many **ferries** is Eminönü, between Sirkeci railway station and the Galata Bridge. The jetty nearest the bridge is marked '3 Boğaz Hattı' (Bosphorus Lines), for trips along the Bosphorus; next are the '2 Üsküdar' and '1 Kadıköy' jetties, for boats across to the Asian side; then comes the car ferry to Harem, near Haydarpaşa railway station, also on the Asian side; and finally, off to the right through a gate, is the 'Adalar' (Princes' Islands) jetty. For all ferries, buy a ticket or *jeton* from the ticket desk (*gişe*) before departure. Prices and timetables are displayed at the ticket desks. There are also ferries along the Golden Horn, which depart from jetties near the large Chamber of Commerce building west of the Galata Bridge.

The city's **taxis** are bright yellow. They can be hailed in the street, picked up at a rank, or ordered by phone from your

hotel. All taxis have meters, and are required by law to use them. Most drivers are honest, but a few may try to rip you off, especially on the trip from the airport to the city centre; if you want to pay in foreign currency, you will probably be charged more than the going rate. Note that fares increase by 50 per cent between midnight and 6am. If you take a taxi across the Bosphorus Bridge, you will have to pay the bridge toll on top of the fare. Tipping is not compulsory, but is often expected from tourists; the normal practice is simply to round up the fare. Few drivers speak English, so it's worth writing down your destination on a piece of paper, especially if it's off the main tourist trail.

Suburban **trains** run from Sirkeci station westwards along the coast to Yeşilköy. For the visitor, it is useful for getting to Yedikule and Ataköy. Buy a flat-rate *banliyö* (suburban) ticket on the platform, and keep it until the end of your journey.

Air

Turkish Airlines (*Türk Hava Yolları,* or THY) provides an extensive network of internal flights, with the main hubs at Istanbul and Ankara. These flights are complemented by the services of Istanbul Airlines, Turkish Air Transport (*Türk Hava Taşımacılığı,* or THT) and Greenair. Air transport is particularly useful for reaching the far-flung cities of the east, such as Van and Erzurum. Flights can be very busy during the summer, so book your seat as far in advance as possible, reconfirm your reservation the day before your flight, and check in at least an hour before departure. You can get information on fares and schedules from tourist information offices (see p.14-15), and buy tickets from any travel agent. Timetables, reservations and tickets are also available from Turkish Airlines offices, a few of which are listed here:

London: 11-12 Hanover Street, London W1R 9HF, tel. (0171) 499 4499.
Istanbul: 3rd Floor, Cumhuriyet Caddesi 199/201, Harbiye, tel. (212) 248 2631.
Ankara: Atatürk Bulvarı 167/A, Bakanlıklar, tel. (312) 312 4900.
Izmir: Gazi Osman Paşa Bulvarı 1/F (beneath Büyük Efes Hotel), tel. (232) 425 8280.
Antalya: Özel İdare İşhane Altı, Cumhuriyet Caddesi, tel. (242) 242 3432.

There are also THY offices at all Turkish airports. Note that Turkish Airlines offers discount fares for parents travelling with children, for young people who are under 24 years of age, and for senior citizens over 60 years old.

Buses

Long-distance buses are the most important form of public transport in Turkey. They are cheap, frequent and reliable, and those on the main inter-city routes are often air-conditioned. Buses are generally comfortable, except for cigarette smoke and hot sunshine; try to get a seat on the shady side, or take a night bus on long hauls. Most towns and cities have a bus station (*otogar*) located on the outskirts; Istanbul has several. There are a number of national and regional bus companies, and they often compete for business on the more popular routes; the two main national companies are Ulusoy and Varan. Routes, fares and timetables are displayed at the various company offices in the *otogar* – check times and prices before you buy. You are recommended to buy your ticket the day before you intend to travel; buses fill up quickly on popular routes.

Dolmuş

The *dolmuş* is one of the great institutions of Turkish public transport. It is basically a shared taxi – a large saloon car or minibus that shuttles back and forth along a set route for a fixed fare. The departure and destination are shown on a sign in the windscreen. The driver waits at the departure point until all the seats are taken, then drops you off wherever you want along the way (*dolmuş* stops are marked by a sign with a 'D'). You pay the driver once you are inside. In Istanbul, many of the vehicles used as *dolmuş* are beautifully preserved American cars of 1950s vintage.

Trains

The Turkish rail network is fairly extensive, linking most of the country's principal cities (except those in the southwest). The trains, run by Turkish State Railways (*Türkiye Cumhuriyeti Devlet Demiryolları* – TCDD), offer first- and second-class coaches, couchettes, sleeping cars, restaurant cars and buffets. Although more comfortable, rail travel is generally slower than the bus, except on a few express routes. The principal route is Istanbul–Ankara, which is served by the *Fatih Ekspresi* (Conqueror Express), a luxury air-conditioned train which leaves each city daily at 10.30am and arrives at 6pm. (Note that Istanbul has two main railway stations: Sirkeci on the European side, and Haydarpaşa on the Asian side.) There is a twice-daily boat-train service between Istanbul and Izmir (*Marmara Ekspresi*). A ferry leaves Istanbul at 9am and 9pm for Bandırma on the south shore of the Sea of Marmara, where you board a train for the rest of the journey, arriving in Izmir around 11 hours later.

You can get information on fares and timetables from tourist information offices, or from TCDD at the following numbers – Istanbul Sirkeci, tel. (212) 527 0050; Istanbul Haydarpaşa, tel. (216) 336 0475; Ankara Tandoğan, tel. (312) 311 0620; Izmir Basmane, tel. (232) 484 8638.

Ferries

Sea travel offers an appealing alternative to long overland routes, especially during the heat of summer. In addition to the Bosphorus ferries (see above), Turkish Maritime Lines (TML, or TDI – *Türkiye Denizcilil İşletmeleri*) runs a number of car and passenger ferries along the Aegean and Black Sea coasts, south to Izmir and east to Trabzon. The Black Sea car ferry departs every Monday from June to September, calling at Sinop, Samsun, Giresun, Trabzon and Rize. The Izmir ferry leaves Istanbul around 5.30pm and arrives the following day about noon. Tickets are in great demand, and you should make a reservation as far in advance as possible.

A fast and comfortable passenger hydrofoil skims daily across the Sea of Marmara from Istanbul to Yalova, where you can catch a connecting bus to İznik or Bursa. If you are heading south from Gallipoli, you will have to take the ferry from Eceabat to Çanakkale. Ferries depart hourly between 6am and 11pm for the 25-minute crossing. Buy your ticket from the office at the jetty gate before you board.

You can get information on fares and timetables from tourist information offices, from the head office of TML in Rihtim Caddesi, Karaköy, Istanbul, tel. (212) 249 9222, or from TML's UK agent (see HOW TO GET TO TURKEY – BY SEA).

A number of small, independent operators run ferry services from certain Aegean resorts to the Greek Islands (for more information see p.19)

Many ferry services ply the waters along the Turkish coast, with services linking Istanbul to Trabzon and Izmir, Izmir to Venice and Ancona, and the Aegean resorts to the Greek islands. This hydrofoil links Alanya and Cyprus.

Car Hire

Renting a car is a good, though expensive way of getting around Turkey, giving you the freedom to travel at your own pace, and to explore places inaccessible by public transport. There are numerous car-hire firms in Istanbul and the main tourist resorts. Rates vary considerably – local firms often charge considerably less than the big international chains – and you should shop around for the lowest price, but be warned that hiring a car in Turkey is an expensive business. The best rates are to be had by booking and paying for your car before you leave home, either directly through the UK office of an international rental company, or as part of a 'fly-drive' package deal. Check that the quoted rate includes Collision Damage Waiver, unlimited mileage, and VAT (KDV in Turkey), as these can increase the cost considerably. Note that rental car insurance never covers you for broken windscreens and burst tyres – you will have to pay for these repairs out of your own pocket. Unless you hire a 4WD vehicle, you will not be insured for driving on unsurfaced roads.

Normally you must be over 21 to hire a car, and you will need your passport, a full, valid driver's licence (EU model) which you have held for at least 12 months, and a major credit card – cash deposits are prohibitively large.

Driving in Turkey

The first rule of driving in Turkey is that nobody obeys the rules. Be prepared for vehicles overtaking dangerously, jumping red lights, and not giving way when they ought to; this is not a country for the timid driver. Drive on the right, and pass on the left. Speed limits are 130kph (80mph) on motorways, 90kph (55mph) on highways, and 40 or 50kph (25 or 30mph) in towns and cities. Traffic joining a road from the right has priority, unless signs or markings indicate otherwise. One local quirk to be aware of is that drivers making a left turn on a two-lane road often move over to the wrong side of the road before turning – this can be rather disconcerting if you are travelling in the opposite direction.

Driving conditions outside of the cities are generally good on the main roads, except on the inter-city routes between Istanbul, Izmir, Ankara and Antalya, which are plagued with slow-moving trucks. Minor roads (and main roads in the east) are often in poor condition, and occasionally unsurfaced with few signposts. Even on main roads, beware of pedestrians, donkey carts and mopeds, especially near towns where the former often wander across the road with no apparent concern for their safety. They also make driving after dark particularly hazardous.

There are excellent new **toll motorways** between Istanbul, Edirne and Ankara, and around Izmir, which are very fast and often nearly deserted compared to the lorry-choked toll-free roads. You take a ticket from the barrier at the entrance, and pay when you leave the motorway. They are indicated by green road signs, and the words *geçis üçreti* (pay to enter).

In western Turkey, there are plenty of **petrol stations**, and many are open 24 hours a day, so there is little danger of running out of gas. However, there are as yet very few service stations on the toll motorways; make sure you fill the tank before using these roads. Most rental cars run on *normal* (also called *benzin*); premium grade petrol is called *super*, and diesel is *motorin*. Lead-free petrol (*kurşunsuz*) is still not widespread, but can be found in and around Istanbul and Izmir. In the east, petrol stations are fewer and further apart, so always fill up whenever you can.

Parking in town centres is difficult and is tightly controlled. Indeed, in traffic-packed Istanbul and Ankara a car is more of a liability than a luxury. Watch out for signs saying *park yapılmaz* or *park yasaktır* (no parking) – the local police enforce parking regulations rigidly, and will tow away any illegally parked vehicles within a very short time. You will have to pay a fine to retrieve your car from the pound. Your best bet is to look for an official car park (*otopark*).

You can recognize the Turkish **traffic police** (*Trafik Polisi*) by their black and white baseball-style caps and two-tone Renault patrol cars. They patrol city streets and highways, and have the power to issue on-the-spot fines for traffic offences. The main highways have frequent control points (*kontrol bölgesi*), though these are mainly concerned with trucks and commercial vehicles – watch carefully to see whether the officer in charge wants you to stop. If you *are* stopped, smile politely, and show him your registration and rental documents and passport. When he sees you are a tourist, you will probably be waved on. In eastern Turkey there are also many **military road-blocks**, where your papers will be checked and questions

ROAD SIGNS	
These follow European conventions. Main routes are well signposted; sights of interest to tourists are marked by special yellow signs with black lettering, and most warning signs use standard international pictographs. Some common Turkish-language signs are listed below:	
Dikkat	*Caution*
Dur	*Stop*
Girilmez	*No Entry*
Park Yapılmaz	*No Parking*
Şehir Merkezi	*Town Centre*
Tek Yön	*One Way*
Tırmanma Şeridi	*Overtaking Lane*
Yavaş	*Slow*
Yol Ver	*Give Way*
Yol Yapımı	*Roadworks*
24 Saat Açık	*Open 24 Hours*

asked about your intentions. If there is military activity in the area, you may be turned back.

In most towns there should be no problem finding a mechanic to carry out minor **repairs**, especially for Fiats and Renaults, the most common makes. Larger towns and cities have full repair shops and towing services. However, if you break down in the more remote parts of the country, you will probably have to rely on assistance from passing cars, or carry out repairs yourself. If you have a rental car, follow the procedure laid down by the rental company – there will usually be a 24-hour emergency telephone number you can call, and the company will arrange for repairs or a replacement. For tyre repairs, look for a sign saying *lastikçi*, usually painted on an old tyre at the roadside. A repair or replacement can usually be had in less than an hour, and is very cheap by Western standards.

Motorbikes, Scooters and Mopeds

Most major tourist centres in southwest Turkey, such as Kuşadası, Bodrum and Marmaris, have agencies which rent out motorized, two-wheeled transport. Mopeds and scooters are ideal for pottering around the back roads over short distances, but for exploring more than a few miles from town, especially in hilly areas, a motorbike with at least a 50cc engine is necessary. Bigger bikes of 150-200cc are often available, but you will need a motorcycle licence for these, while an ordinary driving licence is sufficient for bikes up to 50cc. Helmets are compulsory.

Check that the quoted rates include the compulsory tax and insurance – they usually don't, and it's a hefty extra. Inspect the bike carefully before taking it, as you will be responsible for repairing and returning it if it breaks down. Remember that motorbikes and scooters are potentially very dangerous. Go slowly and keep to quiet back roads until you get the hang of it – every year there are many bad accidents involving tourists.

Accommodation

The more popular tourist areas of Turkey, such as Istanbul, Cappadocia, and the Aegean and Mediterranean coasts, offer the traveller a wide range of accommodations, from simple pensions to luxury international hotels. Away from the big cities and coastal resorts, however, you are likely to find only low- to middle-grade hotels. Remember, too, that many resort hotels close down for the winter (November to March), making accommodation there more difficult to find. Prices are low compared to western Europe.

The official grading system for **hotels** runs from one to five stars. One-star hotels provide clean, basic rooms with a minimum of frills, though most can offer private bathrooms. At the three-star level, you

The Pera district of Istanbul has a number of grand, turn-of-the-century hotels, such as the Pera Palas and the Londra. The grandeur is faded, but the character remains.

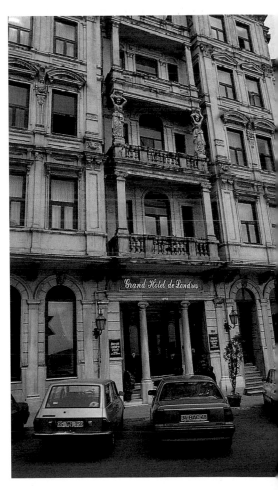

can begin looking for air-conditioning and TV. Five-star establishments are on a par with similar hotels around the world, and charge similarly exorbitant prices. Booking ahead is not normally required for the lower and middle-range hotels, but if you want to be sure of getting a conveniently located hotel during the peak months of July and August, you are advised to make a reservation well in advance.

By law, room rates must be displayed in reception and in the rooms. The quoted rates usually include VAT (KDV in Turkish) at 15 per cent and breakfast. However, these are maximum prices, and you can normally negotiate a reduction, especially for a stay of more than a few days; during the low season, rates drop considerably. It is normal practice to inspect a room before taking it, and this is well worth doing; traffic noise can be a problem in cities, so if the offered room overlooks a busy street, you might like to request another. A list of hotels rated by the Turkish Ministry of Tourism is available from their overseas offices (see TOURIST INFORMATION OFFICES).

The cheapest accommodation on the Aegean and Mediterranean coasts is the **pension** (*pansiyon* in Turkish), a popular choice for backpackers and budget travellers. Rooms are very basic, and toilet and shower facilities are shared. Hot water is rare, and may cost a little extra. If you are travelling on a shoestring, some pensions will allow you to roll out your sleeping bag on the roof for a rock-bottom rate.

First-time visitors should be warned about the vagaries of Turkish plumbing. In the coastal resorts many hotels and pensions have solar-powered water heaters. This means that you are more likely to get a hot shower in the early evening than in the morning. Also, hot and cold taps are often wrongly marked – if the red tap

produces only cold water, try the blue, and be prepared to wait for up to five minutes for hot water to come through. In some cheaper pensions you have to ask the owner to light a fire under the boiler if you want a hot shower.

If your WC has a waste bin beside it, this is for disposing of used toilet paper. Whatever you do, don't put toilet paper (or anything else) in the loo, or you might block not only your own toilet, but your neighbour's as well! However, this is rarely a problem in new and upper grade hotels.

Tap water is considered to be unsafe throughout Turkey, and you are recommended to avoid drinking it. Bottled mineral water is easily obtainable everywhere, carbonated mineral water is called *moden suyu*, still water is *memba suyu*. The electrical supply is 220V/50Hz AC, the same as the UK, but sockets are the standard Continental two-pin type. An adaptor will be needed for UK plugs (buy one before you leave home).

Camping is best enjoyed at official campsites, which provide fresh water, toilets and showers, and often have much-needed shade. In Cappadocia and the coastal resort areas, there are many cheap campsites associated with pensions and small hotels, but these are usually very basic and can be uncomfortable. Rough camping is not illegal, provided you seek permission from the landowner, but you will probably be checked out by the local police and be subject to endless scrutiny by curious village children.

Most campsites are open from April to October. For a full list of campsites, and further information on camping in Turkey, contact the Turkish Ministry of Tourism office in your home country – see TOURIST INFORMATION OFFICES.

Money

The unit of currency in Turkey is the Turkish Lira, usually abbreviated to TL. Notes come in denominations of 5,000, 10,000, 20,000, 50,000, 100,000, 250,000, 500,000 and 1,000,000TL, and coins in 500, 1,000, 2,500 and 5,000TL.

Exchanging Money

Banks are generally open 8.30am to noon and 1.30 to 5pm Monday to Friday. The most efficient banks are the Türk Ticaret Bankası, the Yapı ve Kredi, and the AkBank. Rates of exchange and commission vary considerably, so it can be worth shopping around, and the rate in Turkey is always better than in the UK – so don't change large amounts of money before you leave home.

In the more popular tourist resorts such as Kuşadası and Bodrum, the banks have exchange booths which open independently of the main bank, often 8am to 8pm including weekends. You will find the best rates of exchange at the many independent currency dealers called *döviz*, which stay open late in the evening and at weekends, and are often crowded out with local people. They deal only in cash, not traveller's cheques. You can also change cash and traveller's cheques at the PTT office (see POST AND TELEPHONE, P.30).

Traveller's cheques are generally accepted by middle- and upper grade hotels, and by the banks mentioned above, though smaller branches may refuse to cash them and will direct you elsewhere. Unfortunately, the banks usually charge an outrageous commission of around 3 per cent, while some of the more expensive hotels offer a very poor exchange rate.

In popular tourist resorts like Marmaris and Bodrum, changing money is rarely a problem. In more remote areas, facilities are rare, so plan ahead.

Thomas Cook and American Express are the most widely accepted brands; US dollars, pounds sterling and Deutsche Marks are the preferred currencies. You will need your passport when changing traveller's cheques.

Major **credit cards** – Visa, Access/Mastercard, American Express and Diners Club – are accepted in the more expensive hotels (three-star and above) and restaurants in the larger cities, and by tourist shops and car-hire firms. If you are unsure whether an establishment will accept credit cards, ask first. Visa and Access/Mastercard can also be used in banks to obtain cash advances, and in automatic teller machines to withdraw cash (Turkish Lira only). A credit card and an ATM is the fastest and easiest way of getting cash in Turkey, and is usually cheaper than using traveller's cheques.

Post and Telephone

Post offices handle mail, parcels, telegrams and telephone calls, and often currency exchange too; they are marked by a yellow sign with the letters 'PTT'. If you want to buy stamps, look for the counter marked *'pul'*. Hours are generally 8.30am to 8pm for postal services, and until midnight for telephone and telegrams. The main post office in Istanbul is in Yeni Postane Sokak (turn left, facing the ferries, at the Sirkeci tram stop); other convenient branches are in the Grand Bazaar and at Galatasaray Square, half way along İstiklal Caddesi. Postage stamps can also be bought at tourist shops that sell postcards. Post boxes are few and far between – you can post your mail at your hotel desk or at a PTT office. There are usually three slots: *şehiriçi* for addresses within the city;

yurtiçi for destinations within Turkey; and *yurtdışı* for international mail. Letters and cards to the UK take about five days to arrive.

If you want to receive mail **poste restante** while you are in Turkey, arrange to have letters sent to you with your surname underlined, c/o Poste Restante, (name of town), Turkey, and it will be held for you at the main post office. In Istanbul your letters will end up at the head post office on Yeni Postane Sokak (see above). Take along your passport when you go to claim your mail.

Domestic and international **telephone** calls can be made from public telephones at PTT offices, or from phone boxes on the street. These accept either telephone cards (*telekart*) or a metal token called a *jeton*. Cards and *jetons* can be bought at the PTT, and at some newsstands and kiosks. *Jetons* come in three sizes, small (*küçük*), medium (*orta*) and large (*büyük*), and are best for local and inter-city calls. Simply drop a jeton in the slot before dialling, and add more if necessary when the red light comes on and a warning tone sounds. Cards come in five sizes, of 30, 60, 100, 120 and 180 units. The largest sizes are best for international calls. To make a local call, lift the receiver, insert your card or tokens, and simply dial the seven-digit number. For inter-city calls (which include calls across the Bosphorus from European to Asian Istanbul), dial 0, then the area code, then the number. The ringing tone is a single long tone.

To make an international call, dial 00 and wait for a second tone, then dial the country code (44 for the UK, 353 for Ireland, 1 for the USA and Canada), and the full number including area code, minus the initial zero. To make a reverse-charge (collect) call, dial 115 for the international

operator, and ask to be connected to an operator in your home country. You can contact a UK operator direct by dialling 00 800 44 1177 to make a reverse-charge call, or to bill the call to a BT Chargecard or credit card. You will need a *jeton* or telephone card, but it will be refunded after the call.

Eating Out

Turkey has one of the world's richest cuisines, with influences derived from the many cultures of the former Ottoman Empire, and top-quality produce from Anatolia's lush farmland and fertile seas. Many dishes originated in the kitchens of the Ottoman sultans – in the time of Süleyman the Magnificent there were over 150 recipes for aubergines alone. Most tourists, however, will be exposed to only a small range of Turkish dishes, unless they are lucky enough to be invited into a Turkish home, or get the chance to eat at one of the country's better restaurants. The vast majority of eating places in Istanbul and the coastal resorts concentrate on the standard but tasty fare of bread, salads, kebabs and seafood.

Meal Times
The standard Turkish breakfast, served between 7 and 10am, usually consists of fresh bread, butter, jam and honey, with cucumber, tomato, olives, white cheese and

*F*ood, drink and conversation are favourite Turkish pastimes. Çiçek Pasaji in Istanbul is lined with lively bars and cafés, many offering light meals.

perhaps a hard-boiled egg, washed down with sweet black tea. Ask for *menemen,* a delicious dish of scrambled eggs with tomatoes, green peppers and onion.

In Turkey, people eat out regularly, and as a result there are many restaurants, cafés and food stalls that are open all day and late into the evening. There are no set times for lunch and dinner, especially in tourist areas, and you can eat at almost any time of day.

A typical Turkish meal begins with a spread of *meze* (starters), washed down with *rakı,* followed by grilled meat, fish or kebabs, and rounded off with fresh fruit or milk puddings, and cups of strong, black coffee. When ordering, it is customary to be taken to the kitchen to look at the various dishes – you will find printed menus only in tourist restaurants. Don't order a main course until you have finished the *meze* – you may be too full to appreciate it. It is perfectly acceptable to have a meal composed entirely of *meze*.

Where to Eat

Turkey has a vast range of different eating places, many of which specialize in serving a certain kind of dish. An average restaurant, offering a variety of typically Turkish food and drink, freshly prepared, is called a *lokanta* or *restoran*, and may or may not be licensed. A *gazino* is a restaurant that definitely serves alcohol, and usually offers an evening floor show of folk music and belly-dancing. *Hazır yemek* ('ready food') means that you choose your meal from heated trays of pre-cooked food.

A *kebapçı* specializes in grilled meats, especially kebabs, served with *pide* (unleavened bread) and salad, while a *pideci* or *pide salonu* is a Turkish-style pizza parlour, dishing up tasty *pide* topped with minced lamb, eggs or cheese. You can enjoy lamb meatballs in a *köfteci,* tripe in an *işkembeci,* soup in a *çorbacı,* and milk puddings in a *muhallebici.* A *büfe* is a street kiosk which sells snacks, soft drinks and sandwiches.

What to Eat

Starters (meze)

Meze is the collective name given to a wide selection of appetizers, both hot and cold. These are usually presented on a tray at your table, or in a glass-fronted display case, and you can choose as few or as many dishes as you like. The more popular offerings include *kuru fasulye* (haricot beans in tomato sauce), *patlıcan kızartması* (aubergine fried in olive oil and garlic), *şakşuka* (aubergine, tomato and hot peppers in oil), *cacık* (yoghurt with cucumber and garlic), *biber dolması* (green peppers stuffed with rice, raisins and pine nuts), *sigara böreği* (cheese-filled pastry rolls), and a range of salads. *Çerkez tavuğu* (Circassian chicken) is a classic dish of chicken fillet cooked in a sauce flavoured with ground walnuts and paprika. *Meze* are served with fresh white bread to soak up the tasty oil and juices.

Soups (çorba)

Turkish soups are usually thick and substantial. Try *mercimek çorbası* (red lentil soup), *düğün çorbası* ('wedding' soup, a mutton broth flavoured with lemon juice and cayenne, and thickened with egg), or *işkembe çorbası* (tripe soup, a traditional hangover cure). *İşkembecis* stay open until the early hours of the morning to serve bowls of tripe soup to late-night revellers on their way home.

Turkish meals traditionally begin with a spread of meze, *or starters – in this case* kuru fasulye *(haricot beans in tomato sauce), courgette fritters, Russian salad, and fresh bread.*

Main Courses

The best-known of Turkish dishes is *kebap* – grilled, broiled or roasted meat. The most common varieties are *şiş kebap* (cubes of lamb threaded on a skewer and grilled over charcoal); *döner kebap* (literally 'revolving' kebap – a stack of marinated, sliced lamb and minced mutton roasted on a vertical spit, with slices cut off as the outer layers cook); *Adana kebap* (spicy minced beef moulded around a skewer and grilled); and *fırın kebap* (fillet of lamb marinated in yoghurt and roasted in an oven).

The ubiquitous *İskender kebap* is a dish of *döner kebap* served on a bed of diced *pide* bread with tomato sauce and yoghurt, topped with a sizzling splash of browned butter. *Çiftlik kebap* is a casserole of lamb, onion and peas. Meatballs of minced lamb, usually served with a tomato sauce, are called *köfte*. A classic Turkish dish, well worth asking for, is *mantarlı güveç*, a delicious stew of tender lamb, mushrooms, peppers, tomatoes and garlic baked in a clay dish and topped with melted cheese.

Seafood

The seas around Turkey abound with fish, and waterfront restaurants serve up the catch of the day, sold by weight. Choose your own fish from the display and find out how much it will cost before having it cooked. Some of the tastiest species are *levrek* (sea bass), *barbunya* (red mullet), *palamut* (bonito), *uskumru* (mackerel), and *lüfer* (bluefish). The best way to enjoy your fish is simply to have it grilled over charcoal; the waiter will remove the bones if you ask. Look out for *kılıç şiş*, a grilled skewer of juicy swordfish chunks with onion, pepper and tomato.

Other kinds of seafood more commonly appear as *meze* – *ahtapod* (octopus), *kalamar* (squid), *karides* (prawns), *sardalya* (sardines) and *midye* (mussels). Mussels are either coated in flour and fried (*midye tava),* or stuffed with rice, pine nuts, raisins and cinnamon (*midye dolması).*

Desserts

Fresh fruit is often served to round off a meal – succulent *karpuz* (watermelon) and *kavun* (musk melon), *kiraz* (cherries), *kayısı* (apricot), *incir* (figs), *düt* (mulberries) and *erik* (sour plums) – but when it comes to prepared desserts, the Turks have a very sweet tooth. The best-known is *lokum* (Turkish delight), a soft jelly flavoured with rosewater and sprinkled with icing sugar. Another classic sweet is *baklava,* made of alternating layers of thin pastry and ground pistachios, almonds or walnuts, saturated with syrup. Many other sugary confections have names which betray their origins in the harem – *dilber dudağı* ('lips of the beloved'), *hanım göbeği* ('lady's navel') and *bülbül yuvası* ('nightingale's nest').

A traditional Turkish pudding shop (*muhallebici*) serves milk- and rice-based desserts such as *fırın sütlaç* (baked rice pudding), *zerde* (saffron-flavoured rice pudding) and *tavuk göğsü* (an unlikely combination of rice, milk, sugar and chicken breast). A more unusual dish is *aşure* 'Noah's pudding' in English, a kind of sweet porridge made with cereals, nuts and fruit sprinkled with rosewater.

Drinks

The Turkish national drink is tea (*çay*). It is drunk throughout the day, in shops, cafés and offices, oiling the wheels of commerce, and sealing many a business deal. If you bargain for a carpet in the Grand Bazaar you will get through two or three glasses of *çay* before a price is agreed. Tea is usually served black in small tulip glasses.

Turkish coffee (*kahve*) is strong and black, served grounds and all in a small espresso cup, with a glass of water on the side. Sugar is added while brewing, so order *sade kahve* (no sugar), *orta kahve* (sweet), or *çok şekerli kahve* (very sweet). Leave it for a moment for the grounds to settle, and remember not to drain your cup. If you want instant coffee, ask for Nescafé.

You should avoid drinking tap water and instead stick to bottled mineral water, which is easily available everywhere – *maden suyu* is carbonated mineral water, *memba suyu* is still. A traditional Turkish thirst-quencher is *ayran,* a 50/50 mixture of yoghurt and mineral water, seasoned with a pinch of salt.

The national alcoholic drink is a potent anise liquor called *rakı.* It is drunk as an aperitif, and indeed throughout the meal. It should be mixed half and half with iced water, with a glass of water on the side (when mixed with water it turns a pearly white, hence its nickname, *aslan sütü* – lion's milk). Turkish-made beer is also popular and of good quality.

Turkish wines (*şarap*) have a history going back to 7000 BC, and European vinestocks may well have originated here. Nevertheless, despite good quality local wines, the Turks are not great wine drinkers, preferring beer and *rakı.* You can choose from a wide range of Turkish reds, whites, rosés and sparkling wines at very reasonable prices (foreign wines are not available in Turkey). The two largest wine producers in the country are Doluca and Kavaklıdere – there is not a Turkish restaurant worth its salt that does not stock Villa Doluca red and white. Another Doluca to ask for is Moskado, a semi-dry, slightly sparkling white. From the Kavaklıdere cellars, try the fruity red Yakut, the dry white Çankaya, or the refreshing rosé, Lâl. Much harder to get hold of, but definitely worth asking for in Istanbul or Ankara, are the wines produced by the small Diren winery in Tokat – the red Karmen is reckoned to be the best wine in Turkey; Diren Vadi is a semi-sweet white.

Shops and Services

Opening Hours

The times given below are a guide to opening hours, though variations do occur, especially in the cities where some banks and post offices open later and at weekends.

Archaeological sites: generally 8am to 6pm daily. Ephesus 8am to 6.30pm daily (5.30pm in winter). Pergamum 8.30am to 7pm (5.30pm in winter).
Banks: 8.30 to noon and 1.30 to 5pm Monday to Friday.
Currency exchange offices: 8am to 8pm daily.
Museums: generally 9.30am to 5pm, closed Monday. Ayasofya 9.30am to 5pm, closed Monday. Topkapı 9.30am to 5pm daily, closed Tuesday in winter (Harem 10am to 4pm) Dolmabahçe Palace, 9am to 4pm daily (3pm October to February).
Post offices: main offices 8am to midnight Monday to Saturday, and 9am to 7pm Sunday.
Shops: generally 9.30am to 7pm Monday to Saturday, closed 1 to 2pm; tourist shops open later and on Sundays. Grand Bazaar, 8am to 7pm Monday to Saturday.

Public Holidays

There are two kinds of public holiday in Turkey – secular holidays, which occur on the same date each year; and religious holidays, which are calculated by the Islamic

*M*ost *Turkish cities, large and small, have a lively bazaar offering a wide range of attractive souvenirs.*

authorities according to the lunar calendar, and thus occur about 11 days earlier each year. Banks, post offices, government offices and many other businesses will be closed on the secular holidays shown in the panel overleaf.

Movable Dates

There are two national religious holidays, marked by three and four days off respectively, whose dates are calculated according to the lunar calendar. During these times, seaside accommodation and public transport will be booked solid, and it will be almost impossible to change money.

PUBLIC HOLIDAYS

1 January	**Yılbaşı**	New Year's Day
23 April	**Ulusal Egemenlik ve Çocuk Bayramı**	National Sovereignty and Children's Day (anniversary of first meeting of Republican parliament in Ankara in 1920)
19 May	**Gençlik ve Spor Günü**	Youth and Sports Day (Atatürk's Birthday)
30 August	**Zafer Bayramı**	Victory Day (commemorates victory over the Greeks during the War of Independence in 1922)
29 October	**Cumhuriyet Bayramı**	Republic Day (anniversary of proclamation of the republic by Atatürk in 1923)

MOVABLE DATES

2-4 March 1995	**Şeker Bayramı**	'Sugar Festival', the end of the month of Ramazan
10-13 May 1995	**Kurban Bayramı**	'Feast of the Sacrifice', commemorating the sacrifice of Abraham

The dates given are the approximate dates for 1995; these will fall roughly 11 days earlier with each succeeding year.

The holy month of Ramazan, during which devout Muslims fast from sunrise to sunset, occupies the four weeks preceding Şeker Bayramı. See FESTIVALS, p.39.

Pharmacies
See HEALTH AND MEDICAL CARE, p.12-14.

Newspapers and Magazines
Most foreign dailies, including the principal British newspapers and the *International Herald Tribune,* appear on newsstands in Istanbul (Sultanahmet, Laleli and Taksim), Izmir and Ankara the day after publication, at a rather stiff price. There is also a good selection of foreign magazines from most other European countries. In the coastal resorts, supply is tailored to demand, and in summer you'll find a good selection of British newspapers, European periodicals and the major American news weeklies. In winter there are few if any foreign publications on sale outside the big cities. The English-language *Turkish Daily News* is published Monday to Saturday, and offers national and international news and features.

Books and Maps
You can find English-language bookshops in Istanbul, at the Tünel end of İstiklal Caddesi in Beyoğlu, in Sultanahmet and in the Galleria shopping centre in Ataköy. There are a number of small English-language bookshops and book

exchanges in the big coastal resorts such as Kuşadası and Bodrum.

Tourist information offices can provide free maps of the various cities, resorts and regions, though these can be frustratingly short of detail. Large-scale maps for walkers and climbers are few and far between, and very difficult to get hold of. More detailed road maps can be bought from bookshops in the UK before you leave home. The biggest selection is at Stanford's, 12-14 Longacre, London WC2 9LP, tel. (0171) 434 4744.

Photography

Major brands of film are widely available, but are more expensive than in the UK, so stock up before you leave. Photoshops in the major cities and resorts can process your colour prints in 24 to 48 hours at reasonable prices, and some provide a 1-hour service. Protect your film from the effects of heat, and never leave a camera or film lying in direct sunlight. The use of flash or tripod is forbidden in many museums, so always check before snapping away. Taking pictures of military subjects and active archaeological excavations is forbidden. If you want to take photos of the local people outside of the main tourist resorts, ask permission first to avoid causing offence – some country people, especially women, may object to having their picture taken.

For handy tips on how to get the best holiday snaps, purchase a copy of the BERLITZ-NIKON GUIDE TO TRAVEL PHOTOGRAPHY (available in the UK only).

Guides

Official, English-speaking guides can be hired at the local tourist office (see TOURIST INFORMATION OFFICES) or through travel agencies and the better hotels. They are usually friendly and knowledgeable, and are in-valuable if your time is limited. Freelance guides also hang around at the entrance to Topkapı Palace in Istanbul (be sure to agree on a price before hiring one).

Complaints

The manager or owner of the hotel, restaurant or shop in question, or your holiday company representative (for package tours), should be your first recourse if you want to complain about anything. Otherwise, the local tourist information office will be interested to hear of any problems. If you do want to make a complaint, be pleasant about it and try not to lose your temper. To avoid problems, prevention is better than cure – always establish a price in advance, especially when dealing with guides, taxi drivers and porters at stations.

Embassies and Consulates

You should only get in touch with your consulate in the event of a *serious* emergency, such as losing your passport, getting into trouble with the police, or being involved in an accident. The consul can issue an emergency passport, give advice on obtaining money from home, and provide a list of lawyers, doctors and interpreters. He *cannot* pay your bills, lend you money, fly you home, find you a job, or obtain a work permit for you.

Australian Embassy: Nene Hatun Caddesi 83, Gaziosmanpaşa, Ankara, tel. (312) 436 1240.
Australian Consulate: Tepecik Yolu Üzeri 58, Istanbul, tel. (212) 257 7050.
Canadian Embassy: Nene Hatun Caddesi 75, Gaziosmanpaşa, Ankara, tel. (312) 436 1275.
Canadian Consulate: Bükükdere Caddesi, Bengün Han 107, Kat 3, Gayrettepe, Istanbul, tel. (212) 272 5174.

British Embassy: Şehit Ersan Caddesi 46/A, Çankaya, Ankara, tel. (312) 427 4310.

British Consulates: Meşrutiyet Caddesi 34, Tepebaşı, Beyoğlu, Istanbul, tel. (212) 252 6436; 1442 Sokak 49, PK 300, Alsancak, Izmir, tel. (232) 421 1795; Kazin Özalp Caddesi 149/A, Antalya, tel. (242) 241 1815.

Irish Consulate: Cumhuriyet Caddesi 26A, Elmadağ, Istanbul tel. (212) 246 6025.

US Embassy: Atatürk Bulvarı 110, Kavaklıdere, Ankara, tel. (312) 426 5470.

US Consulates: Meşrutiyet Caddesi 104-8, Tepebaşı, Beyoğlu, Istanbul, tel. (212) 251 3602; Atatürk Caddesi 92, Alsancak, Izmir, tel. (232) 484 9426; Atatürk Caddesi, Vali Yolu, Adana, tel. (322) 234 2145.

Emergencies

Except in out-of-the-way places, you should be able to find someone who speaks English to help you out. But if you're alone and near a telephone, here are some important numbers to remember in an emergency (you will need a *jeton* or phonecard to call these numbers from a public telephone).

Police	155
Ambulance	112
Fire	110

See also EMBASSIES AND CONSULATES above.

Language

At first glance, the Turkish language can appear formidably difficult to learn. But a little perseverance will bring great rewards, and make your trip more interesting. The fact that the Turks use a Latin-based alphabet (introduced by Atatürk in the 1920s), and that words are pronounced exactly as they are spelt makes things a little easier. The grammar

TURKISH PRONUNCIATION					
A	a	like the **u** in b**u**n	L	l	as in long
B	b	as in **b**ig	M	m	as in **m**an
C	c	j as in **j**ob	N	n	as in **n**o
Ç	ç	ch as in **ch**ap	O	o	as in pond
D	d	as in **d**id	Ö	ö	like **eu** in French,
E	e	as in test			e.g. d**eu**x
F	f	as in **f**at	P	p	as in **p**en
G	g	always hard, as in **g**a**g**	R	r	rolled
Ğ	ğ	silent, but lengthens	S	s	as in **s**ea
		preceding vowel,	Ş	ş	**sh** as in **sh**ort
		e.g. *dağ* = 'daa'	T	t	as in **t**ea
H	h	always sounded	U	u	as in p**u**ll
İ	i	as in **s**it	Ü	ü	an 'ew' sound, like the
I	ı	like the **er** in lett**er**			**u** in the French t**u**
J	j	a soft zh, like the **s**	V	v	as in **v**iolet
		in lei**s**ure	Y	y	as in **y**et
K	k	as in **k**ite	Z	z	as in **z**oo

is rather complex, but you can make yourself understood even with a very limited vocabulary.

It is quite possible to enjoy a trip to Turkey without knowing any Turkish at all – in the main tourist destinations many people are fluent in English. All the same, it is polite to learn at least a few basic phrases. Local people will welcome and encourage any attempt you make to use their own language. The Berlitz TURKISH PHRASE BOOK AND DICTIONARY will cover most situations you are likely to encounter.

FESTIVALS

January	Selçuk	Camel-wrestling Festival
April	Istanbul	Istanbul International Film Festival – new Turkish and foreign films
	Kaş	Kaş Tourist Festival – folk music and dancing
April-May	Ankara	International Ankara Festival of Music and Art
May	Kuşadası/Selçuk	Ephesus International Festival of Culture and Tourism
	Emirgan, on the Bosphorus	Tulip Festival
	Marmaris	International Marmaris Yacht Festival
June	Ürgüp	Wine Festival
	Bergama	Bergama Festival
	Marmaris	Music and Art Festival
	Bursa	International Bursa Festival
June-July	Çeşme	Sea and Music Festival
	Istanbul	Istanbul International Arts Festival
July	Foça, near Izmir	Foça Festival of Music, Folklore and Watersports
	Avanos	Handicrafts Festival
	Edirne	Kırkpınar Greased Wrestling Competition
	Antakya	Culture, Tourism and Arts Festival
August	Çanakkale	Çanakkale-Troy Festival – folk dancing and music
	Antalya	Antalya Festival of Music and Dance
September	Cappadocia	Cappadocia Festival – grape harvest and folklore shows
	Bodrum	Bodrum Culture and Art Week
	Izmir	Izmir International Fair
October	Konya	Troubador's Week – folk music and poetry competitions
	Bodrum	International Bodrum Cup – yacht races
December	Kale (Demre)	St Nicholas Festival – services in Church of St Nicholas (Santa Claus)
	Konya	Mevlana Festival – Whirling Dervishes

A Welcome Awaits in the Land Where the Traveller is a Gift from God

The traditional Turkish greeting, *'Hoş Geldiniz!'*, translates literally as 'glad you came'. In Turkey, it is said, the visitor is 'a gift from God', and one of the lasting impressions most visitors take home is of the genuine friendliness and hospitality of the Turkish people. Wherever you go, especially in rural areas, you will be met with smiles and the offer of tea, or a glass of spring water, and a share of whatever there is to eat.

Since the earliest days Turkey has been a land where different peoples have met and mingled, and absorbed influences from both east and west. The country's position astride so many major trade routes, has also given it a long tradition of tolerance and respect for travellers from other countries.

You should reciprocate by showing a similar respect for local customs and sensibilities. Most important of all is dress. You will notice that even in Istanbul and

Turkey has a complex and fascinating history. Turks are proud of their past, and commemorate important events with fine monuments, such as this relief at the Atatürk Mausoleum in Ankara.

Ankara local people dress modestly, and usually avoid shorts and skimpy tops even in the heat of summer. If you plan to visit a mosque, you should follow suit and wear long trousers or a skirt reaching below the knee, with a long-sleeved shirt or blouse. Women should cover their heads with a scarf. Mosques are normally open to tourists except during prayer times, especially on Fridays, the Muslim holy day. Remember, too, to take your shoes off before entering a mosque, or a Turkish house or apartment.

Although some small Armenian, Greek Orthodox, Jewish and Catholic communities survive, the overwhelming majority of Turks are Muslims, and adhere closely to the principles known as the 'Five Pillars of Islam' – to believe with all one's heart that 'There is no God but

41

FACTS AND FIGURES

Geography: Lying in the southeast corner of Europe, and the northern part of the Middle East, Turkey covers an area of 780,000 sq km (301,000 sq miles). Its neighbours are Greece and Bulgaria to the northwest, Syria and Iraq to the south, and Iran, Armenia and Georgia to the east. It is a very mountainous country, with a mean height above sea level of 1,100m (3,600ft). The principal rivers are the Kızılırmak, the Sakarya and the Yeşilırmak, draining into the Black Sea; the Gediz and the Büyük Menderes, draining into the Aegean; the Seyhan and Ceyhan, which drain into the Mediterranean; and the Tigris and Euphrates, which flow south through Iraq to the Persian Gulf.

Highest mountain: Mount Ararat (Ağrı Dağı), 5,137m (16,850ft).

Longest river: the Kızılırmak (Red River), 1,182km (734 miles).

Largest lake: Lake Van (Van Gölü), 3,713 sq km (1,434 sq miles).

Population: 60 million (85.7 per cent Turkish; 10.6 per cent Kurdish; 1.6 per cent Arab; 2.1 per cent other).

Religion: Sunni Muslim (99.2 per cent); Eastern Orthodox (0.3 per cent); other (0.5 per cent).

Capital: Ankara.

Major cities: Istanbul, Ankara, Izmir, Adana, Bursa.

Government: multi-party republic with one 450-seat legislative house, the Turkish Grand National Assembly (*Türkiye Büyük Millet Meclisi*). The President is head of state, and the Prime Minister is head of the government.

Economy: principal exports are textiles, agricultural products, iron and non-ferrous metals, food, chemical products, leather and hides, and machinery. Main trading partners are Germany, USA, Iraq, Italy, UK, Iran, France, Japan, Saudi Arabia. Agriculture employs 47 per cent of the labour force, public services 14 per cent, and manufacturing 11 per cent. Turkey is one of the few countries in the world that produces a surplus of food. Principal crops are wheat, sugar beets, barley, potatoes, grapes, maize, apples, onions, sunflower seeds, olives, lentils, chick-peas, tea, and oranges.

Allah, and Muhammad is his Prophet'; to pray five times a day, at dawn, midday, afternoon, sunset, and after dark; to give alms to the poor, and towards the upkeep of the mosques; to fast between sunrise and sunset during the month of Ramazan; and to try to make the pilgrimage to Mecca at least once in one's lifetime. Those who have made the pilgrimage can add the title *haci* before their names, an honour displayed proudly on many shop-owner's signs throughout the city.

Kemal Atatürk, the father of the Turkish Republic, is a national hero. Every town of any size has an Atatürk Caddesi (Atatürk Street), and a statue of Atatürk presiding over the main square. The pedestals of these statues usually bear one of the great man's many sayings, such as *'Ne mutlu Türküm diyene'* ('Happy is he who can call himself a Turk'). You should never make jokes or insulting comments about Atatürk or the Turkish flag, or behave disrespectfully towards them (i.e. don't climb on a statue of Atatürk to have your photo taken, as too many tourists do).

Occasionally, body language can be confusing. If a Turk shakes his head, that means 'I don't understand'; if he asks you a question and you shake your head, meaning 'No', he will probably repeat the question, thinking you have misunderstood. In Turkey, 'No' is indicated by tilting your head back while raising your eyebrows, such as a Westerner might do to say 'Pardon me? I didn't catch what you said'.

History

The modern Republic of Turkey dates only from 1923, but the history of the land within its borders stretches back to the dawn of humanity. Widespread finds of Stone Age implements in cave excavations show that Anatolia was already inhabited during the Middle Palaeolithic Period (about 200,000 to 40,000 years ago). By neolithic times, organized communities had arisen, such as the one at Çatalhöyük, near Konya, Turkey's most important prehistoric site. This town, which flourished around 6500-5500 BC, had flat-roofed houses of mud and timber decorated with wall-paintings, some of which show patterns that still appear on Anatolian kilims.

The advent of the Bronze Age (about 3200 BC) and the spread of city-states ruled by kings is marked by the appearance of royal tombs containing bronze objects in places such as Troy in the west and Alacahöyük near Ankara. Around this time the Sumerian civilization in Mesopotamia (the region between the Tigris and Euphrates rivers in present-day Iraq) developed the cuneiform script, the world's oldest form of writing. The technique was introduced into Anatolia about 1,000 years later by Assyrian traders, where it was soon adopted by the indigenous Hatti people, who had already reached a fairly advanced state of civilization.

The Hittites

The capital of the Hatti was Kanesh (modern Kültepe, near Kayseri, a major archaeological site). Cuneiform tablets discovered here record the arrival in Anatolia of a warlike invaders around the 2nd millennium BC. Their origins remain mysterious (their written language was finally deciphered in 1915), but they came from the direction of the Caucasus mountains, spreading destruction and disorder across Anatolia. Two hundred years later they were firmly ensconced in their newly conquered empire.

The newcomers were the Hittites, and their domination of Anatolia is divided into three periods: the Old Kingdom (*c.* 1600-1450 BC), the New or Empire Period (*c.* 1450-1200 BC), and the Late Hittite Period (*c.* 1200-700 BC). Their first capital city was Hattusa (now Boğazköy, near Ankara),

The Hittites created one of Anatolia's earliest civilizations, with its capital at Hattuşaş, near Ankara. This fine vaulted chamber, decorated with bas-reliefs, was once a royal tomb.

Archaeologists at Hattuşaş discovered thousands of cuneiform tablets that helped them piece together Hittite history. The city was protected by massive walls, pierced by monumental gates.

which dates from the 13th century BC. Huge fortifications enclosed temples, tombs and a citadel containing an impressive library of over 3,300 cuneiform tablets.

During the Empire Period, an ambitious and energetic Hittite king, Mutawallis, defeated the forces of the Egyptian

Treaty of Kadesh, recorded on clay tablets on display in the Museum of the Ancient Orient in Istanbul, is the oldest known example of a written international treaty.

The Hittite Empire eventually collapsed following invasion from the west by the Achaeans, the Phrygians and a mystery force known only as the 'Sea People'. The Hittites were forced south into the mountains, where they remained until they were absorbed by the advancing Assyrians.

Troy and the Greeks

While the Hittite Empire declined, other momentous events were taking place on the shores of the Aegean. The ancient Greeks traditionally took the Fall of Troy, as recounted by Homer, as the starting point of their history. Much academic disputation surrounds the exact date of the Trojan War, if indeed it ever took place. Modern archaeologists studying the ruins of Troy have discovered nine superimposed cities ranging from Troy I (3000-2500 BC) to Troy IX (350 BC AD 400); the city of King Priam, described in the *Iliad* and the *Odyssey*, is thought to be either Troy VI, which was destroyed by an earthquake in 1275 BC, or its successor Troy VIIa. Another school of thought holds that the Trojan War never took place at all, and that the decline of Troy was due to the mysterious 'Sea People' mentioned above.

Whatever really happened, the Mycenaean Greeks who were supposed to have conquered Priam's city soon found their own civilization in decline. A race known as the Dorians gained power in southern Greece, forcing many mainland Greeks to flee their homeland and cross the Aegean to settle on the coast of Anatolia. Their colonization of the coast took place in successive waves of immigration. First came the Aeolians, who settled the region to the north of

pharaoh, Rameses II, at Kadesh (Syria) in 1285 BC. Rameses was too proud to accept his defeat, and even commissioned obelisks celebrating his 'victory'. But he was sufficiently wary of the formidable strength of the Hittite Empire to make peace with the next king, Hattusili III. The

Smyrna (now Izmir), then the Ionians, who settled the coast south of Smyrna as far as the River Maeander. The Dorians followed, installing themselves south of the Maeander, in the region known as Caria.

Around 1000 BC mainland Greece entered a 'dark age' of limited achievements, but not so the Ionians, who developed an outstanding civilization. By the 8th century BC the 12 main city-states of Ionia, including Ephesus, Priene and Miletus, had consolidated themselves into the Pan-Ionic League. Science, philosophy and the arts flourished, and Ionian traders founded colonies as far away as France and Spain.

Lydians and Persians

Inland from Ionia lived the wealthy and powerful Lydians, with their capital at Sardis. They reached their peak during the reign of Croesus (560-546 BC), who owed his legendary fortune to gold panned from the River Pactolus. Croesus lasting legacy was the invention of coinage, which led to the beginnings of our money-based economy. His expansionism brought the bulk of Ionia under Lydian rule, but also resulted in conflict with the advancing Persians in the east, where he was roundly defeated. Driven back to Sardis, Croesus witnessed the sacking of his city by the army of Cyrus the Great in 546 BC.

With Lydia defeated, the Greek cities of the coast lay open to the Persians, who swiftly incorporated them into their empire. Ionia attempted a revolt c. 499 BC, supported by Athens, but was easily subdued. However, Athenian involvement provoked the Persian King Darius to invade the Greek mainland. He was defeated at the famous Battle of Marathon in 490 BC, and ten years later his son Xerxes lost the Persian fleet at the Battle of Salamis. Xerxes suffered a further humiliating defeat in 479 BC, when his army was beaten at Plataea on the same day that his fleet lost to the Greeks at Mycale.

As a result of the Persian Wars, the Greek cities of Anatolia were encouraged to join the Delian Confederacy, paying tribute to Athens in return for protection against the Persians. Athens grew so attached to this source of easy money that dissent soon grew among the member cities, and Sparta took the leadership of the confederacy from Athens following the Peloponnesian War

---

ARCHITECTURAL GLOSSARY

architrave	*lintel resting on top of columns*
bouleterion	*Hellenistic city hall, or council chamber*
caldarium	*hot room of baths*
cavea	*seating area of theatre*
crepidoma	*stepped platform on which a temple stands*
diazoma	*horizontal terrace in cavea of theatre*
frieze	*decorative panel above architrave*
frigidarium	*cold room of baths*
odeon	*small theatre for musical performances and lectures*
opisthodomus	*porch at rear of a temple*
palaestra	*exercise area*
pediment	*low-pitched gable above portico*
peristyle	*row of columns around temple or courtyard*
propylon	*entrance gate to temple precinct*
stoa	*a free-standing portico or colonnade*
stylobate	*top surface of crepidoma*
tepidarium	*warm room in baths*

(413-404 BC). Sensing weakness, the Persians launched another offensive, and the cities of the Aegean coast came under Persian control in 387 BC.

Alexander the Great

Meanwhile, in northern Greece, King Philip II of Macedon dreamed of driving out the Persians and unifying the whole of the Greek world. His dreams were fulfilled, and even surpassed by his son, Alexander the Great, in a brief but action-filled lifetime of only 33 years (356-323 BC). In 334 BC, aged only 22, Alexander led his army across the Hellespont (now the Dardanelles), and paused at Troy to make a sacrifice at the temple of Athena and pay homage to his hero Achilles, before going on to defeat the Persians at the Battle of Granicus and liberating the Ionian cities. After conquering the entire Aegean and Mediterranean coasts of Anatolia, and subduing Syria and Egypt, he took the great prize of Persepolis, the Persian capital, before advancing further still into India. During his 12-year campaign, Alexander established some 70 cities and built the greatest empire the world had yet seen.

After his death, the conquered territory was divided among his generals, whose mutual antagonism and expansionist ambitions led to weaknesses which laid western Anatolia open to the increasing might of Rome.

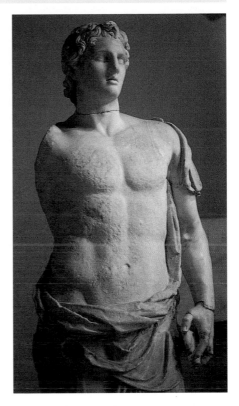

*A*lexander the Great created an empire stretching from Greece to India. He marched through Anatolia with his army in 334-333 BC.

The Romans

One of the most prosperous city-states of the Aegean coast was Pergamum, ruled since 264 BC by the Attalid Dynasty. The last of the Attalid kings, Attalus III, is remembered as something of an eccentric – one of his hobbies was devising new poisons and testing their efficacy on his reluctant slaves. When he died (of natural causes) in 133 BC, his subjects were dismayed to learn that he had bequeathed his entire kingdom to the Romans. Thus Pergamum became the capital of the new Roman province of Asia. Mithridates VI, king of Pontus (on the Black Sea), vigorously resisted Roman occupation, temporarily occupying Pergamum and ordering the massacre of all Romans. But eventually, after a number of campaigns, the power of Rome prevailed.

47

ROMAN ANATOLIA

THRACE
Constantinople
PAPHLAGONIA
BITHYNIA
AND PONTUS
Abydos   Cyzicus
Caïcus   ASIA   Ancyra
                Gordium
Magnesia   Hermus   PHRYGIA
   LYDIA   Sardis
Ephesus
   LYCIA AND   GALATIA
   PAMPHYLIA   PISIDIA   Iconium
   CARIA   LYCAONIA   TAURUS MTS
AEGEAN SEA   Aspendus
   Phaselis   CILICIA
Myra   Selinus

Sinope   BLACK SEA
          Trapezus   N
PONTUS POLEMONIACUS
                ARMENIA
Halys   CAPPADOCIA
Lake
Tatta
                Tigris
                COMMAGENE
          Tarsus
                MESOPOTAMIA
Euphrates
          Antioch
MEDITERRANEAN SEA   Cyprus   SYRIA
          0   100 miles
          0   160 km

In 27 BC Julius Caesar's nephew Octavian took the name Augustus; Rome ceased to be a republic and became an empire. There followed a long period of peace known as the Pax Romana. All of Asia Minor (the Roman name for Anatolia) was incorporated into the Roman Empire. The old Greek cities were embellished with grandiose Roman buildings and subjected to Roman administration, but, except for military bases where Latin was used, the citizens of the Aegean coast continued to speak Greek.

News soon spread of a new religion that was causing trouble for the Roman authorities. Christianity threatened the establishment because it rejected the old gods and denied the divinity of the emperor. The word was carried into Asia Minor by Paul the Apostle, whose voyages between AD 40 and 56 led to the founding of many churches, notably the Seven Churches of Asia addressed in the Revelation of St John – Ephesus, Smyrna, Pergamum, Thyatira, Sardis, Philadelphia and Laodicea.

The Byzantine Empire

Legend claims that the city of Byzantium was founded around 660 BC by a Greek named Byzas, after the Delphic Oracle had bidden him to build his city 'opposite the Land of the Blind'. When he saw that earlier settlers had built a town on the eastern shore of the Bosphorus, he decided they must have been 'blind' to overlook the advantages of an easily defensible point across the water, and founded Byzantium there, on the site now occupied by Topkapı Palace.

In the succeeding centuries Byzantium, like the cities of the Aegean, fell in turn under the sway of Athens, Sparta, Persia, Alexander and Rome. It tried to regain its

Mithrodates VI, ruler of the northern Anatolian Kingdom of Pontus, briefly challenged the might of Rome. The tombs of the Pontic kings can be seen at Amasya, their former capital.

independence from Rome, but proved too small and weak, and was conquered by the emperor Septimius Severus in AD 196. He had the city razed to the ground, but soon saw the advantages of its strategic location, and began a programme of enlarging and strengthening the old defensive walls.

A succession of weak and decadent emperors saw the Roman Empire fall gradually into decline and anarchy. In 286 Diocletian sought to reverse the decline by splitting the administration of the empire in two – he would govern the east, based in Nicomedia, while his friend Maximiian ruled the west from Milan – and later split it further, into four parts. His policy succeeded for a time, but following his abdication in 305 the empire continued to weaken, harassed by invaders and troubled by internal strife. Constantine the Great (who was a convert to Christianity) and Licinius ruled east and west respectively, until in 324 Constantine overthrew his pagan ally and reunited the empire. He chose Byzantium as his new capital to emphasize the break with heathen Rome. The city was inaugurated with great ceremony in 330, and renamed Constantinople in honour of

the emperor. Constantine added new city walls, following a plan he claimed to have been given by Christ in a vision, and commissioned a grand central forum decorated with a triumphal column and other monuments. The 'New Rome' soon achieved a pre-eminence in the Christian world that it would retain for 1,000 years.

In 392 the Emperor Theodosius proclaimed Christianity to be the official religion of the Roman Empire, and on his death in 395 the empire was split again, between his two sons, never again to be reunited. The Western Empire, ruled from Rome, fell to the Ostrogoths in 476, while the Eastern, or Byzantine Empire went on to become one of the longest lived empires the world has ever known (395-1453).

The greatest of the Byzantine emperors was Justinian the Great (ruled 527-65), who introduced an equitable legal system, and extended the boundaries of the empire into Spain, Italy and Africa. He encouraged the arts and commissioned the magnificent basilica of Hagia Sophia.

Following the death of the Prophet Muhammad in 632, Arab armies, united under the banner of Islam, poured out of their homeland and soon took Egypt, Syria and Palestine from the Byzantines; Constantinople itself was besieged from 674 to 678, but survived thanks to its substantial defences. The empire was further diminished by the loss of North Africa and Italy, and was brought to the brink of civil war by the Iconoclastic Crisis, before enjoying another brief golden age under Basil II (976-1025). But the empire's troubles increased as invaders made further incursions into Byzantine territory. Most worrying were the Seljuk Turks, who came out of the east in the 11th century to wrest large parts of Asia Minor from Constantinople's control. Converted to Islam in the 10th century, and fired by religious zeal, the Seljuks overran Anatolia, menacing Christian holy places

*T*he Byzantines created the longest-lived empire the world has ever known, lasting from 395 to 1453. Their wealth and might was symbolized by the magnificent churches they built, such as Hagia Sophia and St Saviour in Chora, and the ornate decoration that covered the churches' interiors.

*S*uccessive Byzantine
emperors endowed Constantinople
with fine buildings and magnificent
monuments. This relief shows the
Emperor Theodosius presiding over
an event in the Hippodrome, the
city's great chariot-racing stadium.

CHURCH GLOSSARY

apse	*semi-circular recess at far end of nave*
basilica	*design of early church adapted from Roman public hall, consisting of nave flanked by two aisles, with apse at far end*
nave	*central aisle of basilica*
synthronon	*curved seating in apse for clergy*

and attacking pilgrims who were bound for Jerusalem.

Reluctantly, Emperor Alexius I sought outside help from the Christian west. The First Crusade was organized to help the Byzantines recapture the Holy Land from the 'infidel' Muslims, and was successful. The Second and Third Crusades, however, were a disaster for the Christians. The Fourth Crusade, launched in 1202 and partly inspired by Venetian jealousy of Byzantium's trading power, became an excuse to plunder Constantinople itself. The city, which had held out against so many attacks by the infidel, was subjected to mindless pillaging by fellow Christians. The crusaders ruled the city from 1204 to 1261, calling their new state Romania, also known as the Latin Empire. A remnant of the Byzantine Empire survived in Nicaea (now İznik), and recaptured Constantinople in 1261, but the city had been shattered, its great monuments stripped of gold, silver, and precious works of art. Constantinople was never the same again.

The Sultanate of Rum

The Seljuk invasion of Anatolia in the 11th century began as an uncoordinated migration of tribesmen led by petty chieftains, who continuously harried the eastern outposts of the Byzantine Empire. They were

*T*he Seljuk sultans established a network of important trade routes, with an infrastructure of roads, caravanserais, and fine bridges.

encouraged by the Seljuk sultan to establish small principalities bound to him by blood ties, in the hope of later uniting them into a greater Seljuk state. Following the defeat of the Byzantine army at Manzikert by Alp Arslan in 1071, the Seljuk tribes overran Anatolia; one prince, Süleyman Shah, advanced right across Asia Minor and in 1078 took İznik, near Bursa.

During the 12th century, the sultans Kılıç Arslan I (1092-1107) and his son Malik Shah (1107-16) gradually consolidated power and established an organized Seljuk state in Anatolia – the Sultanate of Rum (*'Rum'*, derived from 'Rome', was the old Turkish name for the Byzantine Empire). Malik Shah's brother and successor, Masud (1116-55), made Konya the capital city of his new kingdom.

The Sultanate of Rum reached its zenith during the reign of Sultan Alaeddin Keykubad I (1219-37). Its territory extended from the Mediterranean to the Black Sea, and from Afyon to Erzincan. The Seljuk rulers were tolerant of the many races and religions under their control – Armenians, Greeks, Syrians, Turks, Persians, Jews, Christians, Muslims and pagans – and concentrated on developing agriculture and commerce. They endowed their cities, especially Konya, Kayseri and Sivas, with fine architecture, and encouraged the arts and sciences. Literature flourished, and mystical movements such as the Mevlevi Dervishes arose.

But the Seljuk state was short lived. In 1243, only six years after the death of Keykubad, the Mongol armies rampaged across Anatolia, subduing all before them. The Seljuk rulers became vassals, and the unity of the state broke down as provincial emirs fought against one another. In the west, outside the sphere of Mongol influence, independent emirates arose. One of these was led by Osman Gazi, a 'warrior for the faith', who was destined to found an empire that would stretch right from the Caucasus to the Atlas mountains.

The Ottomans

During the 14th century the Turks in Anatolia rallied under the banner of Osman Gazi, who won a great victory over the Byzantines in 1301. Osman Gazi's son Orhan captured Bursa in 1326, and set up his capital there, then moved it to

This Istanbul monument commemorates 29 May 1453, one of the most important dates in Turkish history – the day that Constantinople fell to the young Ottoman sultan, Mehmet II.

OTTOMAN EMPIRE

AUSTRIA

RUSSIA

HUNGARY

SPAIN

ITALY   BALKANS   BLACK SEA

● Istanbul 1453

GREECE

ALGERIA

TUNISIA

IRAN

CRETE   CYPRUS   SYRIA   MESOPOTAMIA

MEDITERRANEAN SEA   PALESTINE

TRIPOLI

ARABIA

Acquisitions 1300-59

Acquisitions 1359-1481   EGYPT

Acquisitions 1512-66
Süleyman the Magnificent (1520-66)

Acquisitions 1566-1683

Boundary of the Ottoman Empire
at its greatest extent. 1683-99

Mecca ●

0   500 miles

0   750 km

MOROCCO   CASPIAN SEA   PERSIAN GULF   RED SEA

N

Adrianople (Edirne), which he took in 1361. By the 15th century the whole of Anatolia and Thrace, except for Constantinople, was under the control of these Osmanli – or Ottoman – Turks. The Byzantine emperor, Manuel II (1391-1425), tried to appease his enemies by allowing a Turkish district, mosque and tribunal within his city, and by courting Turkish goodwill with gifts of gold, but to no avail. The young Ottoman sultan, Mehmet II (reigned 1451-81), set about cutting off Constantinople's supply lines. The huge fortress of Rumeli Hisarı on the Bosphorus was built in just four months in 1452. He then withdrew to his capital in Adrianople to await the spring.

The Byzantines tried to protect the Golden Horn from enemy ships by stretching a huge chain across its mouth, repaired and strengthened the city walls which had saved them so many times in the past, and waited fearfully for the inevitable onslaught. In April 1453 the sultan's armies massed outside the walls, outnumbering the Byzantines by ten to one. The siege and bombardment lasted seven weeks. The Ottoman admiral bypassed the defensive chain by having his ships dragged overland under cover of darkness, opening a second front of attack. The final assault came on 29 May, when the Ottoman army surged through a breach in the walls. The last emperor, Constantine XI, fell in the fighting, and by noon Mehmet had taken control of the city. His first act was to ride to Hagia Sophia and order that it be converted into a mosque; on the following Friday, he attended the first Muslim prayers in what came to be called Ayasofya Camii (Mosque of Hagia Sophia). After allowing his soldiers three days of pillaging he restored order, acting with considerable leniency and good sense. Henceforth he became known as 'Fatih' (Conqueror), and his new capital city was renamed Istanbul.

55

Fatih Sultan Mehmet laid claim to all the territories previously held by the Byzantines, so that his empire took in most of Greece and the Balkans as well as Anatolia. Expansion continued under his successors, but it was during the reign of his great-grandson, Süleyman, that the Ottoman Empire reached its greatest heights. Süleyman the Magnificent ascended the throne at the age of 25 and ruled for 46 years (1520-66), the longest and most glorious reign in Ottoman history. Süleyman's army captured Belgrade in 1521; Rhodes capitulated in 1523. Six years later he reached the gates of Vienna and besieged the city for 24 days (unsuccessfully) before going on to take most of Hungary. Turkish corsairs, notably the infamous Barbarossa, helped to win Algiers and Tunis. By the mid-17th century the Ottoman Empire had reached its greatest extent, stretching from Batumi at the eastern end of the Black Sea to Algeria, taking in Mesopotamia, Palestine, the shores of the Red Sea including Mecca and Medina, Egypt, the North African coast, Anatolia, Greece, the Balkans, Hungary, Moldavia, the Crimea and southern Ukraine. With such far-flung territories, dissolution was inevitable, and began almost immediately – Hungary and other northern possessions had been lost by the close of the 17th century. The decline was long and painful, leaving problems in its wake which have been the source of trouble in the Balkans and the Middle East to this day.

Decline and Fall

The year 1821 marked the beginning of the Greek War of Independence, which resulted in victory for the Greeks in 1832,

The Gallipoli peninsula witnessed one of the most notorious campaigns of World War I. The Allied forces landed at this bay, now known as Anzac Cove, after the Australian and New Zealand Army Corps (Anzac).

and another loss of territory for the Ottomans, whose empire had shrunk significantly. A century of decadence and intermittent wars had left the Ottoman sultanate in serious decline. Attempts at reform came too late – by 1876 the government was bankrupt. Sultan Abdül Hamid II (1876-1909), tried to apply absolute rule to an empire staggering under a crushing foreign debt, with a fragmented population of mutually hostile peoples, and succeeded only in creating ill will and dissatisfaction among the younger generation of educated Turks.

Young army officers and the professional classes were becoming increasingly interested in Western ways of government and social organization. European literature was being widely studied. Robert College, an American school, and the Galatasaray Lycée, the French academy in Istanbul, were turning out young men imbued with dreams of democracy. These new intellectuals formed an underground group known as the Young Turks, centred on Salonica, where revolt finally broke out. In 1909 Abdül Hamid was deposed and replaced by his brother, Mehmet V.

There followed the Balkan Wars in which Turkey lost Macedonia and western Thrace, then World War I, which Turkey entered on the side of Germany. In the notorious Gallipoli campaign of 1915, the Turks, under the leadership of General Mustafa Kemal, defeated the Allied attack on the Dardanelles; but although they won this battle, they finished on the losing side.

At the end of the war, the Treaty of Sèvres formally ended the existence of the Ottoman Empire. Greece was given large concessions, Armenia was to become an independent state in the east, and the Middle East was to be divided among the Arab leaders who had fought with Colonel

These restored World War I trenches at Gallipoli mark the hilltop from which Atatürk commanded his army.

Lawrence (under British and French 'spheres of influence'). The subsequent period of internal strife between the Turks, Greeks and Armenians was dominated by the figure of Mustafa Kemal, who had risen from the status of war hero to become the charismatic leader of the Turkish nationalist movement. In 1920, with army support, he was elected president of the Grand National Assembly in Ankara in defiance of the sultan's government in Constantinople, claiming to speak for the Turkish people.

57

A TRADITIONAL SHAVE

For male travellers, one of the great pleasures of a trip to Turkey is the chance to experience a traditional shave at an old-fashioned barber shop (ask for the local *berber;* when you find him, tell him you want a *tıraş*). Hot towels and shaving soap soften up your beard, and then the *berber* sets to work with his cut-throat razor, deftly flicking the bristle-laden lather onto the heel of his left hand. When not a trace of beard remains, he wipes down your face and splashes on some cologne.

But he's not finished yet. Next, he dips a cotton swab in meths and lights it, and with the flame singes off the small hairs in your ears. Then he begins the massage – fore-head, temples, neck, shoulders and arms, rounding off by cracking all your finger joints one by one. A final trim of your hair, a dust down with talc, and you're ready to face the world. And all for the price of a pint of beer back home!

From 1919 to 1922 he waged war with the Greeks, who had invaded at Smyrna, ulti-mately defeating them and forcing their withdrawal from Asia Minor. He was then faced with the delicate task of abolishing the sultanate, without antagonizing the religious elements within his party. This meant de-posing Sultan Mehmet VI, whose position as caliph (leader of the Islamic world) and sultan stood for the old tradition of com-bined secular and religious power. Kemal handled the problem with his usual vigour and eloquence in a speech to the Assembly, by linking the power of the caliphate with that of the Assembly: 'It was by force that the sons of Osman seized the sovereignty and Sultanate of the Turkish nation...Now the Turkish nation has rebelled and has put a stop to these usurpers, and has effectively taken sovereignty and Sultanate into its own hands. This is an accomplished fact...'

In the early hours of 10 November 1922, Mehmet VI slipped away quietly to a waiting British warship, to end his life in exile. He was replaced as caliph by his cousin, with powers limited strictly by secular laws, until that position too was abolished in 1924.

The Republic of Turkey

In 1923 the Treaty of Lausanne defined the present borders of the Turkish Republic. An exchange of expatriate pop-ulations between Greece and Turkey re-sulted in the movement of thousands of people, and the wholesale desertion of ethnic Greek villages and districts.

The decade 1925-35 witnessed the in-troduction of wide-ranging reforms. President Mustafa Kemal set to work sec-ularizing institutions, adapting the Latin alphabet for the Turkish language, eman-cipating women, reforming the calendar, and improving agriculture and industry. He also introduced the Western idea of surnames – until then Turks had only a single name – and made everyone choose a family name to be handed down to their children. For himself he chose Atatürk – Father of the Turks.

It was an appropriate choice, as Atatürk almost single-handedly forged the modern Turkish state. He was enormously popular with the common Turkish people – when he died in 1938 thousands of mourners lined the railway track to salute the white presidential train as it carried him from Istanbul for burial in Ankara, the new capital of the Republic.

Turkey remained neutral during World War II until 1945, when it entered the war on the side of the Allies; it became a mem-ber of NATO in 1952. The Democratic Party was elected to power in 1950, and remained in control of the country until

1960 when, in the face of increasing social and economic difficulties, it was overthrown by a military coup. A new constitution consolidating liberal reforms was drawn up, and approved by referendum in 1961. But continuing unrest led to further coups in 1971 and 1980, after which yet another, more restrictive constitution was prepared.

Turgut Özal, a former world banker and economist, was narrowly elected as prime minister in 1983, and served until his death in 1993. Under his leadership Turkey moved towards an industrialized, Western-style economy, and even applied for full membership of the European Community in 1987. But his successor, Tansu Çiller, Turkey's first woman leader, inherited many problems, including rampant inflation, and a violent conflict between Kurdish separatists and the security forces in the southeast of the country.

HISTORICAL LANDMARKS

Prehistory to Alexander the Great

6500-5700 BC	Neolithic community at Çatalhöyük.
c. 3000-2500 BC	Earliest level of habitation at Troy.
c. 2500-2000 BC	The Hatti produce Anatolia's earliest civilization, with capital at Alacahöyük.
Early 2nd millennium	The Prophet Abraham and his family arrive in Harran, on their way to Canaan.
c. 1950 BC	Assyrian trading colony at Kültepe, with oldest cuneiform tablets.
c. 1900-1260 BC	Levels VI and VIIa at Troy, perhaps the city of King Priam.
c. 1650-1620 BC	Hittite capital founded at Hattuşaş.
c. 1700-1450 BC	Old Hittite Kingdom.
c. 1450-1200 BC	Hittite Empire flourishes. Treaty of Kadesh between Hittites and Egyptians c. 1299 BC.
c. 1100-1000 BC	Greeks begin to colonize Aegean coast of Anatolia.
c. 900-700 BC	Phrygian culture flourishes, with capital at Gordion. Rise of Lydian, Carian and Lycian cultures. In eastern Anatolia, kingdom of Urartu has its capital at Tushpa (Van).
c. 700	The poet Homer born in Smyrna.
c. 660	Megara the Greek founds city of Byzantium.
560-546 BC	Reign of King Croesus of Lydia, based at Sardis.
c. 540 BC	Temple of Artemis at Ephesus completed.
499 BC	Ionian cities revolt against Persian rule.
499-467 BC	Greek-Persian Wars.
c. 353 BC	Mausoleum of Halicarnassus built.
334-333 BC	Alexander the Great crosses the Hellespont into Asia, marches through Anatolia.
323 BC	Alexander dies in Babylon. His generals battle over the subdivision of his empire.

The Hellenistic Age (323-30 BC)

301 BC	Battle of Ipsus. Lysimachus takes western Anatolia, Seleucus the southeast, and Mithradates founds Pontic kingdom in north.
c. 300 BC	Seleucus founds Antioch (Antakya).
263-241 BC	Eumenes I rules independent Pergamum.
241-197 BC	Attalus I extends Pergamene kingdom, allied with Rome; defeats invading Gauls.
197-159 BC	Eumenes II of Pergamum creates famous Pergamene library. Founds Hierapolis.
159-138 BC	Attalus II of Pergamum founds Attaleia (Antalya).
133 BC	Attalus III dies and bequeaths Pergamum to Rome. Romans create province of Asia in 130 BC.
120-63 BC	Reign of Mithradates VI, king of Pontus, with capital at Amaseia (Amasya).
88 BC	Mithradates VI invades Roman Asia, provokes slaughter of Roman citizens.
c. 69-34 BC	Reign of Antiochus I of Commagene. Builds temple-mausoleum on Nemrut Dağı.
41 BC	Mark Antony and Cleopatra meet at Tarsus.
31 BC	Octavian (later Augustus) defeats Antony, assumes control of Roman Empire. Antony and Cleopatra commit suicide.

The Roman Period (31 BC-AD 395)

31 BC-AD 14	Reign of Emperor Augustus. Beginning of Pax Romana, period of great prosperity in Asia Minor.
c. AD 35	Christian community established at Antioch (Antakya).
c. AD 49-60	The Apostle Paul makes missionary journeys in Asia Minor and Greece.
161-80	Construction of theatre at Aspendos.
c. 350	St Nicholas (later known as Santa Claus) becomes Bishop of Myra.
313	Christianity is legalized by Rome.
325	Council of Nicaea (Iznik).
330	Constantine makes Byzantium the 'New Rome', renamed Constantinople.
380	Christianity becomes the state religion of the Roman Empire.
395	Death of Theodosius I, and the division of the Roman Empire into east (Byzantine) and west.

The Byzantine Era (395-1453)

455	Rome sacked by Vandals. Constantinople becomes centre of civilized world.
527-65	Reign of Justinian the Great, golden age of Byzantine Empire.

532-37	Construction of Hagia Sophia in Constantinople.
636-718	Arabs overrun Syria, Egypt and Iran, and invade eastern Anatolia. Arab armies besiege Constantinople 674-8 and 717-18.
726-843	Iconoclastic Controversy divides Byzantine church and empire.
885-1045	Armenian culture flourishes in eastern Anatolia, with capital at Ani (Kars).
1071	Seljuk Turks defeat Byzantines at Battle of Manzikert (Malazgirt), and invade Anatolia.
1071-1283	Sultanate of Rum, Seljuk state with capital at Konya.
1096	Beginning of First Crusade.
1204-61	Crusaders sack Constantinople and occupy the city for 57 years. The Comneni found a separate Byzantine kingdom at Trebizond.
1243	Seljuks defeated by Mongols at Battle of Köse Dağ, and become vassals. Seljuk state begins to disintegrate.
1326	The Osmanlı Turks take Bursa and make it their capital – birth of the Ottoman Empire.
1453	Mehmet the Conqueror takes Constantinople and makes it his capital, renamed Istanbul.

The Ottoman Empire (1453-1922)

1517	Selim I captures Egypt and assumes title of caliph (leader of Islamic world).
1520-66	Reign of Süleyman the Magnificent, golden age of Ottoman Empire.
1571	Ottoman navy destroyed at Battle of Lepanto.
1683	Expansion of Ottoman Empire stops when siege of Vienna fails. Beginning of decline.
c. 1700-1800	Ottomans lose much territory during a series of wars with European powers.
1839-61	Reign of Abdül Mecid I. Introduction of westernizing reforms known as *Tanzimat*.
1876	Abdülaziz deposed, first constitution and parliament introduced.
1881	Birth of Atatürk.
1908-9	'Young Turks' uprising. Abdül Hamid II deposed.
1914-18	World War I. Turks enter war as German ally. Allies defeated at Gallipoli in 1915. In 1918, Turks surrender to Allies, Istanbul occupied by British.
1919	Atatürk organizes nationalist resistance in east.
1920-2	Turkish War of Independence drives Greeks out of Anatolia.

1923	Treaty of Lausanne guarantees Turkish independence and defines borders. Atatürk proclaims Republic.
Modern Turkey (1923-present)	
1923-4	Ankara becomes official capital of Turkey. Exchange of Greek and Turkish populations. Caliphate abolished.
1925-38	Atatürk's reforms transform the country.
1938	Death of Atatürk.
1939-45	Turkey annexes Hatay from French-controlled Syria. Remains neutral on outbreak of World War II, but joins on side of Allies in 1945.
1952	Turkey joins NATO.
1970-82	Period of instability, with weak government, increasing terrorism, military coups. Turkey invades northern Cyprus in 1974.
1973	First suspension bridge across Bosphorus.
1987	Turkey applies for membership of EC.
1988	Second bridge across Bosphorus.
1995	Turkey plans customs union with EU.

TURKISH GLOSSARY

ada(sı)	*island*
bulvarı	*boulevard*
burun (burnu)	*point, headland*
cadde(si)	*street*
camii	*mosque*
cumhuriyet	*republic*
çay(ı)	*stream (also tea)*
dağ(ı)	*mountain*
ev(i)	*house*
göl(ü)	*lake*
hamam(ı)	*Turkish bath*
haremlik	*private family quarters of Ottoman house*
iskele	*quay*
kaya	*rock, cliff*
kilise(si)	*church*
konak (konağı)	*mansion*
köprü(sü)	*bridge*
köy(ü)	*village*
kral	*king*
külliye	*complex of mosque, medrese, etc.*
ırmak	*river*
medrese	*theological college, seminary*
mezar	*tomb*
mihrab	*prayer niche facing Mecca*
mimber	*pulpit*
müze(si)	*museum*
nehri	*river*
saray	*palace*
savaş	*war, battle*
selamlik	*area of Ottoman house or palace where visitors are received*
sokak (sokağı)	*street, lane*
şadırvan	*ablutions fountain*
şehir	*town, city*
şerefe	*balcony*
taş(ı)	*stone*
türbe(si)	*tomb*

Kemal Atatürk – Father of the Turks (1881-1938)

You cannot travel through Turkey without noticing the statues that grace the main square in every city, town and village. Some are equestrian, some show a figure pointing the way, some are only a head and shoulders bust. But all of them share the rugged profile and steely, determined gaze of Kemal Atatürk, the distinguished soldier and statesman who founded the Turkish Republic.

Atatürk was born Mustafa, the son of a customs official in Salonika (now Thessaloniki, in northern Greece), in 1881. At school he excelled in mathematics, and his teacher suggested he adopt the second name 'Kemal', meaning 'perfection' or 'maturity'. Mustafa Kemal's first great ambition was to join the army, and eventually he graduated from the Harbiye Military Academy in Istanbul in 1902. While at college he developed an interest in politics, and became, like many of his fellow cadets, an enthusiastic nationalist. These were troubled times for the Ottoman Empire, then in a period of terminal decline. The young officer joined the revolutionary Committee for Union and Progress, and took part in the 'Young Turks' movement that deposed the sultan in 1909.

In subsequent years Mustafa Kemal saw action in Libya and in the Balkan War of 1912, before the Ottoman Empire became swept up in the turmoil of World War I. He distinguished himself as a military commander, defeating the Allies at Gallipoli in 1915, repelling the Russians on the eastern front in 1916,

The mansion above Trabzon where Atatürk stayed while visiting the city.

and saving the Turkish 7th Army from disaster in northern Syria in 1918. By the end of the war he had reached the rank of brigadier general, and was a popular hero, acclaimed in the press as the 'Saviour of Istanbul'.

Kemal, now promoted to a post in the Ministry of War, was appalled by the terms of the Armistice that had been imposed by the victorious Western powers, who had negotiated secret deals to carve up the Ottoman Empire in their own interests. Bitterly opposed to the stance of the sultan's government in Istanbul, which wanted to place the country under British protection, he set off for the east with secret plans to establish a nationalist resistance movement. He arrived at Samsun, on the Black Sea coast, on 19 May 1919, and travelled throughout central and eastern Turkey, explaining his plans for independence, and mustering support from the remains of the Turkish army and among the farmers and villagers of Anatolia. At the National Congresses of Erzurum and Sivas a National Pact was agreed, which laid out the movement's objectives – principally the establishment of an independent Turkish state within the country's existing frontiers.

In March 1920 the British formally occupied Istanbul and dissolved the sultan's government. Mustafa Kemal moved his headquarters to Ankara, where he formed an alternative government, the Grand National Assembly, which opened on 23 April 1920. Kemal was elected president, and set about the task of driving out the forces of occupation. The Turkish War of Independence culminated in the Battle of Dumlupınar (west of Ankara) on 26 August 1922, when the Turkish army, under the command of Mustafa Kemal, routed the Greek forces and drove them back to the sea at Izmir. In the face of the nationalist victory, the British

Atatürk, the 'Father of the Turks' in 1923.

handed over Istanbul and the Dardanelles; the frontiers of the Turkish state were confirmed and its independence assured by the Treaty of Lausanne on 24 July 1923. Kemal proclaimed the Republic of Turkey on 29 October and became its first president, ending nearly 600 years of Ottoman rule.

Having achieved an independent Turkish Republic, Kemal then set in motion a series of sweeping reforms. He had had ample opportunity to study the ways of Western society during his spell as a military attaché in Sofia in 1913 and during a convalescent trip to Austria in 1917, and was convinced that Turkey's future lay in Europeanization. He abolished the caliphate in 1924, closed down all religious schools and dervish orders, and replaced the *Sheriat* (Islamic code of law) with a new legal system based on that of the Swiss. Modern secular schools were established, and in 1928 the old Arabic script was replaced by a new Latin alphabet (critics complained that it would take five years to introduce the new alphabet; Kemal accomplished the reform in three months). Women were given equal status with men, and allowed to vote in national elections for the first time in 1934. The wearing of the old Ottoman turban and fez were banned in favour of Western-style headgear, the Gregorian calendar replaced the lunar Islamic calendar for official purposes, and all citizens were required to adopt a family surname. Kemal himself took the name 'Atatürk' which translates literally as 'Father of the Turks'.

Atatürk's body was re-interred in this splendid mausoleum in 1953.

Atatürk's reforms naturally met with opposition from those who sought to cling to the old ways, but they were generally welcomed by the common people, who were fired with a new sense of national pride and patriotism after the dismal years when the ailing Ottoman Empire had been reviled as the 'Sick Man of Europe'. The changes also created a divide between the educated city dwellers who soon adopted a European way of life, and the mass of peasant farmers whose lifestyles continued fundamentally unchanged, a divide which exists to this day. Atatürk's attempts at industrialization were less successful, but he provided the firm foundation on which his successors could build a modern industrial economy.

Kemal Atatürk died on the morning of 10 November 1938, in his apartments in the Dolmabahçe Palace in Istanbul. (All the clocks in the palace were stopped at 9.05, the hour of his death, and 10 November was made a national holiday; each year on that date, streets and houses are decked with the Turkish flag, military parades are organized, and at 9.05 all traffic stops and cars sound their horns.) Atatürk's coffin was placed in the presidential train and taken to Ankara for burial, with thousands of villagers lining the track for a last glimpse of their hero. His body was reinterred in 1953 in the capital's splendid Atatürk Mausoleum.

As a soldier, Atatürk saved his country from extinction, halting the advance of Allied forces in Gallipoli and in northern Syria, and driving the Greek army out of Anatolia. As a statesman he created a nation with a commitment to Western-style democracy, one that has been accepted by Europe and North America as a dependable ally and a valued trading partner. Little wonder that he is revered as the 'Father of the Turks'.

Just the Essentials

On a first-time visit to Turkey, you may be overwhelmed by the sheer wealth of choices you have wherever you start. The major landmarks and places to see and visit are proposed here to help you establish your priorities.

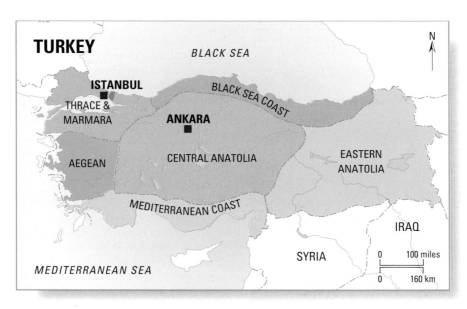

Istanbul

Hagia Sophia: the highest achievement of Byzantine architecture

Topkapı Palace: the former palace of the Ottoman sultans.

Grand Bazaar: the world's largest covered market.

St Saviour in Chora (Kariye Camii): beautiful Byzantine mosaics and frescos.
(2 days)

Aegean Region

Pergamum: ruins of impressive hilltop city.

Manisa: fine old Ottoman city.

Ephesus: Turkey's best-preserved ancient city.

Priene: beautiful ruins in romantic setting.

Didyma: remains of the vast Temple of Apollo.

Bodrum: attractive, bohemian seaside town with huge crusader castle.

Pamukkale: spectacular landscape of travertine terraces.

Aphrodisias: source of ancient Anatolia's finest sculpture.
(4-5 days)

Central Anatolia

Museum of Anatolian Civilizations, Ankara: Turkey's top museum.

Hattuşaş and Yazılıkaya: site of ancient Hatti and Hittite capital cities.

Amasya: beautiful riverside town with impressive rock tombs.

Cappadocia: spectacular landscapes of coloured cliffs and fluted pinnacles.

Mevlana Museum, Konya: home of the famous Whirling Dervishes.
(5-7 days)

Black Sea Coast

Sumela: improbable monastery clinging to high crag.

Ayasofya, Trabzon: beautifully preserved Byzantine frescos.
(1-2 days)

Thrace and Marmara

Bursa: First capital of the Ottoman Empire.

Selimiye Mosque, Edirne: one of the great masterpieces of Ottoman architecture.

Gallipoli: poignant war graves.

Troy: the site of Homer's fabled city.
(2-3 days)

Mediterranean Coast

Dalyan: pretty village with rock tombs.

Fethiye: lively harbour town with good market and Lycian rock tombs.

Ölüdeniz: one of the country's most beautiful beaches.

Kekova: ruined underwater cities.

Myra: impressive theatre and cliff-face riddled with rock tombs.

Arykanda: beautiful ruined city.

Olympos and Chimaera: where eternal flames issue from the rocks.

Termessos: spectacular ruins in a mountainous setting.

Aspendos: world's best-preserved Roman theatre.

Alanya: lively resort with impressive castle crag and extensive Seljuk ruins.

Caves of Heaven and Hell: vast subterranean caverns.

Kızkalesi: beautiful beach framed between two romantic castles.

Antakya Museum: display of Turkey's finest Roman mosaics.
(8-10 days)

Eastern Anatolia

Mount Ararat: Turkey's highest peak, last resting place of Noah's Ark.

İşak Bey Saray: romantic palace commanding route to Iran.

Ahtamar Adası: crowning glory of Armenian church architecture.

Şanlıurfa: ancient biblical city where Abraham may have lived.

Nemrut Dağı: monument to one man's megalomania.
(7 days)

Going Places with Something Special in Mind

If you are planning a trip to Turkey with specific interests in mind, a better idea than taking an off-the-shelf package tour is to design a holiday plan to fit in with your own tastes. Below we offer a selection of routes and themes, some following a specific itinerary, others presenting a list of destinations with a unifying theme. Also detailed are locations where you can pursue particular activities.

Pre-Hellenistic Turkey

The ancient peoples who ruled Anatolia in the centuries before the arrival of the Greeks left many enduring signs of their greatness. Turkey contains the sites of the capital cities of the Hatti, Hittite, Urartian, Phrygian and Lydian kingdoms, as well as many other fascinating remnants of pre-Hellenistic cultures.

Travellers with an interest in architecture will enjoy exploring Turkey's fascinating heritage. This ornately decorated portal at the İnce Minare Medresesi in Konya, is typical of those found on 13th-century Seljuk buildings.

1 KARAIN CAVE
Turkey's most important palaeolithic site, lying in a beautiful setting above the Pamphylian plain. Small museum on site.

2 ÇATALHÖYÜK (6800-5500 BC)
The neolithic site that yielded many of the prehistoric treasures on view in Ankara's Museum of Anatolian Civilizations. There is nothing to see at the site except the huge settlement mound and the eroded remains of the archaeologists' trenches.

3 ALACAHÖYÜK (3rd millennium BC)
The capital of the Hatti kings, whose tombs yielded the magnificent bronze grave goods now exhibited in Ankara's museum (and on which the logo of the Turkish Ministry of Tourism is based).

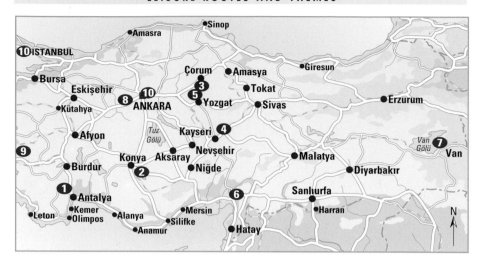

4 KÜLTEPE (c. 2000 BC)

The site of Kanesh, an important Assyrian trading settlement, where Anatolia's earliest written records were recovered.

5 HATTUŞAŞ (1375-1200 BC)

The famous capital of the early Hittite Empire, with impressive city walls and gates. The world's oldest written peace treaty was found here.

6 KARATEPE (8th century BC)

The summer palace of the Neo-Hittite king, Asitawada, adorned with beautiful reliefs depicting life at his court. Set in a scenic national park.

7 TUSHPA (9th-7th centuries BC)

A crumbling citadel on a crag overlooking the shores of Lake Van was the capital of Urartu, the Old Testament kingdom of Ararat.

8 GORDION (8th-7th centuries BC)

A former Hittite settlement which became the capital city of the Phrygians under King Gordios, and reached its peak during the reign of his successor, King Midas.

Central Anatolia is rich in the remains of ancient cultures that flourished in the centuries before the arrival of the Greeks.

9 SARDIS (6th century BC)

The former capital of the ancient Lydians, Sardis was the seat of the famously wealthy King Croesus.

10 ISTANBUL AND ANKARA

Anyone interested in Turkey's ancient sites should pay a visit to the Museum of Anatolian Civilizations in Ankara, and to Istanbul's Museum of the Ancient Orient.

Alexander the Great

Alexander marched through Anatolia in 334-333 BC on the first stage of the famous campaign which gave him an empire stretching from Greece to India. He began his march from Pella in Macedonia in early spring, 334 BC.

1 THE HELLESPONT

Alexander's army crossed the strait from Abydos to Sestos, but Alexander emulated Agamemnon by crossing from the southern tip of the peninsula to Elaeus. As the prow of his galley nudged onto the beach, he threw his spear in the sand to stake his claim on Asia.

2 TROY

Before marching to meet the Persians, Alexander went to Troy to make a sacrifice to Athena and to the dead King Priam. It is said he slept every night with a copy of Homer's *Iliad* beneath his pillow.

3 RIVER GRANICUS

The Persians confronted Alexander's army at the River Granicus (the modern Kocabaş), and were roundly defeated by the Macedonians.

4 SARDIS

The city of Sardis, taken from King Croesus by Cyrus of Persia in 546 BC, surrendered to Alexander, who took the role of liberator, and ordered the construction of a new Temple of Zeus.

5 EPHESUS

At Ephesus Alexander contributed to the costs of enlarging the Temple of Artemis, and of building the new Temple of Athena at Priene.

6 HALICARNASSUS

Halicarnassus (Bodrum) fell to Alexander after a prolonged siege. Alexander became the adopted son of the former Queen Ada, and installed her as ruler of Caria.

7 PHASELIS

Alexander's route along the coast was blocked north of Phaselis, so he sent part of his army inland and led the rest along the shore, where they had to wade around several cliffs. Legend has it that the wind changed, lowering the water level and thus allowing them to pass.

*A*lexander the Great, the legendary Macedonian warrior, created a vast empire. His famous campaign began in Anatolia, at the Hellespont.

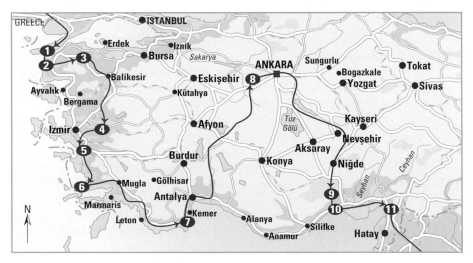

71

8 GORDION

After accepting the surrender of Perge, Alexander marched north to the former Phrygian capital of Gordion, where he solved the problem of the Gordian Knot. By then it was the spring of 333 BC.

9 CILICIAN GATES

Having passed through Ancyra and Cappadocia, Alexander headed south for the Mediterranean. He had expected trouble at the easily defended pass called the Cilician Gates, but the Persian garrison fled at his approach.

10 TARSUS

Alexander arrived in Tarsus in July 333 BC, where he was taken ill after a swim in the river. He had to convalesce until September.

11 ISSUS

After sacrificing to Athena and Asclepius (in gratitude for his recovery), he overcame the forces of the Persian King Darius at the Battle of Issus, opening the way for his conquest of the Persian Empire and the lands beyond. He founded the city of Alexandria ad Issum (now İskenderun) to commemorate his victory.

St Paul in Anatolia

The Apostle Paul was born in the Cilician city of Tarsus. He embraced Christianity after his famous conversion on the road to Damascus, and became an enthusiastic missionary for the new faith. His journeys took him through the territory of modern Turkey, where he founded a number of churches.

1 TARSUS

Paul (or Saul) was born in Tarsus c. AD 10, and trained as a rabbi. He studied as a Pharisee in Jerusalem before his conversion on the road to Damascus, where his first missionary work was carried out.

2 ANTIOCH

Paul lived in Antioch, where there was a small Christian community. After an argument about whether Gentiles should be admitted to this community, he and Barnabas left from the nearby port of Seleucia on the first of their missionary journeys, calling initially at Cyprus.

3 PERGE

'After this Paul and his companions took ship from Paphos and made for Perge in Pamphylia; here John left them and went back to Jerusalem.' *Acts* 13:13.

4 ANTIOCH-IN-PISIDIA

'They passed on from Perge, and reached Pisidian Antioch, where they went and took their seats in the synagogue on the Sabbath day.' *Acts* 13:14 (Antioch-in-Pisidia lies near the modern town of Yalvaç, northeast of Lake Eğirdir.)

5 ICONIUM

Paul and Barnabas then went and preached in the synagogue at Iconium (Konya). St Thecla was converted, but the city was divided about the new faith. On discovering a plot to stone them, they took refuge in nearby Lystra and Derbe.

6 ATTALEIA

They returned to the coast, where 'They preached the word of the Lord in Perge, and went down to Attalia (Antalya), taking ship there for Antioch.' *Acts* 14:24.

7 ALEXANDRIA TROAS

On his second journey Paul went overland towards Bithynia in northwest

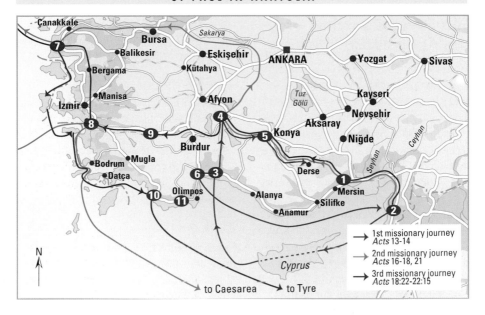

Turkey. But in Alexandria Troas he had a vision: 'A certain Macedonian stood by him in entreaty, and said, Come over into Macedonia and help us...So we put out from Troas, making a straight course for Samothrace [a Greek island]'). *Acts* 16:9-12.

The Apostle Paul made three long missionary journeys through Anatolia, spreading the then new religion of Christianity.

8 EPHESUS

On the return leg of his second voyage he called at Ephesus, and preached in the synagogue. On his third journey, he made the city his base of operations for a time, and wrote many of his letters to other churches here. His preaching enraged the city's silversmiths, who made a living making statues of Artemis. They provoked a riot; Paul spent some time in jail and eventually had to leave.

9 LAODICEA

While Paul was staying in Ephesus during his third journey, he and his colleagues founded churches at Laodicea, and at the nearby towns of Hierapolis and Colossae.

10 PATARA

When Paul was returning from his third journey, in the company of Luke, they changed ships at Patara: '...we made a straight course, sailing to Cos, and next day to Rhodes, and thence to Patara. There, finding a ship crossing to Phoenice, we went on board and set sail.' *Acts* 21:1-2.

11 MYRA

Later, when Paul was being taken to Rome, his ship called at Myra. They 'made a straight course over the open sea that lies off Cilicia and Pamphylia, and so reached Lystra (Myra) in Lycia. There the centurion found a boat from Alexandria which was sailing for Italy, and put us on board.'

The Seven Churches of the Apocalypse

Some of the churches founded by St Paul in western Asia Minor numbered among the famous 'Seven Churches of the Apocalypse', addressed in a letter written by St John of Patmos, the author of the *Book of Revelation*, in about AD 95. Travel agencies in Izmir offer guided tours to the Seven Churches of Asia, as they are also known. Two of the ancient cities have not been excavated. The 'churches' to which he wrote were, of course, congregations, not actual buildings. But in several of the sites you can see church buildings where early Christians once worshipped.

1 SMYRNA
The modern city of Izmir has obliterated most of the remains of ancient Smyrna; there are no early church buildings. To the Christians of Smyrna, St John wrote 'Only be faithful until death, and I will give you the crown of life.' *Revelation* 2:10

2 EPHESUS
St John the Apostle is thought to have lived in Ephesus (his crypt lies in the Basilica of St John in nearby Selçuk), and to have looked after the ageing Mary, Mother of Jesus, who lived in a house at Meryemana on a hill above the city. There is an early Christian basilica at Ephesus, the first ever church to be dedicated to the Virgin Mary.

3 LAODICEA
The sparse ruins of Laodicea lie between Denizli and Pamukkale. The city was castigated by St John in his *Book of Revelation* for its half-hearted embrace of Christianity: 'I know all your ways; you are neither hot nor cold. How I wish you were either hot or cold! But because you are lukewarm, neither hot nor cold, I will spit you out of my mouth…' (*Revelation* 3:15-17).

4 PHILADELPHIA
The modern town of Alaşehir, on the road between Salihli and Denizli, now stands on the site of Philadelphia. But you can visit the remains of the 7th-century Basilica of St John, near the town's Atatürk monument. All that survive are the four brick columns that once supported the central dome.

5 SARDIS
St John berated the Christians of Sardis for not being sufficiently vigorous in spreading the faith: 'though you have a name for being alive you are dead…For I have not found any work of yours completed in the eyes of my God.' *Revelation* 3:1-2.

6 THYATIRA
The site of Thyatira is now occupied by the unremarkable modern town of Akhisar, northeast of Manisa. It has not been excavated and there is nothing to see.

The Seven Churches of Asia that were addressed by St John in the Book of Revelation, *were situated in western Anatolia.*

7 PERGAMUM

Pergamum is referred to in the Book of Revelation as 'the place where Satan has his throne' (*Revelation* 2:13), possibly a reference to the Altar of Zeus on the acropolis. You can visit the remains of a Christian basilica that was built within the walls of the Kızıl Avlu (Red Hall), which was once a pagan temple.

Classical Architecture – Theatres

The great theatres of Turkey's ancient cities, with their curving tiers of marble seats, are often the most impressive part of the ruins.

The ancient cities of Asia Minor were endowed with fine public buildings, the most impressive of which were the theatres, where plays, music, lectures, gladiatorial combats and wild animal fights were staged. Turkey contains many fine examples, varying in style from the early Hellenistic type to the Roman model typified at Aspendos.

1 PRIENE

A classic example of a Hellenistic theatre, thought to date originally from the late 4th century BC, though slightly modified. The *cavea* is greater than a semicircle, and is separated from the 2nd century BC stage building by unroofed *parodoi*. Seats 5,000.

2 PERGAMUM

A stunning piece of Hellenistic architecture, built into a very steep and shallow depression below the summit of the acropolis. No permanent stage building – a wooden stage was erected above the street at its base. Seats 10,000.

3 APHRODISIAS

Built during the late Hellenistic period, with a new stage building added in the late 1st century BC. The orchestra was modified for wild animal shows in the late 2nd century AD. Seats 8,000.

4 TERMESSUS

This Hellenistic theatre enjoys perhaps the most beautiful setting of any in Turkey. A new stage building was added in 63 BC-AD 14, and the seating was extended over the right-hand *parodos*. Seats 4,500.

5 EPHESUS

Originally built in the Hellenistic period, but extensively enlarged and modified, so it is now almost entirely Roman. Stage building were added in the 1st and 2nd centuries AD. Seats 24,000.

6 HIERAPOLIS

Though greater than a semicircle, it was built in the 2nd century AD. Access to the *cavea* was by two *vomitoria* (tunnels giving onto the *diazoma*). It is notable for its ornate stage building, decorated with reliefs of Dionysus.

7 SIDE

Although it was built in the 2nd century AD, it has a Hellenistic-style *cavea,* greater than a semicircle, suggesting that it replaced an older building. Very unusual in that it is not built into a hill, but supported on huge masonry vaults. Seats 13,500.

8 ASPENDOS

The world's best-preserved example of a Roman theatre, built in AD 161-180, with a perfect semicircular *cavea,* two 'royal boxes', and impressive four-storey stage building. Seats 15,000.

Classical Architecture – Temples

The Greeks who settled in Asia Minor brought with them the pantheon of Olympian gods, but often absorbed older indigenous deities into their cults – as at Ephesus, where the Greek huntress Artemis became identified with the ancient Anatolian mother goddess, Cybele. The temples built to house the cult statues of the gods are some of Turkey's finest ancient monuments.

1 ASSOS

The Temple of Athena, perched on a hilltop overlooking the sea, dates from *c.* 530 BC. It is mainly in the old Doric order, with tapered, faceted columns and plain capitals.

2 CLAROS

The ruins of the Hellenistic Temple of Apollo at Claros are in poor condition, but it is another example of the early Doric order, dating from the 4th century BC. There are fragments of the statue of Apollo lying among the tumbled columns.

3 EPHESUS

The Temple of Artemis at Ephesus, built in the 6th century BC, was one of the Seven Wonders of the World. The lower drums of 36 of the massive Ionic columns were decorated with reliefs. Unfortunately almost nothing remains, although the site gives some idea of its vast size.

4 DIDYMA

The Hellenistic Temple of Apollo at Didyma was built in the 4th century BC at the command of Alexander the Great. This huge building, with a double peristyle of Ionic columns, housed a sacred oracle.

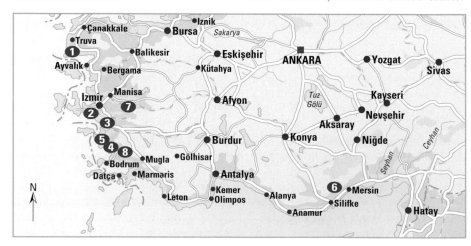

5 PRIENE

Construction of Priene's Temple of Athena Polias (Athena of the City) took place between the 4th and 2nd centuries BC. Five of the elegant Ionic capitals and their whirns that have been re-erected. The temple occupies a beautiful site over-looks the plain below.

6 OLBA/DIOCAESAREA

The Temple of Zeus Olbios is Asia Minor's earliest known example of a temple built in the Corinthian order; it dates from the early 3rd century BC. Thirty columns still stand, four of them bearing their capitals.

7 SARDIS

Work on the Temple of Artemis at Sardis dragged on from the 3rd century BC to the 4th century AD, and even then it was never finished. It has some of Turkey's finest examples of Ionic capitals. Two of the columns still stand to their full height.

8 EUROMUS

The beautiful Corinthian Temple of Zeus at Euromus is one of the best-preserved temples in Turkey; it dates from the reign of the Emperor Hadrian (AD 117-38). Sixteen of the original 30 columns still stand today, bearing both their capitals and long sections of architrave.

The temple was the most important building in a Greek city. Not only was it a house of the gods, it was also a symbol of the city's wealth and power. The earliest temples were made of timber, and when the first stone temples were built, they copied the form of the old wooden structures.

National Parks

Turkey has many national parks, mostly in areas of scenic beauty. Some of them are at sites of historical importance; others provide sanctuaries for wildlife. Most have very basic facilities, such as a car park, picnic area and toilets, although some have museums and restaurants too. Listed below are ten of the best.

1 ADIYAMAN (NEMRUT DAĞI)

Area around the summit of Nemrut Dağı, site of the mausoleum of King Antiochus of Commagene. Hotel and motel.

2 ALTINDERE VALLEY

Beautiful forested river valley in the mountains above Trabzon, around the site of the famous Sumela Monastery. Restaurant, picnic area, camping.

3 BOĞAZKÖY-ALACAHÖYÜK

The excavated ruins of Hattuşaş, the capital of the Hittite Empire, along with sites at Yazılıkaya and Alacahöyük. Museum, camping, picnic area.

4 DİLEK YARIMADASI

The Dilek Peninsula to the south of Kuşadası offers some attractive shingle beaches away from the crowds. Picnic areas, restaurants.

5 KARATEPE-ASLANTAŞ

Lovely wooded site by a man-made lake, with an open-air museum displaying the excavated remains of a Neo-Hittite summer palace. Camping, picnic area.

6 KIZILDAĞ

Beautiful cedar woods, rich in wildlife, in the mountains at the north end of Lake Beyşehir. Camping, picnic area.

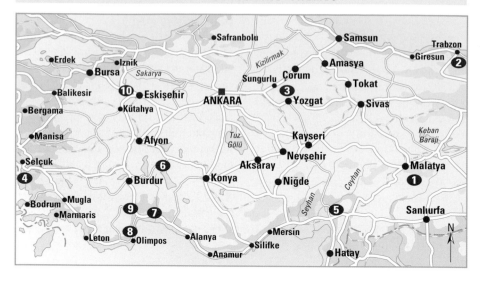

7 KÖPRÜLÜ KANYON

Spectacular canyon, spanned by an old Roman bridge, with a short hiking path along one side. Good scenery and trout fishing. Trout restaurant by river below canyon. Ruins of ancient Selge above. Picnic area, angling, white-water rafting.

8 OLIMPOS BEYDAĞLARI

The Lycian Mount Olympos, overlooking the Gulf of Antalya, offers excellent hiking, with abundant wildflowers in spring. Motel, restaurant, camping, picnic area.

9 TERMESSOS

Spectacular site of ancient Pisidian city set high in the mountains, with a vast necropolis beyond. Good hiking. Restaurant, camping, picnic area.

10 ULUDAĞ

Another ancient Mount Olympos, this time above the historic city of Bursa. Winter sports resort, with limited hiking trails in summer. Pleasant woods in lower part. Cable car from Bursa. Hotels, restaurants, camping, picnic areas.

Turkey has some of Europe's most beautiful landscapes. Many are now protected as national parks.

Seljuk Architecture

When the Seljuk Turks began their invasion of Anatolia in the 11th century, they brought with them a tradition of early Muslim architecture – congregational mosques, tall, decorated minarets, and conical-roofed *türbes* (tombs). Once they had established a Seljuk state within Anatolia – the so-called 'Sultanate of Rum' – their architecture flowered, and left Turkey a legacy of beautiful and distinctive buildings. The following list of sites lies along the Uzun Yol, an old Seljuk trade route.

1 KONYA

As the capital of the Sultanate of Rum, Konya was well endowed with fine buildings, especially *medreses* (religious schools).

78

Sights include: the Alaeddin Camii, which contains the tomb of the great Seljuk Sultan Alaeddin Keykubad I; the İnce Minareli Medrese; and the Büyük Karatay Medresesi.

2 SULTANHANI

Caravanserais were built along the Uzun Yol route to provide a secure lodging for traders' camel caravans at night. The Sultan Hanı here is one of the biggest and best preserved.

3 AKSARAY

On the road from Aksaray to Nevşehir are the ruins of three more caravanserais: Ağzıkarahan (now housing a market), the most interesting; and Örsınhanı and Alayhanı, both of which are rather dilapidated.

4 KAYSERI

Kayseri was an important Seljuk centre of commerce, sited where the route from the Mediterranean through the Cilician Gates joined the Uzun Yol. Sights include the Mahperi Hunat Hatun Medresesi, the Sahibiye Medresesi, the Çifte Medrese, and the Döner Gümbet tomb.

5 SULTANHANI

Northeast of Kayseri lies another smaller caravanserai called Sultanhanı. The arches of the prayer hall in the courtyard are decorated with carved serpents.

6 SIVAS

Another important Seljuk town with a fine legacy of 13th-century architecture. A park in the town centre contains the Çifte Minareli Medrese, the Sifaiye Medresesi and the Bürücüye Medresesi; near by are the 11th-century Ulu Camii and the Gök Medrese, with its beautiful façade.

7 ERZURUM

The eastern outpost of Erzurum has been ravaged by war and earthquakes, but a few

The rich architectural legacy of the Seljuk Sultanate of Rum includes the mosques and medreses of Konya, Kayseri and Sivas, and the hans that lie on the roads between.

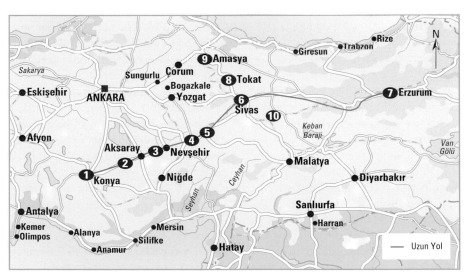

worthwhile monuments remains, notably the Yakutiye Medresesi, built by a Mongol emir in 1310, which shows strong oriental influence.

8 TOKAT

Another trade route branches north from Sivas, following the valley of the Yeşilırmak to the Black Sea. The town of Tokat contains a few buildings worth stopping for, notably the Gök Medrese, which houses the town's museum.

9 AMASYA

The beautiful town of Amasya is better known as the ancient capital city of the Pontic kings, but it also has a couple of Seljuk monuments – the Gök Medrese and the Burmalı Minare Camii.

10 DİVRİĞİ

The out-of-the-way town of Divriği was once the seat of a minor emir, who endowed it with the splendidly idiosyncratic Ulu Camii, which is worth making the effort to see.

Turkish Carpets

Carpets are perhaps Turkey's most famous export. Back in the 16th century, England's Henry VIII couldn't get enough of them – Turkish carpets appear on the floor and in the background in a famous portrait of Henry by Hans Holbein. Different areas of Turkey have become associated with different carpet patterns; below is a brief list of the better known districts.

1 BERGAMA

So-called Yağcibedir carpets have been woven here since the 14th century. The colours are predominantly dark blue (indigo) and red (cochineal), with eagle, triangle, tree of life and pine cone motifs.

2 MILAS

Milas carpets typically have pastel-type shades – pale brown, pink and yellow – and often have a prayer-mat pattern with a *mihrab* panel in the middle. Arrows, goose-feet, clover and carnations are common motifs.

3 BALIKESİR

The carpets woven in the Balıkesir district are called *Sındırgı*. They have a tight weave, and lovely natural shades of blue, red and beige. Common motifs include birds, ram's heads, ears of wheat and the tree of life.

4 YAHYALI

Yahyalı, south of Erciyes Dağı, is one of Cappadocia's most important weaving centres. Natural dyes are extracted from vine leaves, mint, buckthorn and walnut to produce green, gold and black elements that combine with bold blue and red patterns.

5 KARS

The carpets woven in Kars have a reputation for strength and durability, and often incorporate undyed wool from the black- and brown-fleeced sheep which are common in the region.

6 KAYSERİ

Kayseri and Konya are well-known for producing large-size carpets for mosques, halls and reception rooms. They have wool knots and cotton warp and weft, and are tightly woven to create beautiful, hard-wearing, intricately patterned carpets.

7 KONYA

Konya carpets are considered to be among the best carpets woven in Turkey. Those

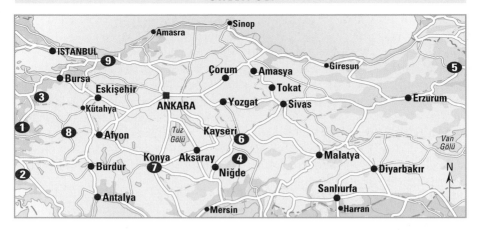

produced by the local nomads are characterized by warm colours, such as brick-red, light brown and beige.

8 UŞAK

Carpets from the Uşak district are sometimes called Holbein carpets, because their patterns resemble those that appear in paintings by the 16th-century artist Hans Holbein. Characteristic colours are cream, yellow, pale blue and beige, which all complement the dominant red.

9 HEREKE

The name of Hereke is synonymous with carpets of the highest quality, produced in workshops set up by the Ottoman sultan in 1891 to produce carpets for the imperial palaces and mosques, and as gifts for foreign potentates. The finest Hereke silk carpets have an average of 100 knots per sq cm (645 per sq in), and would cost several thousand pounds to buy.

Gallipoli

The Gallipoli Peninsula was the site of one of the bloodiest and most notorious campaigns of World War I. The area is now a

Turkish carpets are decorated with traditional patterns that vary from region to region.

national park, dotted with beautifully tended war graves and monuments to those who fell.

1 KABATEPE MUSEUM

The museum has a sad but fascinating collection of articles found on the battlefields, but the most poignant exhibits are the letters written by soldiers in the trenches. Here, too, you can find out about the series of ten bronze plaques that lie scattered around the battlefield explaining the progress of the campaign.

2 ANZAC COVE

The notorious beach where the men of the Australian and New Zealand Army Corps (Anzac) waded ashore in the early hours of 25 April 1915. They had intended to come ashore 1.5 km (1 mile) to the south at Kabatepe, but unknown currents had pushed their boats northwards in the darkness.

3 MEÇHUL ASKER (UNKNOWN SOLDIER)

A massive statue of Mehmetçik (the Turkish equivalent of 'Johnny') remembers all the unknown Turkish soldiers who lost their lives and have no marked grave.

4 CHUNUK BAIR

The ridge that the Turks managed to hold on to, despite Allied attempts to take the summit. Here, the opposing trenches were often only tens of metres apart. Several monuments can be found here, plus a series of reconstructed trenches.

5 KEMAL YERİ

Known to the Allies as the Scrubby Knoll, this was Mustafa Kemal's command post.

6 SUVLA BAY

Suvla Bay was the site of renewed Allied landings in August 1915. This was the offensive that decided the outcome of the campaign; despite three days of fighting, the Allies failed to take Chunuk Bair.

7 CAPE HELLES

While the Anzacs were storming the slopes of Chunuk Bair, the spearhead of the Allied attack was directed at Cape Helles, at the southern tip of the peninsula. The Turkish inscription on the Helles Memorial translates as: 'You soldiers who have fallen while defending this land, may your ancestors descend and kiss your noble brows. Who could dig the grave that could contain you? History itself is too small a place for you.'

8 TURKISH MEMORIAL

To the east of Cape Helles lies the massive, four-pillared stone table of the Çanakkale Martyrs' Memorial (*Çanakkale Şehitleri Abidesi*), which remembers all the Turks who gave their lives at Gallipoli.

Kemal Atatürk

Kemal Atatürk, the 'Father of the Turks', was the distinguished soldier and statesman who founded the Turkish Republic (see p.58). His campaign for Turkish independence took him all over the country, and all major towns and cities have their own Atatürk Museum. To follow in his footsteps is to follow the events that led to the birth of modern Turkey.

1 ISTANBUL

The young Mustafa Kemal was educated at Harbiye Military Academy, next to the Military Museum in Beyoğlu (see p.111). Near by is the Atatürk Museum, set in the house where he lived in 1919 while serving in the Ministry of War.

2 GALLIPOLI

Mustafa Kemal first came to prominence as the brilliant commander who frustrated the Allied campaign at Gallipoli in 1915 (see p.81).

3 SAMSUN

Kemal stepped ashore at this Black Sea port on 19 May 1919 to begin his nationalist resistance movement. The event is commemorated by a 'first step' monument (see p.299).

4 ERZURUM

In July 1919 the eastern city of Erzurum hosted the First National Congress, at which Kemal and his colleagues laid down the minimum acceptable boundaries of a new Turkish state.

5 SIVAS

The Second National Congress was held here in September 1919, the delegates agreeing on a National Pact.

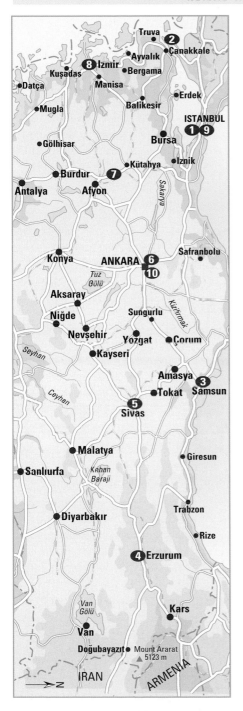

6 ANKARA

Kemal moved his headquarters to Ankara and convened a Grand National Assembly on 23 April 1920. The building is now a museum (see p.260).

7 DUMLUPINAR

The culmination of the War of Independence was the Battle of Dumlupınar, west of Afyon. The battlefield is now a national park, the *Başkomutan Tarihi Milli Parkı,* with monuments marking the important sites.

8 IZMIR

The Greek army, routed at the Battle of Dumlupınar, was driven to the sea at Izmir. A mansion on the waterfront in Alsancak, where Atatürk stayed during his visits to the city, now houses an Atatürk Museum.

9 ISTANBUL

Atatürk died in Istanbul's Dolmabahçe Palace (see p.112) on 10 November 1938. All the clocks in the palace are stopped at 9.05am, the time of his death.

10 ANKARA

Atatürk was reinterred in 1953 in the splendid Atatürk Mausoleum in Ankara, which includes a fascinating museum dedicated to the great man.

*Y*ou cannot travel through Turkey without noticing the statues that grace the main square in every city, town and village. All of them share the rugged profile of Kemal Atatürk – soldier, statesman and founder of the Turkish Republic.

Byzantium, Constantinople, Istanbul – the City that 'with One Key Opens and Closes Two Worlds, Two Seas…'

Istanbul is one of the world's great cities. Its unique setting, at the point where Europe faces Asia across the turquoise ribbon of the Bosphorus, makes it the only city in the world to bridge two continents. Here, where the waters of the Black Sea blend into the Aegean, east and west merge and mingle in the cultural melting-pot of Turkey's largest metropolis.

Istanbul is the only city in the world that has been the capital of both an Islamic and a Christian empire. As Constantinople, jewel of the Byzantine Empire, it was for over 1,000 years the most important city in Christendom. As Istanbul it was the seat of the Ottoman sultans, rulers of a 500-year Islamic empire that stretched from the Black Sea and the Balkans to Arabia and Algeria.

It owes its historic importance to its strategic location on the Bosphorus. From

Istanbul had a strategic position on the Bosphorus. Here, the Fatih Sultan Mehmet Bridge spans the strait beside Mehmet's Rumeli Hisari fort.

here the city could control not only the shipping that passed through the strait on the important trade route between the Black Sea and the Mediterranean, but also the overland traffic from Europe into Asia Minor, which used the narrow strait as a crossing point. In the words of the 16th-century French traveller Pierre Gilles, 'The Bosphorus with one key opens and closes two worlds, two seas'.

That strategic advantage is no less important today than it was 2,500 years ago, when a band of Greeks first founded the city of Byzantium on this very spot. Ankara may be the official capital of modern Turkey, but Istanbul is the country's largest city and busiest port, producing over one-third of Turkey's manufacturing output. The Bosphorus is one of the world's busiest shipping lanes, and the overland traffic is now carried by two of the world's longest suspension bridges.

The city has long since spread beyond the 5th-century Byzantine walls built by Emperor Theodosius II, and now sprawls for miles along the shores of the Sea of Marmara on both the European and Asian sides. Back in 1507 this was the world's largest city, with a population of 1.2 million. That figure has now passed 8 million and is still growing, swollen by a steady influx of people from rural areas looking for work (more than half of the population was born in the provinces). These new arrivals created a series of shantytowns around the edge of the city. Their makeshift homes, known in Turkish as *gecekondu* ('built by night'), take advantage of an old Ottoman law that protects a house whose roof has been built during the hours of darkness. The slums are eventually knocked down to make way for new tower blocks – a new suburb is created, a new shantytown springs up beyond it, and Istanbul sprawls a little further.

At the other end of the social spectrum are the wealthy *İstanbullus* who live in the upmarket districts of Taksim, Harbiye and Nişantaşı, where chunky gold jewellery, Gucci shoes and BMWs are *de rigueur,* and the streets are lined with expensive apartments, fashion boutiques and stylish cafés. These are the lucky few who frequent the city's expensive restaurants and casinos, and retire at the weekends to their restored wooden mansions *(yalı)* along the Bosphorus. But the majority of Istanbul's inhabitants fall between these extremes, living in modest flats and earning an average wage in the offices, shops, banks and factories that provide most of the city's employment.

Just as the Bosphorus separates Asia from Europe, so the inlet called the Golden Horn separates the old Istanbul from the new. The historic heart of the city lies on a small peninsula on the south side of the Golden Horn, known as Saray Burnu, or Seraglio Point. This easily defensible thumb of land is bounded on three sides by the so-called 'Three Seas' – the Sea of Marmara to the south, the Bosphorus to the east and the Golden Horn to the north – and on the fourth by the 5th-century Theodosian Walls. Across its seven hills spreads the Old City, also known as Stamboul or Eski Istanbul, home to the city's richest historic treasures – Hagia Sophia, Topkapı Palace, the Blue Mosque, the Covered Bazaar, the Süleymaniye Mosque and the Church of St Saviour in Chora.

The new Galata Bridge spans the mouth of the Golden Horn, linking Old Istanbul to the 'New City' of Beyoğlu. Here you will find the 14th-century Galata Tower, the stylish shops, cafés and hotels of İstiklal Caddesi and Taksim Square, and the sumptuous splendour of Dolmabahçe Palace.

Ferries cross the Bosphorus to Üsküdar and ply the length of the scenic strait, past the pretty fishing villages of Arnavutköy, Kanlıca, Emirgan and Tarabya, and the imposing fortress of Rumeli Hisarı. And to the south, in the Sea of Marmara, lie the woods and beaches of the Princes' Islands.

The Old City – Stamboul

Istanbul's most popular tourist attractions are concentrated in the Sultanahmet district, near the tip of the Saray Burnu peninsula, and are all within easy walking distance of each other. A new tram line runs from Sirkeci, near the Galata Bridge, through Sultanahmet, past the Grand Bazaar, the hotels of Laleli and

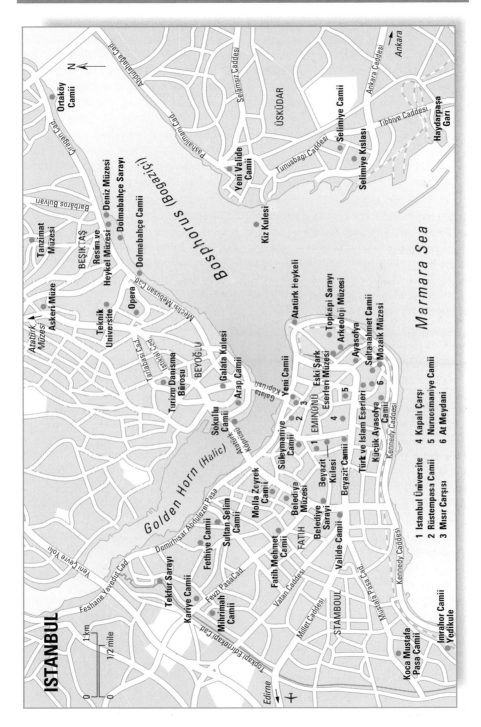

Aksaray, and on to the city walls at Top-kapı bus station (not to be confused with the famous palace of the same name). The outlying sights of St Saviour in Chora and Yedikule are best reached by taxi.

Sultanahmet

The Sultanahmet district occupies the summit of the first of the Old City's seven hills. This was the site of the original Byzantium, founded in the 7th century BC, and of the civic centre of Constantinople, capital of the Byzantine Empire. Here, too, the conquering Ottoman sultans chose to build their most magnificent palaces and mosques. Little now remains of the Byzantine city, but what does is one of the most remarkable buildings ever constructed – Hagia Sophia.

Hagia Sophia (Ayasofya)

For nearly 1,000 years, the **Church of Hagia Sophia** was the greatest church in Christendom, an architectural wonder designed to impress upon the world the might of the Byzantine Empire.

A Christian basilica is thought to have been built here by the Emperor Constantine in AD 325, on the site of a pagan temple. It was destroyed by fire in 404, and rebuilt by Theodosius II, then burnt down again in 532. The building you see today was commissioned by Justinian and completed in 537, though many repairs, additions and alterations have been made over the centuries. The dome has been damaged by earthquakes several times, and the supporting buttresses have coarsened the outward appearance of the church.

The finest materials were used in its construction – white marble from the islands of the Marmara, yellow marble from Africa, verd-antique from Thessaly, gold and silver from Ephesus, and ancient red porphyry

columns which possibly came from Egypt, and may once have stood in the Temple of the Sun at Baalbek. The interior was covered with glowing golden mosaics, lit by countless flickering candelabras.

The last Christian service ever to be held in Hagia Sophia took place on 28 May 1453, the day before Constantinople finally fell to the Turks. Mehmet the Conqueror immediately converted the building to an imperial mosque, and built a brick minaret at the southeast corner.

The magnificent church of Hagia Sophia was for over 1,000 years the most important church in Christendom, and a lasting symbol of the might and wealth of the Byzantine Empire.

Sinan strengthened the buttresses and added the other three minarets during the 16th century; the most recent restoration was carried out in the 1840s. Hagia Sophia continued to serve as a mosque until 1935, when Atatürk proclaimed that it should become a museum.

The entrance path leads past the ticket desk to a shady tea garden outside the main portal, surrounded by architectural fragments from the 5th-century church built by Theodosius; an excavated area to the left of the door reveals a part of this earlier building. You enter Hagia Sophia through the central portal, across a worn and polished threshold of *verd-antique*, and under a 9th to 10th-century **mosaic** of Christ Pantocrator, into the long, narrow

Little now remains of the decoration that once covered the interior of Hagia Sophia. This mosaic, at the east end of the gallery, shows emperor and empress with the Virgin Mary.

narthex, running to right and left (NB the ramp to leading to the galleries is to the left, see below; to the right is the exit). Note the beautiful matched **panels** of red and green marble, and the vaulted, gold-mosaic **ceiling**. As you continue through the huge bronze doors of the Imperial Gate, your eyes will be drawn heaven-wards by the upwards sweep of the vast dome. It is about 31m (100ft) in diameter, and stands 55m (180ft) high – about the same as a 15-storey building.

The sensation of space is created by the absence of supporting walls beneath the dome – it rests instead upon four great arches, which in turn spring from four massive piers. The arches flanking the nave are filled with tiers of columns and window-filled walls, while those above the entrance and the apse are backed by semi-domes, further increasing the interior space. This was the great achievement of the Byzantine architects Isidorus and Anthemius – to transfer the weight of the dome to the pillars using arches and 'pendentives', the four triangular sections of masonry that fill the gaps between arches and dome,

creating the illusion of an unsupported dome floating in space. The Emperor Justinian was so overwhelmed by the first sight of what his architects had achieved, that he cried out, 'Glory be to God that I have been judged worthy of such a work! O Solomon, I have surpassed you!'

The original decoration has long since disappeared. Eight huge medallions, bearing the Arabic names of Allah, Muhammad, two of his grandsons, and the first four caliphs, and a quotation from the Koran in the crown of the dome, are remnants of Hagia Sophia's 500 years of service as an imperial mosque, as are the elaborate *mihrab* and *mimber* in the apse. But a few **mosaics** survive – above the apse is the Virgin with the infant Jesus, with the Archangel Gabriel to the right (his companion Michael, to the left, has vanished save for a few feathers from his wings).

The best mosaics are in the galleries, reached by a spiral ramp at the north end of the narthex. By the south wall is the famous **Deesis**, an extraordinary 13th-century mosaic showing Christ flanked by the Virgin Mary and St John the Baptist. Beyond, on the east wall, are two more images showing Byzantine emperors and empresses making offerings to Christ on his throne (to the left), and to the Virgin and Child.

Back at the east end of the galleries, two small columns and a circle of green marble mark the spot where the empress sat during services; on the floor of the nave below, a circle of coloured stone to the right of centre is the **Opus Alexandrinum**, where the Byzantine emperors were crowned. Go back down the ramp and go through the first door on your left. In front of you is the **Weeping Column**, or the Column of St Gregory, which has a thumb-sized hole covered with a brass plate. If you insert a finger, it comes out damp – the moisture is said to have miraculous healing powers, especially for eye diseases.

As you leave by the door at the south end of the narthex, turn around and look up above the door to see a beautiful 10th-century **mosaic** of the emperor and empress offering symbols of Hagia Sophia and Constantinople to the Virgin Mary and Child.

Topkapı Palace (Topkapı Sarayı)

Between Hagia Sophia and the tip of Saray Burnu stretches the walled enclosure of **Topkapı Palace**, the former residence and seat of government of the Ottoman sultans. Begun in 1462 by Mehmet the Conqueror, it was enlarged and extended by each succeeding sultan until it became a miniature city, including mosques, libraries, stables, kitchens, schools, the imperial mint, treasuries, barracks, armouries, government offices and audience halls, as well as the private chambers of the sultan and his entourage. At its height, it supported a population of nearly 4,000.

Sultan Abdül Mecit moved into the newly built Dolmabahçe Palace in 1853, and by 1909 Topkapı was completely abandoned. In 1924 it was converted to a museum, and has been undergoing a continuous programme of restoration ever since. It is the city's most popular tourist attraction, and deserves a full day to do justice to its many treasures. If you are pushed for time, the 'must-sees' are, in order of importance, the Harem, the Treasury and the Pavilion of the Holy Mantle.

The palace is laid out as a series of courtyards linked by ceremonial gates. You enter through the **Imperial Gate** (built in 1478) into the wooded gardens of the First Court. On the left is the Byzan-

TOPKAPI PALACE

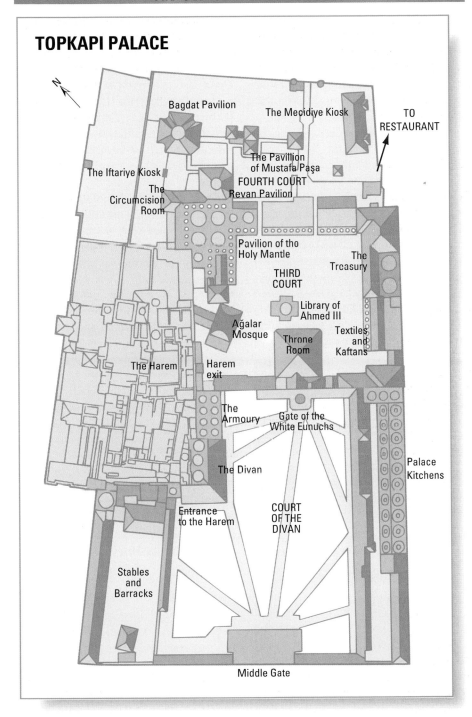

N

Bagdat Pavilion

The Mecidiye Kiosk

TO
RESTAURANT

The Pavillion
of Mustafa Paşa

The Iftariye Kiosk

FOURTH COURT

The
Circumcision
Room

Revan Pavilion

Pavilion of the
Holy Mantle

The
Treasury

THIRD
COURT

Library of
Ahmed III

Ağalar
Mosque

Textiles
and
Kaftans

Throne
Room

The Harem

Harem
exit

The
Armoury

Gate of the
White Eunuchs

Palace
Kitchens

The Divan

Entrance
to the Harem

COURT
OF THE
DIVAN

Stables
and
Barracks

Middle Gate

tine church of **Hagia Eirene** (Divine Peace), rebuilt along with Hagia Sophia after being burnt down in 532 (closed to the public). This area was also known as the **Court of the Janissaries**, after the crack military corps that served as the sultan's bodyguard, who used it as an assembly ground while on duty at the palace (the name comes from the Turkish *yeni çeri,* 'new army'). It originally contained the palace bakery, the armoury and the mint. At the far right-hand corner is the ticket office, which once served as a prison. The fountain beyond is traditionally called the Executioner's Fountain. Here he rinsed his sword and washed his hands after carrying out his orders; examples of his handiwork were displayed on pikes at the Imperial Gate.

Buy your ticket and pass through the turreted Gate of Salutations, better known as the *Orta Kapı,* or **Middle Gate**. Only the sultan was permitted to ride through this gate on horseback; all others had to dismount and bow. It leads into the Second Court, also called the **Court of the Divan**, as this is where the Imperial Council (known as the Divan) carried out the business of governing the Ottoman Empire. Five avenues radiate from the inside of the gate. To the right lie the enormous **Palace Kitchens**, which house a priceless collection of Chinese porcelain, European crystal, and Ottoman cooking implements and serving dishes. Straight ahead is the ornate Gate of the White Eunuchs, which leads into the Third Court and the private quarters of the palace. The avenue on the left leads towards the pointed **Divan Tower** *(Divan Kulesi),* at the foot of which lie the Council Chamber and the Grand Vizier's Office. Here, too, is the entrance to Topkapı's main attraction, the Harem.

The **Harem** housed the private quarters of the sultan, his mother, and his many wives and concubines. Its network of dimly lit staircases, corridors and courtyards linked the sumptuously decorated chambers of the royal household, and harboured a claustrophobic world of ambition, jealousy and intrigue. The Harem is open from 10am to 4pm, and can be visited only on the official 30-minute guided tour, for which you must buy an additional ticket. Try to get there early, as tours sell

Topkapı Palace, once the home of the Ottoman Sultan and his government, is now Istanbul's biggest attraction. You enter through the Orta Kapi, *or Middle Gate, with its twin turrets and tall battlements.*

*T*he magnificent royal apartments in the Topkapı Harem
include the huge and ornately decorated Imperial Hall.

THE HAREM HIERARCHY

The bottom rung of the harem ladder was occupied by the *cariye*, or odalisque, a concubine
of the lowest rank. These women were taken from their families as girls of 12 or 13, variously
captured in war, kidnapped, or even bought as slaves. They came from the non-Muslim parts
of the empire (religion forbade the enslavement of Muslim women), and were chosen for their
beauty. Many were from Georgia and Circassia (in the Caucasus Mountains), where the women
were noted for their black hair and fair skin. The girls were taught Turkish and Arabic,
music, dancing and etiquette, and converted to Islam.

If a *cariye* was fortunate enough to catch the sultan's eye, she became a *gözde* (favourite),
was given servants and a private room, and could concentrate her wiles on winning an invi-
tation to the sultan's bedchamber – the first step on the path to power. If she succeeded she
received the title *ikbal* (success), and if she bore a child, she was a *haseki* (that which belongs
to the sultan).

The next step was to become a *kadın*, one of the four 'official' wives permitted by the laws
of Islam. These were former favourites who had borne male children, and were given a whole
suite of rooms and retinue of slaves. The main aim in life of a *kadın* was to manoeuvre her
son into a position where he would succeed his father as sultan. If successful, she attained the
pinnacle of power and became *valide sultan* (mother of the sultan), the undisputed queen of
the harem and often the power behind the throne.

out quickly on busy days. The ticket will be stamped with the time your tour begins, which may be immediately or a few hours later – ask when you buy. The tours are rushed, and the route may change as restoration work closes off certain areas.

You enter by the **Carriage Gate**, where the women mounted their carriages on the rare occasions they were permitted to venture outside. The only adult males allowed in the Harem were the Black Eunuchs, who were in charge of security and administration. Their quarters opened off the narrow **Courtyard of the Black Eunuchs**, beyond the gate. Windows in the colonnade on the left give a glimpse of their tiny rooms; sticks hanging on the walls were used to beat miscreants on the soles of their feet, a mandatory punishment for all novices.

A long, narrow corridor lined with shelves (for trays of food) leads to the Courtyard of the Women Servants, from which you enter the **Apartments of the Valide Sultan** (the sultan's mother, and the most powerful woman in the Harem). Her domed sitting room is panelled with 17th-century Kütahya tiles, and decorated with scenic views. A raised platform framed by two columns contains divans and a low dining table. The door on the left, beyond the hearth, leads to the *valide sultan's* bedchamber, with a gilded bed canopy and ornate floral faience in turquoise, blue and red. A small adjoining prayer room has scenes of Mecca and Medina.

The right-hand door leads to the **Apartments of the Sultan** himself. First you pass the entrance to the royal bathchambers, designed by Sinan and richly ornamented in marble. There are paired but separate chambers for the sultan and the *valide sultan*, each having a changing room, a cool room and a hot room. The sultan was bathed by elderly female servants, then dried and pampered by groups of younger handmaidens.

Next, you enter the vast and splendid **Imperial Hall**, with three handsome marble fountains and a canopied throne from which the sultan would enjoy the music and dancing of his concubines. The *valide sultan* and the senior wives sat on sofas under the gallery to the left, while the more talented slave-girls played music from the balcony above.

Perhaps the most splendid of all the rooms is the **Salon of Murat III**, with inlaid floors, flowered İznik tiles of the best period, carved fountains, canopied sofas and a superb domed ceiling; its design is attributed to Sinan. On the far side a door leads to the Library of Ahmet I, with cupboard doors and shutters inlaid with mother-of-pearl and tortoiseshell, which in turn opens into the Dining Room of Ahmet III, better known simply as the **Fruit Room**. This tiny, wood-panelled room is covered all over with lacquered paintings of flowers and fruit in rococo style. Ahmet III was known as the 'Tulip King', and celebrated each spring by holding a tulip festival in the palace grounds.

The exit from the Harem opens into the **Third Court**, otherwise reached through the Gate of the White Eunuchs (see above). Immediately inside the gate is the richly decorated **Throne Room** *(Arz Odası),* where the sultan received foreign ambassadors. Head down to the right to the **Treasury**, whose chief attractions are the famous golden Topkapı Dagger, with three huge emeralds set in the hilt, and a fourth forming the lid of a watch hidden in the handle; and the Spoonmaker's Diamond, an 86-carat, pear-shaped diamond set in a gold mount encrusted with 49 smaller diamonds. Other exhibits include gilded thrones studded with precious stones, a pair of solid gold candlesticks set with 666 diamonds (one for each verse of the Koran), and reliquaries containing the hand and part of John the Baptist's skull.

This elaborate fountain lies next to the Pavilion of the Holy Mantle, one of Istanbul's most sacred shrines. It contains relics of the Prophet Muhammad, including his sword and robe.

THE ORIGINS OF WRITING

Cuneiform (i.e. 'wedge-shaped') text was a system of writing that emerged in the Middle East around the end of the 3rd millennium BC, and was used extensively until the 1st century BC. It was produced by pressing the slanted edge of a stylus into a soft clay tablet, producing a wedge-shaped impression. The earliest type of cuneiform, found in Mesopotamia, was pictographic – words were represented by 'pictures' drawn in the clay. Over time these pictographs evolved into formalized patterns of strokes and became true writing.

The thousands of cuneiform clay tablets discovered by archaeologists in the Hittite cities of Hattuşaş (see p.260) and Kanesh (see p.272) are some of the oldest known examples of true writing, and provide most of the information we have on Hittite culture and history. They were stored in sophisticated libraries complete with catalogues and indexes; there were even three-language dictionaries for translating documents from Hittite into Sumerian and Akkadian, the 'international' diplomatic languages of the time. The most famous cuneiform document, found at Hattuşaş and now on display in the Museum of the Ancient Orient in Istanbul, is the bilingual Treaty of Kadesh between the Hittites and the Egyptians – the oldest recorded peace treaty in the world

Across the courtyard is the magnificently decorated **Pavilion of the Holy Mantle**, which houses sacred relics of the Prophet Muhammad, and is therefore a place of great religious importance for Muslims. The relics include a hair from the Prophet's beard, soil from his tomb, his sword and his robe (the Holy Mantle). The **Fourth Court** contains a number of pretty pavilions and terraces, and a restaurant and cafeteria with fine views of the Bosphorus.

Archaeological Museum

From Topkapı's First Court, a narrow cobbled lane leads down beside Hagia Eirene to the Fifth Court, which contains three outstanding museums. The excellent **Archaeological Museum** *(Arkeoloji Müzesi)* has recently been expanded to include galleries devoted to Cyprus, Syria and Palestine, the Phrygians, Troy, and Anatolia from the palaeolithic to the Iron Age. But its main attraction is still its magnificent collection of sarcophagi, especially the Alexander Sarcophagus, decorated with scenes of hunting and battle.

The **Museum of the Ancient Orient** *(Eski Şark Eserleri Müzesi)* displays a rich collection of objects from ancient Near and Middle Eastern civilizations, including Babylonian ceramic panels from the time of King Nebuchadnezzar (605-562 BC), Hittite stone lions, and clay tablets bearing some of the earliest known examples of writing (2700 BC) and the oldest recorded set of laws, the Code of Hammurabi (1750 BC).

The most eye-catching building in the square is the **Tiled Kiosk** *(Çinili Köskü),* built in 1472 for Mehmet the Conqueror, and decorated with turquoise and blue tiles. It houses a valuable display of ceramics ranging in age from Seljuk times to the 20th century.

Hippodrome

This long, narrow park stretching southwest from Hagia Sophia occupies the site of the ancient Byzantine **Hippodrome** *(At Meydanı)*. Inspired by the Circus Maximus in Rome, it was built in AD 203 as a stadium for chariot-racing and other public events. Enlarged by Constantine the Great, it eventually measured 400m long by 120m wide (1,300ft by 400ft), and could hold an audience of 100,000.

The Hippodrome was the setting for the ceremony which proclaimed Constantinople as the 'New Rome' in AD 330, following the division of the Roman Empire, and soon became the civic centre of the Byzantine capital, decorated with imposing monuments and flanked by fine buildings. Unfortunately it was destroyed when the city was sacked during the Fourth Crusade, and left stripped of its statues and marble seats. In the 17th

century its ruins were used as a quarry for the building of the Blue Mosque. Only its outline, a few brick vaults, and three fine ancient monuments survive.

The north end of the *spina,* or central axis, is now marked by an ornate, domed ablutions fountain, gifted to the city by Germany's Kaiser Wilhelm II to commemorate his visit in 1900. At the opposite end rise the three remnants of the original Hippodrome. The **Egyptian Obelisk** was

A narrow lane leads down beside Hagia Eirene to the Fifth Court, where you will find the Archaeological Museum and the Museum of the Ancient Orient. On the north side of the courtyard lies the Cinili Kosku *(Tiled Kiosk), which houses a museum of Ottoman ceramics.*

The Egyptian Obelisk stands at the south end of the Hippodrome. It was brought to the city in AD 390 by the Emperor Theodosius who is depicted in reliefs on the pedestal.

commissioned by the Pharaoh Thutmose III in the 16th century BC, and brought to Constantinople by the Emperor Theodosius in AD 390. This is only the top third of the original – it broke during shipment. The reliefs on the pedestal show Theodosius and his family presiding over events taking place in the Hippodrome, notably (on the side opposite the Serpentine Column) the raising of the obelisk.

The **Serpentine Column** consists of three intertwined bronze snakes; they originally supported a gold vase, but the snakes' heads and the vase have long since disappeared. It is the oldest Greek monument in Istanbul, commemorating the Greek victory over the Persians at Plataea in 479 BC (it was brought here from Delphi by Constantine the Great). A second, deeply eroded stone obelisk is known as the **Column of Constantine Porphyrogenitus**, as an inscription on its base records that the emperor of that name (913-59) had it restored and sheathed in gilded bronze plates.

The six slender minarets of the **Blue Mosque** dominate the skyline above the Hippodrome. Known in Turkish as the *Sultan Ahmet Camii* (Mosque of Sultan Ahmet), it was built in 1609-16 for Sultan Ahmet I, and thereafter became the city's principal imperial mosque because of its proximity to the sultan's palace at Topkapı. Enter the courtyard through the gate that opens on to the Hippodrome to savour the full effect of the architect's skill. As you pass through the portal, the façade sweeps up before you in a magnificent crescendo of domes. (Go out through the door on the left of the courtyard to reach the tourists' entrance to the mosque proper.)

Once inside, you will see how the mosque earned its familiar name. The very

A *graceful cascade of domes meets your eye as you enter the*
courtyard of the Blue Mosque.

air seems to be blue – over 20,000 turquoise İznik tiles glow gently in the light from the mosque's 260 windows, decorated with lilies, carnations, tulips and roses. Four massive fluted columns support a dome 22m (70ft) in diameter, and 43m (142ft) high at the crown – big, but not as big as Hagia Sophia, whose design obviously influenced the architect. The *mihrab* and *mimber* are of delicately carved white marble, and the ebony window shutters are inlaid with ivory and mother-of-pearl. The painted blue arabesques in the domes and upper walls are modern restorations. For a glimpse of the original decoration, take a look at the wall beneath the sultan's loge.

Across the Hippodrome from the Blue Mosque is the **Museum of Turkish and Islamic Arts** *(Türk ve İslam Eserleri Müzesi)*. The collection is housed in the former palace of İbrahim Paşa, the son-in-law of Süleyman the Magnificent, and includes illuminated Korans, inlaid Koran boxes, antique carpets, ceramics and Persian miniatures. The ethnographic section has tableaux of a nomad tent or yurt, a village house, and a traditional carpet loom, with explanations of the natural dyes used to colour the wool.

Across the tram lines from Hagia Sophia lies the entrance to one of Istanbul's more unusual historic sights – the **Yerebatan Saray** (Underground Palace). This amazing construction is actually an underground cistern, one of many that once stored Constantinople's water supply. Aqueducts brought the water from the Belgrade Forest, north of the city, to the cisterns, where it was held in reserve in case the city was besieged. The cistern measures 140m by 70m (460ft by 230ft); its vaulted brick roof is supported by a forest of columns topped by Corinthian

capitals, 336 in all, set in 12 rows of 28. As you peer into the dripping gloom, you can marvel at the fact that it still stands, almost 1,500 years after it was built.

Central Stamboul

The street with the tram lines that leads uphill from Sultanahmet (Divan Yolu) was the main road leading to the city gates in Byzantine and Ottoman times, and it still is today. The next tram stop is called *Çemberlitaş* (Hooped Column), after the stone pillar that rises to the right of the road. Also called the **Burnt Column**, it was charred and cracked by a great fire which ravaged the district in 1770 (the iron hoops help to hold it together). It was erected by Constantine in May 330 to mark the city's new status as capital of the Eastern Roman Empire. Parts of the Cross, and the nails with which Christ was crucified, are reputed to be sealed in the column's base.

The Grand Bazaar

Behind the Burnt Column rises the baroque exterior of the Nuruosmaniye Camii (built in 1755). Walk towards it, turn left through an arched gate into the mosque precinct, and follow the crowds into the bustling **Grand Bazaar**. The *Kapalı Çarşı* (Covered Market) of Istanbul is the world's largest covered bazaar, with about 4,000 shops, as well as banks, cafés, restaurants, mosques and a post office, crammed together in a grid of narrow streets, and protected from summer sun and winter rain by a multitude of domed and vaulted roofs. Mehmet the Conqueror built the first covered market on this site in 1461, and over the centuries it has been rebuilt several times after destruction by fire and earthquake, most recently in 1954.

It is fairly easy to find your way around, as most of the streets follow a regular grid pattern and are well signposted. From the Nuruosmaniye entrance, the main street stretches away to the Beyazıt Gate, lined with jewellers' shops. On your right is the entrance to the 16th-century **Sandal Bedesten**, with lovely brick vaults supported on massive stone pillars. It is quiet and empty for most of the week, but comes alive during the auctions held here at 1pm on Tuesdays, Wednesdays and Thursdays. In the centre of the bazaar is the **Old Bedesten**, where you can find the best quality gold and silver jewellery, brass and copper ware, curios and antiques (the most precious goods were traditionally kept in the Bedesten, as it can be locked at night).

The Beyazıt Gate, at the far end of the the main street (*Kalpakcılar Başı Caddesi*), leads to a crowded street of vegetable and flower stalls. Turn right, and first left up the stairs to the **Book Market** (*Sahaflar Çarşısı*), a shady retreat where students and professors from the nearby university browse among well-stacked shelves. There is a fair selection of English-language books, including many specialist titles devoted to Turkish history, art and architecture.

*A*t weekends the open space of Beyazıt Square is thronged with market stalls and crowds of shoppers.

Beyazıt

Beyond the Book Market lies **Beyazıt Meydanı**, a vast, pigeon-thronged square below the entrance to Istanbul University. At weekends the square hosts a lively flea market, where vendors lay out an astonishing variety of new and second-hand goods, from alarm clocks, transistor radios, cameras and medical equipment to cheese slicers, chainsaws, snorkelling gear and inflatable boats. Old men sell bags of corn to feed to the pigeons, while colourfully dressed water-sellers tout for business with cries of *'buz gibi!'* ('ice-cold!'), and encourage tourists to take a photograph – for a fee.

The east side of the square is dominated by the beautiful **Beyazıt Camii**, built in the early 16th century by Sultan Beyazıt II, son of Mehmet the Conqueror. It is important as the earliest surviving example of classical Ottoman architecture, drawing its inspiration directly from Hagia Sophia. Opposite the mosque is the arched gateway to Istanbul University, and the distinctive landmark of the 50m (164ft) high **Beyazıt Tower**, built in 1828 as a fire lookout point.

The Süleymaniye

Beyond the university campus, on an imposing site high above the Golden Horn, rises the majestic outline of the Süley-maniye, the **Mosque of Süleyman the Magnificent**. The finest Ottoman building in Istanbul, the mosque is a tribute to the 'Golden Age' of the Ottoman Empire, and to the two great men of genius who created it – Sultan Süleyman I, the Magnificent, and his chief architect, Sinan. Süleyman, known in Turkish as *Kanuni* (The Lawgiver), reigned from 1520 to 1566, during which period the empire attained the height of its wealth and power.

The mosque and its extensive complex of attendant buildings was built between 1550 and 1557, employing around 5,300 labourers and craftsmen. Legend has it that jewels from Persia were ground up and mixed in with the mortar for one of the minarets, and that the incredible acoustics were achieved by embedding 64 hollow clay vessels neck-down in the dome. It is also said that Süleyman, recognizing the greatness of his architect's achievement, handed the keys to Sinan at the inauguration ceremony and allowed him the privilege of opening the mosque.

You enter through a grand courtyard, colonnaded with columns of granite, marble and porphyry, with a rectangular *şadırvan* (ablutions fountain) in the centre. The interior is vast and awe-inspiring, flooded with light from the 16th-century **stained-glass windows**. It is square in plan, about 58m (190ft) on a side, capped by a dome 27.5m (90ft) in diameter and 47m (154ft) high. The **tiles** are original İznik faience, with floral designs in turquoise, blue and the then-new coral red; the **woodwork** of the doors and shutters is delicately inlaid with ivory and mother-of-pearl.

Both Süleyman and Sinan (who lived to be almost 100) are buried near by. The tombs of the sultan and his wife Roxelana are in the **walled garden** behind the mosque, both richly decorated with İznik tiles and painted patterns. The garden is an atmospheric spot, where roses and hollyhocks tangle among the long grass between the gravestones, and flocks of sparrows swoop and squabble in the fig trees. Sinan's modest tomb, which he designed himself, stands in a triangular garden at the northern corner of the complex, capped by small dome.

A walk around the **terrace** beside the mosque, which affords a fine view across the Golden Horn, will give you some idea of the huge size of the complex, which included bath-houses, schools, a caravanserai, a library, kitchens, a poorhouse and accommodation for attendants. You can also look up at the four fine **minarets**, two with two balconies and two with three. It is said that the four minarets signify that Süleyman was the fourth sultan to reign in Istanbul, and the ten balconies remind us that he was the tenth ruler of the Ottoman Dynasty.

Outer Stamboul

There are a number of worthwhile sights in the outer reaches of the city between the Süleymaniye and the city walls, but they are widely scattered, and you will probably want to use taxis to reach most of them. Away from the main roads, these mostly residential districts contain a maze of backstreets, cobbled alleys and muddy lanes, where the occasional old wooden house that has survived the city's many fires leans creaking across the crumbling bricks of some forgotten Byzantine ruin. If you choose to walk, be prepared to get lost – often – and to be an object of friendly curiosity to the local people.

The imposing **Şehzade Camii** (Mosque of the Prince) overlooks a grassy park, whose atmosphere is rather spoiled by the roar of traffic from nearby Atatürk Bulvarı. The mosque, one of Sinan's early works (1548), was built in memory of Süleyman the Magnificent's son, Prince Mehmet, who died in 1543 aged only 21.

Spanning the park and the six lanes of Atatürk Bulvarı, are the ruins of the **Aqueduct of Valens** *(Bozdoğan Kemeri)*, whose origins date back to the 2nd century AD. It was rebuilt by the Emperor Valens in the 4th century, and was restored several times by both the Byzantines and Ottomans, and remained in use as recently as the 19th century. It once delivered water to a number of cisterns in the city centre, which supplied the palace of the Byzantine emperors, and later Topkapı.

If you follow the line of the aqueduct away from the city centre, you will soon reach the vast complex of the **Fatih Camii** (Mosque of the Conqueror), perched on top of the city's Fourth Hill. This was the first imperial mosque to be built following the Conquest of Constantinople in 1453, and its *külliye* (mosque complex), the biggest in the whole of the Ottoman Empire, included a hospital, a mental asylum, poorhouses, accommodation for visitors, and a number of schools teaching science, mathematics and history as well as Koranic studies. Built by Mehmet the Conqueror between 1462 and 1470, it was almost completely destroyed by an earthquake in 1766. Only the courtyard and its huge portal survived; the rest was rebuilt to a different plan. The tombs of the Conqueror and his wife are in the walled graveyard behind the mosque.

Further out, dominating the Fifth Hill, is the **Sultan Selim Camii** (Mosque of Selim I), dedicated to the father of Süleyman the Magnificent. Unlike its dedicatee, who was known as *Yavuz Selim* (Selim the Grim), the mosque is one of the most charming in the city, with a sparse but tasteful decoration of beautiful **İznik tiles** from the earliest period in turquoise, blue and yellow, and richly painted woodwork. Its dramatic situation overlooking the Golden Horn commands a fine view across the picturesque districts of Fener and Balat.

The brightest jewel in Istanbul's Byzantine crown is the former church of **St Saviour in Chora**, known in Turkish as the **Kariye Camii**. Restored and opened as a museum in 1958, this small building, tucked away in a quiet corner of the city, is one of

T he unassuming exterior of St Saviour in Chora hides a treasure-house of Byzantine art in the form of beautiful mosaics and several frescoes.

the world's greatest monuments to Byzantine art. The name of the church means 'in the country', because the first church to be built on this site was outside the city walls. Although it was later enclosed within the Theodosian Walls, the name stuck.

The oldest part of the present building, the central domed area, dates from 1120. The church was rebuilt and decorated early in the 14th century under the supervision of Theodore Metochites, statesman, scholar and art-lover, and a close friend and adviser of the Emperor Andronicus II Palaeologus. Sadly, Metochites was reduced to poverty and sent into exile when the emperor was overthrown in 1328. He was allowed to return to the city in 1330 provided that he remained a monk at Chora, which he did, living out the last years of his life surrounded by the magnificent works of art he had commissioned.

Metochites left the central portion of the church untouched, but added the outer narthex and the parecclesion (side chapel). The wonderful mosaics and frescoes, dating 1310-20 (contemporary with those of Giotto in Italy), are almost certainly the work of a single artist, now unknown. Their subtlety of colour, liveliness of posture and strong, lifelike faces record a last remarkable flowering of Byzantine art before its descent into decadence. The church was converted to a mosque in 1511, but thankfully it was not altered substantially. The mosaics were covered with wooden screens, some windows were boarded up, and a minaret was added.

The **mosaics** are grouped into four narrative cycles depicting the lives of Christ and of the Virgin Mary, along with portraits of various saints and large dedicatory panels. The mosaic above the door leading from the narthex into the nave shows the figure of Metochites wearing a huge hat and offering a model of his beloved church to Christ. Each tiny tile is set at a different angle to its neighbours so that the reflected light creates the illusion of a shimmering, ethereal image.

The **frescoes** are all in the parecclesion, which stretches the length of the building and was used in Byzantine times as a funerary chapel. The artist's masterpiece is the *Anastasis* (Resurrection) in the vault of the apse, showing Christ pulling Adam and Eve from their tombs, while the figure of Satan lies bound and helpless beneath His feet.

Fifteen minutes' walk from the Kariye, and marking the summit of the Sixth Hill, is the Mihrimah Sultan Camii, built by Sinan in 1565 for Süleyman's favourite daughter. Next to the mosque are the **Theodosian Walls**, pierced here by the Adrianople Gate (*Edirnekapı*), where Mehmet the Conqueror entered the fallen city in 1453. The double walls were built in the 5th century, during the reign of the emperor Theodosius, and stretch 6.5km (4 miles) from the Sea of Marmara to the Golden Horn. They were defended by 96 towers and had numerous gates, of which seven remain in use. Much of the inner wall and many of the towers are still standing.

At the Marmara end of the Theodosian Walls, a long way from the city's other sights but easily reached by bus or taxi, stands the ancient fortress of **Yedikule** (Seven Towers). It encloses the famous **Golden Gate**, the grand triumphal arch of the Byzantine emperors, which existed before the walls were built and was incorporated into them. In 1470 Mehmet the Conqueror further strengthened the ancient portal by building three towers of his own, linked by curtain walls to the four Byzantine towers flanking the Golden Gate. During Ottoman times the fortress was used as a prison and a treasury.

The Golden Horn (Haliç)

The Golden Horn is an inlet of the Bosphorus, penetrating 7.5km (4½ miles) into the hills behind the city. It forms a natural harbour, and in Ottoman times was the site of the Imperial Tershane (Naval Arsenal), capable of holding 120 ships. Today it is lined with shipyards, factories and industrial development, and its waters are badly polluted.

Eminönü

The mouth of the Golden Horn is spanned by the busy **Galata Bridge**. The first bridge here was a wooden structure, built in 1845. It was replaced in 1910 by the famous old pontoon bridge with its seafood restaurants, which served until the present bridge was opened in 1992. Like the Atatürk Bridge further upstream, its central span is opened at 4am each morning to allow ships in and out. At the Stamboul end of the bridge is the colourful district of Eminönü, a major transport hub where

bus, ferry, tram and train services interconnect. At rush hour, the waterfront becomes a bedlam of bodies as commuters pour off the ferries. The air is loud with blasts from ships' horns, and the water boils white as half a dozen vessels jostle for a vacant berth. Smaller boats equipped with cooking fires and frying pans bounce around in the wash, while their crews dish up mackerel sandwiches to hungry workers on the quayside, apparently oblivious to the violent movement of their floating kitchens. Competing with them for passing trade are the sellers of grilled corn cobs, *lahmacun, simit* and fried mussels, while water-sellers tempt thirsty diners with lemon- and cherry-flavoured drinks.

The wide square opposite the bridge is dominated by the **Yeni Camii** (New Mosque). Commissioned in 1597 by the Valide Sultan Safiye, the mother of Mehmet III, it was not completed until 1663, making it the youngest of Istanbul's great classical mosques. The square is always busy with fruit and vegetable stalls, pedlars of all kinds of goods, and huge flocks of pigeons.

The large archway to the right of the mosque is the entrance to the famous **Spice Bazaar**, also known as the Egyptian Bazaar (*Mısır Çarşısı*). It was opened a few years before the Yeni Camii, and its revenues originally paid for repairs to the

---

LEONARDO'S BRIDGE

The first bridge to be built across the Golden Horn was a wooden one, built at the behest of Bezmialem Sultan, the mother of Sultan Abdül Mecit, in 1845. But a bridge had been proposed much earlier, by Sultan Beyazıt II. In 1502, Leonardo da Vinci heard from an Ottoman delegation to the Borgia court that the sultan was looking for an engineer capable of building such a bridge. He designed a gigantic masonry arch, with a single span of 240m (790ft), and sent his plans to Istanbul; but nothing came of them. In 1952 researchers found in the Topkapı Palace archives a copy of a letter sent to Sultan Beyazıt by 'an infidel named Leonardo' in which he offered to build not only the bridge, but also windmills, and automatic bilge pumps for the sultan's fleet.

---

*T*he new Galata Bridge was opened in 1992, replacing a pontoon bridge that had served since 1910. At the far end is Eminönü with its busy quay, the Yeni Camii, and on the skyline the dome of Nuruosmaniye Camii (following pages).

mosque complex. Inside, the air is heady with the mingled aromas of ginger, pepper, cinnamon, cloves and freshly ground coffee. The L-shaped building has 88 shops, many still devoted to the sale of spices, herbs and herbal remedies, but dried fruit and nuts, *lokum* (Turkish delight), fresh fruit and flowers, apple tea, and more mundane household items occupy the majority of stalls.

If you leave the Spice Bazaar by the gate at the far end of the first aisle and turn right, you will find the **Rüstempaşa Camii** (Mosque of Rüstem Paşa), with its minaret soaring high above the narrow backstreet. This is one of Sinan's smaller works, and one of his most beautiful. The interior is almost completely covered in İznik tiles of the finest period, with floral and geometric designs in turquoise, blue and coral red.

Eyüp

Ferries depart from the upstream side of the Galata Bridge for the half-hour trip along the Golden Horn to the suburb of **Eyüp**, which contains one of Islam's most sacred shrines. The Eyüp Sultan Camii marks the burial place of Eyüp Ensari, the standard-bearer of the Prophet Muhammad. He died in battle while carrying the banner of Islam during the Arab siege of Constantinople, between 674 and 678. Following the Conquest in 1453, his grave was rediscovered, and Mehmet the Conqueror erected a shrine on the spot, followed in 1458 by a mosque, the first to be built in Istanbul. Thereafter each sultan, on his accession, visited Eyüp Camii ceremonially to gird himself with the Sword of Osman, the first Ottoman sultan. The original mosque was destroyed by an earthquake in 1766; the present building dates from 1800. The Tomb of Eyüp Ensari, opposite the mosque, is beautifully decorated with gold and silver, and coloured tiles, and is protected by a gilded grille. Remember that this is a sacred place – dress respectfully (long trousers and long-sleeved shirt; women should cover their head, shoulders and arms), remove your shoes before entering, and keep your camera in its bag.

The hillside behind the mosque is a vast cemetery littered with turbanned headstones. A path winds up to the **Pierre Loti Café**, named in honour of the 19th-century French writer who once lived in the neighbourhood and who wrote a number of romantic novels about life in Istanbul. The café enjoys a splendid view down the Golden Horn to the distant domes and minarets of Stamboul.

The New City – Beyoğlu

The north shore of the Golden Horn was traditionally the quarter where foreign merchants, craftsmen and diplomats made their homes, beginning in the 11th century when the Genoese founded a trading colony in the district of Galata. Following the Conquest, European ambassadors built their mansions on the hills beyond Galata, a place which came to be called Pera (Greek for 'beyond'). Foreigners from all over the Ottoman Empire flooded into Galata and Pera, attracted by the wealth and sophistication of the capital. As the area became more crowded, so the rich merchants and diplomats moved their mansions and embassies further out along the 'Grande Rue de Pera' (now İstiklal Caddesi), forming a focus for the 19th- and 20th-century expansion of the modern, European-style part of Istanbul, known as Beyoğlu.

Galata and Pera

As you cross the Galata Bridge, crowded with shoppers, office workers, water-sellers and anglers, your eyes are drawn naturally to the pointed turret of the Galata Tower, which dominates the skyline. Some time during the 11th century, a rough bunch of coastal traders and dubious drifters from every port in the Mediterranean began to settle the northern shore of the Horn, in the maritime quarter which came to be known as Galata. Genoese merchants had already taken up residence on the hillside above the port, eventually establishing a fortified city within the city.

The **Galata Tower** (*Galata Kulesi*) was the keystone in the colony's defences. Its age is uncertain, but it seems to have been built in its present form around 1349, at the highest point of the city walls. Now restored, with a restaurant and nightclub at the top, it offers a superb panoramic view over the city (open daily 10am to 6pm). Looking across the Golden Horn, you can count off the domes and minarets that embellish Istanbul's famous skyline. From left to right they are: Hagia Sophia; the Blue Mosque; the Nuruosmaniye (above the Galata Bridge); Beyazıt Camii; the Beyazıt Tower; the Süleymaniye, looming over the far shore; the Şehzade Camii (in the distance); the Aqueduct of Valens; the twin minarets of the Fatih Camii (above the Atatürk Bridge); and the Sultan Selim Camii.

You can avoid the steep climb up the hill beyond the Galata Bridge by taking the **Tünel**, the world's oldest (and probably its shortest) underground railway, built in 1875. The trip to the top station just 90 seconds (see GETTING AROUND IN TURKEY p.21). To reach the Galata Tower

The fresh fruit on a street stall adds a splash of colour to a grey Galata street.

from the top station, turn left out of the exit and immediately left down a very steep road. Continue for about five minutes until you see a sign saying 'Kuledibi' on the left, which points to the tower.

109

The distinctive pointed turret of the Galata Tower lies within a maze of narrow alleys on the steep hillside above the Galata Bridge. The view from the top is simply magnificent.

From the Tünel exit, restored 1920s streetcars clang their way along **İstiklal Caddesi**, the former Grande Rue de Pera, once lined with the palatial embassies of foreign powers. The mansions remain, downgraded to consulates since the capital was transferred to Ankara in 1923, and now crowded by turn-of-the-century apartment blocks and modern shops and restaurants. The street is now a pedestrian precinct, and boasts some of the city's most stylish cafés. At Galatasaray Square, where İstiklal Caddesi bends to the right, an elegant wrought-iron gateway marks the entrance to the Galatasaray Lisesi, the takes 19th-century Franco-Turkish *lycée* (secondary school) which educated many of the great names in modern Turkish history. (Incidentally, the district also lent its name to one of Turkey's most famous football clubs.)

Past the square on the left is the entrance to **Çiçek Pasajı** (Flower Alley), a high, glass-roofed arcade lined with bars and restaurants. It is liveliest in the evenings when the tables fill with a mixture of Turks and tourists drinking beer and swapping yarns. The far end of the passage leads into the **Balık Pazarı** (Fish Market), a picturesque block of narrow streets thronged with stalls selling fish, fruit and vegetables, and a local speciality snack – fried mussels on a stick (*midye tava*).

If you turn left at Galatasaray Square, and left again at the British Consulate along Meşrutiyet Caddesi, you will soon reach the **Pera Palas Hotel**, established in 1892 to provide accommodation for Orient Express passengers. Its splendour is a little faded now, but that only adds to the charm of the huge, chandeliered public rooms with their antique mirrors, braziers and samovars, and thick Turkish carpets. The old 'birdcage' lift will take you up to the second floor for a look at the suite used by Atatürk, now preserved as a museum.

The morning's catch from the Black Sea quickly finds its way to the Galatasaray Fish Market, and from there to the tables of Beyoğlu's restaurants.

Taksim

Beyond Çiçek Pasajı, the side streets off İstiklal Caddesi are the focus for Istanbul's raunchier nightlife, lined with seedy bars, 'adult' cinemas and nightclubs – best avoided, unless you want to be relieved of all your spending money in one night. The street, and the trams, end at **Taksim Square** (*Taksim Meydanı*), the heart of modern Istanbul, lined with five-star hotels and the site of the glass-fronted **Atatürk Cultural Centre** (*Atatürk Kültür Sarayı*), sometimes called the Opera House. This is the principal venue for performances during the International Istanbul Festival (see p.39).

At the far end of the square, Cumhuriyet Caddesi leads past the Hilton Hotel to the **Military Museum** (*Askeri Müze*). The many fascinating exhibits include a section of the massive chain that the Byzantines

stretched across the mouth of the Golden Horn to keep out enemy ships, captured enemy cannon and military banners, the campaign tents from which the Ottoman sultans controlled their armies, and examples of uniforms, armour and weapons from the earliest days of the empire down to the 20th century. But the main attraction is the concert given by the **Janissary Band** (*Mehter Takımı*) at 3pm each day (except Monday and Tuesday). The band is a revival of the Ottoman military band that accompanied the sultan's armies on their campaigns, and led the victory processions through conquered cities. The colourful uniforms are exact replicas of the originals, as is the distinctive Janissary march, with the musicians turning to left and right at each alternate step.

Dolmabahçe Palace

Sultan Abdül Mecit (reigned 1839-61), continuing the programme of reform begun by his father, Mahmut II, decided that Topkapı Palace was too old-fashioned for a Westernizing ruler like himself. He therefore commissioned a vast new palace on the shores of the Bosphorus, on the site of a

park which had been created by filling in an old harbour – (*dolmabahçe* means 'filled-in garden'). The **Dolmabahçe Palace** (*Dolmabahçe Sarayı*), finished in 1853, was intended as a bold statement of the sultan's faith in the future of his empire, but it turned out to be a monument to folly and extravagance. Its construction nearly emptied the imperial treasury, and the running costs amounted to £2 million a year, a financial burden which helped contribute to the eventual bankruptcy of the empire in 1875.

Appropriately, the palace witnessed the final act of empire. When Atatürk's government abolished the Sultanate in November 1922, Mehmet VI, the last representative of the dynasty which had ruled the Ottoman Empire for six centuries, was ignominiously smuggled aboard a British

The 19th-century Dolmabahçe Palace cost so much to build and maintain that it brought about the bankruptcy of the Ottoman government. Later it was where Atatürk died.

warship anchored off Dolmabahçe, to spend his last years in exile. Atatürk himself used a small apartment in the palace during the first years of the Republic, and died there on 10 November 1938. All the palace clocks are stopped at 9.05, the hour of his death.

The guided tour of the palace is in two parts – first the *Selamlık* (public rooms) and Throne Room, then the *Harem* (private apartments). The interior of the palace is very dark, and the use of flash is forbidden, so photographers should think twice before paying the extra fee for a camera or video. The highlights of the *Selamlık* include the vast Baccarat and Bohemian crystal chandeliers, 36 in all, and the crystal balustrade of the main staircase, the sultan's bathroom of marble and alabaster, two huge bearskins (a gift from the Tsar of Russia), Sèvres vases, Gobelin tapestries and carpets, and the vast bed used by the 'giant sultan', Abdül Aziz. The Throne Room is huge – the ceiling is 40m (130ft) high – and lavishly decorated. The chandelier, a gift from Queen Victoria, has 750 light bulbs and weighs 4.5 tonnes.

Two kilometres (1 mile) beyond Dolmabahçe you can escape from the city among the wooded walks of **Yıldız Park**. Head up the hill to the **Malta Köskü**, a restored royal pavilion that has been converted to a café, and enjoy tea and pastries on a beautiful terrace looking over the treetops to the Bosphorus. Near by is the **Şale Köskü** (Chalet Pavilion), set among beautiful gardens. It was built by Abdül Hamid II in 1882 to house the guests of the sultan during state visits, but Abdül Hamid liked it so much that he lived there himself until he was deposed in 1909. Its main claim to fame is that it contains the world's largest hand-made carpet, which weighs 7.5 tonnes (guided tours only 9.30am to 5pm, closed Monday and Thursday).

Along the Bosphorus

The Bosphorus (*İstanbul Boğazı*) is the narrow strait that links the Black Sea to the Sea of Marmara, and separates the European part of Turkey from the vast hinterland of Anatolia. The winding channel is 30km (19 miles) long and around 2km (1 mile) wide, narrowing to a mere 750m (820yd) at Rumeli Hisarı; a strong current flows continuously from the Black Sea into the Marmara. The name Bosphorus comes from the mythological character Io, who swam across the strait after being turned into a heifer by Zeus (Bosphorus means 'ford of the ox' in Greek). Jason and the Argonauts passed through the strait in their search for the Golden Fleece, and the Persian army of King Darius crossed it on a bridge of boats in 512 BC *en route* to battle with the Scythians.

Today the strait is busy with commercial shipping, fishing boats and ferries, and its wooded shores are lined with pretty fishing villages, old Ottoman mansions and the villas of Istanbul's wealthier citizens. It is spanned by two impressive suspension bridges. The first bridge ever to link Europe and Asia was the **Bosphorus Bridge** (*Boğaziçi Köprüsü*) at Ortaköy, opened in 1973 and at that time the fourth longest in the world (1,074m, or 3,524ft). It was followed in 1988 by the **Fatih Sultan Mehmet Bridge** at Rumeli Hisarı. Special **ferry tours** of the Bosphorus depart three times a day from Eminönü, calling at Beşiktaş, Kanlıca, Yeniköy, Sarıyer and Anadolu Kavağı. You can stay on the boat for the round trip, or alight anywhere and return by bus or taxi.

The Bosphorus Tour

The ship pulls away from the crowded quay at Eminönü and heads north, past the

The fortress of Rumeli Hisarı was built in only four months, in preparation for the conquest of Constantinople.

dazzling white wedding-cake façades of the **Dolmabahçe Palace** and the neighbouring Çirağan Palace, gutted by fire in 1910 but now restored and serving as a luxury hotel. After stopping to pick up more passengers at **Beşiktaş**, you pass beneath the first of the huge suspension bridges connecting Europe and Asia.

Tucked beneath the western end of the Bosphorus Bridge is the village of **Ortaköy**, recognizable by its baroque mosque right on the waterfront. The village has a rather Bohemian atmosphere, with antique shops, art galleries, bookstalls and trendy cafés. Just beyond the bridge, on the opposite shore, is the **Beylerbeyi Palace**, a summer residence and hunting lodge built for Sultan Abdül Aziz in 1865 (guided tours 9.30am to 4pm, closed Monday and Thursday).

Heading north past the wealthy suburbs of Arnavutköy and Bebek, you soon reach the huge fortress of **Rumeli Hisarı** (9.30am to 5pm, closed Monday). It was built at the command of Mehmet II in 1452 in preparation for his final assault on Constantinople, and was completed in the remarkably short time of four months. Its three massive towers linked by curtain walls now enclose a pleasant park, with an open-air theatre which stages folk-dancing and concerts in summer. On the opposite shore is the smaller and older fortress of **Anadolu Hisarı**, dating from 1390. Just to the south of the fort is the ornate rococo façade of the **Küçüksu Lodge**, an Ottoman summerhouse built on a favourite picnic spot known as the Sweet Waters of Asia. Here, too, a number of old wooden mansions (*yalı*) fringe the shore.

Beyond the Fatih Sultan Mehmet Bridge, the boat stops at **Kanlıca** on the Asian shore, famous for its yoghurt which you can sample at one of the little waterside cafés. The upper reaches of the Bosphorus are lined with picturesque fishing villages – **Tarabya**, **Sarıyer** and

Rumeli Kavağı – where you can enjoy a stroll along the prom, followed by a meal at one of the many excellent seafood restaurants. At Sarıyer you can visit the **Sadberk Hanım Museum**, a very impressive private collection spanning the period from 500 BC to Ottoman times. Last stop for the ferry is **Anadolu Kavağı** on the Asian side, overlooked by an imposing castle built by the Byzantines, and improved by the Genoese in the 14th century.

Üsküdar

Directly opposite Stamboul lies **Üsküdar**, better known to Europeans as Scutari. The ferry from Eminönü passes the **Kız Kulesi** (Maiden's Tower), perched on a tiny island about 200m (220yd) offshore. Originally a 12th-century Byzantine fort, the present tower dates from the 18th century and has served as a lighthouse, customs office and shipping control tower. In Byzantine times, a huge chain could be slung between here and Saray Burnu to close the mouth of the Bosphorus.

The ferry leaves you at Üsküdar's main square, İskele Meydanı. Among the many historic buildings, note the **İskele Camii**, designed by Sinan in 1548 for Mihrimah, daughter of Süleyman the Magnificent, and the **Yeni Valide Camii**, dating from the early 18th century. West of the square is the **Şemsi Paşa Camii** (1580), also designed by Sinan.

Scutari is traditionally associated with the name of Florence Nightingale. During the Crimean War (1854-6) she set up a hospital in the huge **Selimiye Barracks** (*Selimiye Kışlası*). A small corner of the building is kept as a museum in her memory – exhibits include the famous lamp.

Directly inland from the Bosphorus Bridge is the park and lookout point of **Büyük Çamlıca**, capped by a distinctive TV transmitter. The park offers a superb view across the Bosphorus to the Stamboul skyline, which is particularly spectacular at sunset, when crowds converge on the café at the summit.

The Princes' Islands

An hour's ferry trip to the southwest of Istanbul lies the bucolic retreat of the Princes' Islands, known to the Turks simply as *Adalar* – The Islands. This archipelago of nine islands in the Sea of Marmara has been inhabited since Byzantine times by monastic communities and was used as place of exile for deposed rulers. The Emperor Justin II built a palace on the largest island in the 6th century, and it soon came to be called Prinkipo, the Prince's Isle, the name later spreading to cover the whole group.

Today the islands are a weekend retreat for the people of Istanbul, providing pretty beaches, cliffs, pine forests, and wooden villas wreathed with wisteria and bougainvillaea. Motor vehicles are banned, and all transport is by foot, bicycle or horse-drawn carriage. The biggest and most popular island is **Büyükada** (Big Island), with a pleasant town and a picturesque monastery. You can take a tour of the island on a *fayton* (carriage) – to find the 'cab rank', walk uphill from the jetty to the clock tower in the square and turn left. The tour will take you past **St George's Monastery** where you can sample the monks' home-made wine and the healing waters of an *ayazma* (sacred spring). The iron rings in the marble floor of the chapel were used to restrain lunatics who were once brought here hoping to be cured by the waters.

The ferry also calls at the smaller islands of Kinaliada, Burgazada and Heybeliada.

Turkish Carpets

A Turkish carpet is more than a mere floor covering; it is a document, a picture, a record of the beliefs and desires of the woman who made it, written in its own language of patterns and symbols. Every carpet tells its own tale, woven with themes of love, jealousy, hope and happiness.

Origins

Carpets and kilims have their origins among the nomadic peoples of central Asia, who brought their weaving tradition with them as they migrated west into Persia and Anatolia. They were an important part of the nomads' household goods, serving as floor insulation and draught excluders. Kilims (flat-weave rugs) are less hard-wearing than carpets and were used as partitions, seat coverings and wall hangings. The oldest known carpet is the Pazyryk Carpet, which was found frozen in a block of ice in a tomb near the border between Mongolia and Russia. It dates from the 3rd–5th century BC, and is decorated with rows of deer and men on horseback, as well as square geometric patterns. The carpet was woven using the double-knot technique, which still characterizes Turkish carpets today, and is now displayed in the Hermitage Museum in St Petersburg.

The oldest carpets you will see in Turkey are the 13th-century Seljuk carpets from Konya and Beyşehir exhibited in the Museum of Turkish and Islamic Arts in Istanbul (the 13th-century Italian traveller Marco Polo claimed that the best and most beautiful carpets in the world came from the district of Konya, in central Anatolia). Each district in Anatolia developed its own distinct carpet-weaving patterns and traditions, which can often best be seen on the floors of local mosques. The Seljuks and Ottomans introduced the practice of weaving large, intricately patterned carpets for the sultan's palace and imperial mosques, a tradition exemplified in the exquisite silk carpets of Hereke.

Materials and Dyes

The basic material of most Turkish carpets is sheep's wool, ideally the wool of a mature sheep shorn in the spring. The fine court carpets of Kayseri, Konya and Hereke use wool knots on a cotton warp and weft; the finest and most expensive carpets of all are made of silk.

Before the introduction of artificial dyes in the late 19th century, all carpets were coloured using nature's palette of vegetable dyes. The dying of wool was

In popular tourist spots like Istanbul and Marmaris, you will be constantly approached by carpet sellers eager to show you their wares.

an art in itself, requiring a precise knowledge of the various plants and substances, the amount of dyestuff to add to the water, how long to boil it, and whether to add lime or alum. The most commonly used dyes included indigo (blue), madder (red and orange), buckthorn (yellow) and walnut (black and brown). Attempts are being made to reintroduce the use of natural dyes in modern Turkish carpets. (NB There is an excellent exhibit on natural dyes in the Museum of Islamic and Turkish Arts in Istanbul.)

Techniques

Carpets are woven on a wooden frame, on which the warp threads are strung vertically in continuous loops. The bottom edge is begun with a few centimetres of kilim-type flat-weave to stop the ends from unravelling, and then the carpet proper is built up one row at a time.

The weaver takes a short length of wool, loops it over two adjacent warp threads and pulls the ends back between the two threads; this is the classic 'double knot' or 'Gördes knot', which makes Turkish carpets so hard-wearing (the Persian single knot is looped around a single warp thread). The pattern for the carpet is drawn on squared paper, and each knot corresponds to a single coloured square (in earlier times, a woman carried her traditional patterns in her head). When a row of knots is finished, it is tamped down, a weft thread is woven through the warp above it, and the long ends of the knots are trimmed before the next row is begun. As it grows bigger, the carpet is moved down around the loom, so the weaver can keep the 'leading edge' at the same level in front of her. The carpet is finished off with another band of flat-weave, is cut from the loom and is then washed.

The art of carpet weaving in action. As the carpet is woven on the wooden frame, it is moved down so that the weaver keeps the leading edge in front of her.

Patterns

Each tribe that migrated into Anatolia brought with it its own distinctive tribal 'mark', often a stylized bird or animal, and a rich vocabulary of symbols, most of whose original meanings have been lost in the mists of time. Recurring motifs include the camel, eagle, the 'hands on hips' (denoting motherhood and fertility), a row of five dots (usually in the margin, representing the five fingers of the hand, a precaution against the evil eye), the tree of life, flowers, an ear of wheat, pine cones (all symbols of fertility), the goose's foot (good luck), the arrow (courage and heroism), and the scorpion (a talisman to keep live ones out of the nomad's tent). The colour blue, representing the infinity of sky and sea, is a symbol of splendour and nobility, and wards off the evil eye; yellow is the colour of the sun and of ripened wheat, and is associated with love and abundance; red is for wealth and good fortune, while green is the colour

The shape of the central panel shows that this carpet was made originally as a prayer mat.

of spring and of Paradise, symbolizing fertility and happiness.

A special type of carpet is the prayer mat, which has a central panel pointed at one end like the prayer niche in a mosque; some have three medallions where the owner would place his knees and forehead while praying. Prayer mats are often decorated with texts from the Koran, and with a water jug as a reminder of ritual washing.

The distinctive designs of eastern Anatolia include many animal and bird motifs.

119

'Halt, Traveller!...And Listen...In this Silent Mound a Nation's Heart Once Throbbed'

The words of a poem engraved on a hillside overlooking the Dardanelles remind us that the beginnings of the modern Turkish Republic were forged in the heat of the Gallipoli campaign. Six hundred years earlier, but not so far away, the Ottoman Empire had its beginnings in the beautiful city of Bursa. These lands that circle the Sea of Marmara are rich in history. Here you can explore the fascinating architecture of Bursa and Edirne, and ponder the follies of war on battlefields both ancient and modern.

The portion of Turkey that lies within Europe is known to the Turks as *Rumeli*, but it is only a part of the ancient region called Thrace, which stretched from the shores of the Marmara and Aegean seas north to the banks of the Danube. In times past Thrace has been a battleground for Greeks and Persians, Bulgars and Byzantines, and Russians and Turks, for it forms a bottleneck on the main overland route between Europe and Asia.

The lands around the Sea of Marmara formed the nucleus of the early Ottoman Empire. The cities here have a fine legacy of Islamic architecture, such as the Yeşil Camii at İznik.

Down the centuries Thrace has been overrun by the invading armies of King Darius of Persia, the troops of Alexander the Great, the legions of Hadrian, marauding Bulgars, campaigning crusaders, and Ottoman Turks. More recently it was torn by the Balkan Wars of 1912-13, a conflict echoed in the continuing troubles of neighbouring former Yugoslavia. After World War I the present boundaries of Turkey, Bulgaria and Greece were settled by the treaties of Neuilly, Sèvres and Lausanne.

Turkish Thrace has a mostly agricultural landscape of low, rolling hills with few trees, the wide horizon occasionally spiked by the minaret of a small farming town. The E-80 highway leading north west from Istanbul (now paralleled by a fast toll motorway) cuts a straight line across an undulating patchwork of wheat

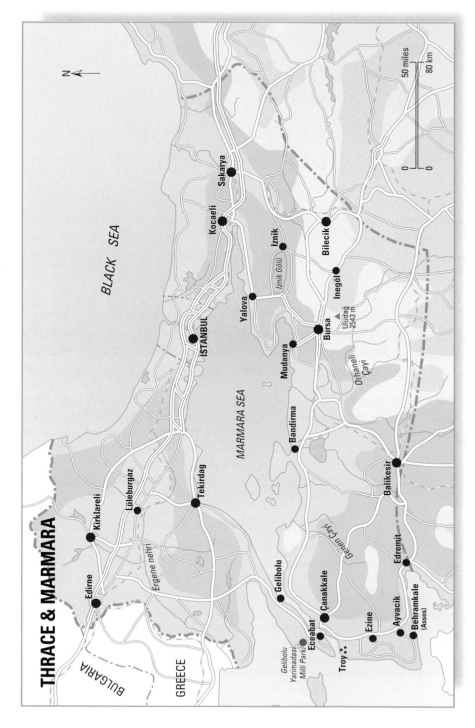

THRACE & MARMARA

BULGARIA

GREECE

BLACK SEA

MARMARA SEA

Edirne
Kırklareli
Lüleburgaz
Tekirdağ
İstanbul
Yalova
Sakarya
Kocaeli
İznik
İznik Gölü
Bilecik
İnegöl
Bursa
Uludağ 2543 m
Mudanya
Orhaneli Çayı
Bandırma
Balıkesir
Edremit
Ayvacık
Behramkale (Assos)
Ezine
Troy
Çanakkale
Eceabat
Gelibolu Yarimadasi Milli Parki
Gelibolu
Ergene nehri
Geren Çayı

50 miles
80 km
0

fields to Edirne, the principal city of Turkish Thrace. This was the route followed by the Ottoman armies as they marched towards Vienna in 1529, but today it has been commandeered by convoys of container trucks bound for Anatolia and the Middle East.

Edirne

Edirne lies 245km (152 miles) northwest of Istanbul, at the confluence of the Tunca and Meriç rivers. In AD 125 the Roman Emperor Hadrian founded a city here, and named it Hadrianopolis (later shortened to Adrianople). Its strategic position, on the main route between Asia Minor and the Balkans, made it a coveted prize; it was taken by the Bulgars in the 10th century, sacked twice by rampaging crusaders, and finally fell to the Ottoman Turks in 1362. The Turks used the city as a base for their final conquest of Constantinople, and it served as their capital from 1413 to 1458.

During Ottoman times, Edirne (as it was named by the Turks) continued to play an important role as an administrative and cultural centre, and served as a forward base for Turkish campaigns in the Balkans. It was a favourite hunting resort of the sultans, who graced it with a number of beautiful mosques, notably the famous Selimiye Camii. The city's fortunes declined after the 1700s as the Ottoman Empire began its long slide into decadence. It was captured and sacked by the Russians in 1829 and 1878, and taken again by the Bulgars in 1913. In 1920, during the Turkish War of Independence, the city fell to the Greeks, but was finally returned to Turkey in 1923 when the Treaty of Lausanne defined the new republic's borders.

Today, Edirne is a pleasant frontier town – the border with Greece (Yunanistan) is a mere 5km (3 miles) away, and the Bulgarian frontier (Bulgaristan) is only 15km (9 miles) to the north. It is a stopover for intercontinental truck drivers, and a shopping centre for Greek bargain hunters (prices are lower in Turkey). As yet it draws only a few tourists, who come to enjoy the fine Ottoman architecture of its historic mosques. Arriving from Istanbul, you reach a roundabout in the centre of the town, with the Eski Camii on your left, and the unmistakable outline of the Selimiye Camii rising to your right.

Selimiye Camii
(Mosque of Selim)

Edirne is dominated by the imposing **Selimiye Camii**, whose graceful silhouette crowns a low hill overlooking the town centre. This beautiful mosque was commissioned by Sultan Selim II and built between 1567 and 1574. It was designed by the architect Sinan, who regarded it as his finest achievement – he was 85 years old by the time it had been completed. Its harmonious form was the result of a lifetime's experience and experimentation, and its sheer size realized one of the architect's greatest ambitions. He wrote, 'With God's help and the Sultan's mercy I have succeeded in building a dome for Sultan Selim's mosque which is four ells greater in diameter and six ells higher than that of St Sophia' (it is in fact only 50cm, or 20in, wider, and is 10m, or 33ft, *lower* than Haghia Sophia). Its four slender, fluted minarets, each with three balconies, are at 71m (233ft) the tallest in Turkey.

A statue of Sinan stands at the foot of the park below the Selimiye; walk up the street to its left (Mimar Sinan Caddesi) to reach the main entrance of the mosque on

*T*he graceful silhouette of the Selimiye Camii overlooks the main square of Edirne, once the Ottoman capital. It is the work of the great imperial architect Sinan, whose statue stands at the foot of the hill.

the right. The gate leads into a courtyard graced with a delicate *şadırvan*, and lined with beautifully decorated domes. Take off your shoes and go inside.

The interior of the mosque is a symphony in space and light. The vast dome, 31.5m (103ft) across and 45m (148ft) high, rests on eight fluted columns connected by arches of red and white stone. It is decorated with flowing arabesques and Koranic verses rendered in colourful calligraphy, and pierced around its base by 40 windows. The tympanum walls and semidomes that support the dome are likewise pierced by dozens more windows, making the interior unusually bright and airy. The sunlight picks out friezes of turquoise İznik tiles, especially around the sultan's loge and the *mihrab,* and highlights the delicate tracery of the *mimber,* intricately carved from thin sheets of marble.

As you leave, turn right and right again to find Edirne's **Archaeological Museum** (*Arkeoloji ve Etnoloji Müzesi*), hidden away behind the mosque in a modern building. The archaeological collection consists mainly of a few Roman finds from the ruins of Ainis (Enez) on the coast near the Greek border, but the ethnology section is more interesting, with a selection of Ottoman clothing, household goods, carpets, farming equipment, coins and medals. Across the street, in the

former *medrese,* is the town's **Museum of Turkish and Islamic Art** (*Türk-İslam Eserleri Müzesi*).

Below the mosque is an arcade of shops called the *Arasta* (Arcade). Although the shops have been taken over by souvenir sellers, the rent goes towards the upkeep of the mosque – as it has done since the 16th century.

Old Town

At the foot of the hill below the Selimiye Camii, across the road from Sinan's statue, is Edirne's oldest mosque, the **Eski Camii**, built between 1403 and 1414. Its 'forest-of-pillars' layout shows Seljuk influence, similar to the Ulu Camii in Bursa (see p.139), though much smaller – there are only nine small domes, arranged three by three. The mosque is famous for its large-scale calligraphic decoration, which was recently restored. Next to the Old Mosque is the **Bedesten** (Covered Market). It was built, like the Eski Camii, at the behest of Sultan Mehmet I, and its revenues went towards the upkeep of the mosque. Today its two rows of seven domes shelter stalls devoted to cheap consumer goods, but if you hunt around you can find a shop selling the fruit-shaped and scented soaps (*sabun*) for which the town is famous.

Across the main square from the Eski Camii rise the four minarets of the **Üç Şerefeli Camii** (Mosque of the Three Balconies). Built between 1440 and 1447, this building is transitional in style between the earlier Seljuk-type mosques of Bursa and Konya and the later imperial mosques of Istanbul, which were influenced by Hagia Sophia. It has a large central dome supported on six pillars, flanked by several smaller ones. The mosque takes its name from the three balconies on its tallest minaret. The other three are splendidly decorated in different Seljuk designs – *baklavalı* (diamond), *burmalı* (spiral) and *yivli* (fluted).

Opposite the Üç Şerefeli Camii is the start of Edirne's main shopping street, Saraçlar Caddesi, lined with little cafés, restaurants and shops. On the right are several entrances to the **Semiz Ali Paşa Çarşısı**, a covered bazaar built by Sinan for one of Süleyman the Magnificent's vezirs in the 16th century. However, the goods are of little interest to visitors except for a few leather and jewellery shops.

About 1.5km (1 mile) northwest of the town centre, at the far end of a 15th-century bridge across the Tunca River, lies the extensive **Beyazıt II Complex** (*İkinci Beyazıt Külliye*). Built by the architect Hayrettin between 1484 and 1488, the complex consists of a mosque, hospital, asylum, medical school, kitchens and bakeries. The buildings were recently restored, and many now house students from the medical and arts faculties of the University of Thrace. The most interesting part of the complex is not the mosque but the hospital to its right. The *darüşşifa*, or treatment centre, is hexagonal in shape, with six wards opening into a circular domed hall, where a tinkling fountain helped soothe the fevered patients. A courtyard, which housed the pharmacy and administrative offices, links this to the *timarhane* (lunatic asylum), with seven cells opening off a porticoed garden, and the medical school at the far end.

The 17th-century traveller Evliya Çelebi records how the physicians attempted to treat insanity by exposing the patients to soothing music and fragrant flowers: 'Patients were given daffodils, jasmine, roses…in whose fragrant benediction the sick people found health…Some of them stamped the blossoms underfoot, others ate

---

THE DERVISH MEHMET

Evliya Çelebi (1611-84), also known as 'Dervish Mehmet', was a famous 17th-century Ottoman writer, who spent 40 years travelling around the lands of the Ottoman Empire. He recorded his impressions in his famous *Seyahatname* (*Book of Travels*), whose fascinating pages offer a glimpse of the day-to-day life of Ottoman times, and provide much useful historical, geographical and ethnological information about the period.

---

them, and still others made uncouth noises…The youth of Edirne would come to watch.' A much more effective treatment was used to provide protection against smallpox. Patients were inoculated by infecting them with matter from the pustules of someone suffering from a mild form of the disease. Lady Mary Wortley Montagu, the wife of the British Ambassador to Turkey from 1716-18, was so impressed by the efficacy of this procedure that she had her four-year-old son Edward treated, making him the first Briton ever to be inoculated against smallpox.

About a kilometre (½ mile) upstream from the Beyazıt Complex lie the ruins of a once-splendid palace, the **Edirne Sarayı**. It was begun in the 15th century by Sultan Murat II, and soon grew to be as sumptuous as the Topkapı Palace in Istanbul. Unfortunately it was destroyed during the Turko-Russian War in 1878, and little remains save a few crumbling archways. The site is more famous today as **Sarayiçi** (Within the Palace), the home of the annual Kırkpınar Greased Wrestling Festival (see box opposite). The games once took place in an open field, but are now held in a purpose-built concrete stadium. Held annually in July, the games attract wrestlers from all over Turkey.

GREASED WRESTLING

Greased wrestling, known as *yağlı güreş*, is Turkey's traditional national sport. The wrestlers wear only a pair of leather breeches, and are smeared liberally from head to foot with olive oil. The competitors are classified by height into nine classes, and are paired off by a random draw; the winner of each bout moves into the next round until only two remain for the final. There are few rules, but they are applied strictly – no scratching, biting, kicking or punching. The winner is the first to pin his opponent's shoulders to the ground, or to lift him off the ground and carry him for three consecutive steps, or to win a submission. Bouts can last from a few minutes up to one hour – if there is no result after one hour, a decision is made on points. (In the old days there was no time limit, and some famous bouts lasted several hours.)

The main wrestling event of the year is the Kırkpınar Festival, held each July at Sarayiçi, in Edirne, when about 1,000 competitors from all over the country meet to do battle. The games have been held annually, wars and occupations permitting, for over 600 years. Legend has it that in 1360 a band of 40 soldiers camped here and began wrestling to pass the time. Eventually only two remained, and they struggled on through the night. In the morning their comrades founded them locked together in a death grip, and when they moved the bodies from the dry and dusty field 40 springs (*kırk pınar* in Turkish) gushed forth, producing a lush meadow. The annual festival commemorates this miraculous event.

Gallipoli

The **Gallipoli Peninsula** (*Gelibolu Yarımadası*), on the north side of the Dardanelles, was the scene of one of the most notorious military campaigns of World War I. The Allied assault, involving Australian, British, New Zealand and French forces, aimed to control the narrow strait of the Dardanelles and capture Istanbul, thus securing an ice-free sea passage to supply arms to Russia and open another front against the Germans. The first landings took place on 25 April 1915, meeting with fierce resistance from the Turks, who were under the leadership of General Mustafa Kemal. The Allies managed to gain a toehold on the peninsula, and then deadlock ensued, with nearly nine months of static trench warfare. The cost in human lives and suffering was terrible, with around 250,000 dead and wounded on each side. The Anzacs (Australia and New Zealand Army Corps) saw some of the worst fighting and suffered the heaviest casualties – the beach where they landed has been named Anzac Cove (*Anzak Köyü*) in their honour.

The whole peninsula is a vast memorial, with plaques describing the progress of the campaign, and monuments to the soldiers of the Allied and Turkish armies. Each war cemetery is signposted in both English and Turkish, and all are beautifully tended, planted with flowers and scented with hedges of rosemary. Travel agents in Çanakkale, across the strait, provide guided tours of the peninsula, but it is best

DAMN THE DARDANELLES!

The plan to take control of the Dardanelles did not win unanimous approval amongst the members of the War Cabinet. Whilst Lord Kitchener and Winston Churchill (then Lord of the Admiralty) were for it, Admiral Fisher wrote in a letter to Churchill on 5 April 1915: 'Damn the Dardanelles! They will be our grave!' Fisher was outvoted, but his words would return to haunt his colleagues as the campaign went disastrously wrong.

if you have your own transport. Each year, on Anzac Day (25 April), a moving memorial service is held here.

Heading south from Edirne, the road cuts through unremarkable farmland and small towns, until you catch your first glimpse of the Aegean at the head of the Gulf of Saroz. The first town on the peninsula is **Gelibolu**, a small fishing port on the Dardanelles. The town has a tiny, picturesque harbour overlooked by a squat medieval castle, and lined with fish stalls and restaurants. The castle is thought to date from the 8th century, but is more interesting as being the first ever Ottoman conquest in Europe – Süleyman, son of Orhan Gazi, captured this and another nearby castle in 1354 on his way to Adrianople and, ultimately, Constantinople. There is a statue and small museum devoted to Piri Reis, the famous 16th-century Ottoman navigator, whose book of charts included one of the North American coast. The town is a pleasant place to stop for lunch – try some of the fresh *sardalya* (sardines) or *uskumru* (mackerel) – and to pick up a guide to the peninsula from the small tourist office.

A few kilometres before the town of Eceabat, a road on the right (signposted 'Kemalyeri') leads into the **Gallipoli Peninsula Historic National Park** (*Gelibolu Yarımadası Tarihi Milli Parkı*). Remember that within the park boundaries you are not allowed to camp, swim, light fires or pick flowers. The first place of interest you will see is the **Kabatepe Museum**, about 6km (3½ miles) along the road. The museum has a sad but fascinating collection of articles found on the battlefields – fragments of shrapnel and ammunition, canteens, tobacco tins, knives and forks; the most gruesome relics include a skull with a bullet embedded in its fore-

The Gallipoli campaign wore on for nine long months of trench warfare, with terrible casualties on both sides. Plaques have been placed at strategic positions, explaining the progress of the campaign.

head, and a boot with the remains of a foot inside. But the most poignant exhibits are the letters written by soldiers in the trenches – one moving letter was written by a Turkish soldier to his mother only two days before he was killed. Here, too, you can find out about the series of ten bronze plaques that lie scattered around the battlefield and that explain the progress of the campaign.

Beyond the museum the road leads to Arıburnu and **Anzac Cove** (*Anzak Köyü*), the notorious beach where the men of the Australian and New Zealand Army Corps (Anzac) waded ashore in the early hours of 25 April 1915. They had intended to come ashore 1.5km (1 mile) to the south at Kabatepe, but unknown currents had pushed their boats northwards in the darkness. Instead of flat land they were confronted by a steep scrubby cliff backed by a maze of gullies and ravines, overlooked by the Turkish lines commanding the heights above. In the ensuing battles the Anzacs suffered terrible casualties. A memorial above the cove records the words of Atatürk, sent in 1934 to the first visitors who had come from New Zealand and Australia to pay their respects. It reads:

Those heroes that shed their blood and lost their lives…You are now lying in the soil of a friendly country. Therefore

rest in peace. There is no difference between the Johnnies and the Mehmets to us where they lie side by side here in this country of ours…You, the mothers, who sent their sons from faraway countries, wipe away your tears; your sons are now lying in our bosom and are in peace. After having lost their lives on this land they have become our sons as well.

Return towards the museum and take the road on the left uphill towards **Chunuk Bair** (*Çonk Bayırı*). The top of the ridge to the left of the road was reached by Australian soldiers on the first day of the land-ings, but they advanced no further during the next nine months. At the point known as Courtney's and Steele's Posts, the Allied and Turkish trenches were separated by only 5-10m (15-30ft). The modern road follows the line of 'no man's land'. At the top of the hill is the huge obelisk of the Anzac Monument, and a statue of Mustafa Kemal Paşa. Mustafa Kemal, later to become Atatürk, was the general who saved Gallipoli for the Turks with his shrewd tactics and inspirational leadership. He commanded many of the battles from this hilltop, and a number of trenches and an observation post have been restored. A sign marks the point where, on the first day, he addressed his men, saying, 'I am not ordering you to attack, I order you to die. In the time which passes until we die, other troops and commanders will come to take our places.' Thousands of Turkish soldiers died, but the time their bravery had bought allowed reinforcements to arrive and the day was saved. Another sign marks the place where Kemal was struck by a piece of shrapnel, but saved by his pocket watch.

War cemeteries and monuments, maintained by the War Graves Commission, dot the hillsides and beaches of the Gallipoli peninsula.

While the Anzacs were storming the slopes of Chunuk Bair, the spearhead of the Allied attack was directed at **Cape Helles**, at the southern tip of the peninsula. However, the Allies fared no better here, and captured nothing more than the barest toehold on the peninsula. There are two imposing monuments: the **Helles Memorial** is a tall white obelisk commemorating the Allied troops who fell here; and the huge, four-pillared stone table of the **Çanakkale Martyrs' Memorial** (*Çanakkale Şehitleri Abidesi*), which remembers all the Turks who gave their lives at Gallipoli. The Turkish inscription translates as: 'You soldiers who have fallen while defending this land, may your ancestors descend and kiss your noble brows. Who could dig the grave that could contain you? History itself is too small a place for you.'

Returning north along the east side of the peninsula, you pass through the small village of Kilitbahir, with its massive castle, before reaching the ferry terminal at **Eceabat**. There is nothing to do here except wait for the ferry to take you across the water to Çanakkale. As you make the crossing look back to the hillside where you can see the giant white figure of a soldier laid out in white stones. Beside him are the first lines of a famous Turkish poem by Necmettin Halil Onan:

Dur yolcu! Bilmeden gelip bastığın
Bu toprak bir devrin battığı yerdir.
Eğil de kulak ver, bu sessiz yığın
Bir vatan kalbinin attığı yerdir.

Halt, traveller! This earth you tread unthinkingly
Once witnessed the end of an era.
Bend low and listen. In this silent mound
A nation's heart once throbbed.

Çanakkale

The Gallipoli campaign was fought over control of the Dardanelles (*Çanakkale Boğazı*), the narrow strait that links the Aegean with the Sea of Marmara, and separates the Gallipoli Peninsula from Asia Minor. The strait is 61km (38 miles) long, and varies in width from 6km (4 miles) to 1,200m (1,300yd); a strong current flows from the Marmara into the Aegean. In ancient times it was known as the Hellespont, after the mythological character Helle. According to legend, Helle and her brother Phrixus were trying to escape from their wicked stepmother, who planned to sacrifice them to the gods. They flew across the strait on the back of a winged ram with a golden fleece, but Helle fell off into the swirling currents and was drowned. Phrixus continued to Colchis on the Euxine (Black Sea), where he was rewarded with the fleece of the ram. He hung the golden fleece in a grove of oaks sacred to Ares, where it was later discovered by Jason and his Argonauts. (The name Dardanelles arose in Renaissance times, after Dardanus, a city near Troy named for one the ancestors of Virgil's hero Aeneas.)

It was at the narrowest point of the strait, just north of the town of Çanakkale, that the Persian King Xerxes led his army across a bridge of boats on his way to conquer the Greeks in 480 BC. At the same point, between the ancient towns of Abydos and Sestos, Alexander the Great crossed in the opposite direction in 334 BC, becoming the first Macedonian ever to set foot on Asian soil. As his boat nudged the beach, he flung his spear into the sand, thus staking his claim to the Persian Empire.

The largest town on the strait is **Çanakkale**, with its massive 15th-century

---

HERO AND LEANDER... AND BYRON

The tragic tale of Hero and Leander was set on the shores of the Hellespont. Hero, a handsome youth from the town of Abydus on the south shore, was madly in love with Leander, a priestess in the Temple of Aphrodite at Sestus, across the strait. Every night, Hero would swim across the perilous waters to be with his love, guided by a lamp that she hung by the shore. But one night the lamp was blown out by the wind, and Hero lost his way and was drowned. Finding her lover's body washed up on the beach, the heartbroken Leander flung herself into the sea.

On 3 May 1810, inspired by Hero's tale, the poet Lord Byron swam across the Hellespont between the sites of ancient Abydos and Sestos. In a letter to a friend he described his feat: '...the immediate distance is not above a mile but the current renders it hazardous, so much so, that I doubt whether Leander's conjugal powers must not have been exhausted in his passage to Paradise.'

---

fortress. There is not much to see here, but there is a good selection of hotels; if you're visiting Gallipoli you'll probably be staying here. The most interesting part of town is the **Military and Naval Museum** (*Askeri ve Deniz Müzesi*) beside the castle; to find it, turn right as you come off the ferry and go past the clock tower to a park. You will immediately notice a large mock-up of the Turkish minesweeper *Nusrat*. The original ship was instrumental in preventing Allied ships forcing the Dardanelles at the beginning of the Gallipoli campaign, by re-mining the strait at night after it had been swept by the British and French.

The small museum beside the ship has an interesting collection of Gallipoli memorabilia, including the shattered pocket watch which saved the life of Mustafa Kemal, and thus, perhaps, the Turkish nation. (Kemal went on to become Atatürk, founder of the Turkish Republic.) The hulking fortress next to the park, the **Sultaniye Bahir**, was built in the late 15th century by Mehmet the Conqueror. It is still used by the Turkish military as part of the straits' defences and is therefore off limits to the public.

On the way out of Çanakkale, heading towards Troy, you will pass the town's **Archaeological Museum** (*Arkeoloji Müzesi*). The exhibits include finds from ancient sites throughout the surrounding region, but especially from nearby Troy, an extensive coin display, and a collection of Atatürk's military clothing. Highlights include a crystal lion's head and a black-glaze cup with owl decoration from Troy, and the fretboard of a lute from the Dardanos Tumulus.

Troy (Truva)

There can be few people in the western world who have not heard of the stories and characters in Homer's *Ilia*: beautiful Helen, 'the face that launched a thousand ships', and the handsome Paris with whom she eloped to Troy; Agamemnon, who led the Greeks against the Trojans, and Achilles, his finest warrior, who was killed when Paris shot an arrow into his heel, (the only part of his body which had not received divine protection when his mother dipped him in the River Styx); the ruse dreamed up by Odysseus to hide Greek soldiers in the belly of a wooden horse, and the sack of Troy that followed.

The exact location of the legendary city of Troy remained a mystery until an amateur archaeologist with a passion for Homer began excavations in 1871. Heinrich

Schliemann found the fabled city of the *Iliad,* and discovered 'Priam's treasure', a cache of gold beside the city walls. He smuggled it back to Germany, but it vanished during World War II, only to make a dramatic reappearance in Moscow in 1993. (Negotiations are taking place between Russia, Germany and Turkey as to where the treasure should finally be displayed.)

In his eagerness, Schliemann dug carelessly down to the bottom of the mound with little regard for scientific excavation. Later archaeologists using modern techniques have since uncovered nine superimposed cities, from Troy I, an Early

---

HEINRICH SCHLIEMANN

As a seven-year-old boy, Heinrich Schliemann (1822-90) saw a picture of Troy in flames in a history book given to him by his father. The image planted in his imagination a seed which grew into an overriding ambition – to discover the true site of the city of King Priam, famed in Homer's epic story. The young Schliemann made a fortune in business before retiring, at the age of 36, to devote himself to archaeology. Entirely self-taught, he travelled extensively in Greece and Asia Minor before deciding that a large mound near the village of Hisarlık must conceal the ruins of Troy. He began digging in 1871, and within two years had found remains of massive fortifications, and a cache of gold jewellery which he believed to be King Priam's treasure.

Schliemann has been criticized for digging haphazardly and for smuggling his finds out of the country, but we must remember that he was a pioneer – this was the first time such a mound had ever been dug. He also discovered and excavated the sites of Mycenae and Tiryns in Greece, and popularized archaeology with his books and newspaper articles. Many regard him as the father of prehistoric Greek archaeology.

The tale of the Wooden Horse of Troy is known throughout the world. This modern version stands at the entrance to the archaeological site.

Bronze Age settlement (3000-2500 BC), to Troy IX, the Hellenistic and Roman metropolis, known as Ilium Novum, which stood here from 334 BC to AD 400. American scholars identify the level known as Troy VIIa as King Priam's city, and place its destruction around 1260 BC; some eminent Turkish archaeologists disagree, opting for the preceding level, Troy VI. Then there are those who claim that the Trojan War of the *Iliad* was a fiction, cobbled together in Homer's imagination from memories of various different conflicts, and has little or no basis in fact. Whatever the truth of the matter, there is no doubt that this was the site of an important and long-lived city.

The site is near the village of **Tevfikiye**, marked by a large modern replica of the famed wooden horse. The village contains a number of small pensions and restaurants, and a bigger hotel; there are also two places that claim to be 'Schliemann's House', containing collections of digging tools and photographs of the excavations.

The **excavations** are less impressive than most other Turkish sites, but for those who

THE FACE THAT LAUNCHED A THOUSAND SHIPS

Paris, the son of King Priam of Troy, was chosen to judge which of the three goddesses Aphrodite, Athena and Hera was the most beautiful. Aphrodite persuaded Paris to choose her, in return for the promise that he would win the most beautiful woman in the world – Helen, the wife of King Menelaus of Sparta.

Soon after, Menelaus arrived on a visit to the Trojan court, and invited Paris to stay with him in Sparta. Paris, emboldened by Aphrodite's promise that the beautiful Helen would be his, heaped gifts on Menelaus' wife and flirted outrageously with her. He ostentatiously drank from her goblet at the very spot where her lips had touched it, and traced 'I love you' in wine on the table top. Helen was swept off her feet, and when the king went off to Crete for his grandfather's funeral, Helen promptly eloped with Paris, and returned with him to Troy. In an attempt to win back his wife, Menelaus launched the famous 'thousand ships', thus beginning the Trojan War and inspiring one of the world's best-known stories.

The ancient walls of Troy, revealed by the archaeologist's trowel. A well-marked trail leads around the site.

have enjoyed Homer's epics this is a magical place, where the stones are haunted by the spirits of Helen and Paris, Achilles and Agamemnon. There is a fine view across the surrounding plains of the Troad (as the region surrounding Troy is known), and on

You enter the excavation proper through a grove of pines, where you will find the first of 12 information boards (1), which explain each feature clearly. (The various superimposed levels can be confusing, so take a look at the map and model in the display room to the right of the entrance before beginning your tour.) Climb up the steps to the top of the mound on your right (2). This is part of the wall of Troy IX, and affords a good view over the site. At your feet you can see the massive **fortifications** of Troy VI, with a gap that was the east gate. Descend and go through this gate to reach the trail which heads anticlockwise around the site (there are convenient shady benches at intervals if you are in need of a rest). The main sights are the remains of the Roman **Temple of Athena** (4), now little more than a bare platform; the rough, drystone walls of Troy I, laid in a herringbone pattern (7); the famous **ramp** (8) at the southwest gate of Troy II, now crossed by a wooden footbridge (this is where Schliemann found 'Priam's treasure'; he also believed the wooden horse had been pulled up this ramp); a **sanctuary** (10) outside the walls of Troy VI with several altars and sacrificial pits; and the semicircular rows of seats in the **odeum** (11) of Troy IX.

Assos (Behramkale)

The Turkish village of Behramkale and the neighbouring ruins of ancient Assos are actually on the Aegean, but we have included them here because they are most easily visited from Troy and Çanakkale, and a visit here is often included on tours to Troy.

Assos lies about 70km (44 miles) south of Troy, perched spectacularly on a craggy hilltop overlooking the Gulf of Edremit

a clear day you can even see the massive Turkish Memorial on Cape Helles away to the north. Here, where the farmers' fields are splashed with scarlet by the blossoms of spring poppies, Achilles slew Hector and Agamemnon marshalled his army.

and the Greek island of Lesbos (*Midilli* in Turkish). You leave the main road at the town of Ayvacık and follow a minor road through scrubby hills until the acropolis of Assos comes into view. A graceful, hump-backed 14th-century Ottoman bridge carries the road over the Tuzla stream and on to the village of Behramkale, whose ramshackle houses tumble down the slope below the ancient fortifications. As you enter the village, take the left fork to reach the obvious large mosque which lies below the entrance to the ruins on the acropolis.

Assos was founded in the 7th century BC by Greek colonists from Lesbos. The city's heyday was in the 4th century BC, when it ruled the surrounding region, and it was even home to the great Aristotle from 347 to 344 BC. The massive Hellenistic **fortifications** of dark brown stone date from the mid-4th century BC. They enclose the summit of the hill, where you will find the only building worth looking at, the partially restored **Temple of Athena**. The temple is thought to have been built in the 6th century BC, and it is the only surviving example of Doric architecture in Asia Minor; some of the tapering, fluted columns, with their distinctive plain capitals, have been rather inelegantly restored, the pale concrete clashing with the natural brown of the volcanic stone.

Return to the fork in the road and take the right branch, which leads past the best-preserved section of the city wall, with the **main gate** flanked by two towers. The cobbled road continues steeply downhill to the picturesque **harbour**, which is lined with seafood restaurants and a number of hotels. In AD 53 St Paul met up with Luke and other companions here before setting sail for Lesbos.

Bursa

The historic city of Bursa lies scattered picturesquely across the wooded slopes of Uludağ (Great Mountain) to the south of the Sea of Marmara. It was founded in the 3rd century BC by King Prusias of Bithynia, and named Prusa in his honour. In 1326 it was taken by Orhan Gazi, and became the first capital of the new Ottoman Empire. Although the capital was moved to Edirne in 1362, and then to Istanbul, Bursa remained an important town, with a rich legacy of religious architecture – the founder of the Ottoman Dynasty and five of his successors

are buried here. Its other attractions include hot springs, a fine market, and the forests and ski-slopes of nearby Uludağ.

To get to Bursa from Istanbul, you can take a hydrofoil (*deniz otobüsü*, or 'sea bus') from the quay at Kabataş (just south of Dolmabahçe) to Yalova or Mudanya, where you catch a bus for Bursa. Alternatively, you can arrange an organized tour through your hotel or any travel agency. To see the city properly you will need to stay for at least one night, preferably two. The main axis of the city stretches horizontally across the mountainside, and all the main sights can be explored on foot in one long day. However, this involves a lot of walking, and you may prefer to use public transport. Don't try to use a car as the traffic in central Bursa is horrendous, with many narrow one-way streets, and there is very little parking.

The beautiful city of Bursa (known as Yeşil Bursa, or Green Bursa, to the Turks) was the first capital of the Ottoman Empire, and the burial place of the founder of the Ottoman dynasty.

Yeşil Camii (Green Mosque)

Bursa's most famous building is the **Yeşil Türbe** (Green Tomb), which takes its name from the beautiful turquoise tiles which cover its walls, both inside and out. (Many tiles have been dislodged by earthquakes and replaced with modern ones; the new tiles are easily spotted because they do not match the originals in depth and richness of colour.) A simple octagonal building with a domed roof, the tomb houses the sarcophagus of Mehmet I (ruled 1413-21), which is itself ornately decorated with patterned İznik tiles of blue, yellow, green and turquoise, and surrounded by the smaller tombs of family and court members.

Below the tomb is the **Yeşil Camii** (Green Mosque), commissioned by Mehmet I in 1419. It remains unfinished, as work on a mosque traditionally stopped after the death of the sultan who began it. It too once had dazzling green tiles on its dome and minarets, now gone. But the interior is still breathtakingly beautiful, decorated with the best İznik tiles, with geometric and arabesque designs in turquoise, green, white and deep blue. It is very different in form to the imperial mosques of Istanbul, with a ground plan in the shape of a 'T', the entrance in the middle of the 'cross-piece' and the *mihrab* at the far end of the 'upright'. The sultan's loge is above your head as you enter; the two rooms in the wings to either side were used for meetings of the sultan's court. The huge *mihrab* is ornately decorated, like a Seljuk portal. An inscription records that the tile-makers came from Tabriz in Persia, 1,600km (1,000 miles) to the east (these are the craftsmen who founded the famous tile-making industry of nearby İznik). The Yeşil Camii marks the emergence of a truly Turkish style in mosque design; earlier buildings had drawn on Seljuk and Persian influences.

The octagonal Yeşil Türbe (Green Tomb) is covered with turquoise tiles. It houses the richly decorated sarcophagus of Mehmet I.

The *medrese* beside the mosque houses the town's **Museum of Turkish and Islamic Art** (*Türk ve İslam Eserleri Müzesi*). This contains an interesting display of Karagöz shadow puppets, made from coloured, translucent camel skin. Although this type of shadow play probably originated in China, the stories which made it popular in Turkey were based on the exploits of two Bursa peasants. Karagöz and Hacivat were fellow labourers whose practical jokes incurred the wrath of Sultan Orhan. They were put to death on his orders, but their earthy humour lives on in the puppet plays which became popular throughout Turkey, and especially in Bursa.

The terrace cafés behind the Yeşil Camii enjoy a magnificent panorama over the eastern end of the city. Prominent down to the left, with two domes and a single minaret, is the **Yıldırım Beyazıt Complex**, Turkey's earliest example of a complete *külliye,* or mosque complex, including a mosque, Sultan Beyazıt's mausoleum, a *medrese,* soup kitchen and *hamam.* It was built between 1398 and 1403, and originally included a hospital, a Dervish monastery, and a caravanserai in addition to the existing buildings. The inverted-T plan of the mosque prefigures that of the Yeşil Camii.

City Centre

From the Green Mosque you can walk to the city centre in about ten minutes, past the equestrian statue of Atatürk and the traffic jams of the main street to the pleasant pedestrian plaza of Koza Parkı right in the heart of Bursa. The far end of the square is bounded by the **Ulu Camii** (Great Mosque), built between 1396 and 1399 with honey-coloured stone quarried from the slopes of Uludağ. It was not an imperial mosque but a municipal one, designed as a place where the townspeople could gather for communal prayers every Friday. Hence it has a huge rectangular prayer hall, with 20 domes in four rows of five,

supported by 12 great pillars. Legend has it that Sultan Beyazıt vowed that he would build 20 mosques if he was granted victory in his next battle against the crusaders. The sultan won, but thought better of his extravagant promise and used his war spoils to build the 20 domes of the Ulu Camii instead. Nevertheless, the Great Mosque of Bursa was, at that time, the largest Ottoman mosque ever built.

An archway leads from the centre of the plaza into the **Koza Hanı**, an arcaded 15th-century caravanserai which is the centre of Bursa's silk trade. In June and July you can watch dealers haggling over heaps of white silkworm cocoons piled in the courtyard, before browsing among the colourful scarves and shawls in the shops

*B*ursa is the centre of Turkey's silk industry. Each year, in June and July, you can see silk dealers haggling over piles of silkworm cocoons in the courtyard of the Koza Hanı.

THE SECRET OF SILK

Silk (*ipek* in Turkish) is a fibre produced by the larva of the silkworm moth as it spins its cocoon. Sericulture (the production of silk as a textile) involves breeding silkworm moths and their larvae, which feed on mulberry leaves. The larvae are killed inside their cocoons using steam, and several cocoons (each of which contains a single filament 600-900m, or 650-1,000yd long) are unravelled and their fibres twisted together to form a single strand of silk. Several of these strands are in turn twisted together to make a still stronger yarn, which is woven into a fabric. At this stage it is called raw silk; it is boiled in soapy water to remove a gummy substance called sericin, thus producing the soft, slinky, lustrous material we know as silk.

Sericulture originated in China, perhaps as long ago as 3000 BC, and remained a jealously guarded secret for thousands of years. However, during the reign of the Byzantine emperor Justinian (527-65) two Persian monks succeeded in smuggling several silkworm cocoons out of China, hidden in hollow bamboo canes, thus breaking China's monopoly of the silk trade. In Turkey, Bursa became the centre of silk production, and despite a slump in the 19th century, continues to be so today. Most of the silk produced is used in the weaving of high-quality Hereke silk carpets.

that line the upper colonnade. The small octagonal building in the centre of the courtyard is a tiny mosque. Stairs at the far end of the gallery lead down to the courtyard, from which an arch on the left leads to another yard with a pleasant café.

Beyond the *han* sprawls Bursa's **Bazaar**, which is every bit as interesting to explore as Istanbul's. The original Bedesten was built in the 14th century by Sultan Beyazıt, but was destroyed by an earthquake in 1855. The entire market area was devastated by fire in 1955, so most of what you see today is restored. But don't let the bright new shopfronts fool you into thinking that this is a tourist bazaar – almost all the shoppers here are local people. Shops selling similar goods are often gathered together in one area of the market – there is even an entire alley devoted to wedding dresses. There are bargains to be found in gold and silver jewellery, silks and antiques. Look out for the **Eski Aynalı Çarşısı**, which is crammed with shops selling antiques, ethnic goods, and Karagöz puppets.

From the far side of the Ulu Camii, take the pedestrian underpass to Yiğitler Caddesi, the road which rises steeply from left to right at the far side of the busy intersection. This leads beneath the remains of the walls of Bursa's ancient **Hisar**, or fortress, parts of which contain old Roman or Byzantine columns. This is the oldest part of town, and the earliest fortifications date from Hellenistic times, although they have been much repaired by the Byzantines and Ottomans.

At the top of the hill, on the right, you can enjoy a fine view over the city from the terrace park that holds the **tombs of Orhan Gazi and Osman Gazi**. Osman Gazi was the founder of the House of Osman, the dynasty that ruled the Ottoman Empire for 600 years. He died in 1324 in the neighbouring town of Söğüt, but was buried here in 1326 after the city had been

Like all Turkish towns, Bursa has its Atatürk statue. This one is a local landmark, so much so that the surrounding district is called Heykel – 'statue'.

captured by his son, Orhan Gazi. Osman's tomb was formerly a Byzantine baptistery, and his son's tomb is in the nave of the neighbouring church – fragments of its ancient mosaic pavement can be seen on the floor of the tomb. There are a number of pleasant cafés here in the shady park making it a good spot to break for lunch.

The tombs of sultans and princes lie amid the shady gardens of the Muradiye Complex. If they are locked, look for the caretaker, who will open them for you.

Muradiye Complex

To find the **Muradiye Complex**, just follow your nose for a mile or so along the main road beyond the tombs of Orhan and Osman, as it sweeps through a neighbourhood of old wooden Ottoman houses, many crumbling in picturesque decay. The complex, or *külliye,* is a peaceful rose garden shaded by pine and magnolia trees, with a mosque and ten *türbes,* including that of Sultan Murat II (ruled 1421-51), the last sultan to be buried in Bursa. Murat was considered a wise and strong leader, and gave much of his time to study and contemplation. His *türbe* is plain and undecorated save for the painted ceiling of the wooden portico; as was his wish, his earth-filled sarcophagus lies beneath an opening in the crown of the dome, so that 'the rain of heaven might wash my face like any commoner's'.

The Ottoman rule of succession gave no favour to the eldest son – any of the sultan's male offspring had the right to claim the throne. Following the death of the sultan, the prince who had negotiated the strongest position in court would often have his brothers put to death rather than risk a challenge to his authority. Many of the princes laid to rest in the Muradiye Complex met their deaths at the hands of close relatives. Near to Murat's tomb is that of **Şehzade Ahmet** and his brother, who were murdered by their cousin Selim I; it is handsomely decorated with blue and white İznik tiles. Beyond is the tomb of **Şehzade Mustafa** (1515-53), the son of Süleyman the Magnificent, who was executed at his father's orders. The sultan had ordered the killing at the insistence of his favourite wife Roxelana, and later bitterly regretted his actions. The magnificent floral tilework that graces the tomb was perhaps a small token of Süleyman's remorse. The most colourful tomb is that of **Cem Sultan** (1459-95), the youngest and favourite son of Mehmet the Conqueror, who was driven from the empire by his brother Beyazıt II. Cem lived in exile for 14 years, trying to raise support amongst Christian leaders for a campaign against his brother, but he died in Italy unavenged (see box, p.239).

Across the street from the Muradiye is a restored **17th-century Ottoman house** (*17YY Osmanlı Evi Müzesi*), with original decor and furnishings. Note how the wooden house is divided into two parts: the *haremlik,* the private family quarters; and the *selamlık,* the public area where visitors were received. Bursa's **Archaeological Museum** (*Arkeoloji Müzesi*) can be found downhill from the Muradiye Complex, amongst the trees and lawns of the Kültür Park. There are the usual displays of Roman and Byzantine artefacts and fragments of sculpture, but the most interesting exhibit is the collection of Anatolian jewellery.

Çekirge

Further west Bursa merges into the affluent suburb of **Çekirge**, a place famous for its **hot springs** and spa hotels. The restorative powers of Uludağ's hot, mineralized waters, rich in iron and sulphur, and with temperatures ranging from 37 to 75°C, have been known since antiquity. The Romans and Byzantines built baths here, and the Ottomans continued the tradition. Bursa's top hotels, the Çelik Palas and Kervansaray Termal, can be found here; both have their own private baths, pools and massage rooms, although the general public can use the facilities for a fee.

There are also some historic public baths. The **Eski Kaplıca** (Old Spa), next to the Kervansaray Hotel, is a restored 14th-century *hamam*, built on the site of an earlier Byzantine bath. The marble-clad hot room has a large, spring-fed pool of scalding water beneath a dome supported by eight Byzantine columns. Opposite the hotel is the **Hüdavendiğar Murat I Camii** (Mosque of Murat I, Creator of the Universe), built 1359-89. The mosque is unique in having both mosque and *medrese* under a single roof, and in having many Byzantine and Italianate features, such as alternating bands of brickwork and stone, and pointed-arch arcades. Tradition maintains that it was designed by a captured Italian architect.

Back towards the city centre, at the west end of the Kültür Park, is the **Yeni Kaplıca** (New Spa). This was originally a Byzantine bath built by the Emperor Justinian, but it was restored in 1522 by Rüstem Paşa, Grand Vizier to Süleyman the Magnificent, after the sultan was cured of gout by its waters. The hot room has a deep plunge pool and fragments of ancient mosaic in the marble floor. The Yeni Kaplıca is for men only, but near by you will find the Kaynarca Kaplıca for women, and the Karamustafa Kaplıca, which has family rooms.

Uludağ National Park

Uludağ (2,543m; 8,344ft), one of many peaks known to the ancients as Mount Olympus, rises majestically above Bursa, its pine-clad slopes giving way to alpine flowers and bare scree near the summit. It is snow capped in winter, making it a popular skiing area for *İstanbullus* and *Bursalıs*. In summer its cool forests, abundant wildlife and expansive views attract weekend walkers and picnickers.

The **ski season** lasts from December to April, and there are more than a dozen over-priced hotels at the 1,800m (6,000ft) level that cater to the ski trade. Six chairlifts and six T-bars give access to the

İznik

The pine forests that cover the slopes of Uludağ, above Bursa, provide shady picnic spots and pleasant wooded walks.

İznik is a sleepy farming town about 70km (43 miles) northeast of Bursa. It wakes up at the weekend, when city folk descend to enjoy its beach and lakeside restaurants, then returns to dusty somnolence, a centre for the farmers who grow wheat, maize, sunflowers, olives and fruit in the lush hills around the lake,

But İznik's crumbling city walls testify to the former importance of the town. This was once Nicaea, capital-in-exile of the Byzantine Empire for the six decades when Constantinople was occupied by the crusaders (1204-61). The city was founded long before, around 300 BC, and later became one of the most important cities in the Roman province of Asia. It played a major role in the development of the Christian church, hosting two ecumenical councils. The first, in 325, promulgated the Nicene Creed, a fundamental statement of the Christian faith that is accepted by the Roman Catholic, Anglican, Eastern Orthodox and major Protestant churches. The second Council of Nicaea, in 787, was called to resolve the Iconoclastic Controversy, which had raged since 726 when Emperor Leo III decreed that the worship of icons was blasphemous. The council decided that icons deserved reverence and veneration, but not adoration.

The city was taken by the Ottoman Turks in 1331, and became famous for its magnificent faience tiles during the 15th century, when skilled craftsmen brought from Persia by Mehmet I set up their kilns in the town. İznik tiles were used to decorate mosques, palaces and other important buildings all over the Ottoman Empire, and by 1575 there were 375 working kilns in the town. But when war broke out between Turkey and Persia at

slopes – the runs are less than challenging for experienced skiers, but can be good fun for beginners and intermediates. Most of the hotels close for the summer, but a few stay open to accommodate weekend hikers and tourists. There are a few marked **hiking trails**, and it is possible to walk to the summit and back from the hotel area (allow 6-7 hours for the round trip, and take full hill-walking equipment – even in summer the weather can turn bad very quickly, and it would be all too easy to get lost).

There are two ways to reach the hotel area (Oteller). A **cable car** (*teleferik*) runs from Bursa to a picnic area and campground called Sarıalan, about 6km (10 miles) from Oteller. The *teleferik* runs every half-hour or so between 8am and 9pm all year round, and takes about 30 minutes, with a brief stop half way up at Kadıyayla. (In bad weather or high winds the service may be suspended.) From Sarıalan you can catch a *dolmuş* to Oteller.

Alternatively, you can take a *dolmuş*, taxi, or your own car up the winding 36km (22-mile) road that leads from Çekirge to Oteller. At the 20km (12-mile) mark you will reach the national park entrance, where you must stop and pay an admission fee. The upper half of the road is paved with rough stone blocks which keep your speed down, so allow an hour for the trip to the top. There are a number of appealing barbecue restaurants on the way up.

the end of the 16th century, many of the Persian craftsmen were banished, and İznik entered a long decline. The city was damaged extensively during the Turkish War of Independence in 1922.

A main street shaded by tall pines and plane trees leads from the tea gardens of the flower-bedecked lakeside to a crossroads in the town centre. Here you will find the ruins of the **Church of Hagia Sophia** (*Ayasofya*), marked by the brick stump of a minaret topped with the tangled twigs of a stork's nest. The original church here was built in the 6th century, and replaced in the 11th century when it was destroyed by an earthquake; when the Ottomans arrived, they converted the church to a mosque. The church hosted the second Council of Nicaea in 787.

Just inside the door you can see (under glass) a part of the original 6th-century mosaic floor; a fragment of a contemporary fresco survives in a tomb niche low on the left wall. There are two aisles and a nave, with a synthronon in the apse; the reliquary to the right of the apse contains traces of frescoes. In the right-hand aisle you can see some Arabic inscriptions on the arches, and the angled *mihrab* that was added when the church was used as a mosque.

Follow the main street away from the lake, past shady cafés, a little square and shops selling agricultural goods, to a large, well-tended park on the left. The multi-

coloured minaret you see belongs to İznik's **Yeşil Camii** (Green Mosque, 1378-91), which took its name from the brilliant green İznik tiles which once covered the minaret (the present tiles are modern replacements from Kütahya). Across the park from the mosque is the Nilüfer Hatun Imareti, which translates as the 'Soup Kitchen of Lady Nilüfer'. Nilüfer was the mother of Sultan Murat I, who commissioned the building in her honour in 1388. The kitchen provided food for students and poor townspeople, and offered accommodation for travellers. Today it houses İznik's attractive **Archaeological Museum**, and provides a nesting site for storks on top of its ample domes. The museum exhibits include a fine Roman

sarcophagus, Roman glass objects, coins, Ottoman weapons, calligraphy and İznik faience. There is an interesting display on recent excavations in the town, which have unearthed some of the original pottery kilns.

You can see all that remains of Roman Nicaea by returning to Hagia Sophia and turning left, then right at a sign a few blocks down reading 'Tiyatro' (a sign on the left, 'Çini Fırınları', leads to the pottery kiln excavations described in the museum). Little is left of Nicaea's **Roman theatre**. The seats are gone, but you can make out the shape of the *cavea* and the base of the stage building.

The most impressive legacy of İznik's past is undoubtedly the Byzantine **city wall**, which runs largely unbroken around the town for a distance of about 5km (3 miles). The older, outer wall dates from the 3rd century, but the main inner wall, which originally had more than 100 watchtowers, dates from the 13th century. There were four main gates, of which two are reasonably well preserved. The **Lefke Kapısı**, on the main road beyond the Yeşil Camii, is a triple gate, with statue niches flanking the middle arch; an inscription records that it was dedicated to the Emperor Hadrian in AD 123. You can climb to the top of the crumbling ramparts to see a part of the aqueduct that once supplied the city with water. The **Istanbul Kapısı**, on the road north, is a double gate, the inner of the two decorated with carved stone masks.

*T*he ruined church of Hagia Sophia in İznik dates from the 11th century. The minaret stump shows that it was converted into a mosque after İznik was captured by the Ottomans.

A Treasure House of History on the Shores of the Aegean

The lands around the Aegean gave birth to the great civilizations of Crete and ancient Greece, and are generally considered to be the cradle of modern Western culture. The west coast of Asia Minor was one of the most densely populated parts of the ancient world, with many famous cities to its name: Smyrna, the birthplace of Homer; Sardis, seat of the wealthy King Croesus; Ephesus, where St Paul preached the gospels; and Halicarnassus, birthplace of the historian Herodotus. The sites of two of the Seven Wonders of the World – the Temple of Artemis at Ephesus, and the Mausoleum of Halicarnassus – can also be found here.

The coast to the north of Izmir (ancient Smyrna) was called Aeolis in very early times, and was first settled by migrant Greeks towards the end of the 2nd millennium BC. A second wave of immigration took place around 1000-900 BC when Ionic Greek refugees, escaping war and invasion in their homeland, founded settlements on the coast to the south of Izmir, a region that came to be known as Ionia. The 12 major cities of Ionia formed themselves into a powerful allegiance called the Panionion,

Turkey's Aegean coast is famed for its wealth of ruined Greek and Roman cities. The Temple of Hadrian can be seen at Ephesus, one of the best of the ancient sites.

and their trading fleets founded colonies as far away as the Black Sea coast, France and Spain. Anatolia came under Persian rule during the 6th century BC, and it was the famous revolt of the Ionian cities against the Persians in 499 BC that marked the beginnings of the Greco-Persian Wars.

The cities of the Aegean regained their independence following the campaigns of Alexander the Great, but later became part of the Pergamene Kingdom that was bequeathed to Rome in 133 BC. The Ionian cities flourished under Roman rule, and many of their most magnificent ruins date from this period. Smyrna, Pergamum, Ephesus and Miletus in particular were among the most splendid cities in the whole of the Roman Empire, and continued to prosper under the Byzantines. However, coastal cities such as Miletus and Ephesus turned

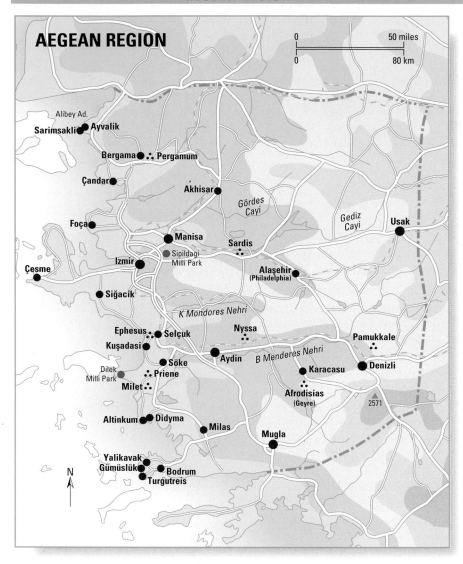

AEGEAN REGION

0   50 miles
0   80 km

Alibey Ad.
Sarimsakli Ayvalik
Bergama Pergamum
Çandar
Akhisar
Gördes Cayi
Gediz Cayi   Usak
Foça
Manisa
Sardis
Izmir   Sipildagi Milli Park
Çesme
Alaşehir (Philadelphia)
Siğacik
K Mondores Nehri
Ephesus Selçuk   Nyssa
Kuşadasi   Pamukkale
Söke Aydin   B Menderes Nehri   Denizli
Dilek Milli Park Priene   Karacasu
Milet
Afrodisias (Geyre)   2571
Altinkum Didyma
Milas
Mugla
Yalikavak
Gümüslük Bodrum
N   Turgutreis

out to be victims of their river-mouth locations. As the centuries passed, the rivers on which the cities had been built poured millions of tonnes of silt into the sea, filling up the harbours and extending the land. Today Ephesus's ancient harbour lies high and dry, 8km (5 miles) from the modern coastline, long since cut off from the sea by the alluvial plain of the River Cayster.

North of Izmir

The coast from the Gulf of Edremit south to Izmir is fringed by narrow gravel beaches, backed by olive groves and farmland. There are a few small, well-established resorts, which cater mainly to Turkish tourists, but new development in the form of holiday villages and apartment complexes is gradually spreading along the shoreline. The old backwater atmosphere of this part of the country is slowly disappearing amid the dust of new roads, building sites, and a forest of fences and power cables. However, the old fishing village resorts of Ayvalık and Foça are still worth visiting, and the hilltop city of Pergamum is the most evocative ancient sites in Turkey.

Ayvalık

The old town of **Ayvalık** makes a living from tourism, fishing and olives – nearly three-quarters of Turkey's olive-oil production comes from the surrounding area. The setting is attractive, on a bay hemmed in by islands. During summer there is a daily boat service from Ayvalık to Mytilene on the Greek island of Lesbos, and a more frequent ferry to Alibey, the largest island in the bay.

Ayvalık was founded nearly 400 years ago by Ottoman Greeks, a fact reflected in the abundance of old stone buildings (the Turks usually built in wood), and a number of Orthodox churches. During the exchange of populations that took place following the Turkish War of Independence in 1920-2, the mainly Turkish speaking Greeks were moved out and replaced by Greek-speaking Turkish refugees from Thrace, Crete and the Aegean islands. The old churches were converted to mosques – take a look at the **Saatlı Camii** (Mosque with a Clock), which used to be the Church of St John; it lies a few blocks inland from the main square.

The centre of town has a number of waterfront restaurants and hotels, but there are quieter and more pleasant alternatives on Alibey Island and on the bay to the south. You can get to **Alibey** (also known as Cunda) by taking a boat from the quay opposite the main square, or by driving over the causeway that links the island to the mainland just north of town. Alibey town is a smaller and quieter version of Ayvalık, with good seafood restaurants and some peaceful pensions, as well as a ruined Greek Orthodox cathedral. There are some good sandy beaches in the north.

If you follow the road south from Ayvalık you will eventually reach the new resort of **Sarımsaklı**, which has an excellent sandy beach but suffers from overdevelopment, with lots of ugly apartment blocks and building sites. A far more pleasant spot is **Şeytan Sofrası** (The Devil's Dinner Table), a flat-topped, wooded hill northwest of the beach; a road leads to all the way to the summit, where

The hill called Şeytan Sofrası, above Ayvalık, bears a rocky hollow said to be the devil's foot-print. Votive ribbons ward off any evil spirits.

there is a small café-restaurant. A hollow in the rocks at one side of the summit, enclosed by an iron cage, is supposed to be Satan's footprint. The iron bars and the bushes all around are covered in votive ribbons tied by local people to ward off evil spirits, and the 'footprint' is full of coins thrown for luck. The hill commands a splendid view over the island-filled bay, and is famous for its spectacular sunsets.

Pergamum (Bergama)

The modern Turkish town of Bergama lies 8km (5 miles) west of the main road, about 60km (37 miles) south of Ayvalık. It is an agricultural market town, serving the rich farmland that lines the valley of the Havran River (the ancient River Caicus). Each year in early June it hosts the Bergama Festival, a five-day celebration of traditional music, dancing and handicrafts. But Bergama's main attraction sits atop the craggy hill that towers 300m (1,000ft) above the town – the ruins of ancient Pergamum.

The easily defended hilltop was probably settled by Aeolian Greeks as long ago as the 8th century BC, but the city of Pergamum does not enter the history books until 300 years later, and did not become important until the break-up of Alexander the Great's empire in 323 BC. It gained its independence under Eumenes I, the founder of the Pergamene royal dynasty, whose successor, Attalus I, defeated the marauding Gauls and allied himself with the Romans against the Seleucids of Syria.

At the height of its power, in the 2nd century BC, Pergamum was one of the most splendid cities on the Aegean coast. During the reign of Eumenes II (197-160 BC) the Pergamene kingdom inherited the territory of the defeated Seleucids, and stretched from the Sea of Marmara to the Maeander Valley, and east as far as Iconium (modern Konya). The vast riches of the empire were spent on developing the arts and sciences, and on embellishing the acropolis hill with magnificent new buildings. One of the city's greatest innovations was the use of treated animal skins as a writing material. The finished product was called *pergamene* (*charta pergamena* in Latin), and has been handed down to us as 'parchment'. This invention enabled the scribes of Pergamum to amass a great library, which rivalled that of Alexandria in its size and scope. (Plutarch, writing in the 1st century AD, tells us that Mark Antony gave most of Pergamum's library to Cleopatra as a gift, after the Alexandrian library was destroyed by fire in 41 BC.)

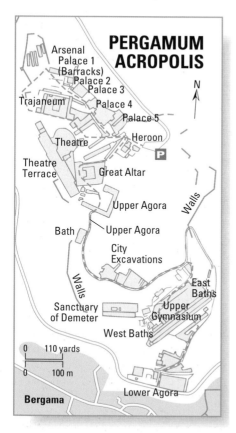

PERGAMUM ACROPOLIS

N

Arsenal
Palace 1 (Barracks)
Palace 2
Palace 3
Trajaneum
Palace 4
Palace 5
Heroon
P
Theatre
Theatre Terrace
Great Altar
Upper Agora
Bath
Upper Agora
City Excavations
Walls
East Baths
Walls
Sanctuary of Demeter
Upper Gymnasium
West Baths
0 110 yards
0 100 m
Bergama
Lower Agora

PAPYRUS AND PARCHMENT

Legend maintains that parchment was invented as a result of the rivalry between Ptolemy V of Egypt and Eumenes II of Pergamum. Fearing that Pergamum's library might grow to equal that of Alexandria, Ptolemy banned the export of papyrus, the universal writing material of the time. Undaunted, the Pergamenes perfected the art of preparing animal skins for writing. The skins of calves, goats and sheep were washed and depilated, then stretched on a frame and scraped to remove any remaining traces of hair and flesh. The skins were then whitened with chalk and smoothed with pumice stones. The finished material, which became known as *charta pergamena*, or parchment, was smooth, flexible and durable, and both sides could be written on. The finished pieces of parchment were much larger than papyrus sheets, and could be folded, allowing the development of the *codex*, or bound book, which eventually replaced the scroll, or rolled manuscript.

The last king of Pergamum was the eccentric Attalus III, who died without an heir and bequeathed his kingdom to Rome in 133 BC. Under Roman rule the city flourished again, but was damaged by an earthquake during the 2nd century AD and slipped gradually into decline. The ruins were discovered by a German railway engineer in 1871; excavations began in 1878 and are still continuing today. The four separate sites will take a full day to explore, and should be visited in the following order – take a taxi to the summit of the acropolis, then walk downhill through the ruins to the Kızıl Avlu (Red Courtyard). Break for lunch in one of the restaurants in central Bergama before visiting the Archaeological Museum, then take another taxi out to the remains of the Asclepion.

Acropolis

To reach the **acropolis** (*Akropol*), take the main street through the town centre and across the river, and on up the hill in a long loop, passing old fortifications on the way. The car park at the top is surrounded by souvenir stalls, a café and a ticket office (if you bring your own vehicle there is a separate fee for parking).

From the car park a ramp leads up to the remains of a **monumental gateway**, passing the foundations of the **heroon**, a monument dedicated to the kings of Pergamum. Ahead on the left you will see an open space littered with column stumps; this was the precinct of the **Temple of Athena**. A statue of the Roman Emperor Augustus once stood on the circular pedestal in the centre of the precinct. All that remains of the 4th-century BC Doric temple is the *crepidoma* (the stepped base), set way back at the far edge of the precinct below a fragment of standing masonry; marks on the *stylobate* (top surface of the *crepidoma*) show that it originally had a single row of columns, ten by six, around the outside edge. Along the north side of the precinct (currently fenced off and undergoing restoration) is Pergamum's famous **library**.

The stone-paved main street continues uphill. On the right are the remains of five **royal palaces**, each with its rooms arranged around a central, colonnaded courtyard. There are two deep water-storage **cisterns**: one close to the right of the path, beneath a low arched roof; and one higher uphill (beneath the modern radio shack), which has a pillar in the centre. Ignore the sparkling white columns of the Trajaneum for the moment, and climb up to the **city walls** at the top of the hill. You can distinguish the relatively hastily built Byzantine walls, with rough stone and brickwork, sitting on top of the earlier, cleanly finished masonry of the Hellenistic walls. Go through the gap in the walls to a spur where you can see the foundations of narrow storerooms known as the **arsenal**. The archaeologists found 900 rounds of stone shot stored here. From the end of the spur you can enjoy a fine view over the Caicus River valley, and down to a 2nd-century AD Roman **aqueduct**. The aqueduct was part of a system that supplemented the original Pergamene pipeline, providing extra water for the growing population, and especially for the new Roman baths.

From the arsenal take the path (marked by spots of blue paint) which passes beneath the right-hand corner of the walls, to reach the most imposing of the monuments on the acropolis. The **Trajaneum** was erected during the 2nd century AD in honour of the deified emperors Trajan and Hadrian. It is built on a large terrace supported by huge vaults. Six of the original 26

*G*littering marble columns mark the site of Pergamum's Trajaneum, a temple from the 2nd century AD dedicated to deified Roman emperors.

THE PERGAMENE PIPELINE

One of the problems of living on a mountain top is securing a reliable water supply. Around 180 BC, the engineers of Pergamum solved this problem by constructing a pipeline that carried water to the city from the mountain springs of Madra Dağ, 45km (28 miles) to the north. A three-channelled, low-pressure, terracotta pipeline, in 240,000 sections, brought the water by gravity to settling tanks on a spur 3km (2 miles) east of, and 40m (130ft) higher than the city. From there, a high-pressure pipeline, called a siphon, dipped 180m (590ft) into the intervening valley and up the other side to the cisterns on the acropolis summit. The lower sections of this final pipeline had to be capable of carrying water at pressures of 20 atmospheres (300 psi); they were probably made of bronze, or perhaps lead.

columns that once formed the Corinthian temple have been re-erected by the German archaeological team; the glittering white marble of the columns and cladding contrasts with the grey stone of the foundation.

From the terrace of the Trajaneum you can admire the impressively steep *cavea* of the **Hellenistic theatre**, set in a shallow

*T*he theatre at Pergamum was built in a shallow depression in the steep hillside below the Temple of Athena. At its foot runs a terraced street, with a Temple of Dionysus at one end.

154

depression in the hillside. Lack of space forced the Pergamene architects to build upwards, and to provide a movable stage. The wooden stage was supported on posts which fit into holes in the stone pavement; between performances the stage was dismantled to allow free movement along the narrow terrace street at the foot of the theatre. At the near end of the street is a small **Temple of Dionysus** dating from the 2nd century BC, which was clad in marble during Roman times and re-dedicated to the Emperor Caracalla. The emperor donated funds for the marble and other gifts after recuperating from an accident at Pergamum's Asclepion.

Return to the monumental gateway and turn right down the stone-paved road that leads past the stepped base of the **Altar of Zeus**, built to commemorate the defeat of the Gauls in 190 BC. The edge of the altar was positioned carefully so that it was aligned with the Temple of Athena on the terrace above. The altar was entered by a wide staircase on the west side, and was once decorated with a remarkable frieze depicting the Battle of the Gods and Giants (symbolizing the victory of Attalus I over the Gauls), one of the finest existing examples of Hellenistic sculpture. The remains of the frieze, which was over 2m (6ft) tall and more than 100m (330ft) long, were removed during the 19th century and now reside in Berlin's Pergamon Museum.

The ancient road continues downhill and curves round to the left towards the lower city, past an area called the City Excavations (remains of an auditorium, gymnasium, restaurant and latrine), before doubling back right along a terrace street above the colonnaded *palaestra* of the Upper Gymnasium. At the far end, beyond a small temple to Hera, the path leads down through jumbled ruins to the gymnasium terrace.

To the right you will find the entrance to the **Sanctuary of Demeter**, marked by two Doric columns. To the left of the entrance is a sacrificial pit, and to the right the remains of a fountain for ritual ablutions. Demeter was the Greek 'earth mother', goddess of agriculture, associated with corn and the harvest. It is thought that the sanctuary at Pergamum was used for the performance of secret rites associated with the cult of Demeter, similar to the Eleusinian Mysteries, which conferred a blissful afterlife on the initiates. The temple building is towards the far end of the precinct, with a large altar of huge stone blocks in front of it; the right-hand side of the sanctuary has stepped seating for about 1,000 spectators.

To the left is the **Upper Gymnasium**, with large baths complexes at either end; if you look in the rooms at the southwest end you will find some surviving marble washbasins. At the back of the *palaestra* is a small auditorium, and a marble-lined room with an apse at either end which was reserved for the use of the emperor. Immediately below the terrace, and accessible by narrow stairs, is the long, narrow **Cellar Stadium**, which was used as a race track.

The Upper Gymnasium was used by the young men of the city. The Middle Gymnasium, on the terrace below, was for teenagers, while the Lower Gymnasium still further downhill was for younger boys. Near the bottom of the hill, the stone road is polished and rutted by the wheels of ancient carts. Above on the right is the **House of Attalus**, with well-preserved wall-paintings and floor mosaics protected by a modern roof.

Kızıl Avlu (Red Court)

Pergamum's most unusual monument lies at the foot of the acropolis hill, where the road crosses the river. The **Kızıl Avlu**, also known as the Red Basilica, is a huge red-brick edifice flanked by two circular towers, set in a wide precinct that sits astride the river (the water is carried in an ancient tunnel beneath the courtyard). The walls still stand to a height of nearly 20m (60ft), and are home to flocks of screaming swifts.

The building dates from the 2nd century AD, but its original purpose remains a mystery. The most popular theory is that it was a temple to the Egyptian deities Isis and Serapis, who were associated with the underworld; their worship involved mysteries and rites similar to those observed in the Sanctuary of Demeter on the acropolis. The hollow cult statues of the gods sat atop a podium at the far end of the temple; the chamber beneath the pedestal (entered by stairs to the left) was used by priests to get inside the statues and deliver divine pronouncements. The courtyards in front of the towers to either side of the hall each contain a rectangular pool, and are riddled with more tunnels which may have played a part in the performance of the secret rites.

However, some experts disagree with this interpretation and claim that the building may have been the home of

The massive brick walls of the Kızıl Avlu (Red Court) are home to flocks of screaming swifts. In ancient times they may have housed a temple to the gods Isis and Serapis.

Pergamum's library, or even a university, during Roman times. Whatever its original function, the Byzantines built a basilica within the main hall, dedicated to St John the Apostle; you can see the remains of the walls and marble floors, and the curved outline of the apse at the far end. The Basilica of St John was one of the Seven Churches of Asia mentioned in the Book of Revelation, and was the seat of a bishopric from the 4th to the 15th centuries.

Archaeological Museum

In the centre of the modern town is the Bergama **Archaeological Museum**, with a large collection of material from Stone Age to Byzantine times. Its fine collection would be even finer if 19th-century archaeologists had not removed all the best works from the acropolis to the Pergamon Museum in Berlin. Take a look at the model of the Altar of Zeus, the architrave from the entrance to the precinct of Athena, the frieze from the Temple of Dionysus below the theatre, and the plaques listing graduates from the gymnasia. There is a pleasant tea garden in the courtyard where you can rest before heading for the Asclepion.

Asclepion

From the summit of the acropolis the **Asclepion** is visible on the plain below. This was one of the ancient world's leading medical centres, rivalling similar sites at Epidauros, Kos and Ephesus. Dedicated to Asclepius, the god of healing, the Asclepion provided its patients with hot baths, massages, primitive psychiatry, dream interpretation and draughts of water from a sacred spring (recently found to be mildly radioactive). The physician Galen (AD 130-200), whose fame in the ancient world was second only to Hippocrates, practised here.

THE GOD OF HEALING

Ailing citizens from all over the Aegean came to Pergamum to seek a cure from the doctor-priests of Asclepius, the god of healing. Asclepius was the son of Apollo and the nymph Coronis, and was taught the secrets of medicinal herbs by the centaur Chiron. Asclepius became so skilled in the art of healing that Zeus became afraid that he would make men immortal, and struck him down with a thunderbolt. He is revered as the founder of the study of medicine, and his symbolic attribute of a serpent coiled around a staff is still recognized as the emblem of medicine today.

The worship of Asclepius began at Epidauros in Greece, and was brought to Pergamum some time in the 4th century BC. The treatments dispensed at the Asclepion were recorded by a 2nd-century hypochondriac named Aelius Aristides, who spent 13 years in therapy there. They included herbal preparations, mud baths, exercise, special diets, and massage. Some patients slept in the temple, where Asclepius would appear in their dreams. The dream events were interpreted by the doctors, who then prescribed a suitable treatment. The theatre, like the bandstands and casinos of modern spas such as Baden-Baden and Montecatini, was intended to provide a little therapeutic entertainment.

As you approach Bergama from the main road, you pass the tourist information office on the left; the side road which branches left here leads to the Asclepion. The entrance to the site is along a colonnaded street, the **Sacred Way**, which leads to a *propylon*, or monumental gateway, with steps down into the medical precinct. On the right you can see the remains of the **library**, and the well-preserved colonnade which leads to the 3,000-seat **theatre** (entertainment was part of the therapy). In front of the theatre is a square pool holding the healing waters of the **sacred spring**, where you can still drink to this day. Near the centre of the courtyard a tunnel leads to the circular **treatment room**, where you can see stone bathing tubs and niches for cult statues. Near by is the **Temple of Asclepius**, also circular in plan, which was capped with a dome 24m (79ft) in diameter. A statue of the god once occupied the large recess facing the entrance; patients who had been cured would come here to sacrifice a cockerel in thanks.

Foça and Çandarlı

South of Bergama lie two fishing villages-turned-holiday resorts, frequented mainly by the residents of nearby Izmir. **Çandarlı** is a small town dominated by a restored 14th-century Genoese fortress, and has some pleasant gravel beaches. **Foça** is livelier and has been extensively developed, with apartment complexes and holiday villages sprawling along the rocky coastline. It is a major fishing port, with a sizeable fleet moored in the bay to the south of the castle.

Foça's castle is also Genoese, and sits picturesquely on a promontory overlooking the harbour. But the town's origins are far older, for this was the site of **ancient Phocaea**, founded around 1000 BC by Ionian Greeks. The city's name comes from the hump-backed islands in the bay, which reminded the original inhabitants of seals – *phoce* in Greek. Seals also appeared on Phocaean coins. The Phocaeans were famous seafarers; in the words of Herodotus, 'The Phocaeans were the pioneer navigators of the Greeks, and it was they who showed their countrymen the way to the Adriatic, Tyrrhenia, and the Spanish peninsula as far as Tartessus. They used to sail not in deep, broad-beamed merchant vessels but in fifty-oared galleys.' The Phocaeans founded the colonies of Massalia, Nicaea and Antipolis on the Mediterranean coast of France, which are now the cities of Marseilles, Nice and Antibes.

Unfortunately, almost nothing remains of Phocaea. On the road between Foça and the main highway you will see an impressive 8th-century BC rock tomb known locally as the **Taş Kule** (Stone Tower).

Izmir and Around

Known to the Greeks as Smyrna, and to the Turks as *Güzel Izmir* ('Beautiful Izmir'), Turkey's third-largest city and second-busiest port sprawls around the head of the finest natural harbour on the Aegean coast. The city was founded in the third millennium BC on the north shore of the bay, making it a contemporary of the earliest settlement at Troy. It reached its peak between the 10th and 7th centuries BC, when it was one of the most important cities in the Panionion, with massive fortifications and blocks of two-storey houses; the poet Homer may have been born in Smyrna during this period. The city lost its importance after the Lydian conquest of the 6th century BC, but was re-founded by Alexander the Great on the slopes of Mount Pagus (now Kadifekale), and under the Greeks and Romans it became one of the principal centres of Mediterranean trade. It was also an important religious centre during the early days of Christianity.

When the Ottoman Turks took control in the 15th century, Izmir grew wealthy as a merchant city, handling Smyrna figs and Turkish tobacco from the farms of the interior, and allowing the establishment of

European trading colonies. It prospered as a Levantine port until the close of the Greco-Turkish War in 1922, when it was almost completely destroyed by fire. Rebuilt around the site of Alexander's city, it is once again a bustling port and industrial town, and is home to the headquarters of NATO's southern command. Each year the city hosts the Izmir International Arts Festival (mid-June to mid-July) and the Izmir International Trade Fair (late August to early September); at these times accommodation can be hard to come by, so book in advance.

Izmir's fine hotels and pleasant atmosphere make it an ideal base for exploring the surrounding countryside and the ancient cities that lie scattered around it – Pergamum, Sardis, Ephesus, Priene, Miletus and Didyma – as well as the beaches of the Çeşme Peninsula and the Ottoman architecture of Manisa.

Izmir

At the heart of the city is **Konak Meydanı** (Mansion Square), a busy pedestrian precinct named after the Ottoman mansion which housed the local government. The square lies next to the main bus station and the ferry to Karşıyaka across the bay, and is distinguished by two famous monuments: the **Saat Kulesi** (Clock Tower), an elaborately decorated structure dating from 1901, is the unofficial symbol of Izmir; nearby stands the tiny **Konak Mosque**, built in 1756 and decorated with colourful Kütahya tile panels.

Inland from the Konak Mosque is Izmir's **bazaar**, one of the best in Turkey. The bazaar district was the Turkish quarter of Smyrna, the only part of the old town to escape destruction in the great fire of 1922 (see box). Its narrow, crowded lanes, rich with the smells of coffee and

The tiny, 18th-century Konak Mosque, in busy downtown Izmir, is a well-known local landmark.

kebabs, are packed with men and boys selling household items – coat hangers, plastic bags, clothes pegs, string, baby's bibs, sticky tape, Band-Aids – and tourist touts offering bargain jeans and leather jackets. Of more interest are the antique, jewellery and metalwork stalls, and the locally made *nargiles* (hubble-bubble pipes). If you want to take home a taste of Izmir, try a kilo of the figs or olives for which the city is famous. Ask the way to

THE GREAT FIRE OF SMYRNA

In the closing stages of the Turkish War of Independence in 1922, the Turkish army under Mustafa Kemal (later Atatürk) routed the Greek invasion forces in Anatolia and drove them back to the coast at Izmir. As the Greeks retreated they burned crops and destroyed the towns and villages in their path – Alaşehir was razed to the ground, and of the 18,000 buildings in the historic Ottoman city of Manisa, only 500 survived. Ottoman Greek villagers, afraid that the advancing Turks would wreak a terrible revenge, fled their homes and headed for the coast. When the Turkish army finally took Izmir on 9 September, there were 50,000 Greek refugees camped on the waterfront, still waiting to be evacuated.

A few days later a fire began in the Armenian quarter of the city. No-one will ever know for sure how it started – some say the Greeks started it, some the Armenians, some the Turks. One story claims that Turkish soldiers started a fire to burn out Armenian rebels who were hiding in a house, and that it got out of control. Fanned by a strong breeze, the flames spread rapidly, and by nightfall the whole city was ablaze. As the fire spread towards the waterfront it drove the escaping crowds before it. Many jumped into the water and were drowned, though many more were rescued by the boats of the foreign warships anchored in the harbour. The fire died down the next day when the wind changed, but it smouldered on for three days. Almost three-quarters of the city had been completely destroyed, and thousands of people had died.

*I*zmir's bazaar offers some of the best shopping in Turkey. This shop sells nargiles, or 'hubble-bubble' pipes.

the **Kızlarağası Hanı**, a restored Ottoman caravanserai whose ancient courtyard now houses modern shops and cafés. It was built in the 18th century for Beşir Ağa, the chief black eunuch (*kızlarağası*) in Istanbul's Topkapı Palace during the reign of Mahmut I. Near by is the **Hisar Camii** (Castle Mosque), Izmir's oldest mosque, built in 1597.

On the hill to the south of Konak stands the **Archaeological Museum** (open 9am to 5.30pm daily), whose superb collection of antiquities from Smyrna, Ephesus, Sardis, Miletus and other Aegean sites is labelled in both Turkish and English. The highlights include Roman statues of Poseidon and Demeter that once stood in the *agora* of ancient Smyrna; a bronze statue of a runner, which was dredged up from the sea bed near the site of Kyme, north of Foça; a Roman mosaic from Smyrna showing Aphrodite and Eros; a 4th-century BC bronze head of Demeter, found in the sea near Bodrum; and a fine selection of sarcophagi and funerary monuments.

Across the street from the Archaeological Museum is the **Ethnographic Museum** (open 9am to noon and 1 to 5.30pm), housed in an old Ottoman building. Its varied tableaux re-create the interiors of traditional Turkish and Ottoman Greek houses, a 19th-century Ottoman bridal chamber and circumcision room, an Ottoman pharmacy, and a ceramics kiln for producing the traditional blue and white 'evil-eye' beads for warding off evil spirits. Other exhibits explain carpet-weaving, felt-making, embroidery, metalwork and other crafts.

If you follow Mithatpaşa Caddesi for 1km (½ mile) southwest from the foot of the hill below the museums you will find Izmir's old **Jewish Quarter**. The narrow cobbled streets are lined with restored traditional houses and cast-iron street

---

INFIDEL SMYRNA

The Ottomans used to refer to Izmir as '*Gâvur Izmir*', or 'Infidel Smyrna', because of its large population of Jews, Christian Greeks and Armenians, as well as foreign merchants and their families. After the Treaty of Lausanne (1923), which settled the boundaries of modern Turkey, there was an exchange of ethnic minorities between Turkey and Greece: all the ethnic Greeks in Anatolia were moved to Greece, while the ethnic Turks in Greece were moved to Anatolia. Thus the city that arose from the ashes of the great fire of 1922 was a thoroughly modern, but also thoroughly Turkish one. It is known by the Turks today as '*Güzel Izmir*', or 'Beautiful Smyrna'

---

lamps, tucked beneath a rocky cliff. Dominating the view is the **Asansör** (from the French *ascenseur,* meaning elevator), a 50m (164ft) high red-brick tower, which houses a 19th-century lift connecting the lower streets with those at the top of the cliff. There is a pleasant café at the top, with a grand view across the bay.

North of Konak Meydanı, the palm-fringed promenade of Atatürk Caddesi, more commonly called the **Kordon**, runs along the waterfront to the ferry port at Alsancak, 3km (2 miles) away. A horse-drawn phaeton will take you for a tour, passing through **Cumhuriyet Meydanı** (Republic Square), the centre of modern Izmir, surrounded by glittering luxury hotels and expensive shops and restaurants. Near by is the **Kültür Parkı**, a huge, shady pleasure garden, site of the annual International Trade Fair.

Uphill to the south of the park lies the **Agora**, one of the few remaining traces of ancient Smyrna. This colonnaded square, built during the 2nd century AD, was once the city's bustling market-place. At the top of the hill is the imposing fortress of **Kadifekale**. This was the ancient Mount Pagus, where Alexander the Great commanded his generals Lysimachus and Antigonus to found a new city back in the 4th century BC. No trace remains of their original fortifications, but the view from the medieval ramparts across the city is particularly fine, especially at sunset.

Manisa

Forty kilometres (25 miles) northeast of Izmir lies the attractive Ottoman town of **Manisa**. It occupies the site of (and takes its name from) the ancient city of Magnesia ad Sipylum, which is said to have been founded in the 12th century BC by the Magnetes of Thessaly (warriors from northeastern Greece), after they had fought with Agamemnon's army during the Trojan War. The city was taken by the Persians in the 6th century BC, and came under the control of Pergamum in 190 BC, when it enjoyed a period of prosperity as a commercial centre. It was captured from the Byzantines in 1313 by a Turkmen tribe led by Saruhan Bey, who renamed it Manisa and made it the capital of his principality. The Ottoman Turks took control of Manisa in 1390, and the town became a favourite of the sultans, who graced it with many fine buildings.

In the centre of town you will find the **Sultan Camii**, also called the Valide Camii, a fine Ottoman mosque built in 1522 for Süleyman the Magnificent, in honour of his mother. The portico contains a number of columns taken from the ruins of ancient Magnesia, and is decorated with colourful paintings of local scenes. Each year in late March the mosque precinct is the setting for the **Mesir Şenlikleri** (Sweetmeat Festival), which commemorates the invention of a sweet paste that cured Süleyman's mother of a mystery illness. The paste (called *mesir macunu*) is made from sugar mixed with a blend of 41 spices, and is reputed to give protection from illness, as well as having an aphrodisiac effect. During the festival, quantities of the sweet paste are thrown from the minaret of the Sultan Camii to the crowds of townspeople gathered below.

Across the street is the **Muradiye Camii** (Mosque of Murat III), built in 1583-5, and designed by the great architect Sinan. It has an ornate *mihrab* decorated with blue floral İznik tiles, and a delicately carved marble *mimber*. The stained-glass windows are also lined with İznik tiles. The adjacent *imaret* is occupied by Manisa's **Archaeological Museum**, which has some fine mosaics from Sardis. In the garden of the mosque is the **Saruhan Bey Türbesi**, the tomb of

---

TANTALUS AND NIOBE

Tantalus was the legendary king of Sipylus who was punished in the underworld for offending the gods. His punishment consisted of standing up to his neck in sweet water which flowed away from his mouth when he tried to drink it; above his head hung delicious fruits that swayed out of his reach when he tried to grasp them. His name lives on in the English word 'tantalize'.

Tantalus had a daughter, Niobe, who bore six sons and six daughters to her husband, King Amphion of Thebes. Niobe taunted Leto, who had borne only two children, boasting of her superior fertility. But Leto's offspring were the divine twins Apollo and Artemis, who killed all Niobe's sons and daughters in revenge for the insult against their mother. Niobe, in her grief, could not stop crying, and begged Zeus to turn her into stone to end her pain. The Weeping Rock of Niobe on Mount Sipylus, above Manisa, is supposed to be the petrified remains of Tantalus' tragic daughter.

the Turkmen leader who captured Magnesia from the Byzantines in 1313.

On the hillside high above the museum is Manisa's oldest surviving mosque, the **Ulu Camii** (Great Mosque). It was built in 1366 by İşak Bey, the grandson of Saruhan, on the site of a Byzantine church; there are Byzantine capitals from the older building on some of the columns. The mountain rising above the mosque is Sipil Dağ, the ancient Mount Sipylus, which is associated with the myths of Tantalus and his daughter Niobe (see box on p.163). A strangely shaped rock formation on the hillside about 500m (550yd) to the west of the Ulu Camii is called the **Weeping Rock of Niobe** (*Niobe Ağlayan Kaya*). From a certain angle it resembles the profile of a long-haired woman; local legend maintains that it is the petrified remains of Niobe, turned to stone by Zeus, and who continues to weep for her lost children.

About 7km (5 miles) east of Manisa, on the road towards Sardis and Uşak, is Akpınar. On the cliffs to the right above the road is the **Taş Suret** (Stone Figure), which can be reached by a short scramble up the hillside. The deeply weathered figure of a seated woman, about 8m (26ft) high, is thought to date from the 13th century BC, and represents the Hittite fertility goddess, later known as Cybele and adopted by the Greeks as Artemis. A panel to the right of the figure contains badly worn Hittite hieroglyphics.

Sardis

The site of **Sardis** lies 100km (60 miles) east of Izmir near the village of Sartmustafa, on the road to Uşak and Afyon. The former capital of ancient Lydia, Sardis reached its peak during the reign of King Croesus (560-546 BC). The Lydians invented the world's first-ever coinage, producing coins of gold

and silver stamped with the royal emblem – a lion's head. The gold was washed down from the hills by the River Pactolus; according to legend, King Midas of the 'golden touch' had once bathed in the headwaters of the river (see box). The Greek historian Herodotus relates how sheepskins were spread in the streambed, trapping flakes of the precious metal in the fleece, a practice which perhaps gave rise to the legend of the Golden Fleece.

During its 'golden age' Sardis was the one of the wealthiest cities in the world, hence the expression 'as rich as Croesus'. Intent on expanding his empire into Persian-held territory, Croesus consulted the oracle at Delphi. It told him that if he attacked the Persians he would destroy a great empire. He attacked, and was crushed – the empire he destroyed was his own. The city became part of the kingdom of Pergamum, and later flourished under Roman rule; the monuments you see today date from Roman and Byzantine times.

Sardis was an important episcopal see during the early days of Christianity, and was one of the Seven Churches of the Apocalypse that were addressed by St John in the Book of Revelation. It was sacked by the Sassanids in the 7th century, and again by Tamerlane in 1401, and never recovered, declining over the years into a humble village surrounded by the tumbled ruins of its past splendour.

Baths–Gymnasium Complex

The principal remains of Sardis are in two parts. Just beyond the village of Sartmustafa, on the left-hand side of the main highway, you will find the **Baths-Gymnasium Complex**, which formed the centre of Roman Sardis. From the car park you pass a Byzantine public toilet and follow a long line of ancient **shops** to a gate at the far

THE MIDAS TOUCH

Midas was a Phrygian king (see p.263), who won the favour of the god Dionysus for his kind treatment of the satyr Silenus. The drunken satyr, a close companion of the wine god, had become lost and stumbled into the gardens of King Midas, where he was found sleeping off a hangover by the king's servants. Midas entertained Silenus for five days and nights before appointing an escort to guide him back to the court of Dionysus.

The god was so pleased to see his friend safe and well that he granted Midas a wish. 'Grant that all I touch should turn to gold', was the greedy king's reply. His wish was granted, and Midas delighted in watching the stones and flowers of his garden turn to gold, but soon realized his foolishness when his food and water also turned to gold. Half-starved, he begged Dionysus to release him from his wish. The god told him to travel to Mount Tmolus and bathe himself in the headwaters of the River Pactolus. Midas was delivered of his golden touch, but the waters of the Pactolus were for ever after bright with gold dust – the gold which created the vast wealth of King Croesus of Sardis.

end, which leads into the **synagogue**. This hall was given to the city's prosperous Jewish community during the late 3rd century AD, and is the biggest known ancient synagogue. The floor was richly decorated with mosaic patterns, fragments of which remain.

The gymnasium complex itself, dating from the 2nd and 3rd centuries AD, is approached through the huge open square of the *palaestra,* lined with the stumps of colonnades. It is dominated by the magnificently restored **Marble Court**, decorated with ornate marble columns and

Sardis, the ancient capital of wealthy King Croesus, was endowed in Roman times with many fine public buildings, such as the Marble Court, which has been extensively restored.

In the 4th century AD a small church was built next to the Temple of Artemis, in the shadow of and dwarfed by its huge Ionic columns.

niches; originally the entire façade would have been faced with marble. The huge central niche above the arched gateway once held a cult statue of the emperor. Behind the court lie the ruins of a huge Roman and Byzantine **baths complex**. Go through the central door and you will find yourself in the *frigidarium* (cold room), which has a large swimming pool, and smaller bathing pools in niches along the sides. The *caldarium,* as yet unexcavated, lies further west, back towards the car park.

Temple of Artemis

Back in the village, a side road leads south for 1km (½ mile) to the imposing ruins of the **Temple of Artemis**, overlooked by the deeply eroded slopes of the acropolis hill. This huge building was one of the seven biggest temples in the ancient Greek world, rivalling those at Didyma and Ephesus. (It was far bigger than the Parthenon in Athens, measuring 99m × 46m (325 × 150ft) compared with 70 × 31m (230ft × 100ft). It was begun around 300 BC on the site of an older Lydian altar dedicated to Artemis, which can still be seen at the near end of the site. Construction was repeatedly interrupted over the following six centuries, and the design was changed more than once. The enormous structure had a *peristyle* of 52 Ionic columns (20 by 8), of which only two still stand to their full height. It was finally abandoned, still unfinished, some time during the 4th century;

a small Byzantine church was built in the shadow of the columns at the far end.

The abandoned temple's marble masonry was quarried to provide lime, and the ruins were gradually buried beneath landslides from the acropolis hill, until only the tops of the two standing columns could be seen above ground level; it was excavated by American archaeologists in 1910-14.

Çeşme

A brand-new, six-lane, toll motorway leads 80km (50 miles) west from Izmir to the small resort and ferry port of **Çeşme**, where boats cross daily to the Greek island of Chios, a mere 12km (7½ miles) away. The town was a quiet spa and beach resort (its name means 'drinking fountain') until the motorway's arrival brought it within commuting distance of the city; now it is set to become a busy seaside suburb of Izmir, and a terminal for international ferries from Italy.

Çeşme is dominated by a brooding **fortress** built in the 14th century by the Genoese, and repaired and enlarged by the Ottomans. Beside it lies an 18th-century **caravanserai**, which has been converted into a hotel, and now hosts regular 'folklore evenings' of Turkish dance and music. On the main shopping street you will find an attractive art gallery housed in the old Greek basilica of Ayios Haralambos. There are few other sights to see – the main attractions are the golden-sand **beaches** at nearby Altinkum and Ilica, and the **hot springs**. The warm, sulphurous waters (around 35-50°C; 95-122°F) are said to be good for treating rheumatism and respiratory complaints.

The landscape around Çeşme is rather desolate – low rocky hills covered with a stubble of thorny scrub, relieved by the

The beach and spa resort of Çeşme, dominated by a huge 14th-century Genoese fortress, is the port for ferries to Chios.

brilliant turquoise of the sea. About 9km (5½ miles) southeast of Çeşme is the old Greek farming village of **Alaçatı**, with its three windmills and a Saturday market. But even here development is encroaching, with villas and apartments springing up on the

168

A minor road leads northeast along the coast from the beach resort of Ilıca, through the little spa village of Şifne, to the village of Ildır, which lies huddled beneath the acropolis hill of ancient **Erythrae**. The city was one of the 12 members of the Panionion, and was famous for its Heracleion, a shrine to Heracles (Hercules). The shrine contained a miraculous statue of the god that was found floating in the sea, but no trace of it remains. All that can be seen today are a few fragments of walls, parts of the theatre, a tomb and a Roman villa, but the view over the island-studded bay is worth the climb.

South of Izmir

A fast highway leads south from Izmir, lined with farmers' stalls piled high with succulent peaches, and shaded by rows of cypress and oleander. The rampart-capped hill of Ayasuluk guards the approach to Selçuk, where a right turn leads to the celebrated ruins of Ephesus and the bustling holiday resort of Kuşadası.

An alternative route from Izmir to Kuşadası lies along the Ionian coast, reached by turning off the Çeşme–Izmir highway at Urla and heading south for 30km (19 miles) through Seferihisar to the yacht harbour of **Sığacık**, clustered within its Genoese fortifications. There is little to see in town, but a road west leads to the pleasant beach at nearby Akkum, and continues for a few more kilometres to the ancient city of Teos.

Teos was an important member of the Ionian Federation, and famed as the birthplace of the poet Anacreon (*c.* 570-485 BC), who wrote of love and the pleasures of drink. His diet of wine, women and song sustained him into his eighties, when he

outskirts of the village. The road south from Alaçatı leads to a shallow inlet of the sea, with an ugly new fishing harbour at its head. The coast beyond has several small rocky coves with sandy beaches, but nothing to compare with the strand at Altınkum.

choked to death on a grape seed during a banquet. He was honoured with a monument in Athens, which showed the poet 'singing in his cups'. Appropriately, the city was also famous for its **Temple of Dionysus**, the god of wine, fertility and fruitfulness, and of the theatre. The ruins of the Ionic temple can still be seen, with three of the original 30 columns still standing amid the olive trees – the perfect place to take a picnic, and drink to Dionysus with a bottle of Turkish wine.

Return to Seferihisar and take the minor road that follows the coast south towards Pamucak. On the way you will pass the scant remains of several more Ionian cities, though they are overgrown and rarely visited: the miniature Gibraltar of **Myonessus**, connected to the mainland by a sunken causeway and best visited by boat from Sığacık; the crumbling walls and watchtowers of **Lebedus**; the hilltop ruins of **Notium**, with their grand view

across the bay to Samos; and the flooded fragments of Doric columns in the Temple of Apollo at **Claros**. The lack of spectacular ruins is made up for by a number of excellent beaches.

Kuşadası

Eighty kilometres (50 miles) south of Izmir lies **Kuşadası** (Bird Island), one of Turkey's liveliest and most popular holiday resorts. The town has a large yachting marina, and is a regular port of call for Mediterranean cruise ships. Its attractions include some pleasant beaches, a bustling bazaar, lively nightlife and the nearby ruins of Ephesus.

Whitewashed houses climb the hill above the harbour, where ferries depart daily for the Greek island of Samos, and bustling bars and restaurants line the streets of the old quarter. The busy **bazaar** clusters around the walls of a 17th-century caravanserai, now converted into a hotel;

across the street, seafood restaurants line the quay of the old harbour. Beyond the modern ferry port, a 350m (382yd) causeway connects the town to the pretty **Güvercin Adası** (Pigeon Island), topped by a 13th-century Byzantine castle, and ringed with gardens and cafés.

The town beach is a man-made sandpit, but better sunbathing spots can be found near by. A *dolmuş* service links the town to **Ladies' Beach** (*Kadınlar Plajı*), a narrow and crowded strand 3km (2 miles) to the south, but you will need your own transport to reach the wide, long and relatively deserted beach at **Pamucak**, 15km (9 miles) to the north. At Pamucak the tarmac ends right on the beach, and development is as yet limited to two hotels and a craft centre.

The prettiest beaches are to be found in the **Dilek Peninsula National Park** (*Dilek Yarımadası Milli Parkı*), 25km (15½ miles) from town. A number of pleasant, pebble-fringed bays backed by attractive pine-shaded picnic areas, each with its own little restaurant, line the north coast of this narrow finger of land, nestling beneath the craggy, forested slopes of Samsun Dağı (1,237m; 4,060ft), the ancient Mount Mycale. The park is a nature reserve, created to protect the rare bears, wild boar and lynx that inhabit the forest. It is not unusual to spot sea eagles soaring overhead as you lie sunbathing on the beach.

*L*adies' Beach, to the south of town, is Kuşadası's most popular sun-bathing spot. There are other good beaches at Pamucak, 15km (9 miles) north, and Dilek Peninsula National Park, 25km (15 miles) to the south.

Ephesus (Efes)

Ephesus, 17km (10½ miles) inland from Kuşadası, is one of the best preserved and most visited of Turkey's ancient cities. Its marble streets and monuments have been excavated and restored extensively by archaeologists – with a little imagination it is easy to transport yourself back to Roman times.

Ionian Greeks from the island of Samos settled in Ephesus around 1000 BC. The site was associated with the worship of Cybele, the Anatolian mother goddess, who was eventually merged with the Greek Artemis. The great Temple of Artemis at Ephesus, one of the Seven Wonders of the World, was erected in her honour. The city was ruled in turn by the Lydians, the Persians and the Attalid kings of Pergamum, until 133 BC when Attalus III bequeathed his kingdom, and Ephesus with it, to the Romans. Ephesus, with a population of 200,000, was one of the most important cities in the new Roman province of Asia, and grew wealthy on the proceeds of trade. But its greatness was linked to its fine natural harbour, and when this silted up in the 3rd century AD the city went into decline. The site was rediscovered by a British archaeologist in 1869 after six years of searching. Most of the ruins that you can see today date from the Roman period, between the 1st century BC and the 2nd century AD.

Most guided tours begin at the **Magnesian Gate** and head downhill along the main street, to be picked up at the main entrance near the theatre. However, if you have your own transport you can make a circular walk back to your car via the Cave of the Seven Sleepers.

The first buildings inside the gate are the well-preserved **Odeon** (council chamber), with its semi-circular seats, and the

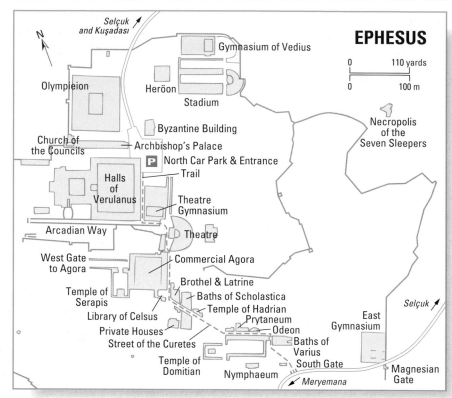

EPHESUS

Selçuk and Kuşadası

Gymnasium of Vedius

0   110 yards
0   100 m

N

Olympieion

Heröon

Stadium

Church of the Councils

Byzantine Building

Archbishop's Palace

P North Car Park & Entrance

Trail

Halls of Verulanus

Theatre Gymnasium

Arcadian Way

Theatre

West Gate to Agora

Commercial Agora

Brothel & Latrine

Temple of Serapis

Baths of Scholastica

Library of Celsus

Temple of Hadrian

Private Houses

Prytaneum

Odeon

Street of the Curetes

Temple of Domitian

Nymphaeum

Baths of Varius

South Gate

Meryemana

Necropolis of the Seven Sleepers

Selçuk

East Gymnasium

Magnesian Gate

Prytaneum, where archaeologists found the two statues of Artemis now on display in the Selçuk Museum.

The marble-paved **Street of the Curetes**, its stone slabs rutted by the wheels of ancient carts, leads downhill through the **Gate of Hercules**, decorated with a relief of the god clad in the skin of the Nemean lion. On the right is the **Fountain of Trajan**, partly restored, and beyond it the graceful **Temple of Hadrian**, its arched doorway capped by the head of Tyche, goddess of fortune. Across the street a mosaic pavement lies at the foot of the **terrace houses** which rise up the hillside above, protected from the elements by a modern roof. This was a residential district, and the houses provide a glimpse of everyday life in ancient Ephesus. The windowless rooms are arranged around a central courtyard, decorated with mosaics and frescoes of mythological scenes and geometric patterns. Unfortunately, the houses are usually closed to the public, in order to protect the delicate frescoes from damage.

At the corner of Marble Street, a flight of steps on the right leads into the public latrines in the **Baths of Scholastica**. The latrines were built in the form of a courtyard with marble seats around the perimeter, above a channel of constantly flowing water which carried the effluent into a sewer and down to the sea. The building below the baths, right on the street corner, is thought to have been a **brothel**. It consists of a series of rooms around a central courtyard, and has some mosaic floors, including one of the Four Seasons; the clay figure of Priapus on display in the Ephesus Museum in Selçuk was found in the well here.

Rising across the square from the baths is the imposing façade of the **Library of Celsus**, built in AD 110 by a Roman consul as a memorial to his father, and restored

*E*phesus is one of the largest and best-preserved of Turkey's ancient cities. Its main street (left) is paved with marble and lined with splendid buildings and monuments such as the Library of Celsus (right). The library was built in the early 2nd century AD by a Roman Consul as a memorial to his father. Its elegant façade is decorated with columns and statues.

THE LIBRARY OF CELSUS

The library was built between AD 110 and 135 by the consul Gaius Julius Aquila as a memorial to his father, Gaius Celsus Pole-maeanus, who had been a Roman senator and proconsul of Asia. His remains were discovered in a sarcophagus beneath the semicircular niche in the back wall, which once held a statue of Athena; they still lie there today. The library contained up to 12,000 scrolls and books, stored in rectangular niches around the walls. An air-gap between the shelves and the main wall protected the books from dampness.

*T*he statues that decorate the façade of the Library of Celsus represent the Four Virtues of Wisdom (or Sophia in Greek), Valour, Thought and Knowledge.

during the 1970s. Statues of the four virtues – *Sophia* (Wisdom), *Arete* (Valour), *Ennoia* (Thought) and *Episteme* (Knowledge) – adorn the niches between the columns. This is a good place to try to imagine what Ephesus might have been like during its heyday – sit on the steps of the library and fill the square with milling crowds, the clatter of donkey carts on the stone-paved streets, the smoke of cooking fires and the shouts of vendors in the *agora*.

Marble Street leads from the library to the **Great Theatre**, the probable setting for the riot of the silversmiths described in the Bible (Acts 19:24-41). Its vast *cavea* provided seating for 25,000 people, and still accommodates the crowds who gather for performances during the annual Ephesus International Festival (see p.000). From the top rows of seats you can enjoy a grand view of the **Arcadian Way**, the city's colonnaded main street, which was once lined with fine statues and lit by oil lamps at night. At its far end a scrub-filled depression marks the site of the city's harbour, long since silted up.

A path on the right leads out of the site into the car park at the main entrance,

lined with souvenir stalls, currency exchange booths and a post office. Through the fence on the left of the car park you can see the long, narrow outline of the **Church of the Councils**, also called the Church of the Virgin Mary. A church was built here in the 4th century, on the foundations of an older building which may have been a corn exchange or a college. This was the first church in the world to be dedicated to the Virgin Mary; it hosted the Third Ecumenical Council in 431, and also the so-called 'Robber Council' of 449, which deposed the Patriarch of Constantinople and was condemned as heretical by the Orthodox Church. Pope Paul VI visited Ephesus in 1967 and led prayers here on the very spot where some of the earliest Christian services had been held.

To return to the Magnesian Gate, continue past the car park and turn right along a minor road signposted **Grotto of the Seven Sleepers**. The road passes through groves of orange and fig trees at the foot of Mount Pion for about 1km (½ mile), before reaching a drinks stand where you pay for admission. A path leads uphill to a grotto of catacombs cut into the rock on two levels, filled with tomb recesses and vaulted chambers, some with traces of mosaic floor, red and blue frescoes, and painted lettering in Greek. Return to the road and follow the track for another kilometre (½ mile) to the main road; the Magnesian Gate is uphill to the right.

ΣΟΦΙΑ
ΚΕΛΣΟΥ

THE TALE OF THE SEVEN SLEEPERS

Legen has it that seven young Christian men of Ephesus were persecuted during the reign of the Roman Emperor Decius (AD 149-51) for refusing to sacrifice to the emperor. They sought refuge in a cave on Mount Pion, but were walled in alive by Roman soldiers. They fell into a deep sleep, and when they awoke and wandered into town to buy food, they found that two centuries had passed and Christianity was now the state religion. When they died they were buried in the cave, and a church was built over their graves. News of the miracle spread throughout the empire, and many pilgrims came to the church, and were buried there themselves. The grotto remained a Christian sanctuary and catacomb until the 15th century.

According to legend, St John the Apostle brought the Virgin Mary to Ephesus around AD 37-48. At **Meryemana** in the hills above the city is the house where she is thought to have lived out the last years of her life. It was discovered during the 19th century by priests from Izmir following instructions given by a German nun, Anna Katharina Emmerich, who had seen it in a vision. A chapel now occupies the site, which has long been a place of pilgrimage; experts believe that the building's foundations may indeed date from the 1st century.

This tiny chapel at Meryemana is thought to rest on the foundations of a 1st-century house that was once occupied by the Virgin Mary, the mother of Christ.

Selçuk

The small town of **Selçuk**, a short distance
from Ephesus, has an interesting museum
and several noteworthy monuments. The
6th-century **Basilica of St John**, on Ayasuluk Hill, has been extensively restored.
The basilica is the biggest Byzantine monument on the Aegean, 110m long by 60m
wide (360 by 197ft). Red-brick walls and
marble columns, whose capitals bear the
monogram of the Emperor Justinian and
his wife Theodora, have been re-erected.
Four columns in the transept mark the site
of the crypt that holds the remains of St
John the Apostle; an octagonal baptistery
lies north of the nave, with a marble-lined
baptismal pool in the centre. The fortress
on the hilltop above dates from Byzantine
times, but is now closed to the public.

From the terrace in front of the basilica
you have a good view over the impressive
İsa Bey Mosque (1375), and beyond it to
the low hill of Mount Pion, which marks the
site of Ephesus. To the left of the mosque,

a solitary column marks the site of the once-great **Temple of Artemis**. It is hard to believe that this was one of the Seven Wonders of the World – all that remain are the flooded foundations and that single reconstructed column. The original temple was built in the 6th century BC on the site of an altar to Cybele, and measured 115 × 55m (377 × 180ft) – three times the area of the Parthenon in Athens – and had a double row

From the terrace of St John's Basilica there is a fine view over İsa Bey Mosque to Mount Pion and Ephesus.

The hill of Ayasuluk, at Selçuk, is capped by the ruins of a huge Byzantine basilica dedicated to St John the Apostle. St John, who brought Mary, Christ's mother, to Ephesus, is buried in the apse.

of columns 18m (60ft) in height. It was destroyed by fire in 356 BC by a madman called Herostratus, who (successfully) sought to immortalize his name. A new temple was erected on the site of the old, but was destroyed by invading Goths in AD 262 and never rebuilt.

The statue of Artemis which stood in the *cella* of the temple is thought to have resembled the 1st and 2nd century AD Roman statues found in the Prytaneum at

Ephesus, and now displayed in the **Ephesus Museum** (*Efes Müzesi*) in Selçuk (open 8.30am to 6pm, closed Monday). These statues present a very different image to that of the Greek goddess of the hunt. It is thought that the Artemis of Ephesus assimilated a very ancient Anatolian mother goddess, Cybele. She appears standing stiff and straight with arms extended, wearing an elaborate headdress, her chest covered with several rows of smooth protuberances. No one knows what these represent – they could be breasts, eggs, bulls' testicles, bees or grapes – but they are probably a symbol of fertility. There is also a tiny gold statuette of Artemis that was found in the temple.

The rest of the museum contains a fascinating collection of statues, reliefs and artefacts from Ephesus and other ancient sites, well laid out and clearly explained in English.

South from Ephesus

Between Selçuk and Bodrum lie three important archaeological sites that can all be seen in one day.

Priene

Once one of the most active ports in the Ionian Federation, **Priene** now stands several miles inland due to the silting up of the River Maeander (*Büyük Menderes*). It enjoys a magnificent setting on a terrace overlooking the plain, backed by the steep, 250m (80ft) high crag of its acropolis. The theatre, *bouleterion* (council chamber) and *agora* are worth exploring, but the main attraction is the great **Temple of Athena**. Alexander the Great, who passed through the city in 334 BC, paid for its completion; five of the original 30 columns have been restored to their full height. At the entrance to the *cella,* marks in the paving show where metal gates once swung back and forth.

Miletus (Milet)

The silt of the River Maeander has also stranded the once mighty city of **Miletus**. Its harbour, from which Miletan ships set forth to found over 100 colonies during the 7th and 8th centuries BC, is now a frog-filled marsh. Some inkling of its former glory can be gleaned from the ruins of the theatre, the *agora* and the Baths of Faustina. Take a look in the baths' *frigidarium* – water poured into the swimming pool from ornamental spouts; at one end is a reclining statue of the river god Maeander, at the other is a lion's head.

Didyma (Didim)

The most impressive of the three sites is **Didyma**. No city ever stood here, just the colossal **Temple of Apollo**, one of the largest and most elegant temples in the ancient world. Only two columns still stand, but the forest of massive marble stumps gives some idea of the grandeur of the original building. People would travel many miles to consult the oracle of Apollo, seeking advice on marriage, business ventures and military campaigns. When the Persians destroyed Miletus in 494 BC they also razed the Temple of Apollo at Didyma. Reconstruction of the temple was begun by Alexander the Great (his decisive victory over the Persians at Gaugamela in 331 BC was predicted by the oracle), and continued for many centuries, but it was never actually completed – note that some of the columns visible today remain unfluted.

The road continues beyond Didyma to the busy resort of **Altınkum**. The name means 'golden sands' in Turkish, and the beach is indeed one of the best that can be found on the Aegean coast. If you feel like staying the night, there is no shortage of hotels, pensions and restaurants.

Other sites

Continuing south towards Bodrum you enter the region known in ancient times as Caria. Stretching from Aydın to Fethiye, this is one of the most beautiful regions of Turkey, and contains some of its most interesting archaeological sites.

The main road skirts the southern shore of attractive Lake Bafa (*Bafa Gölü*), an arm of the sea that has been isolated by the silt deposits of the Maeander River. The hill slopes are covered in groves of silver-leaved olive trees, while across the water rises the jagged ridge of Mount Latmus, associated since ancient times with the legend of Endymion (see box). On the far side of the lake lie the ruins of **Heracleia ad Latmus**, one of the most romantic

spots in Aegean Turkey. Heracleia flourished during the Hellenistic period, but slipped into decline from the 1st century BC as its harbour was gradually cut off from the sea. The ruins are scattered picturesquely among rocky outcrops beside the lake, overlooking an island bristling with Byzantine fortifications.

The site of **Euromos** can easily be explored by even the laziest of travellers – there is only one building worth seeing, and it sits right beside the main road. The 2nd-century AD **Temple of Zeus** is one of the best-preserved temples in Asia Minor. Sixteen of the original 36 Corinthian columns still stand, supporting long sections of the architrave; 12 of them bear dedicatory plaques which show that they were presented by wealthy citizens of Euromos. If you are lucky the guardian will offer you sweet water from the springs at Labraynda and juicy pears from the trees that grow around the temple.

A much more difficult prospect is the sanctuary of Zeus at **Labraynda**, which occupies a magnificent site on wooded terraces high in the hills above Milas. A dirt road branches off to the left a short distance after Euromos, and leads steeply uphill for 13km (8 miles) to the ruins (this road is best attempted in an off-road vehicle, and may be impassable after heavy rain). Labraynda was not a city, but a religious centre dedicated to the worship of

---

ENDYMION'S ENCHANTED SLEEP

In Greek mythology, Endymion was the beautiful shepherd who remained forever young, cast by Zeus into eternal slumber in a cave on Mount Latmus. Selene, the moon goddess, fell in love with the sleeping youth, and lay with him every night, eventually bearing him 50 daughters.

The anchorites who retreated to the caves of Latmus during Christian times altered the pagan myth to make Endymion a mystic who had learned the secret name of God by gazing at the moon. Once a year they would open his tomb, and his bones would give off an unearthly humming sound, Endymion's attempt to pass on the secret name to other men.

The myth inspired Keats to write his famous lyric poem entitled *Endymion*, which begins with the immortal lines:

A thing of beauty is a joy forever:
Its loveliness increases; it will never
Pass into nothingness; but will keep
A bower quiet for us, and a sleep
Full of sweet dreams, and health,
and quiet breathing.

---

*T*he Temple of Zeus at Euromos is one of the best-preserved temples in Asia Minor, with 16 of its original 36 columns still standing. The ruins of a theatre lie nearby, but are overgrown and hard to find (overleaf).

Zeus Stratius (the warlike), also called Zeus Labrayndus (the axe-wielder); images of the god show him carrying a spear and a double-headed axe, the symbol of divine royalty on Minoan Crete, suggesting a historic link between Caria and Crete. His chest is adorned with 'multiple breasts' like the Artemis of Ephesus. Some experts have suggested that their appearance on a male deity proves that the objects are not breasts at all, but represent the testicles of sacrificial bulls, which were once hung on the cult statue.

The ruins, most of which date from the 4th and 5th centuries BC, include a Temple of Zeus; several androns (literally 'men's halls', used for religious banquets), one of which is complete except for its roof; a monumental staircase; and the remains of a building which may have housed Labraynda's 'fish oracle' (see box).

Milas

The small, drab market town of Milas is usually ignored by tourists heading for the bright lights and bars of Bodrum. But this was the site of ancient **Mylasa**, an important Carian city that was linked to the Sanctuary of Zeus at Labraynda by a

---

THE FISH ORACLE OF LABRAYNDA

A number of ancient writers refer to an oracle at Labraynda, in the form of a pool inhabited by sacred fish. Pliny the Elder (a 1st-century AD Roman author) goes on to say that the sacred fish were adorned with jewellery and earrings in their pierced fins, and that they responded to calls and could be fed by hand. To consult the oracle, the supplicant threw grains of wheat into the pond. If the fish took the wheat, the answer to his question was favourable; if they refused, he should reconsider his intentions.

---

sacred road. Its famous marble quarries produced many fine buildings, but little remains to be seen today except the well-preserved tomb called **Gümüşkesen** ('silver purse'). It is a square Corinthian colonnade with an ornate ceiling and a stepped-pyramid roof. Because of its shape and its proximity to Bodrum, it has been suggested that its design was influenced by the Mausoleum of Halicarnassus.

Bodrum

The picture-postcard resort of **Bodrum** occupies the site of ancient Halicarnassus, famed as the city of King Mausolus, whose mausoleum was one of the Seven Wonders of the World, and as the birthplace of Herodotus, the 'Father of History'. Little remains of Halicarnassus, however, and the town's main attractions today include its laid-back, bohemian atmosphere, its beautiful double bay backed by white-washed, flower-bedecked houses, and the magnificent crusader castle which dominates the harbour.

The **Castle of St Peter** was built in the 15th century by the Knights of St John (see box on p.185) using stone quarried from the ruins of the Mausoleum of Halicarnassus. It fell to the Ottomans in 1523, and its various buildings now house a fine collection of antiquities, including a fascinating **Museum of Underwater Archaeology**. The various towers offer splendid views across the town and harbour. In the **English Tower** the banqueting hall has been restored, and you can sip a glass of Turkish wine while you read the centuries-old graffiti carved in the window niches by homesick knights.

The site of the **Mausoleum of Halicarnassus** is set a few blocks in from the

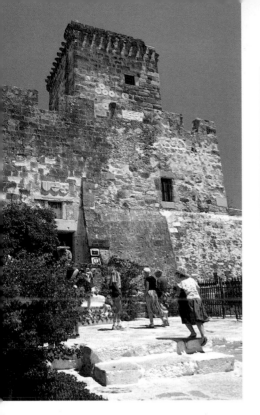

The huge Castle of St Peter, built by Crusaders in the 15th century, dominates Bodrum harbour. Its various towers now house a fascinating museum.

harbour. It was begun around 355 BC at the behest of King Mausolus (the word 'mausoleum' is derived from his name), and survived until at least the 12th century. By the time the crusaders arrived in 1402 it was in ruins, destroyed by an earthquake. Today, nothing remains save the foundations. An exhibition hall displays several versions of how the building may once have looked, and plaster casts of the friezes of battling Amazons and Greeks which once decorated its walls – the originals are in the British Museum.

There are no good beaches in Bodrum itself, but you can take a boat trip from the harbour to one of the myriad coves that lie hidden along the coast of the peninsula to the west, or catch a *dolmuş* to the pretty fishing villages of Turgutreis, Gümüşlük, Yalıkavak and Türkbükü.

Excursions Inland

Pamukkale

One of the most popular excursions from the Aegean resorts goes to the spectacular travertine terraces of **Pamukkale**, which lie above the town of Denizli, about 200km (125 miles) inland from Kuşadası. This remarkable natural formation has been created by mineral-rich hot springs cascading down the hillside and depositing layers of calcium carbonate. The resulting pools, terraces and 'petrified waterfalls' of dazzling white travertine are one of Turkey's most famous sights. (The name Pamukkale means 'cotton castle', this referring to the whiteness and softness of the limestone ramparts.) In the grounds of the Pamukkale Motel you can bathe in the **Sacred Pool**, where the warm spring waters will float you above a picturesque jumble of tumbled columns and Corinthian capitals.

Hierapolis

The ruins of ancient **Hierapolis** lie scattered on the hillside above the travertine terraces. The city is first mentioned in the 2nd century BC, and prospered during Roman times as a commercial centre and spa town.

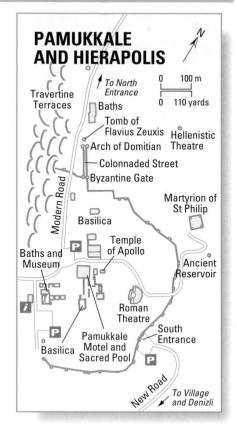

PAMUKKALE AND HIERAPOLIS

To North Entrance
Travertine Terraces
Baths
Tomb of Flavius Zeuxis
Hellenistic Theatre
Arch of Domitian
Colonnaded Street
Byzantine Gate
Modern Road
Martyrion of St Philip
Basilica
Temple of Apollo
Baths and Museum
Ancient Reservoir
Roman Theatre
South Entrance
Pamukkale Motel and Sacred Pool
Basilica
New Road
To Village and Denizli

0   100 m
0   110 yards

A road leads uphill behind the modern Pamukkale Motel. On the right are the remains of a restored 4th-century AD

THE BREATH OF HADES

The Plutonium of Hierapolis was as big a tourist attraction in Roman times as Pamukkale is today. Built around a narrow cave beneath the Temple of Apollo, the sanctuary took the form of a square, marble-paved pit, which at one time had an auditorium built around it. A poisonous gas, which was heavier than air, flowed from the cleft into the pit, where it could kill animals as big as a bull. Ancient writers reported that only the eunuch priests of Cybele, who tended the sanctuary before the temple was built, were immune to the gas, but whether this was due to divine intervention, an ability to hold their breath, or simply to be able to keep their heads above the level of the invisible 'pool' of gas is not known.

The gas still issues from the vent, and until recently local guides indulged in the grisly habit of placing caged birds in the cleft to demonstrate the vapour's deadly effect. Those who have braved the cave describe the gas as sharp and stinging, making your eyes water; it is most probably carbon dioxide.

The days of bathing on the terraces at Pamukkale may soon be over, as conservation efforts intensify.

nymphaeum, and beyond it the foundations of the **Temple of Apollo**. On the far side of the staircase leading up to the temple is the famous **Plutonium**, a sanctuary dedicated to Pluto, god of the underworld, where noxious vapours issue from a cleft in the rock. Although the opening has been fenced off with an iron grille to prevent inquisitive visitors from gassing themselves, you can still hear the sound of running water and an ominous hissing emanating from the bowels of the earth (see box, p.186).

Further uphill is the **theatre**, which is exceptionally well preserved, with much of the stage building still standing. It is decorated inside with a frieze showing scenes from the life of Dionysus. Above the theatre you can climb to the Byzantine city walls and follow a track left across the hillside to the **Martyrium of the Apostle Philip**. This unusual building, with its octagonal central hall, was erected in the 5th century AD in memory of the Apostle Philip, who lived in Hierapolis. He was martyred in AD 80 by being nailed upside-down to a tree and stoned to death.

The road that leads to the north entrance to Pamukkale passes through the extensive **necropolis** of Hierapolis. This is one of the biggest and best-preserved ancient cemeteries in Asia Minor, with over 1,200 tombs dating from the Hellenistic period to early Byzantine times.

Laodicea

Little remains of this once magnificent city – most of its stone has been pilfered – but it was famed in ancient times for its school of medicine and for its fine black wool. The mineral springs of nearby Pamukkale are said to have been responsible for the black fleeces of the local sheep, and were certainly the reason for the founding of a medical centre.

The ruins lie to the left of the road between Denizli and Pamukkale, but there is little to see – two theatres, a *nymphaeum*, a baths complex and the outline of the stadium which, at 350m (1,150ft) long, was one of the biggest in Asia Minor. The few people who do come to pick over the crumbling stones do so because **Laodicea** was one of the Seven Churches of Asia. It was castigated by St John in his Book of Revelation for its half-hearted embrace of Christianity: 'I know all your ways; you are neither hot nor cold. How I wish you were either hot or cold! But because you are lukewarm, neither hot nor cold, I will spit you out of my mouth…' (*Revelation* 3: 15-17).

Nyssa

On the road from the coast to Pamukkale, between Aydın and Nazilli, a left turn leads through the village of Sultanhisar to the ruins of **Nyssa**, a city famed in Roman times as a centre of learning – the Greek geographer and historian Strabo (*c.* 63 BC-AD 24) was educated here (see box p.266). The **theatre** is the main attraction, beautifully set on a hillside overlooking the valley of the River Maeander, with olive trees sprouting among the ancient seats. It's a perfect spot for a picnic, peaceful and picturesque, with only a child's shout or a dog's bark floating up from the village below to break the silence. As you admire the view, try to fit it to Strabo's description:

'Nyssa …is a double city, so to speak, for it is divided by a torrential stream that forms a gorge, which at one place has a bridge over it, joining the two cities, and at another it is adorned with an amphitheatre with a hidden underground passage for the torrential waters. Near the theatre are two heights, below one of which is the gymnasium of youths; and below the other is the market-place and the gymnasium for older persons'.

Just left of the theatre (facing downhill) a path leads down to the Roman **tunnel** (Strabo's 'underground passage') which carried the stream beneath the city. Beyond the downstream end, on the right bank, are the scant remains of the amphitheatre; the waters in the tunnel could be diverted to flood the arena for mock sea battles.

Aphrodisias

A trip to Pamukkale usually includes a visit to the ancient city of **Aphrodisias**, set high on a mountain-ringed plateau above the valley of the Maeander. The city was dedicated to the worship of Aphrodite, goddess of love, nature and fertility, and was famous for its superb sculpture. The site, on a fertile plain, had been occupied since neolithic times, and was probably associated with the worship of an ancient fertility goddess who was later assimilated into the Greek cult of Aphrodite. The city was venerated by the Romans, too, who claimed descent from Aphrodite (Venus) through her son Aeneas, founder of Rome. Aphrodisias flourished from the 1st century BC to the 5th century AD, when its famous school of sculpture, sustained by abundant supplies of excellent marble from the quarries of nearby Mount Salbakos (Baba Dağ), was famed throughout the Roman Empire. The city was extensively damaged and flooded by major earthquakes in the 4th and 7th centuries AD, and fell into decline; it was finally abandoned in the 13th century after falling to the Selçuk Turks.

The **archaeological site** is beautifully set amid groves of poplars, and is best visited in the early morning or late afternoon when the peaceful atmosphere is less likely to be shattered by tour groups; accommodation is available in the nearby village of Geyre. The ruins are undergoing a continuing programme of excavation and restoration, with the intention of creating an archaeological park to rival Ephesus, which means that certain parts of the site may be off limits while work is in progress.

T he Greek city of Aphrodisias, set on a high plain above the Maeander, was famed in ancient times for its superb sculpture. Its many fine public buildings include the Tetrapylon, a ceremonial gateway.

The path opposite the museum (between the postcard stand and the café) leads to the top of the acropolis hill (actually a mound of debris from prehistoric settlements), from where you can look down on the **theatre**. Until excavations began in 1966, the entire structure lay buried beneath the old village of Geyre, which was evacuated to allow digging to commence. (The villagers were re-housed in a new village near by.) The theatre was built in the 1st century BC, but 200 years later it was modified so that gladiatorial contests and wild animal fights could be staged. The lowest few rows of seats were removed and the stage raised to form the semi-circular pit you see today; originally, the pit would have been surrounded by a wooden paling to further protect the spectators.

On the other side of the path, an Ionic colonnade among the poplar trees marks the north edge of the so-called **Portico of Tiberius**. Recent excavations have revealed that this is actually a 200m (650ft) long pool, with stepped margins like stadium seating and semi-circular recesses at each end, stretching from the 'Agora Gate' below you to the Baths of Hadrian away to the left.

The *agora* proper lies beyond this pool, and at its right-hand end a modern roof protects the **Sebasteion**, Aphrodisias's most unusual and spectacular monument. This was a shrine to the cult of the deified Emperor Augustus (*Sebastos* in Greek) and his descendants, and to Aphrodite, from whom they claimed descent. It is in the form of a processional way leading from the *agora* to the cult temple, lined with three-storey colonnades (Doric at ground level, Ionic in the middle, Corinthian on top). The porticoes were decorated with beautiful marble reliefs depicting mythological scenes, imperial

figures and various emperors defeating personifications of the many peoples subdued by the Romans (one of them shows Claudius overwhelming Britannia).

The path continues beyond the acropolis mound to the massive masonry arches of the **Baths of Hadrian**, complete with marble-lined pools and a few fragments of mosaic; an inscription discovered here in 1904 warned bathers not to leave their valuables unattended! A gateway at the far end of the complex (with a marble gaming board to its left) leads through some trees to the **Bishop's Palace**, with an attractive courtyard of blue marble columns. On the far side of the palace is the well-preserved **odeon**. Fourteen fluted Ionic columns mark the site of the **Temple of Aphrodite**, the religious focal point of the city. It was built on the site of an older shrine, and eventually converted into a Christian basilica during the 5th century – religions may change, but sacred ground remains sacred ground.

A path on the left wanders off for a few hundred metres to the **stadium**. This is probably the best-preserved stadium in Turkey, 262m (860ft) long, with seating for 30,000 spectators. If you stand at one end and look down its length, you will notice that the side terraces bulge slightly in the middle. This was intentional, so that people sitting in the middle would still have a clear view of both ends of the arena. The way back to the museum leads past the **Tetrapylon**, an ornate gateway that marked the intersection of a north–south street with the ceremonial way leading to the Temple of Aphrodite. Near by is the grave of Professor Kenan Erim, who supervised the excavations at Aphrodisias from 1961 until his death in 1990. The **museum** contains a fine collection of sculpture found on the site.

The Ancient Cities of Asia Minor

The ruins of the great cities of Asia Minor, while impressive, can often seem bewildering to the casual tourist with little knowledge of Hellenistic and Roman culture. Here we offer a lay-person's guide to the principal public buildings of ancient Greek and Roman cities. (Most of the ancient cities of Turkey were Greek foundations that were later taken over by the Romans, whose wealth allowed them to build many splendid public buildings; most of the best preserved monuments in Asia Minor date from the Roman period.)

The social centre of the Greek city was the *agora*, an open square often surrounded by colonnades, where the citizens gathered to buy and sell, to negotiate business deals or just to catch up on the local gossip. Near by would be the temple, the most important building in the city, and the theatre, where the people would share in the communal enjoyment of religious rituals and plays. The other buildings – houses, workshops, storerooms etc – would be made of timber.

When the Romans arrived in the 1st century BC, they brought with them their own ideas about civic architecture. They were interested in grand assemblages of public buildings and impressive urban landscapes – look, for example, at the acropolis of Pergamum, where the Trajaneum was designed to complement the older Temple of Athena and Altar of Zeus, or at Ephesus, where the architect of the Library of Celsus used clever perspective effects to make the building's façade blend harmoniously into an awkward space. They also introduced the Roman baths complex which was later adopted on a smaller scale by the Ottomans, and which survives today as the *hamam*, or Turkish bath.

Temples

The most important building in a Greek city was the temple. Not only was it a house of the gods, it was a symbol of the city's wealth and power. The oldest Greek temples appeared in the 8th century BC, and were simple structures of mud-brick, rubble and timber, built to house an image of a god. They were built facing east, overlooking a pre-existing altar which may originally have been a simple block of stone, but which grew to be a larger rectangular platform (there are good examples at the Temple of Artemis in Sardis, and in Pergamum's Sanctuary of Demeter). Sacrifices were made at the altar, and offerings and libations were taken into the temple by the priests and priestesses. There were also storage rooms for the gifts of gold

Detail of a Hellenistic wall.

and other precious objects given to the gods by kings and wealthy citizens.

When the Greeks began making trading expeditions to Egypt around 650 BC, they were impressed by the monumental stone architecture they saw there, and they began building their temples with masonry. The earliest stone temples copied the form of the old wooden ones, which had timber posts supporting lintels and a pitched roof covered with clay tiles.

These late 7th-century BC temples were the prototypes of the so-called Doric order of Greek architecture, with squat columns and plain capitals supporting an unornamented entablature, topped by a tiled timber roof. This style was predominant in mainland and western Greece, but there are a few examples in Turkey, notably at Assos and Clarion. The plan of a typical Greek temple was rectangular, with a row of columns (the *peristyle*) set around the perimeter of a raised, stepped platform (the *crepidoma*); the upper surface of the *crepidoma*, which supported the columns, is called the *stylobate*. The *peristyle* enclosed the walls of an inner chamber called the *cella*, which housed the cult statue on a podium at the far end. The porch at the entrance of the *cella*, often framed by two columns, is called the *pronaos*; the rear porch is the *opisthodomus*.

The Ionic order was developed in the cities of the Ionian coast from about 600 BC. Ionic temples were characterized by slender, fluted columns, topped by capitals with horizontally spreading volutes (spiral, scroll-like ornaments). Many examples of this order appeared during the spate of temple building that took place in Asia Minor during the 4th century BC – the Temples of Artemis at Ephesus and Sardis, the Temple of Apollo at Didyma, and the classic Temple of Athena at Priene.

The late 5th century BC saw the invention of the Corinthian order by the architect Callimachus in mainland Greece. This was an ornate variation on the Ionic – the Corinthian capital is carved with rows of overlapping acanthus leaves. The earliest known example was found in the Temple of Apollo at Bassae in the Greek Peloponnese (450-425 BC); the oldest Corinthian temple in Asia Minor is the Temple of Zeus Olbios at Uzuncaburç near Silifke (early 3rd century BC). Other fine examples of Corinthian architecture in Turkey include the Trajaneum at Pergamum (2nd century AD), the Temple of Zeus at Euromos (2nd century AD), and the Tetrapylon at Aphrodisias. (Examples of all three orders can be seen in the Sebasteion of Aphrodisias; here the processional way is lined with three-storey colonnades – Doric at the bottom, Ionic in the middle and Corinthian at the top.)

Theatres

The origins of Greek tragedy are obscure, but performances probably evolved out of ancient religious rituals and dances. The first plays were most likely performed in the *agora*, using a cart as a stage, but the increasing popularity of this kind of entertainment led to the development of the theatre. The first theatres consisted simply of wooden seats ranged on a convenient hillside, with a flat, circular orchestra below. This evolved into the classical Hellenistic theatre, with terraced stone seats cut into the hillside (the *cavea*) surrounding the orchestra. The *cavea* was usually greater than a semi-circle, and there was no stage or backdrop. Theatre construction flourished during the Hellenistic Age, when the stage building was developed to provide a raised stage and a backdrop with three or five doorways (the *skene*, from which the word 'scene' is derived); the actors' dressing rooms lay behind the *skene*.

This improved the acoustics of the theatre, and gave the playwright more flexibility in staging the entrances of his characters.

The audience entered the theatre through the *parodoi* (singular *parodos*), the openings between the stage building and the *cavea*, and climbed to their seats via narrow staircases which divided the *cavea* into segments called *kerkides*, or *cunei*. A good example of this kind of theatre can be seen at Priene. The Roman theatre differed from the Greek in

The Temple, of Apollo at Side is a fine example of Corinthian style; note the frieze of Gorgon heads.

having a raised stage and a high backdrop called the *scaenae frons*, which was often decorated elaborately with columns, niches and statues. So that everyone could get a good view, the *cavea* was limited to a semi-circle whose ends abutted onto the stage building; the

parodoi ran through vaulted tunnels beneath. Unlike the Greeks, the Romans preferred to support the *cavea* on a structure of vaults and arches rather than building it into the hillside.

Many Roman theatres in Asia Minor were remodelled from older Greek ones, such as the one at Termessos, where a high stage building was added in the 2nd century AD and the seating at one side was extended over the *parodos* to meet it. The Roman theatre at Side was built on top of an older and smaller Hellenistic one – the *cavea* is greater than a semi-circle, but the seats are supported by vaults above the level of the low hillside, and there was a substantial stage building. Where the Romans built a brand new theatre, as at Aspendos, it assumed the classic form described above.

In many parts of the Roman Empire amphitheatres were built for the staging of popular entertainment such as gladiatorial combats, mock naval battles and wild animal fights; the classic example

The theatre at Hierapolis – you can see Roman stage building and the deepened orchestra pit.

is the Colosseum in Rome. There are no surviving amphitheatres in Asia Minor, but many theatres here were altered so that they could be used for these purposes. Usually the front rows of seats were removed, and the orchestra pit was deepened and surrounded by a wooden paling to prevent animals (and cowardly gladiators) from escaping. The theatres at Miletus, Aphrodisias and Hierapolis were altered in this way.

Baths

Public baths existed in both the ancient Egyptian and early Greek cultures, but it was the Romans who developed a standard architectural form in the great imperial baths of Rome in the 1st century AD, a form which was copied on a smaller scale throughout the empire.

The general plan was of an open exercise yard called the *palaestra*, surrounded by a colonnade with club rooms and perhaps a swimming pool. The main block of buildings contained an *apodyterium* (changing room), *frigidarium* (cold room), *tepidarium* (warm room) and *caldarium* (hot room); the larger baths complexes would contain several of each type of room, plus several vestibules and *exedrae* (semicircular recesses with seats) where citizens could mingle and gossip. There were plunge pools and swimming pools in the *frigidarium*, and hot baths in the *caldarium*. The floor of the *caldarium* (and sometimes the *tepidarium*) were heated from beneath by hot air from a furnace, which circulated through a space called the *hypocaust*. The baths of wealthy cities were richly decorated with marble walls and floors, stucco reliefs, gilded bronze doors, frescos, mosaics and abundant sculpture.

As in a modern Turkish bath there was a fairly standard procedure for using Roman baths. You would undress in the *apodyterium* (in the Baths of Hadrian in Aphrodisias, an inscription was found which warned bathers not to leave valuables with their clothes – nothing changes!), then have an attendant rub you down with oil before you went into the *palaestra* for some exercise – perhaps a bout of wrestling. After that, you would head for the *sudatorium* (sweat room), where you would sweat for a bit before another attendant scraped the oil, dirt and dead skin from your body with a metal blade called a *strigil*. A hot bath in the *caldarium*, a cold plunge in the *frigidarium* swimming pool, and a final massage would round off your visit.

There are large and fairly well-preserved Roman baths at Perge, Aphrodisias, Miletus and Sardis.

In the Roman baths at Perge, the floor of the caldarium *has fallen in to reveal the brick arches supporting the* hypocaust.

From 'Whirling Xanthos' to the Cave of Typhon – A Coastline Steeped in Myth and Magic

The ancient Greeks peopled Turkey's Mediterranean coast with mythical monsters, gods and heroes. Every cave, every valley and every pile of crumbling stone has a story attached to it, from the tomb of Bellerophon at Tlos to the grove of Harbiye, where the amorous Apollo chased after Daphne. Here you can climb to the eternal flames of the Chimera, and the brave can descend into the cave of Typhon and listen in the darkness for the monster's roar.

The gnarled finger of the Dorian peninsula, poking 80km (50 miles) westwards from Marmaris, marks the traditional boundary between the Aegean and Mediterranean seas. From here, Turkey's Mediterranean coast stretches for over 600km (370 miles) to Antakya, offering some of the best beaches and most spectacular scenery in the country. There are many historic sites, too, from Hittite ruins and Lycian cities, to Seljuk strongholds and crusader castles.

*T*he Mediterranean resort *of Alanya combines beautiful beaches and lively nightlife with a dash of history – the harbour has some of Turkey's finest Seljuk fortifications.*

Marmaris to Fethiye

Marmaris

The **Bay of Marmaris**, an almost circular inlet ringed by steep, pine-clad hills, is one of the finest and most beautiful harbours in southwest Turkey. It was here that Süleyman the Magnificent assembled a fleet in preparation for the siege of Rhodes, a six-month campaign which succeeded in driving the Christian Knights of St John out of Turkey. Lord Nelson called here in 1798 while pursuing the French fleet through the Mediterranean, and recommended it to the Admiralty as a first-class anchorage. Today the harbour shelters a 900-berth yachting marina, and **Marmaris** rivals Bodrum and Kuşadası as one of the most popular holiday resorts on the Turkish coast.

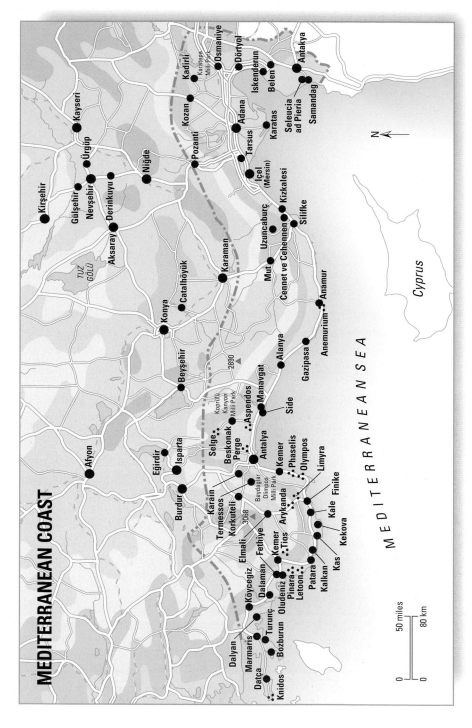

A TASTE OF HONEY

The Marmaris region is famous for its pine honey (*çam balı*), which the villagers collect from beehives specially placed in the pine forests that cover the surrounding hills. You can buy jars of this delicious honey from village houses, or from one of the countless stalls that line the roads around Marmaris. Some villages, such as Bayır in the Loryma Peninsula, produce other flavours such as orange blossom, thyme and wildflower honey. In Bayır you will see beehives outside almost every house, and there is even a workshop which specializes in making them. They are simple wooden boxes, usually painted pale blue.

museum; there are good views from the ramparts. The narrow streets around the castle are all that remain of the old town, most of which was destroyed by an earthquake in 1957.

The **bazaar** sprawls behind the castle, a regular grid of streets roofed with green canvas shades, where you will run a gauntlet of insistent shopkeepers imploring you to look at their wares – mostly carpets, leather and jewellery. If their prices are too low, you can empty your purse at the modern Netsel Shopping Mall beside the marina; Bodrum has a reputation for attracting bohemians and intellectuals, but in Marmaris you'll be mixing with serious money.

Town

When Süleyman the Magnificent massed his fleet in the Bay of Marmaris, he had a castle built on a small promontory at the head of the harbour. The **castle** was restored in 1985, and now houses a pleasant garden with an open-air stage and a small

*T*he little Ottoman castle at Marmaris has been restored and now houses a museum, with an open-air theatre and attractive gardens tucked within the walls.

The main street is the **Kordon**, a restaurant-lined prom that stretches from the tourist information office to Atatürk Meydanı, where the pedestal of the Atatürk statue proclaims *'Ne mutlu Türküm diyene!'* ('Happy is he who can call himself a Turk!'); beyond, the town extends round the curve of the bay in a sprawl of modern hotels and apartment blocks, fringed by a narrow beach of brown sand.

Far more attractive beaches can be found at the satellite resorts of **İçmeler** and **Turunç**, 10km (6 miles) and 16km (10 miles) south of Marmaris. But the best swimming and sunbathing is to be found in the rocky coves further south, which can be reached by taking one of the many **boat trips** on offer along the waterfront. In summer you can take a day trip to the Greek island of **Rhodes**, a mere 40km (25 miles) to the south; boats leave from the jetty near the tourist information office.

Dorian Peninsula

The land to the west of Marmaris is a wild and wooded mountainous peninsula, more easily accessible by sea than by land, a fact reflected in its popularity as a cruising ground for charter yachts. One delightful spot that can be visited as a day trip from Marmaris is *Sedir Adası* (Cedar Island), better known as **Cleopatra's Beach**. The island lies off the village of Taşbükü, about 15km (9 miles) north of Marmaris – you can hire a boat from here, or from nearby Çamlıköy. The island is littered with the crumbling walls of ancient **Cedreae**, including a well-preserved but overgrown theatre. The main attraction, however, is the pretty beach of pink sand which, according to local legend, was brought from Egypt at the command of Mark Antony to impress his famous consort (see box p.246).

A narrow roller-coaster of a road climbs out along the serrated spine of the Dorian Peninsula to the attractive harbour of **Datça**, 75km (47 miles) west of Marmaris. This compact little town, with most of its activity concentrated around the harbour, caters mainly to the yachts that cluster along the quay in high season. It has a handful of lively bars and restaurants, and an infamous open-air disco, shaped like an ancient amphitheatre, in an old quarry above the town. There is a ferry service to Bodrum from Körmen Limanı, 10km (6 miles) north of Datça.

Beyond Datça, the peninsula broadens and rears up in a Tolkienesque landscape of strangely shaped mountains. A road of sorts continues as far as Cnidus, passing a few small fishing and farming villages, but it should only be attempted in a jeep; the best way to get to Cnidus is to hire a boat in Datça.

Cnidus (Knidos)

In ancient times, sailing ships rounding Cape Crio at the tip of the Dorian Peninsula often had to wait for a fair wind. During the 4th century BC the citizens of Cnidus, a settlement near present-day

---

THE APHRODITE OF CNIDUS

The cult statue that graced the Temple of Aphrodite at Cnidus was one of the great tourist attractions of the ancient world. Created by the Athenian sculptor Praxiteles c. 360 BC, the naked figure of the goddess was celebrated for its beauty, and many people came from afar just to see it. The statue was displayed in an unusual circular temple with 18 Doric columns surmounted by a cupola; such was its popularity that it was enclosed within a precinct whose doors were locked at night. A number of copies of the statue were made for wealthy citizens in Greece and Rome, and the king of Bithynia even offered to pay off Cnidus' considerable debts in exchange for the original. The harbour built by the Cnidians still exists, and is much used by yachts and excursion boats; you can see the remains of the ancient breakwaters at the entrance. The ruins are scattered up the hillside – the theatre, the foundations of temples and other public buildings, a Byzantine basilica, and the stepped, circular base of the Temple of Aphrodite.

Datça, decided to take advantage of this by building a harbour at Cape Crio, and founding a new city there. The new port was also called Cnidus, and soon grew to be both prosperous and famous. It was renowned throughout the ancient world for its **Temple of Aphrodite Euploia** (Aphrodite of Safe Voyages – see box).

Loryma Peninsula

A stumpy, double-headed peninsula projects southwest from Marmaris towards the Greek island of Symi. A tarmac road penetrates as far as the village of **Bayır**, where the villagers sell jars of pine-, thyme- and flower-scented honey; beyond, a dirt road continues to the scenic harbour of **Bozburun**, a popular port of call for cruising yachts and a busy boat-building centre. The peninsula contains many attractive coves and overgrown ruins, best explored by boat, such as the beautiful bay of Bozukkale, with the ruined fortress of ancient **Loryma** perched on the headland to the west.

Dalyan

The Turkish word *dalyan* means 'fish-trap', and until the advent of tourism this sleepy little town made its living from the fish-traps on the Dalyan River. Today, the riverfront is lined with blue and white motor boats waiting to carry visitors on day trips to the local sights: the hot springs and mud baths of Köyceğiz Gölü; the rock tombs and ruins of ancient Caunus; and the magnificent strand of İztuzu Beach.

*M*any of the small harbour villages on the coast of the Loryma Peninsula (such as Bozburun, overleaf) are more easily reached by sea than by land.

The town itself is a pleasant place to stay. Dinner at a waterside restaurant offers a sunset silhouette of the craggy limestone hills across the river, merging into the twilight above the reeds. As the light fades, swooping swallows give way to fluttering bats, both feasting on the insect life over the water. (Mosquito repellent recommended!) Many of the hotels have rooftop restaurants, where you can linger over breakfast as the morning sun picks out the details of the rock tombs downstream before heading for the quay and hiring a boat. Don't bother shopping around – the boatmen have formed a co-operative, and all charge the same rates. The head man will approach you on the quay, ask where you want to go, quote you a price and assign you a boat; it's a straightforward and hassle-free arrangement.

Köyceğiz

Upstream from Dalyan lies the large freshwater lake of Köyceğiz Gölü, with the attractive village of Köyceğiz at its far end. The picturesque lake is only 10m (33ft) deep, but is a rich spawning ground for grey mullet and sea bass. (The fish-traps of Dalyan were built to catch the fish as they swam upstream to breed.) At the south end of the lake, where it flows into the Dalyan River, there are **hot springs** on the shore and open-air mud baths, which are said to relieve rheumatism.

Caunus (Kaunos)

The boat trip to **Caunus** takes you downstream from Dalyan, past a series of 4th-century BC **rock tombs**. They are carved into the cliff face in the shape of Greek temple façades; the chambers within have three stone benches to hold the bodies of the deceased. (Note that the largest one is unfinished – only the top half has been completed.) You then pass through the wooden palings of an old fish-trap before heading into a looping maze of reed-lined channels. Fish jump, steel-blue dragonflies and swallows skim the water, and basking terrapins disappear with a plop as your boat chugs lazily between the reeds. After half an hour you arrive at a jetty beside a modern fish-trap, from which a path leads to a café and ticket office at the entrance to the ruins.

Caunus was something of a backwater of the ancient world. Though most of the ruins date from Roman times, the settlement was founded by the native Carians around the 9th century BC. Although prosperous, it was a notoriously unhealthy city; then, as now, it was surrounded by marshes, and the sickness that afflicted its citizens was probably malaria. (The malaria has gone, but the mosquitoes remain.)

As you walk up the path from the entrance, you will see the **theatre** on the right. If you are feeling fit, you can climb above it through the medieval and Hellenistic fortifications to the summit of the **acropolis** hill. The view from the top is fantastic: the ruined city far below, a circular, marshy lake marking its ancient harbour; the green river meandering through its wide, flat flood-plain to the distant golden curve of İztuzu Beach; and upstream the red roofs of Dalyan nestling in a curve of the riverbank, and a patchwork of fields backed by hazy mountains.

The path below the theatre continues past a well-preserved **Byzantine basilica** to the massive ruins of the **baths**. From the big tree beside the baths a small path leads downhill to an unusual building with a circular colonnade, which may have been a temple, a fountain or a bathing pool; no-one knows. Keep an eye open for the abundant wildlife – snakes and lizards sun themselves on the ancient stones, while tortoises crop the grass and herons stalk the reeds beside the lake. On the far side of the lake, one of the best-preserved **city walls** in Turkey stretches away up the skyline to finish at a cliff that overlooks Dalyan town.

İztuzu Beach

After visiting Caunus, you can continue downstream to reach the sea at the beautiful, 4km (2½-mile) strand of golden-brown sand called **İztuzu Beach**. The beach, which can also be reached by road from Dalyan, is famous as a breeding ground of the loggerhead turtle (*Caretta caretta*). These giants of the sea lumber ashore on summer nights to lay their eggs in the sand, but are today under threat from the pressures of tourism. The beach

THE TURTLES OF İZTUZU

İztuzu hit the headlines in 1987 when the foundations for a luxury hotel were laid at the south end of the beach. There was a storm of protest from conservationists throughout the world (including Britain's David Bellamy), backed by public opinion in Turkey, and eventually the Turkish government scrapped the project and declared the beach a protected area. The beach is closed to the public from 8pm to 8am during the nesting season (1 May to 1 October), and anything that might disturb the eggs, such as beach umbrellas or digging in the sand, is prohibited.

The sands of İztuzu Beach are a breeding ground for rare loggerhead turtles.

205

is officially closed at night, but you may be offered an 'unofficial' trip to watch the turtles coming ashore. If you really care about conservation, you will turn down such an offer and leave the animals in peace. There is an information booth, explaining İztuzu's place in the turtles' life cycle, at the south end of the beach (see box on p.205).

Fethiye

East of Dalyan the main road passes Dalaman Airport before climbing over the Göçek Pass and swooping down a series of hairpin bends towards the Bay of Fethiye. The town of **Fethiye** straggles along the shore of its attractive harbour, overlooked by the Lycian rock tombs of ancient Telmessos. It is both a traditional Turkish market town and a popular holiday resort – lively bars and restaurants line the quayside, while the bustling market sprawls among the backstreets a few blocks inland.

The boats along the waterfront offer the classic 'Twelve-Island Tour' of Fethiye Bay. The most popular stops are: Şövalye Adası (Knights' Island), which blocks the entrance to the harbour, and has a pleasant beach; Tersane Adası (Dockyard Island), with the ruins of an ancient lookout tower and an ornately decorated rock tomb; and **Gemiler Adası** (Island of Ships), also known as Aya Nikola Adası (St Nicholas's Island). Archaeologists exploring Gemiler Adası believe that they have found the 4th-century tomb of St Nicholas, Bishop of Myra, better known in the west as Santa Claus. On the island are the ruins of five churches dating from the 4th to 6th centuries, about 50 Christian tombs, and a 350m (380yd) long processional way; the tomb of St Nicholas is thought to be in the church that sits on the highest point of the island.

Fethiye is also an important scuba-diving centre, and there are a number of reputable companies offering dive excursions, equipment hire and instruction.

Telmessos

There is little left to see of ancient **Telmessos**, on which the modern town of Fethiye was built. A **Lycian sarcophagus** sits next to the town hall, and the **theatre** has recently been dug out of the hillside behind the tourist information office. The most conspicuous relics are the rock tombs that honeycomb the cliff above the town, especially the **Tomb of Amyntas**, which is floodlit at night. The tomb, which is reached by a concrete staircase, takes the form of an Ionic temple; on the left-hand pillar is an inscription that reads 'AMHNTOU TOU ERMAGIOU' ('Amyntas, son of Hermagios'). Unfortunately we know nothing of Amyntas and his father.

Where the steps to Amyntas's tomb head left, the road to the right leads towards the **acropolis** hill. A steep scramble leads past some smaller rock tombs to the remains of the 16th-century castle that once capped the hill; it is thought to have been built by the Knights of St John. You can also reach the acropolis from the far end of town, via a steep road that leads past the Hotel Pırlanta then along the hillside to a dusty village beside the ruined castle walls.

Fethiye's **museum** is down a side street between Atatürk Caddesi and the quayside, below the Tomb of Amyntas. Its collection of antiquities from Telmessos and other sites in the surrounding district includes a beautiful 3rd-century BC headdress from Pinara, with gold laurel leaves and turquoise berries, and an important trilingual stele from the Letoön. The stele, which dates from 358 BC, bears an inscription in Greek, Aramaic and Lycian, and played a crucial part in the deciphering of the Lycian language.

Kaya

The village of **Kaya**, about 15km (9 miles) south of Fethiye, is the largest ghost town in Turkey. Until 1923 it was known as Levissi, and supported a thriving Ottoman Greek population of 3,000 people. But the village was emptied during the exchange of populations that took place after the Turkish War of Independence, and its houses and churches have lain abandoned ever since. There were plans to restore the stone cottages and develop Kaya as a holiday village, but it

*O*n *a hillside near Fethiye stands the deserted town of Kaya. Its houses were abandoned during the exchange of populations that took place after the war of 1922-3.*

is now being preserved as a historical monument. You can wander through the deserted streets and take a look inside the church of Panayia Pirgiotissa, with its fading frescoes and marble carvings.

Ölüdeniz

The south side of the Fethiye Peninsula has a number of good beaches, but none can compare with the beautiful bay of **Ölüdeniz**, one of the prettiest beaches in the country. In the height of summer this broad strand of sand, gravel and pebbles can become uncomfortably crowded, but early or late in the season you can have the place almost to yourself. The north end of the beach extends into a spit with a lagoon behind, hence the name 'Ölüdeniz', which means 'dead (as in calm, not moving) sea'. This part of the beach, the most attractive, is fenced off, and you have to pay an entrance fee to get in.

You will soon notice that the main part of the beach also serves as a landing site for paragliders and hang-gliders. In recent years, Ölüdeniz has become very popular with devotees of paragliding, who take advantage of a take-off site on the nearby peak of Baba Dağ (1,976m; 6,480ft) to soar the thermals rising from the sun-warmed rock-faces. If you fancy having a go, there are several agencies in the village that offer tandem flights with an experienced pilot.

The Turquoise Coast

The rugged, mountainous region between Fethiye and Antalya was known in ancient times as Lycia. According to Herodotus, the Lycians came originally from Crete, arriving in Anatolia around 1500-1400 BC. They were renowned as fierce warriors and accomplished seafarers, and although they were later Hellenized they maintained a large degree of autonomy. So fiercely did they believe in independence that the citizens of Xanthos twice destroyed their city and fought to the last man rather than live under the rule of an invader.

Twenty-three cities joined together to form the Lycian League – the largest of these were Xanthos, Patara, Pinara, Olympos, Myra and Tlos. Their most distinctive features are the unusual stone sarcophagi and rock-cut tombs that litter their necropolises. These are copies in stone of the houses and temples the Lycians inhabited in life; the sarcophagus lids, carved from a single block of stone, mimic steeply pitched wooden roofs complete with projecting beam-ends. Many bear inscriptions in the Lycian alphabet, a curious script based on Greek.

Tourist brochures promote the region as the 'Turquoise Coast', a reference to its limpid blue waters. The scenery here is spectacular, with mountains pressing close to the sea and a sprinkling of tiny islands off shore. Until the early 1970s there was no proper road along this stretch of coast, and the fishing-village resorts of Kalkan, Kaş and Finike are thus quieter and less developed than those further west.

The Xanthos Valley

The fertile valley of the Xanthos River (now called the Eşen Çayı) was the most populous part of ancient Lycia. Its swirling, silt-laden waters (*xanthos* is Greek for yellow) have laid down a thick deposit of rich alluvial soil, which today nourishes crops of olives, wheat, maize and sesame. Things were much the same over 2,500 years ago, when Homer described the land of the Lycian warriors, Sarpedon and Glaucus, as 'a great demesne by the banks of Xanthos, of orchard land and wheat-bearing tilth'. Today the ruins of five Lycian cities can be explored along the Xanthos.

Tlos

To reach the spectacular hilltop site of Tlos, turn left (for Denizili and Korkuteli) at the main road junction of Kemer, about 23km (14 miles) from Fethiye. Within a few hundred metres you will cross a bridge; turn right immediately after the bridge, then 9km (5½ miles) later, at the village of Güneşli, turn left up a dirt road (sign for Tlos Park Trout Restaurant) for a further 4km (2½ miles). This brings you to the village of Yaka, also called Asar Kale, which lies among the ruins. Little is known of Tios's history, but it is one of the most ancient and important of Lycian cities – it is mentioned in Hittite records of the 14th century BC, and by the 2nd century BC was a leading member of the Lycian League.

As you drive up the winding approach to the village you will see the rocky **acropolis** hill rising to your right, crowned by an Ottoman **fortress** that was still occupied as recently as the 19th century. On the cliff below the summit are several rock tombs, reached by a path leading right from the ticket office, below the city walls. A scramble downhill brings you to a ladder below the **Tomb of Bellerophon**, which has an impressive Ionic façade similar to the Tomb of Amyntas in Fethiye. Above the left-hand door is a faded carving of a lion, and to its left is the relief that gives the tomb its name, showing the hero Bellerophon riding Pegasus, the winged horse (see box). Other ruins rise beyond the fields below the acropolis, the best preserved of which is the fine, 2nd-century AD Roman **theatre**.

About 9km (5½ miles) along the road beyond Güneşli a track on the left marked **Saklıkent** leads to the mouth of a deep limestone gorge. A wooden walkway leads above the river to where a huge spring gushes forth at high pressure from the foot of a cliff. A number of cafés and trout (*alabalık*) restaurants beside the river make this a pleasant spot to stop for lunch.

BELLEROPHON

Bellerophon was the grandfather of Glaucus and Sarpedon, the leaders of the Lycian warriors in Homer's *Iliad*. Anteia, wife of King Proteus of Tiryns, fell in love with him, but when he rejected her advances she falsely accused him of impropriety. Proteus then sent Bellerophon to his father-in-law Iobates, king of Lycia, bearing a sealed letter which read, 'Pray remove the bearer from this world; he has tried to violate my wife, your daughter.' Unwilling to slay a royal guest, Iobates instead asked him to destroy the Chimera, described by Homer as 'of ghastly and inhuman origin, her forepart lionish, her tail a snake's, a she-goat in between. This thing exhaled in jets a rolling fire'. Bellerophon first tamed the winged horse Pegasus with a magic bridle given him by the goddess Athena, then flew over the Chimera and forced a lump of lead down the beast's throat with his spear. The lead melted in the monster's fiery breath and trickled down its throat, killing it.

Iobates set Bellerophon other 'impossible' tasks in the hope that he would be killed, but with the help of Pegasus the hero always won through. The king eventually accepted that Bellerophon must be favoured by the gods, gave him his other daughter in marriage, and made him heir to the Lycian throne. But Bellerophon's fortunes took a downward turn when he presumed to fly to Olympus, the home of the gods. Zeus sent a gadfly to sting Pegasus, and the winged steed threw its rider to earth, where he wandered grief-stricken, lame and blind until his death.

Pinara

About 25km (15½ miles) south of the Kemer roundabout, a paved road on the right leads in 3km (2 miles) to the village of Minare; just before the village, turn sharp left on a dirt track (signposted for Pinara; jeep recommended) for another 3km (2 miles) to the site. **Pinara** is another Lycian city whose early history in unknown; according to one 4th-century BC historian it was founded by the citizens of Xanthos when that city became overpopulated.

The most impressive sight at Pinara is the 500m (1,600ft) high, flat-topped **acropolis** hill; the huge, reddish-brown cliff that drops from the summit is riddled with rock tombs. The main ruins of the city – temples, baths, *odeon* and theatre – are on a smaller rise below the acropolis, but are overgrown and difficult to explore. The site guardian will lead you to the **Royal Tomb** (*Kral Mezar*), which has faded bas-reliefs inside showing four fortified Lycian cities.

Letoön

The Letoön was not a city, but a shrine dedicated to Leto, and to her children Apollo and Artemis, which became the principal sanctuary and meeting place of the Lycian League. The site lies 4km (2½ miles) from the highway, along a side road on the right 1km (½ mile) before Kınık. You can clamber over the foundations of three ancient temples: in the middle, a small 4th-century BC **Temple of Artemis**; to the right, the slightly later **Temple of Leto**, built in Ionic order; and to the left, the Doric **Temple of Apollo and Artemis**, with a floor mosaic of a lyre, bow and quiver (the traditional attributes of Apollo and Artemis). Beyond the temples are a Byzantine **basilica** (with a mosaic of a stork or ibis), and the flooded remains of

*T*he watery ruins of the Letoön are home to countless frogs. They are supposedly the spirits of shepherds punished by the goddess Leto.

a **nymphaeum**, where frogs and terrapins haunt the precincts of the sacred spring. Directly behind the parking area is the **theatre**. The seating is well preserved but the stage building is gone, replaced by a field of crops. The outer face of the vaulted entrance on the far side is decorated with a frieze of masks above the arch.

210

LETO AND THE WOLVES

The nymph Leto, daughter of the Titans, fell pregnant by Zeus. His wife Hera was jealous, and sent the serpent Python to harry Leto to prevent her from giving birth. Eventually Leto was borne by the south wind to the island of Delos, where she gave birth to the twins Apollo and Artemis. Then she went to Lycia, where friendly wolves led her to the River Xanthos so that she might refresh herself and wash her new-born children. The local shepherds tried to stop her, but the wolves drove them off. She repaid this kindness by naming the land Lycia (from the Greek *lykos*, meaning wolf), and she turned the shepherds into the frogs which haunt the Letoön to this day.

Xanthos

At the village of Kınık a road leads left across the Eşen Çayı and uphill, past the 1st-century AD **Arch of Vespasian** to the ruins of **Xanthos**, the greatest of Lycia's ancient cities. Its first mention in print is in Homer's *Iliad,* where he describes the contingents lined up on the side of the Trojans: 'Sarpedon led the Lycians, with Glaucus, from Lycia afar, from whirling Xanthos' – a reference to the turbulent river that swirls past the foot of the acropolis hill.

The principal ruins are to the left of the road. Xanthos is famous for its funerary monuments, two of which are prominent at the far end of the theatre. The so-called **Harpy Tomb** is a square pillar 7.5m (25ft) high with protruding eaves at the top, dating from the early 5th century BC. The burial chamber was decorated with marble reliefs (now kept in the British Museum), which have been replaced with concrete casts of the originals. They show winged female figures (originally thought to be harpies) carrying small children in their arms – these represent the Sirens bearing the souls of the dead to the underworld. Near by stands a traditional Lycian sarcophagus set atop a pillar.

Directly across the road from the car park, in an excavated area down to the right, is the famous **Inscribed Pillar**. This was originally similar in appearance to the Harpy Tomb, but the burial chamber on top has disappeared. The remaining pillar is notable for bearing the longest-known inscription in the Lycian language.

The Roman **theatre** is in fairly good condition, although a Byzantine defensive

FREEDOM OR DEATH

The Lycians were noted for their refusal to submit to an outside power, a code of honour that was gruesomely demonstrated when the city of Xanthos was attacked by the Persian army under the general Harpagus in 546 BC. Herodotus describes what happened:

When Harpagus advanced into the plain of Xanthos, they [the Xanthians] met him in battle, though greatly outnumbered, and fought with much gallantry; at length, however, they were defeated and forced to retire within their walls, whereupon they collected their women, children, slaves, and other property and shut them up in the inner fortified ring of the city, set fire to the place and burnt it to the ground. Then having sworn to do or die, they marched out to meet the enemy and were killed to a man.

Only 80 families, who happened to be away from home on that day, escaped the holocaust. This was not a unique event. When the city was besieged by the Roman legions of Brutus in 42 BC, the Xanthians destroying themselves and their city rather than surrender to the oppressor.

wall has been built along the top. If you scramble over the back of the theatre you will find yourself on the **Lycian acropolis**, the site of the Xanthians' mass suicide in 546 BC (see box on p.211). You can make out the outlines of a Byzantine church, a temple dedicated to Artemis, and a shrine overlooking the river.

Crossing back over the road, a path leads out of the back of the car park to a large Byzantine basilica with extensive geometric floor mosaics, then heads uphill to the left towards the **necropolis**. The hillside here is pocked with rock tombs and Lycian sarcophagi, some decorated with scenes of hunting and battle. The city walls lead up to the summit of the **Roman acropolis**, capped by the ruins of a Byzantine monastery, and offering a fine view of the site and of the valley of the Xanthos River.

Patara

Patara was the finest harbour on the Lycian coast, and the seat of a well-known oracle of Apollo. According to Herodotus, the prophesies were delivered in dreams to a priestess who spent the night in the temple. In Christian times, St Paul set sail from Patara to Phoenicia during his third journey (Acts 18:22-22:15), and St Nicholas of Myra was born here around AD 300.

The road to Patara passes a ticket office and barrier, before continuing past a triple-arched Roman gateway and a series of newly excavated tombs. The ruins are rather spread out and very overgrown – no trace

*T*he theatre at Xanthos is overlooked by two unusual pillar tombs. Marble reliefs from the Harpy Tomb can now be found in the British Museum, London.

FROM ST NICHOLAS TO SANTA CLAUS

Little is known for certain about the life of St Nicholas, except that he was born in Patara, and became the Bishop of Myra during the 4th century. He was credited with many miracles and good deeds, the most famous of which involved three young girls, the daughters of a poor merchant, who were about to be forced into a life of prostitution because their father could not afford marriage dowries. Nicholas rescued their honour by coming to their house in the middle of the night and throwing three bags of gold through the window (or down the chimney), thus allowing the girls to be married. This was commemorated in medieval times by the giving of anonymous gifts on the eve of St Nicholas's feast day (6 December). Nicholas was enormously popular, and many pilgrims came to visit his tomb on Gemile Adası (see p.206). When the island was threatened by Arab raiders in the 7th century, his bones were removed to the church of St Nicholas in Myra; later, in 1087, his relics were stolen by a group of Italian merchants and taken to the city of Bari, where they were enshrined in the cathedral.

Nicholas became the patron saint of children, sailors, travellers and prisoners, and of Russia and Greece. He was venerated all over the world, and thousands of European churches were dedicated to him. In Holland he was known as *Sinter Claes*, a name that 17th-century Dutch emigrants took across the Atlantic to New Amsterdam (soon to become New York). It was in 19th-century America that he evolved into Santa Claus, the bringer of Christmas gifts, thanks largely to a poem, *A Visit From St Nicholas*, written in 1822 by Clement Clark Moore for his children.

---

has yet been found of the Temple of Apollo. The easiest part to explore is the Hellenistic **theatre**, which lies at the end of a short track on the right, just before the parking area near the beach. The *cavea* is half full of drifted sand, but much of the stage building still stands, and bears an inscription recording alterations made in AD 147.

An easy climb leads to the top of the hill behind the theatre, where you will find a deep cistern cut into the rock and the ruins of a tower which may have been a lighthouse. From the summit there is a fine view of the ruins scattered among the fields; the marshy fen to the left is the site of Patara's ancient harbour, long since cut off from the sea by sand dunes. The dunes are part of Patara's famous **beach**, one of the biggest and best in the Mediterranean – 15km (9 miles) of fine golden sand curving away into the haze. Like İztuzu, this is a favourite nesting site of the loggerhead turtle; the small fee you pay to use the beach goes towards conservation work. There are a couple of small restaurants at the beach parking area, but most new development is concentrated in the village of Gelemiş on the approach road.

Beyond the Patara turn-off the highway narrows and climbs up into the hills, before twisting down to the beautiful bay of Kalkan.

Kalkan to Kale

Kalkan

The little town of **Kalkan** clings precariously to the steep hill above its harbour. Despite encroaching tourist development, it has managed to retain some of the charm and character of the Ottoman Greek fishing village it once was. It makes an excellent base for exploring the sights of western Lycia, offering a wide range of accommodation, from package-tour hotels to tiny pensions.

About 6km (4 miles) east of Kalkan is the pretty little beach of **Kapıtaş**, a narrow strand of sand and gravel hemmed in between two cliffs at the mouth of a narrow gorge – the pale sand here makes the sea a stunning turquoise colour. Steps lead down to the beach from a parking place; you can walk back under the road bridge and explore the floor of the gorge, which is over 50m (165ft) deep, but so narrow you can almost touch the sides with outstretched arms. A marble plaque by the roadside commemorates four workmen who were killed during the construction of this dangerous stretch of road.

Kaş

Kaş is a booming tourist resort set between an attractive harbour and a steep cliff riddled with rock tombs, overlooking the small Greek island of Megisti; like Kalkan, Kaş was once an Ottoman Greek fishing village. It occupies the site of ancient Antiphellos, whose few remains lie scattered around the town. The best known of these is the **Lion Tomb**, which sits at the top of the main shopping street behind the tourist information office. It consists of a beautiful Lycian sarcophagus, with four lions' heads on the lid, set on top of another burial chamber which has a long inscription in Lycian. Heading west from the main square, you pass the foundations of a 1st-century BC temple on the left and the town's main mosque on the right (converted from a 19th-century church), before reaching the small but well-preserved **theatre**.

There are no decent beaches in Kaş; the nearest good one is at Kapıtaş (see above). The boats moored in the harbour offer a wide range of interesting day trips: west to the Blue Grotto (*Mavi Mağara*), Kapıtaş, Kalkan and Patara, east to Kekova, and across the bay to the Greek island of Megisti. Known as **Meis Adası** in Turkish, this tiny island lies a mere 5km (3 miles) off the coast, and over 100km

(60 miles) from Rhodes, its nearest Greek neighbour. The main town, Kastellorizo, clusters around a fine harbour beneath the remains of a crusader castle.

Kekova (Üçağız)

Daily boat trips run from Kaş to Kekova island and the village of Üçağız. The village can also be reached via 20km (12 miles) of newly paved road which leaves the highway at a roundabout some 10km (6 miles) east of Kaş. This stretch

The fishing village and resort of Kaş has been built among the ruins of ancient Antiphellos.

of coast is famous for its sunken cities – the land has been thrown down by earthquake movements, leaving the ruins of ancient towns submerged beneath several metres of water.

215

The sheltered bay of Üçağız is fringed by the necropolis of ancient Teimiussa. Lycian rock tombs lie tumbled along the shore, and even extend underwater.

Üçağız sits on a sheltered bay beside the necropolis of ancient Teimiussa. East of the village you can scramble over a picturesque jumble of rock tombs and tumbled sarcophagi, many hewn direct from the living rock. The village sports a handful of restaurants and pensions, and a small fleet of 'glass-bottomed' boats offering trips to the sunken ruins. The standard tour first visits nearby **Kale**, an impossibly picturesque village topped by a medieval castle, with a Lycian sarcophagus poking up in the middle of the harbour.

The boat then crosses to **Kekova** island and chugs along the north shore, where you can see low walls, stairways, rock-cut houses, drainage channels and narrow alleys that run down the steep hillside to disappear beneath the waves. Through the boat's glass viewing panel you can see these features extending under the water (choose a calm, sunny day for the best viewing conditions), along with a sunken harbour mole, much broken pottery and even some human bones. Your boatman will take much pleasure in pointing out the bones, but they are almost certainly not ancient. The black dots you can see are spiny sea urchins; watch out for them when you are swimming or wading. (Note that swimming, snorkelling and diving are not allowed on this part of Kekova, to prevent the theft of antiquities.) The trip usually ends with a stop at **Tersane**, an attractive bay at the south end of the island where swimming is permitted. The ruins of a Byzantine basilica stand right on the beach.

Kale (Demre)

East of Kaş the highway cuts inland for 35km (21 miles) before arriving at a viewpoint overlooking the flood-plain of the ancient Androkos River. The plain is covered with a patchwork of white houses, deep green citrus orchards and acres of glasshouses glinting in the sun. This is the market-garden town of **Kale** (also called Demre), which sits below the ruins of Myra, home of St Nicholas and site of some of the most impressive rock tombs in Lycia.

In the centre of town is the **Church of St Nicholas** (*Noel Baba Kilisesi*). The

Turkish name means 'Father Christmas Church', and in the garden by the gate there is a statue of the saint in his modern incarnation as Santa Claus (see box p.213). A ramp leads down from the entrance to the south side of the church, which has undergone many alterations, extensions and restorations since its founding in the 4th century. The layout of the building you see today – a basilica with a double aisle on the south side – probably dates from the 8th century, though it was rebuilt by the Byzantine Emperor Constantine IX in the 11th century. It was restored by Tsar Nicholas of Russia in the 19th century, and more recently by the Turkish authorities. At the foot of the modern ramp is a long chapel stretching leftwards, lined with tombs and faded frescoes. At its far end, turn right to find the main entrance to the church – the nave has a decorated marble pavement, with a *synthronon* in the apse and four broken columns marking the altar. At the far end of the left-hand aisle is a dome with a fresco of the 12 apostles. The right-hand aisle is double – in the outer one, at the far end, is the marble sarcophagus that is thought once to have held the remains of St Nicholas.

The site of **Myra** lies 1.5km (1 mile) north of town, and is famous for the elaborate **rock tombs** that honeycomb the cliff face above the theatre. The façades of the

The rock-cut tombs of Myra mimic the appearance of Lycian timber houses, complete with panelled doors and log roof-beams.

tombs are copies of the wooden houses that the Lycians lived in, complete with panelled walls and roof timbers. Inside there are stone benches on three sides, where the bodies of the deceased once lay. Several of the tombs are decorated with reliefs – one shows a figure reclining on a couch, attended by his wife, a musician and a servant carrying a bowl; to the left are two naked youths and a bearded warrior donning his armour. The theatre is large and fairly well preserved; it was rebuilt following an earthquake in AD 141. Large vaulted passageways on either side of the *cavea* give access to the *diazoma,* where you can see the head of Tyche, goddess of luck, carved in the wall near the centre.

A road on the south side of town leads beside the Androkos River to **Andriake** (now called Çayağzı), the ancient port of Myra. In Roman times, Andriake played a vital part in the distribution of grain throughout the empire. To the left of the road, across the marshy basin that marks the silted-up harbour, you can see the ruins of **Hadrian's Granary**, the huge warehouses where the grain was stored before being shipped to Rome or wherever else it was needed. At the road end is a fine sandy beach with a restaurant, and a handful of boats offering trips to Kekova.

The road to Elmalı

The highway east of Kale passes a series of tiny sandy coves in a rock-bound coast-

line, until a new fishing harbour marks the approach to **Finike**, an unprepossessing seaside resort rapidly being taken over by new holiday apartments. There is little to see in Finike, but you may want to make a detour along the scenic road which climbs through the mountains to Elmalı, about 70km (45 miles) inland.

The road passes two attractive ruined cities. First comes **Limyra**, 10km (6 miles) from Finike. A minor road through the village of Turunçova leads to the **theatre**, set at the foot of the acropolis hill. The remains of the walled Roman and Byzantine city lie on the marshy ground to the right, but the main attraction here is the rock tombs that riddle the hillside above the road. Above and to the right of the theatre is the 4th-century BC **Tomb of Xatabura**, a free-standing sarcophagus whose pedestal is decorated with reliefs depicting a warrior and chariot, a funeral feast and the judgement of the deceased. A sweaty 45-minute hike leads to the top of the acropolis (signposted 'Heroön') above the tombs, where you will be rewarded with a grand view back towards the sea. Here, too, is the **Mausoleum of Pericles**, the Lycian ruler who successfully withstood Persian expansionism in the 4th century BC. His tomb is in the form of a temple, decorated with caryatids (female statues serving as columns) similar to those of the Erechtheum on the Athenian Acropolis; however, the figures wear lion-headed bracelets, showing Persian influence alongside the Greek.

Higher up in the mountains, above the village of Arif, lies the beautiful site of **Arykanda**, drowsing peacefully among the pine trees. A rough road leads up from the highway to a parking area and information board (the guardian, who speaks English, will offer to show you around). Arykanda was founded before the 5th

219

century BC, and continued to flourish well into Byzantine times, when it was important enough to have its own bishop.

The city is spread over a series of terraces in the steep mountainside. To the right of the information board is a street with a small Corinthian **temple**, which was converted for Christian worship – there are a number of crosses and religious inscriptions carved on the right wall. On the terrace below is the grassy sward of the **palaestra** and the high walls of the **baths**, with the distinctive bay windows of the *caldarium* enjoying a fine view over the valley. A path leads uphill to the left of the information board, to the wide open space of the **agora**; three arches on the north side give access to a small **odeon**. Above the *agora* is the **theatre**, and above that the recently excavated **stadium**, with seats on the uphill side only.

The main road continues up a series of hairpin bends to crest the Avlan Beli pass at a height of 1,120m (3,700ft), before descending gently into a huge, flat-floored basin. Surrounded by the snow-capped peaks of the Ak Dağ and Beydağları mountain ranges, this vast, dried-up lake bed is intensively cultivated and cradles, at its northern edge, the market town of **Elmalı**. This pleasant country town has a fine 17th-century Ottoman mosque and a number of traditional wooden Ottoman mansions. There are several good restaurants and a couple of hotels, but the only tourists you are likely to see here will be Turkish.

The Olympian Shore

East of Finike the highway cuts inland before entering the **Mount Olympos Coastal National Park** (*Olimpos Beydağları Sahil Milli Parkı*). The park stretches from the Çavuş Peninsula almost to Antalya, embracing the 2,375m (7,790ft) peak of Tahtalı Dağ. In ancient times this was one of the many peaks around the Aegean that was given the name Olympos, which may simply have been an archaic, pre-Greek word meaning 'mountain'. The national park offers some excellent hiking amid the limestone peaks and pine woods of Tahtalı Dağ, while on the coast you can choose between the backpackers' beaches at Olympos and the bustling modern resort of Kemer.

Olympos

The origins of the ancient city of Olympos are shrouded in mystery. It is recorded as being a member of the Lycian League in the 2nd century BC, but unlike its fellow members it has no inscriptions in the Lycian language, and none of the characteristic Lycian rock tombs and sarcophagi that grace the other cities. It was ruled briefly by pirates during the 1st century BC before enjoying a period of prosperity under Roman rule. The city slipped into decline after the 6th century. Although it was used as a port by the Genoese during the 11th and 12th centuries, it had been completely abandoned by the time the Ottomans came to power.

Approaching from Finike, the first side road to Olympos is signposted 'Adrasan-Çavuş-Olympos'. After 8km (5 miles) you turn left on to a dirt track which wanders down a lovely wooded river valley to a parking area near the ruins. A path continues down the riverbank for a few hundred metres to an attractive gravel beach. To the left of the main path a muddy track follows an ancient aqueduct past a ruined temple to a **baths** complex with mosaic floors, hidden among lush vegetation. Nearby, but hard to find, is an enormous marble doorway, 5m (16ft) tall. Just before the beach, a newly excavated recess houses

The ruins of Olympos occupy an idyllic riverside setting in a lush, wooded valley.

house and other buildings. The city's **necropolis** stretches up the hillside across the river from the parking area. The tombs are not typical of Lycia, taking the form of vaulted chambers with a small square opening at the front, closed by a sliding stone slab. The biggest tomb, high up to the right, is inscribed with a 'letter oracle'. This is a series of verses, each of which begins with a different letter. When a citizen wanted to seek the advice of his ancestors, he would draw a letter of the alphabet from a bag, and follow the course of action prescribed in the verse beginning with that letter.

The Chimera (Yanartaş)

The principal deity of Olympos was Hephaistos, the divine blacksmith, god of fire. The reason for this is to be found in the hills to the north of the ruined city, in the eternal flames of the **Chimera**, known in Turkish as *Yanartaş* (firestones'). In a clearing in the trees, yellow flames flicker among the scorched rocks of the bare hillside, fed by a seepage of natural gas. The flames have burned for as long as man can remember, though in ancient times the pressure of the gas was much greater and the fire roared with frightening ferocity – it was this, no doubt, that gave rise to the legend of the Chimera, the fire-breathing Lycian monster defeated by the hero Bellerophon (see box p.209), and inspired the worship of Hephaistos.

The Chimera is best visited at dusk. This means coming back down in darkness, so be sure to take a powerful and reliable flashlight as it is all too easy to lose the path. (You can borrow a torch from any of the nearby hotels and pensions.) To reach the start of the path, take the turn-off signposted 'Çıralı-Yanartaş-Chimera', which leads in 7km (4 miles) to

two **sarcophagi**, one of which bears a detailed relief of a large ship. A steep scramble up to the left will take you to the summit of the **acropolis**, adorned with remains of Genoese fortifications. From the top you will have a good view of the valley and the beach below, with ruined walls poking up among the trees.

On the far side of the river you can wander through the woods to discover the remains of the theatre, a basilica, a warehouse and other buildings. The city's

The flames of Chimera, fed by natural gas, have been burning for as long as man can remember.

the village of Çıralı (which can also be reached from Olympos by walking north along the beach for 20 minutes). Turn left across a bridge and follow signs for the Chimera along a dirt track for a few kilometres to a parking area among the trees. A path leads uphill, marked by piles of stones and red paint marks on the rocks, to the clearing; the climb takes about 20 minutes. The ruins of a small temple to Hephaistos and a Byzantine church lie at the edge of the clearing.

Phaselis

The ruins of **Phaselis** enjoy a picturesque setting on a wooded peninsula, about 20km (12 miles) north of Olympos. The city was founded in the 7th century BC by Greek colonists from Rhodes, and grew rich on the proceeds of trade, finally joining the Lycian League in the 1st century BC. Like Olympos it suffered occupation by pirates, but it flourished under Rome and became an important Byzantine port.

The site is at the end of a short side road, with a ticket office, snack bar and extensive parking area. (Its ease of access makes Phaselis a popular day trip from Kemer and Antalya.) The arches of an **aqueduct** stand among the trees beside the car park; beyond is the small, circular bay of the **central harbour**. An ancient breakwater runs out to a rock on the north side of the bay, and on the beach to the south you can see the remains of the quay, complete with a mooring bollard carved into the stone. The marble-paved **main street** runs from here across the neck of the peninsula to **Hadrian's Gate** and the attractive sandy beach of the south harbour, with the signposted ruins of public buildings on either side – baths, basilica and *agora* to the right, theatre and acropolis hill to the left.

Kemer

Phaselis marks the boundary between the wild country of Lycia and the package-holiday paradise that fringes the Gulf of Antalya. From here on the beach is lined with huge holiday villages and resort complexes, and there is little reason to stop until you reach Antalya. The town of **Kemer** was purpose built in the 1980s as a yacht marina and beach resort, a function it performs well if rather soullessly. There are a number of pleasant restaurants beside the marina, and the usual gamut of carpet, leather and jewellery shops.

Antalya to Alanya

Antalya is the biggest city on Turkey's Mediterranean shore. Thousands of holidaymakers jet in to its international airport every year to enjoy the beaches and resorts of the 'Turkish Riviera'. The beaches are backed by alluvial plains that were as fertile in ancient times as they are now, supporting some of the richest cities in the Roman Empire. Today, exploring the majestic ruins of Perge, Aspendos and Side provides a cultural alternative to soaking up the sun.

Antalya

Approaching from the west, the modern highway cuts through two tunnels before breaking out on to the Pamphylian Plain. It drags for miles through the modern concrete suburbs of Antalya, past the new commercial port, before finally reaching the tiny, ancient heart of the city, clustered around the old harbour. This sheltered cove beneath the cliffs led Attalus II, king of Pergamum, to found a port here in the 2nd century BC. It was named Attaleia, after the king, and was bequeathed to Rome along with the rest of the Pergamene kingdom in 133 BC (see p.153). The Emperor Hadrian visited the city in AD 130, an event that was commemorated by a triumphal gate which still survives today.

In the Middle Ages Antalya was a Byzantine stronghold, and an important staging point for shipping troops and supplies to the Holy Land during the crusades. It was captured by the Seljuk Turks in the 12th century and soon grew to become the most important port on the Mediterranean coast, finally falling under Ottoman control in the late 15th century. After World War I it was occupied briefly by Italian forces, before being liberated by Atatürk's army in 1921.

Old Town

The historic heart of Antalya is the district called **Kaleiçi** (meaning 'within the fortress'), centred on the old harbour. This pretty cove, encircled by low cliffs, now serves as a haven for local *gülets* and fishing boats, and sports a number of attractive restaurants along the quayside. Stairs above the breakwater on the far side of the quay lead into the maze of streets above the harbour, where old wooden Ottoman houses, many of which have been restored as attractive pensions and small hotels, crowd the lanes and alleys. Find your way to a square marked by the ruined stump of a minaret; this is the **Kesik Minare Camii** (Mosque of the Cut-Down Minaret), a 5th-century church that was converted to a mosque by the son of Sultan Beyazıt II. Turn left along Hesapçı Sokak, and you will emerge from the maze at the triple archway of **Hadrian's Gate** (*Hadrianus Kapısı*), the most impressive remnant of Roman Attaleia. Down to the right is Karaali Parkı, a pleasant cliff-top garden containing the **Hıdırlık Kulesi**, a massive

Roman structure of the 2nd century AD, thought to be the tomb of a local dignitary.

From Hadrian's Gate follow the busy thoroughfare of Atatürk Caddesi leftwards to the bazaar at the intersection with Cumhuriyet Caddesi and then go left; this takes you back above the old harbour, where the skyline is pierced by the fluted spire of the **Yivli Minare** (Grooved Minaret), built in 1230 during the reign of the Seljuk Sultan Alaeddin Keykubad. The view across the harbour and the Gulf of Antalya to the wild mountains of Lycia is superb, especially at sunset.

Archaeological Museum

Two kilometres (1 mile) west of Kaleiçi, on the north side of the main road, is Antalya's fine Archaeological Museum (open 9am to 6pm, closed Monday). The collection ranges from prehistoric to Roman times, and includes an ethnographic section devoted to the Seljuk and Ottoman periods. Room 2 displays primitive tools and artefacts from Karain Cave (see below), while Room 3 contains a priceless hoard of Phrygian silver figurines. The museum's best pieces, however, are the marble statues and sarcophagi recovered from the nearby site of Perge. The **Gallery of the Gods** is a pantheon in stone dominated by a huge statue of Zeus; around the walls are representations of Apollo, Artemis, Athena, Aphrodite, Hermes, Hygeia, Tyche and Nemesis, and the Egyptian deities Isis, Serapis and Harpocrates, who were worshipped in Asia Minor until the advent of Christianity (see p.157). Beyond is the **Hall of the Emperors**, with figures of Trajan, Hadrian and Septimius Severus, and of Plancia Magna, a leading woman citizen of Perge. There is also a beautiful statue of a dancing girl, her swirling garments rendered in blue-grey marble; next door are

The Yivli Minare (Grooved Minaret) is old Antalya's most prominent landmark. Beyond, across the bay, lie the mountains of Lycia.

two magnificent sarcophagi depicting the labours of Hercules. The **Mosaic Room** does not begin to compare with Antakya's magnificent collection, but there are one or two interesting pieces – one from Xanthos shows the nymph Thetis dipping her son Achilles in the River Styx; and one from Seleucia is decorated with portraits of ancient writers (Thucydides, Herodotus and Solon, among others, and is notable for having Homer's name in the middle (in Greek; the inscription reads 'ΙΛΙΑΣ ΟΜΗΡΟΣ ΟΔΥΣ…').

Termessos

Before you move on from Antalya, don't miss the opportunity to visit the ruins of **Termessos**, which lie 25km (15 miles) inland. Take the highway towards Burdur and İsparta for 10km (6 miles), then turn left on the road to Korkuteli for another 15km (9 miles), where you will find the entrance to Termessos Milli Parkı (Termessos National Park). The ruined city lies high on the slopes of Güllük Dağı (ancient Mount Solymus), at an altitude of 1,000m

The Pisidian mountain stronghold of Termessos occupies a spectacular setting high in the hills behind Antalya. The theatre (following pages) overlooks a deep ravine.

(3,280ft), reached by 9km (5½ miles) of narrow, winding tarmac. Quite apart from its historical interest, Termessos is notable for the wild beauty of its mountain setting; take along a picnic lunch and allow a full day to explore the ruins and the hills above.

The inhabitants of Termessos were neither Lycians nor Greeks, but Pisidians from the mountains of central Anatolia. Originally called the Solymi, they are mentioned in the *Iliad* as the second hurdle to be overcome by the hero Bellerophon (see box p. 209): 'His second test was battle with Solymi, formidable aborigines. He thought this fight the worst he ever had with men.' Even Alexander the Great found the Solymi to be fierce adversaries, and failed to capture Termessos. The city remained largely autonomous during Roman times and into the Byzantine era, but seems to have been abandoned during the 5th century.

From the parking area a path leads up the left side of the valley, following the **King's Way**, the ancient road that led to the city, and passes beneath an aqueduct and cistern cut into a cliff high above. Beyond the **city gate**, with its fine watchtower, you can see the upper city wall stretching across the valley to the right, and you soon arrive at the extensive remains of the **gymnasium**, with a path leading horizontally left. Ignore this for the moment and continue to the next path on the left, which climbs uphill past a cistern to reach the *agora,* and beyond it the theatre. (The path at the gymnasium leads beneath the retaining wall of the theatre to the east gate of the city and the eastern necropolis; it is possible to scramble steeply up from here to the theatre's stage building.)

The **theatre** of Termessos enjoys one of the most dramatic settings in Turkey, cut into the edge of a cliff and looking across a deep valley to the limestone peak of Mount Solymus. Built in the Greek style (*cavea* greater than a semi-circle), it could seat an audience of more than 4,000. Pick your way across the *agora,* keeping an eye open for five deep water-storage cisterns. The earthquake-toppled buildings are overgrown and difficult to interpret, but signposts mark the *odeon,* the 'founder's house', the Stoa of Osbaras and the Stoa of Attalos.

The King's Way continues uphill as an easily followed footpath, leading through the vast **upper necropolis** to a forest-fire lookout tower on the ridge at the head of the valley. The hillsides are littered with tombs and sarcophagi as far as the eye can see, their sides smashed by grave robbers, their massive lids levered off, and some tumbled from their pedestals by earthquakes.

THE TRAGEDY OF ALCETAS

After Alexander the Great's death in 324 BC, his vast empire was divided among his generals. The young warriors of Termessos took sides with one of these, Alcetas, against another, Antigonus, who sought to control Pisidia. But Alcetas was defeated in battle and took refuge in Termessos. Antigonus demanded that Alcetas be surrendered to him. The young men refused, but the city elders were afraid of Antigonus's power, and secretly arranged with him to lay a trap – Antigonus's army would retreat, and while the young Termessians pursued them, the elders would hand over the renegade. But Alcetas discovered the plot and committed suicide rather than fall into enemy hands. The elders gave the corpse to Antigonus, who vented his anger by mutilating the body of his former adversary, until after three days the young warriors rescued the body of their hero and buried it in an elaborate rock tomb to the west of the city.

Many bear inscriptions and reliefs, usually of warlike motifs such as shields and spears. Beyond the fire lookout is a deep quarry, where the Termessians cut the stone for the necropolis tombs.

The cliffs on the far side of the valley are pock-marked with rock tombs; one of these, the **Tomb of Alcetas**, is believed to be the burial place of Alexander's general (see box). To its left is a relief of a soldier on horseback, his right hand raised as if to throw a spear.

Karain Cave

Karain Cave, one of the most important prehistoric sites in Turkey, lies 10km (6 miles) north of Termessos. From the small museum at the car park, you climb for 15 minutes up a steep, well-marked trail to a terrace at the cave entrance. Slippery steps cut in the earthen floor lead down past deep archaeological trenches to an inner chamber, but there is little to see inside. Of more interest are the Greek inscriptions and votive niches carved in the rock above and to the left of the entrance; apparently the cave was used as a temple during the Hellenistic and Roman periods.

The Pamphylian Plain

East of Antalya a broad, well-watered plain separates the mountains from the sea. This region was settled by a mixed group of Greek settlers some time after the Trojan War, around the end of the 2nd millennium BC, hence its ancient name, Pamphylia – land of the mixed tribes. In Greek and Roman times the fertile plain supported the five major cities of Attaleia, Perge, Sillyon, Aspendos and Side. Attaleia has disappeared beneath the concrete sprawl of Antalya, and most of Sillyon was carried away by a landslide in 1969, but the ruins of Perge, Aspendos and Side rank among the most interesting (and most popular) archaeological sites on the Mediterranean coast.

A few kilometres before Perge, a road on the left leads to **Kursunlu Şelalesi**, a beautiful waterfall set in a cool green ravine. Its shady riverside walks and picnic tables provide a welcome escape from the summer heat.

Perge

In contrast to the spirited defiance of Termessos, the Pergeans surrendered willingly to Alexander the Great in 333 BC, and even sent out guides to lead him to their (then unwalled) city. Perge was famous for its Temple of Artemis Pergaea (still undiscovered), described by one

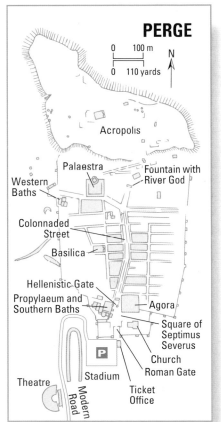

THE GREAT GEOMETER

The most famous son of Perge was Appollonius (*c.* 262-190 BC), known to his contemporaries as 'The Great Geometer'. His treatise on conic sections is regarded as one of the greatest scientific works of the ancient world, introducing and defining the now familiar terms ellipse, parabola and hyperbola. He also introduced the idea of 'epicycles', or wheels within wheels, to describe the motion of the planets, a theory later developed by Ptolemy of Alexandria (2nd century AD), who placed the Earth at the centre of the solar system. The 'Ptolemaic System' remained the accepted view of the universe in the West until the 15th century, when it was challenged by the heliocentric (sun-centred) theory of Copernicus. Ironically, the German astronomer Johannes Kepler (1571-1630) finally confirmed that the Earth and planets moved around the Sun in orbits that take the form of an ellipse – a curve first defined by Appollonius of Perge 1,800 years earlier.

Pergeans. The steps of the *propylaeum* (a columned portico) lead into the colonnaded *palaestra,* where the citizens would take exercise, such as wrestling and boxing, before washing the sand from their feet in the trough at the left-hand edge, and perhaps taking a swim in the adjoining pool. A door leads into the marble-tiled *frigidarium,* with a cold pool in the windowed bay to the left, and another footbath in front of the entrance to the next room. This is the *tepidarium,* with a long, narrow warm bath at the left end; at the right end, the floor has fallen in to reveal the *hypocaust,* an underfloor space heated by the hot air from a furnace. The final room is the *caldarium,* with a marble bench and steps up to a hot pool on the left, and three more hot pools in the arched recesses on the far wall; the *hypocaust* here is supported on arched vaults. The furnace that heated the baths was situated at the right-hand end of the *caldarium.*

To the right of the Hellenistic Gate is the Roman **agora**, a large colonnaded square surrounded by shops, with a circular building in the centre, which may have been a fountain, or perhaps a temple of Hermes (patron of merchants as well as messenger of the gods). From the corner of the *agora*, a grand **colonnaded street** leads for about 450m (500yd) to a fountain at the foot of the acropolis hill. This was a 'dual carriageway', with a raised canal in the middle, crossed by raised walkways. The fountain is crowned with a reclining statue of a river god, beneath which the water cascaded into a basin, then flowed along the canal, cooling the hot city air and soothing the citizens with the sounds of running water. The marble paving of the street is scored with ruts from the wheels of ancient carts. Half way along on the right are four columns with carved reliefs

ancient writer as 'a temple of wonderful size, beauty and construction'. The goddess was originally an Anatolian deity whose identity became merged with that of the Greek Artemis; she was represented as a block of stone (possibly a meteorite) surmounted by a female bust (there is an example in the Antalya Museum).

The road to **Perge** passes the theatre (closed for restoration) and loops around the end of the stadium to reach a huge parking area. You enter the site through the **Roman Gate** – the walls were extended in Roman times to enclose the Square of Septimius Severus, on the far side of which you can see the twin towers of the older **Hellenistic Gate**. On the left side of the square is a very well preserved Roman **baths** complex, where you can follow in the footsteps of the ancient

Aspendos

A fine Seljuk bridge across the Köprü Çay (the ancient River Eurymedon) marks the beginning of the road to Aspendos, once an important Pamphylian port, but now famous for possessing the most perfectly preserved Roman theatre in the world. It was built during the reign of Marcus Aurelius (AD 161-80), and has survived remarkably unscathed for nearly two millennia. You enter, as the citizens of Aspendos once did, through a vaulted *parodos* leading into the orchestra, from where staircases lead up through the rows of seats; the theatre can hold an audience of 20,000. There is a 'royal box' above each *parodos,* reached by a staircase inside the stage building. The *cavea* is a perfect semicircle, topped by a gallery with 59 arched vaults. The stage building is huge – 24m (79ft) high and 100m (328ft) wide – and was ornately decorated with columns and statues; a horizontal row of sockets above the main façade held the beams that once supported a wooden roof.

Köprülü Canyon

About 5km (3 miles) east of Aspendos, a side road heads north into the mountains along the valley of the Eurymedon River towards the **Köprülü Kanyon Milli Parkı** (Köprülü Canyon National Park). After 37km (23 miles) of twisting through pine forests and limestone crags the tarmac ends at the village of Beşkonak, and a dirt road continues for another 5km (3 miles) to the Köprülü Kanyon Restoran. Here you can park your car and enjoy a lunch of fresh trout at a tree-shaded table overlooking the river, before exploring the canyon. A few hundred metres upstream from the restaurant the road crosses an old **Roman bridge** (*köprülü* means 'with a bridge'); on the far

A canal in the middle of Perge's main street once carried water from a fountain straight through the city centre, cooling the hot summer air.

that once adorned the portico of a church; the figures are of Tyche (goddess of fortune), Artemis, Apollo and Calchas (one of the mythical founders of Perge).

231

side, a footpath leads to the right along the far bank of the river. You can follow this path, scrambling over and around large rocks at times, for about 30 minutes. The scenery is impressive, with steep cliffs of conglomerate (also called 'pudding-stone', composed of rounded pebbles cemented together), and springs gushing from the foot of the crags, adding their clear water to the muddy, swirling torrent of the main river.

The dirt road continues uphill steeply for 13km (8 miles) to the village of Zerk and the remote ruins of ancient **Selge**; local children will offer to guide you around the site in exchange for a small tip.

Side

The most prosperous of the Pamphylian cities was Side, a harbour town built on an easily defended peninsula. Founded in the 7th century BC, it grew rich on the profits of the slave trade, and by the time the Romans took control it was one of the most important merchant cities in the eastern Mediterranean. It retained its prominence during the Byzantine era, when it became the seat of a bishop, but Arab raids and earthquakes caused a gradual decline, and the city was abandoned by the 12th century.

However, the late 20th century has seen Side flourish once again, this time as one of Turkey's most popular holiday resorts. Hotels, pensions, restaurants and shops have risen among the classical ruins of Roman Side, catering to the thousands of tourists who come to enjoy the magnificent beaches that stretch eastwards from the town. The place has become so popular that traffic has been banned from the town centre; if you are driving, you will have to leave your vehicle in one of the car parks at the edge of town and then explore on foot.

In Köprülü Canyon you can follow a trail along the side of the gorge, upstream from the old Roman bridge. Downstream is a trout restaurant, with a shady terrace above the river.

The road into Side follows the line of the ancient main street, with the stumps of a colonnaded portico visible on one side, and ruined houses with mosaic floors beyond. The most obvious relic of ancient Side is the huge bulk of the **theatre**, which rises on the left as the road dog-legs through a monumental Roman arch. Built during the 2nd century AD, it is unusual in that the *cavea* is not built into a hillside, but is supported on huge masonry vaults and arches, which still stand to a height of 14m (46ft). From the top row there is a fine view over the town – beyond the stage is the main **agora**, full of broken columns, with the circular foundations of a temple of Tyche; to the left across the road is Side's museum, housed in a restored 5th-century Byzantine bathhouse.

You enter the **museum** (open daily 8am to 7pm) at the far end, through what used to be the *apodyterium* (changing room). Straight ahead is the *frigidarium,* with a circular cold plunge pool in the far wall. Turning right, you pass through the small *sudatorium* (sweat room) into the large hall of the *caldarium;* the hot pools here are still lined with their original pink marble. The *caldarium* contains some fine sculptures recovered from the ruins, notably a muscular, bearded Hercules and a lovely rendering of the Three Graces (unfortunately incomplete). The neighbouring *tepidarium* houses a number of fine sarcophagi.

Beyond the Roman arch, the main street leads down through the touristic heart of modern Side, a crowded maze of carpet shops, kebab stalls and moneychangers. At the far end is the old harbour, protected by half-submerged antique breakwaters, half silted up and used only by small fishing boats. A stroll along the prom to the east leads to the **Temples of Apollo and Athena**. Little remains apart from the foundations, but archaeologists have managed to restore five columns and part of the architrave and pediment of the Temple of Apollo; the frieze is decorated with carved heads of the gorgon Medusa, smaller versions of the giant one that can be seen at Didyma (see p.180).

This ancient sculpture of the Three Graces can be seen in the museum at Side. A modern version, by Canova, was recently acquired by London's Victoria and Albert Museum.

THE THREE GRACES

In Greek mythology, the Three Graces were the daughters of Zeus and Eurynome. As described by Hesiod in his *Theogony*, '...Eurynome, daughter of Ocean, beautiful in form, bore him three fair-cheeked Graces: Aglaea, Euphrosyne, and lovely Thaleia, from whose eyes as they danced flowed love...' They were a favourite subject for ancient artists, and were usually portrayed with their arms around each others' shoulders, the one in the middle facing in the opposite direction to the other two. The three sisters were held to personify the qualities of beauty, friendship and gentleness.

The Cilician Coast

East of Side the scenery becomes wilder as the Taurus Mountains sweep down to the coast. You are now entering the ancient region of Cilicia; its rugged western part, from Alanya to Mersin, was known as *Cilicia Tracheia* (Rough Cilicia), while the fertile flatlands around Adana were called *Cilicia Campestris* (Smooth Cilicia). Rough Cilicia, a harsh mountain country with difficult roads and few towns, a remote and little-visited area with some impressive scenery; the new coastal highway has improved access, but it still takes almost a full day to drive the narrow and twisting 265km (165 miles) from Alanya to Silifke.

Alanya

New hotels and holiday villages line the long, sandy beaches that stretch between Side and Alanya. As the hills press closer to the sea, the striking, Gibraltar-like silhouette of Alanya's castle crag looms ahead. This prominent and easily defended peninsula must have been inhabited since men first sailed this coast, but

The summit of Alanya's impressive castle rock is defended by Seljuk fortifications. Within the walls are a small village, a mosque, and a caravanserai-hotel.

little is known of its early history. In the centuries before Christ it was occupied by the city of Korakesion. This was notorious as a pirates' den until 67 BC, when the Romans challenged the freebooters and destroyed their fleet in a sea battle off Alanya. The Byzantines called the city *Kalonoros* (Beautiful Mountain), and held it until the Seljuk Turks overran eastern Anatolia in the 11th and 12th centuries. Kalonoros fell to the Seljuk Sultan Alaeddin Keykubad I around 1221; today nothing remains of the ancient city except some fragments of the Hellenistic wall beneath the Seljuk fortifications.

The Seljuks built a massive citadel and defensive walls on top of the promontory, and renamed their new possession Alaiye. Under Keykubad and his successors the city prospered as a timber-trading port and cultural centre until it was taken over by the Ottomans in 1471.

Modern **Alanya** is busy international resort, sandwiched between two long stretches of glorious golden sand. The seafront is lined with expensive hotels and restaurants, and the bars and nightclubs stay open into the small hours. But you can escape from the hustle and bustle by taking a boat trip to the sea caves that pock the cliffs around the peninsula, or by climbing up to the Seljuk fortress at the top.

Kale (Castle)

A narrow road winds up the steep hill, passing an arched gate in the fortifications, to reach the **İç Kale** (Inner Castle) at the summit. The ramparts of Sultan Keykubad's fortress are in good condition (they were restored in 1951), and command magnificent views along the coast. Inside are several large cisterns, the Seljuk barracks, and the ruins of a Byzantine church with traces of frescoes inside. On the west

side there is a brick platform poised above a giddy drop; known as *adam atacağı*, 'the man-thrower', this is where condemned prisoners were hurled to their deaths.

Harbour

At the foot of the castle hill, beside the modern harbour, is the **Kızıl Kule** (Red Tower), an octagonal red-brick redoubt which once guarded the Seljuk port. It was designed by a Syrian architect in 1227, and has special apertures in the parapet from which defenders could drop boiling oil or missiles onto their attackers (note the many antique columns from Kalonoros incorporated into the walls). There is a small museum on the ground floor.

From the tower you can walk along the ramparts of the sea wall to the **Tersane**, a Seljuk shipyard; descend from the parapet at the second tower, and follow a path inside the wall to a hole at the far end, where you can clamber through to the shore. The room to the left of the entrance was a tiny mosque, the one on the right a storeroom or office. The five vaulted chambers beyond were used for building and repairing the ships of the Seljuk fleet.

Anamur

Beyond Alanya you leave the trappings of package tourism behind and head into wilder country. The road passes through terraced hillsides planted with bananas, twisting high above the sea then dropping steeply to small river-mouth villages, before climbing again across the rocky, pine-clad flanks of the Taurus. About 30km (18 miles) from Alanya you pass through the tumbledown ruins of **Iotape**, a small Roman settlement set around an attractive inlet. But apart from a swim or a picnic, there is little reason to stop until you reach Anamur. The town itself is of no interest,

The Seljuk harbour at Alanya was defended by the imposing bastion of Kızıl Kule – the Red Tower.

but near by are the Roman and Byzantine ruins of Anemourion, and the magnificent medieval castle of Mamure Kalesi.

Anemourion

Where the highway sweeps down to the broad flood-plain of Anamur, a road on the right at the foot of the hill leads to a car park, restaurant and beach beside the extensive ruins of **Anemourion**. This modest trading town, which occupies the most southerly point of Anatolia, flourished between the 1st and 3rd centuries AD. Beyond the car park, to the left of the road, you can clamber through the remains of a **baths** to the *palaestra,* which has mosaic floors hidden beneath a protective layer of sand. On the right you can make out the *cavea* of the **theatre**, though all the seating has long since gone; further on, across the road, is the much better preserved **bouleterion**, with 14 rows of seats (there are traces of mosaic floor in the vaulted passage beneath the seats). Where the road bends left is another **baths**, still roofed over, with some intact pools and traces of fresco and mosaic. The hillside above the road is littered with the vaulted tombs of the **necropolis**. A few have frescoes and are protected by locked gates – the site guardian will open these for you if you ask. It is a long, hot climb to the **acropolis**, but on a clear day you can see the mountains of Cyprus 80km (50 miles) away across the sea.

Mamure Kalesi

At the far side of the Anamur Plain, between the road and the sea, rise the crenellated ramparts of **Mamure Kalesi** (Castle of Anamur). This huge, fairytale castle, with its 36 towers of all shapes and sizes – square, round, half-round, octagonal and dodecagonal – was built by the Seljuk Sultan Keykubad I in the 13th century on the site of an earlier fortress. The entrance is at the far (eastern) end, across a turtle-filled moat; its dog-leg design made it easier to defend. You can climb to the top of

THE EXILED PRINCE

Mamure Kalesi was the last hiding place of Cem Sultan before his long exile from the Ottoman Empire. Prince Cem was one of the most tragic figures in Ottoman history, a poet, a man of culture and the favourite son of Mehmet the Conqueror. After the sultan's death he lost the battle for succession to his brother Beyazıt II, but escaped death at the hands of his brother's men and persisted with his claim to the throne. He held out for a month at Mamure Kalesi before setting sail for Rhodes, to seek the support of the Knights of St John in an attempt to oust Beyazıt from Istanbul. But the Knights intrigued with Beyazıt and sent Cem to France, where he was kept in captivity until his death in 1495, supposedly poisoned at the request of his brother.

Cem's body was returned to Bursa for burial (in the Muradiye Complex, see p.142), an event colourfully recorded by the Ottoman writer Evliya Çelebi:

> The corpse of Cem, together with his property, amongst which was an enchanted cup...a white parrot, a chess-playing monkey, and some thousands of splendid books, were delivered up...Beyazıt ordered the remains of Cem to be buried at Bursa, beside his grandfather Murat III. While they were digging the grave there was such a thunderclap and tumult in the sepulchral chapel, that all who were present fled...not a soul of them was able to pass its threshold till ten days had passed when, this being represented to the Sultan, the corpse of Cem was buried by his order in his own mausoleum, near to that of his grandfather.

Beyazıt must have been suitably impressed by this display of fraternal displeasure from beyond the grave, because Cem's mausoleum is the most elaborately decorated in the Muradiye.

---

the octagonal tower in the southeast corner (it has a cistern in the middle, like Alanya's Kızıl Kule), for a good view of the fortifications. The keep, in the southwest corner overlooking the sea, is in ruinous condition, but you can follow the ramparts round most of the way.

Silifke

The dull and dusty town of **Silifke** marks the eastern limit of Rough Cilicia. Here the high mountains fall back from the sea and

The fairytale towers of Mamure Kalesi, near Anamur, were built in the 13th century. Today, the romantic castle is frequently used as a location for shooting historical films.

THE DEATH OF BARBAROSSA

Silifke lies at the junction of the coastal road with the ancient route north through the Taurus mountains to Konya. In the summer of 1190 the Emperor Frederick I (Barbarossa), then aged 67, led the armies of the Third Crusade south along this route on their way to the Holy Land. On 10 June the great host arrived on the plain of Seleucia, and the emperor rode forward to cross the river and enter the city. But he never made it – either he was thrown by his horse, or he deliberately jumped into the river to escape the heat and was swept away by the current. Whatever happened, he was pulled under by the weight of his armour and drowned. Barbarossa's death dealt an enormous blow to the morale of the crusaders. The old emperor's body was pickled in vinegar and taken to Antioch (Antakya), where it was buried in the cathedral. A plaque beside the modern road about 7km (4 miles) north of Silifke marks the spot where he perished.

the coastal plain widens. There is not much to see in town, aside from the **Byzantine castle** and the single standing column of the **Temple of Zeus**. The temple is a remnant of Seleucia ad Calycadnus, founded in the 3rd century BC by Seleucus I Nicator, one of Alexander the Great's generals. Some bronze figurines from the temple are displayed in Silifke's **museum**, but the main attraction here is the Gülnar hoard, a stash of over 5,000 silver coins dating from the 3rd and 4th centuries BC.

Ayatekla

A few kilometres south of Silifke, a side road leads to the **Grotto of St Thecla** (*Ayatekla* in Turkish). St Thecla was a native of Iconium (Konya), and was converted to Christianity by St Paul. To escape persecution she fled to Seleucia where she lived in this grotto, praying, meditating and spreading the new faith. The site is marked by the remains of the apse of a 5th-century basilica built in the saint's honour. The guardian will unlock

the gate and show you around the grotto, which lies beneath the basilica. It contains a nave and apse with Doric columns, a confessional, a martyrium, and a baptistery with a mosaic of four fish in the shape of a cross.

Uzuncaburç (Olba/Diocaesarea)

From the centre of Silifke yellow signs point the way to **Uzuncaburç**, 28km (17 miles) distant. This village, tucked away in the hills, is the site of ancient Olba (re-named Diocaesarea by the Romans), a cult centre for the worship of Zeus founded by Seleucus in the 3rd century BC. The road winds up into a limestone gorge stubbled with scrub and dwarf pines, emerging into a scenic upper valley with fields of dark red earth bordered by piles of white stones, and black goats foraging along the dry stream beds. Near the village of Demircili there are several ornate Roman tombs.

The approach to Olba/Diocaesarea is marked by the tall Hellenistic watchtower that gives the modern village its name (*uzuncaburç* means 'tall tower'). When you arrive, one of the men from the local tea house will wander over to sell you a ticket and offer a guided tour. The village houses and fields straggle picturesquely among the ruins – straight ahead from the parking area a colonnaded street leads to the main attraction, the **Temple of Zeus Olbios**. Built in the 3rd century BC, and later converted to a church (you can see the remains of an apse at the east end), it stands amid a patchwork of vegetable gardens, with 30 of its columns still standing; it is the oldest known example of a Corinthian temple in Asia Minor. The tops of the columns are cracked and damaged on the inside, suggesting that the building was destroyed by fire. Other remains include a temple of Tyche, a monumental gate and a ruinous theatre.

*T*he villagers of Uzuncaburç have planted vegetable gardens among the ruins of Olba/Diocaesarea. The Temple of Zeus Olbios, with most of its columns impressively intact, is the earliest example of Corinthian architecture in Turkey.

Caves of Heaven and Hell
(Cennet ve Cehennem)

The Corycian Caves, known in Turkish as *Cennet ve Cehennem* ('heaven and hell'), were thought by the ancient Greeks to be one of the entrances to the Underworld, and the home of the monster Typhon. The caves are really huge pits in the limestone bedrock, caused by cavern collapses. They are a popular weekend picnic spot for the citizens of nearby Mersin and Adana, who are catered for by a large car park, a restaurant and souvenir shops.

The **Cave of Heaven** (*Cennet*) is a vast crater, 200m (656ft) long, 90m (295ft) wide and 70m (230ft) deep, with vertical sides; a long flight of concrete stairs leads down to the sunny, tree-covered floor. At the south end a path heads down a slope to a 5th-century Byzantine chapel dedicated to the Virgin Mary (unfortunately its frescoes have been almost obliterated by vandals), and the gaping entrance to the Underworld. You can follow the slippery earthen floor down into the dank depths of the huge cavern (flashlight necessary)

until the roof dips down to meet the floor (about 135m, or 443ft, beneath ground level). Here, if you stop and listen, you can hear Typhon's roar – the muffled thunder of an invisible underground torrent.

The **Cave of Hell** (*Cehennem*) lies a short distance beyond the car park. It is a circular pit about 50m (164ft) across and 120m (394ft) deep, with overhanging sides, accessible only to experienced cavers with special abseiling equipment. The bushes all around the caves are covered with strips of cloth tied by locals as talismans to ward off evil spirits.

A HELLISH BROOD

Typhon was the offspring of Gaea (the Earth) and Tartarus (the Underworld), a hideous monster with a hundred dragon heads and coiled serpents instead of legs. He was sent against Zeus in revenge for his destruction of the giants, but Zeus defeated the monster and cast him back into the Underworld, confined beneath Mount Etna (where his raging caused eruptions), or in the Corycian Caves of Cilicia (where his roars can still be heard). He fathered several other monsters, including the Hydra, Cerberus (the three-headed hound that guarded the entrance to hell), and the Chimera (see p.221), and summoned up dangerous winds and volcanic eruptions.

The seaside town of Kızkalesi has a good sandy beach, with a picture-postcard castle stranded offshore.

A tiny Byzantine church guards the entrance to the Cave of Heaven, a gateway to the Underworld (opposite).

On the coast below the caves is the village of **Narlıkuyu**, with several seafood restaurants. There is also a ruined Roman bath, with a fine mosaic depicting the Three Graces (see box p.234).

Kızkalesi

The town of **Kızkalesi** is the biggest and best beach resort on the Cilician coast, very popular with Turks from Adana and Americans from the nearby USAF base at

243

MAIDENS AND CASTLES

The name *Kızkalesi* (Maiden's Castle) derives from an old folk legend, which tells the tale of a king and his beautiful daughter, whom he loved tenderly. But a soothsayer predicted that the princess would die of a snake bite. Horrified, the king sent her to a castle on an island without snakes, hoping thus to prevent the prophecy from coming true. All was well until one fateful day when the king sent a basket of rare fruits as a treat for his beloved daughter. Unknown to him, a viper was hidden among the fruit; it struck at the maiden, and she died. The story, which reflects a traditional Muslim belief that you cannot cheat fate, is very popular in Turkey, and has become attached to a number of isolated castles and towers, such as the Kızkalesi at Sarıseki north of İskenderun, and Kızkule in Istanbul.

İncirlik. It takes its name, which means 'maiden's castle', from the picturesque medieval castle that sits on a low rocky island off the fine sandy beach. There is a second castle on the mainland at the north end of the beach, and this was once connected to the island by a causeway.

LITTLE ARMENIA

Following the Seljuk invasion of the 11th century many Armenians were forced from their homeland in northeastern Anatolia and moved to Cilicia, where they founded the kingdom of 'Little Armenia'. Its capital was at Tarsus, where King Leo II was crowned in 1199 (the capital was later moved to Sis, now called Kozan, northeast of Adana). As Christians, the Armenians allied themselves with the crusaders, and established many trading and cultural links with the west. The kingdom finally lost its independence when Sis fell to the Muslim Mamelukes in 1375.

Both fortresses were built during the 12th century by the rulers of the medieval kingdom of Little Armenia (see box); the walls of the land castle contain reused masonry from the Roman city of Corycus, whose overgrown ruins lie near by. You can take a boat trip out to the island and explore the castle. There is an inscription in Armenian above the gate recording the date of construction as 1151; inside there are water-storage cisterns cut into the rock and the remains of a small church.

Kanlıdivane (Kanytelis)

Three kilometres (2 miles) beyond Kızkalesi a side road leads up to the ruins of ancient **Kanytelis**, which was built around a huge limestone sinkhole similar to, but smaller than the Cave of Heaven. The site was originally sacred to Zeus, and obviously retained its religious significance in later times, judging by the number of Christian churches that were built around it (at least four). A fine Hellenistic watchtower stands on the near side of the pit; on the cliff face below it is an interesting relief showing six robed figures who may have been priests of Zeus.

The unusual Turkish name for Kanytelis (*Kanlıdivane*, which means 'place of blood and madness'), derives from the belief that wrongdoers were hurled into the pit to be torn apart by wild animals.

Adana

Beyond the port city of Mersin (ferries to northern Cyprus), the highway leaves the coast and follows the junction between the low hills to the north and vast flood-plain of the Seyhan and Ceyhan rivers. This is one of the most densely populated corners of Turkey, and a principal centre of the country's textile industry. Cotton is grown in huge quantities on the fertile alluvial soil of the river delta, and processed in the factories that sprawl along the highway between Tarsus and Adana. The marshes at the seaward edge of the plain provide a paradise for birdwatchers.

Adana, with a population of over 1.2 million, is Turkey's fourth-largest city and is still growing rapidly. The site, on the banks of the Seyhan River, has been occupied since Hittite times, and its strategic location on the main land route between Syria and Anatolia made sure that it remained an important city throughout the Roman, Byzantine and Ottoman periods. Very little has survived of ancient Adana; its most impressive monument is the **Taş Köprü** (Stone Bridge), built by the Romans and maintained by the Arabs and Ottomans. Other reminders of the past have been gathered in the city's Archaeological Museum.

Tarsus

Forty kilometres (24 miles) west of Adana lies the city of **Tarsus**, commanding the southern end of the ancient route through the mountains known as the Cilician Gates. In Roman and Byzantine times it was an important centre of trade and agriculture, known for its school of Greek philosophy. Today it is a drab, modern industrial town, unremarkable save for two historical associations – it was here, in 41 BC, that Mark Antony first met with Cleopatra (see box on p.246); and it was here, about 50 years later, that the Apostle Paul was born (see box). But there is almost nothing to see of ancient Tarsus, only a Roman gateway known as **Kancık Kapısı** (Gate of the Bitch, also called the Gate of Cleopatra); and **St Paul's Well**, a Roman well which has no authenticated connection with the saint.

THE APOSTLE PAUL

Paul was born in the cosmopolitan trading city of Tarsus around AD 10. He was a Jew (hence his Jewish name, Saul of Tarsus) and a Roman citizen, and spoke fluent Greek as well as Hebrew. Trained as a rabbi, he was at first severely critical of the Christian movement, but after his famous conversion on the road to Damascus he became one of the most energetic missionaries for the new faith. He made three long journeys through Asia Minor and Greece, preaching the gospel and establishing new churches across the eastern Roman Empire. His great achievement was to promote the acceptance of Gentiles (non-Jews) into the early Christian church, thus ensuring that Christianity developed into a world religion, rather than a sect of Judaism.

He was eventually arrested in Jerusalem for allegedly bringing a Gentile into the forbidden inner court of the Temple. When brought before the Roman commandant, he showed some pride in his home town, declaring 'I am a Jew, from Tarsus in Cilicia, a citizen of no mean city'. He was imprisoned in Rome in AD 60, where he wrote his famous letters to the Philippians, Colossians, and Ephesians before being sentenced to death.

Karatepe

East of Adana the highway scythes through the rolling wheat fields of the Cilician Plain, passing the impressive castles of Yılanlı Kale and Toprakkale. At Osmaniye, take the road north towards Kadirli, turn right after 8km (5 miles) on a badly potholed road, and then left on a dirt road for 9km (5½ miles) to reach the Karatepe–Aslantaş National Park. Situated on a pleasant wooded hill above the green waters of the Aslantaş Dam, **Karatepe** was the site of the summer palace of the Hittite ruler Asitiwada. The excavated ruins form an open-air museum, with the monumental sculptures

---

ANTONY AND CLEOPATRA

Mark Antony (81-30 BC) was, with Octavian and Lepidus, a member of the Second Triumvirate, the coalition that attempted to rule the Roman Empire in the troubled times that followed the murder of Julius Caesar. Antony took up the administration of the eastern provinces, and summoned Cleopatra, queen of Egypt, to face allegations that she had assisted his enemies. The meeting took place at Tarsus; the scene, as Cleopatra sailed up the river to the city, was described by Plutarch, whose words inspired Shakespeare's famous rendering in *Antony and Cleopatra*:

> The barge she sat in, like a burnished throne
> Sat on the water. The poop was beaten gold;
> Purple the sails, and so perfumèd that
> The winds were love-sick with them. The oars were silver,
> Which to the tune of flutes kept stroke, and made
> The water which they beat to follow faster,
> As amorous of their strokes. For her own person,
> It beggared all description. She did lie
> In her pavilion – cloth of gold, of tissue –
> O'er-picturing that Venus where we see
> The fancy outwork nature.

Antony was bewitched by the Egyptian queen, and became her lover and, some say, dupe; Shakespeare put these words in the mouth of Antony's friend Demetrius:

> Take but good note, and you shall see in him
> The triple pillar of the world transformed
> Into a strumpet's fool.

Antony and Cleopatra entered into an alliance in the civil war that finally destroyed both themselves and the Roman Republic. Defeated by Octavian and driven back to Egypt, the doomed couple eventually committed suicide.

---

and reliefs displayed *in situ*. Many reliefs show scenes of palace life, with the feasting king surrounded by attendants, musicians, pet monkeys and dancing bears. Take along a picnic and enjoy lunch under the shady pines overlooking the lake.

Hatay

The grim, brown ramparts of Toprakkale overlook the junction between the Adana–Gaziantep highway and the road south to Antakya. This corner of Turkey, squeezed between the Gulf of Alexandretta (*İskenderun Körfezi*) and the Syrian border, is called **Hatay**, and is noticeably more Arabic in nature that the lands to the west. Hatay, along with Syria, came under French administration following the post-World War I break-up of the Ottoman Empire, but was returned to Turkey in 1939.

The road follows the narrow coastal plain that formed the ancient trade route between Syria and Anatolia. The route was also used by invading armies, and it was here, in 333 BC, that the forces of Alexander the Great won a famous victory against the Persian army of King Darius. The **Battle of Issus** took place somewhere to the south of the modern town of Dörtyol; the exact site is not known. Though Alexander's army was outnumbered (100,000 to 35,000), the Persians were routed. Darius fled in panic, hotly pursued by Alexander, who gave up the chase only when darkness fell. He captured the king's chariot and arms, and the richly furnished royal tent where the queen and her children cowered. Alexander commanded his men to treat the royal prisoners with respect, then removed his armour saying, 'Now, let us cleanse ourselves from the toils of war in the baths of Darius'.

To commemorate his victory Alexander built altars to Zeus, Athena and Hercules, and commanded that a new city, Alexandria ad Issum, be founded near by. That city grew to become Alexandretta, now called **İskenderun** (*İskender* is Turkish for Alexander). İskenderun is an important trading port and industrial centre, but little remains of its history. It has a number of good hotels and restaurants, and an attractive waterfront boulevard. South of İskenderun the road climbs into the mountains across the pass known as the Syrian Gates, before dropping to the fertile Amik Plain and Antakya, the provincial capital of Hatay.

Antakya

Antakya, the ancient Antioch, was once one of the greatest cities in the Hellenistic world, rivalling Rome and Alexandria in splendour and sophistication. In 64 BC it was made capital of the Roman province of Syria, and was described by the historian Ammianus Marcellinus as 'the fair

crown of the Orient'. Antioch played an important role in the early days of Christianity, serving as a headquarters for the missionary journeys of St Paul (see p.72 and box p.245); St Peter lived here, too, between AD 47 and 54. The prosperous Byzantine city was a ripe target for invading Persians and Arabs, and changed hands several times. In 1098 it was taken by the crusaders who founded the Principality of Antioch, a European outpost that lasted for nearly two centuries before falling to the Mamelukes of Egypt; it became part of the Ottoman Empire in 1517. The modern city's prosperity is based on the rich farmland of the Amik Plain to the north; the wheat, cotton, olives, grapes and rice grown there are processed in Antakya's factories and sold in its markets.

Archaeological Museum

The glory that was ancient Antioch has sadly disappeared, a victim of earthquakes, fires and sackings, but a fragment of the past survives in the magnificent **mosaics** on display in the city's Archaeological Museum (*Arkeoloji Müzesi*) (open 8am to noon and 1.30 to 5.30pm, closed Monday morning). Most of the mosaics were found in Antakya and Daphne, and date from late Roman and Byzantine times. They once decorated the floors of villas belonging to wealthy citizens, and depict mythological scenes, hunting scenes, and tableaux of wild animals, birds and fish. A list of highlights follows: Room I: **The Four Seasons**, a large floor mosaic with nine panels, including winged figures representing Spring, Summer, Autumn and Winter; an octagonal panel from the floor of a bath portraying Soteria (ΣΩΤΗΡIA), or Salvation. Room II: **The Buffet Mosaic**, with a circular medallion showing the Rape of

Ganymede, surrounded by trays of food and loaves of bread. Room III: the sea gods **Oceanus and Thetis**, surrounded by cherubs fishing or riding dolphins; an overweight infant **Hercules** strangling two serpents. Room IV: the **Drunken Dionysus**, depicting the god of wine supported by a young satyr, with a sacred panther lapping the wine that spills from his cup; **Orpheus** with his lyre, charming an audience of wild beasts, including an eagle, a lion, a tiger, a leopard, a boar and an antelope. The museum's collection of sculpture includes Hittite lions, some fine Roman bronzes of Mars, Venus and Helios, and several statues of Venus. In the garden there is a lovely mosaic of **Eros and Psyche** – Eros is asleep beneath a tree, while Psyche creeps up and tries to steal his bow and quiver.

St Peter's Church

The Apostle Peter came to Antioch sometime after the death of Christ, and with Paul and Barnabas founded one of the world's first Christian communities. The early Christians were severely persecuted, however, and worshipped in secret. This simple **church** was built into a grotto on the hillside above the city, and may well be the oldest Christian church in the world. The façade was added by the crusaders during the 12th century, but the mosaic floor inside is much older, perhaps 4th or 5th century. At the back is an altar and a small figure of the saint; to the left is a tunnel in the rock which allowed the congregation to escape if the church was raided. Mass is celebrated in the church on 29 June, the feast day of St Peter.

The stone façade of Antakya's Church of St Peter was built by the Crusaders. It encloses a grotto used for worship by the earliest Christians.

Daphne (Harbiye)

The picturesque village of **Harbiye** lies about 10km (6 miles) south of Antakya, set above a cool, shady valley full of orchards, cypresses and groves of laurel. Springs and waterfalls cascade down the sun-dappled hillsides between tea gardens and restaurants, a favourite weekend retreat from the summer heat of the city. In ancient times this valley was called Daphne, after the nymph who captivated Apollo. It was a sacred suburb of Antioch, with sanctuaries dedicated to Zeus, Apollo, Artemis, Aphrodite and other gods. The lush surroundings attracted wealthy citizens, who built their summer villas here (many of the mosaics in Antakya's museum came from Daphne). No trace remains of Daphne's past, but the sylvan

---

A PILLAR OF THE CHURCH

Atop a mountain peak to the left of the road from Antakya to Seleucia are the ruins of a monastery dedicated to St Simeon Stylites the Younger (521-92). Inspired by the exploits of his elder namesake, Simeon spent most of his life sitting atop a tall pillar, fasting, praying and delivering sermons to the pilgrims who came to see him.

The ascetic practice of column-sitting was begun by St Simeon Stylites the Elder (*c.* 390-459), who retreated to the top of a 15m (49ft) column to escape the clamour of crowds seeking demonstrations of his miraculous powers. He spent the rest of his life on top of the pillar (which was about 50km, or 30 miles east of Antioch, on the road to Aleppo), exposed to sun and rain, prevented from falling by a small railing and supplied with gifts of food by his followers. Eventually his column became a site of pilgrimage, and has inspired imitators ever since; even today there are dedicated column-sitters, though some are more concerned with getting into the *Guinness Book of Records* than Paradise.

APOLLO AND DAPHNE

Daphne was a mountain nymph, a priestess of Mother Earth and daughter of the river god Peneus. Apollo had mocked Eros, who took revenge by piercing him with one of his arrows. The love-struck god was captivated by Daphne and pursued her relentlessly, but the arrow that had pierced *her* heart had been tipped with lead, so that she could love neither god nor mortal. When Apollo finally caught her, Daphne cried out to Mother Earth for help, and she was turned into a laurel tree. To console himself, Apollo decorated his lyre with leaves from the laurel, and decreed that prize-winning musicians should be crowned with a wreath of laurel.

---

atmosphere can be enjoyed just as much today as it was in Roman times.

Seleucia ad Pieria

Antioch was founded around 300 BC by Seleucus I Nicator, one of the generals who inherited the empire of Alexander the Great. He named the city after his father, Antiochus; **Seleucia**, named after himself, was the port of Antioch, 32km (20 miles) to the southwest. This was the harbour where St Paul and St Barnabus embarked on their first missionary journey, but it is difficult to picture the site as it was then, as the port is silted up and few ruins remain. But there is one spectacular work of Roman civil engineering that must be seen. The **tunnel of Titus and Vespasian** was cut during the 1st and 2nd centuries to divert the flood waters of the local stream away from the city. Hacked laboriously through the solid rock, the channel runs for 1,400m (1,530yd); an inscription at the far end records its dedication to the emperors Titus (AD 79-81) and Vespasian (AD 69-79). Near by is **Beşikli Cave**, which contains many rock-cut tombs.

Exploring the Legendary Landscapes of Anatolia's Historic Heartland

Across the plains of central Turkey lie scattered the former capitals of once-mighty empires: Hattuşaş of the Hittites; the Phrygian city of Gordion; Amasya, the seat of the Pontic kings; and Konya, the centre of the Sultanate of Rum. Their days of glory may have passed, but the achievements of their artists and architects live on. Many of their greatest treasures have been gathered together in Turkey's top museum, in Ankara – the modern capital of the Turkish Republic.

Ankara

On 13 October 1923 Atatürk's Grand National Assembly passed a bill that proclaimed 'The seat of the Turkish State is the town of Ankara'. With these few words Istanbul, for 1,500 years the imperial capital of the Romans, Byzantines and Ottomans, lost its prime administrative role, and a little-known town in the middle of the central Anatolian steppe became the capital of the new Turkish Republic.

Central Anatolia's varied landscapes include the volcanic wonderland of Cappadocia, with its fluted, coloured cliffs, 'fairy chimneys' and underground cities.

The site of Ankara has been inhabited since prehistoric times. The Hittites founded a city called Ankuwash here, which was succeeded by a thriving Phrygian settlement around 1000 BC. Following the Persian invasion, the city, by then called Ancyra, took advantage of its position on the Royal Road between Susa and Sardis. Alexander the Great conquered it in 334 BC after dealing with the Gordian Knot (see box on p.263), and in 25 BC it became part of the Roman Empire.

Ancyra sat astride the crossroads of several overland trade routes, and soon grew into a prosperous city of 200,000 people; under Nero it was made capital of the province of Galatia. But during Byzantine times the city was turned into a fortress as waves of invaders swept across the Anatolian plains. Persians, Arabs,

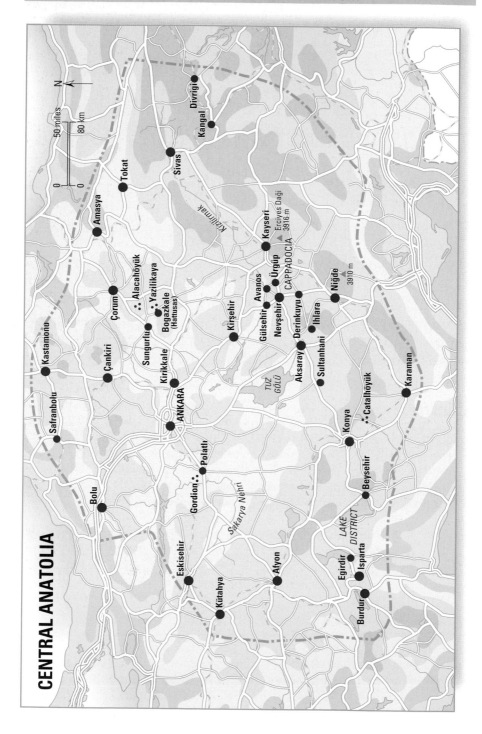

CENTRAL ANATOLIA

Seljuk Turks and crusaders all battled for control of Ancyra, until finally it fell into Ottoman hands in 1360.

When Kemal Atatürk established the headquarters of his nationalist movement in Ankara in December 1919, the town was little more than a primitive backwater

When Ankara became capital of Turkey in 1923, it was a small town clustered around the citadel. The population has now passed 3 million, and the suburbs sprawl for kilometres.

with neither sewers nor street lighting. Lord Kinross (Atatürk's biographer) described it thus:

Angora at this time was little more than a pair of twin hills, rising like nipples from the bosom of the Anatolian plateau. Crowning one of them were the half-ruined walls of a citadel which had seen and survived notable Turkish conflicts. Clambering up to it and around it and within it was a human warren of mud-brick houses and ruins of houses, huddled lattice to lattice and roof above roof amid dunghills and winding precipitous lanes. Rough with stones and, at this season when rain was frequent, awash with mud, they provided a hard climb for the horses and the ramshackle carriages which, apart from the long peasant bullock-carts with their spoke-

less wailing wheels, were Angora's only means of transport.

With its harsh, snowy winters and baking, dusty summers, Ankara was an unlikely choice for the nation's capital. But since 1923 the city has grown explosively, from around 20,000 to today's population of over 3 million. It is a planned city of broad boulevards, parks and pedestrian malls, but growth has outstripped infrastructure and residents complain of living in a building site as city councillors struggle to keep the traffic flowing. A new metro system is under construction, causing chaos in the city centre. Nevertheless, the old city is a fascinating place to explore, and Ankara can boast at least two 'must-see' attractions – the superb Museum of Anatolian Civilizations and the Atatürk Mausoleum.

The Old Town

The old town of Ankara lies beneath the twin hills of the ancient citadel, centred on the huge traffic intersection of Ulus Meydanı. A giant statue of Atatürk on horseback gazes across the square to two modest buildings that witnessed the birth of the Turkish Republic. **The War of Independence Museum** (*Kurtuluş Savşı Müzesi*) and the **Republic Museum** (*Cumhuriyet Müzesi*) housed Atatürk's Grand National Assembly during the early years of the Republic. Photographs and

One of the few places where you can experience the atmosphere of old Ankara is in the maze of narrow streets within the fortress walls. But even here the 20th century encroaches, as old houses are restored as restaurants.

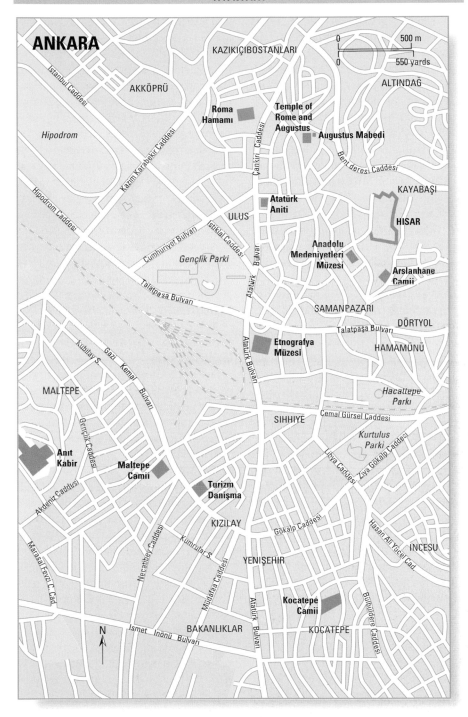

ANKARA

KAZIKIÇIBOSTANLARI

0   500 m
0   550 yards

ALTINDAĞ

AKKÖPRÜ

İstanbul Caddesi

Hipodrom

Kazım Karabekir Caddesi

Roma
Hamamı

Temple of
Rome and
Augustus

Çankırı Caddesi

Augustus Mabedi

Bent deresi Caddesi

KAYABAŞI

Hipodrom Caddesi

ULUS

İstiklal Caddesi

Cumhuriyet Bulvarı

Gençlik Parki

Atatürk
Aniti

HISAR

Anadolu
Medeniyetleri
Müzesi

Arslanhane
Camii

Atatürk Bulvarı

Talatpaşa Bulvarı

SAMANPAZARI

DÖRTYOL

Talatpaşa Bulvarı

Atatürk Bulvarı

Etnografya
Müzesi

HAMAMÜNÜ

Kübilay S.

Gazi   Kemal   Bulvarı

MALTEPE

Hacattepe
Parki

SIHHIYE

Cemal Gürsel Caddesi

Gençlik Caddesi

Kurtulus
Parki

Libya Caddesi

Ziya Gökalp Caddesi

Anıt
Kabir

Maltepe
Camii

Akdeniz Caddesi

Turizm
Danişma

Mareşal Fevzi C. Cad.

KIZILAY

Gökalp Caddesi

Hasan Ali Yücel Cad.

INCESU

Kumrular S.

Necatibey Caddesi

YENIŞEHIR

Müdafaa Caddesi

Atatürk Bulvarı

Kocatepe
Camii

Bülbüldere Caddesi

N

İsmet İnönü Bulvarı

BAKANLIKLAR

KOCATEPE

255

documents (captions in Turkish only) record the battle for Independence and the early history of the Assembly.

Urban sprawl has obliterated almost all signs of Roman Ancyra, but a few monuments remain. North from Ulus, along Çankırı Caddesi, are the **Roman baths** (*Roma Hamamı*). Dating from the reign of Caracalla (AD 212-17), only the foundations survive, with the circular clay bricks that supported the *hypocaust* (underfloor heating space). Cross the road from the baths and turn right along Çiçek Sokağı, then right again at the far end. In a square on the right you will see the **Column of Julian** (*Julianus Sütunu*) with a stork's nest on top; it was erected in AD 362 to commemorate a visit from the emperor.

To the left, broad steps lead up to a new pedestrian plaza. On the far side, next to the 15th-century Mosque of Hacı Bayram is the **Temple of Rome and Augustus** (*Augustus Mabedi*), one of Turkey's most important Roman relics. The temple was probably built around 25 BC on the site of an older shrine, and dedicated to the emperor and to the goddess Roma (the divine personification of the empire). Only the walls of the *cella* still stand, but they bear an inscription of great historical importance – the world's most complete surviving copy of the *Res Gestae Divi Augusti*, the political testament of Augustus, written by the emperor himself. The 3,000-word Latin inscription begins, 'RERUM GESTARUM DIVI AUGUSTI, QUIBIS ORBEM TERRARUM IMPERIO POPULI ROMANI SUBIECIT...' 'The achievements of the divine Augustus by which he brought the world under the rule of the Roman people...'

The oldest part of Ankara is the **Citadel** (*Hisar*), which rises above the bazaar district to the east of Ulus Meydanı. A taxi will take you up the hill, or you can walk up via Hisarparkı Caddesi or narrow Konya Caddesi. The Byzantine fortifications enclose a maze of narrow, twisting alleys, the remains of the 'warren of mudbrick houses' described by Lord Kinross. Much renovation has taken place recently, and many of the houses have been restored as pensions and restaurants. The more expensive restaurants have terraces perched atop the ramparts, offering a fine view across the city. It is possible to climb to the highest point of the ancient walls for a panoramic view over Ankara.

A good plan is to explore the old town and citadel in the morning, have lunch in one of the restaurants on the citadel walls, and then escape the afternoon heat in the Museum of Anatolian Civilizations.

Museum of Anatolian Civilizations

A restored 15th-century *bedesten* (covered bazaar) below the south gate of the citadel houses Ankara's famous **Museum of Anatolian Civilizations** (*Anadolu Medeniyetleri Müzesi*), one of the best museums in Turkey (open 8.30am to 5pm, closed Monday). The collection contains the best finds from pre-classical sites all over Anatolia, and is arranged in chronological order around the perimeter of the building. A display of Hittite sculpture stands in the central hall.

The highlights of the collection include: palaeolithic tools from Karain Cave, near Antalya (see p.229); a reconstruction of a neolithic house from Çatalhöyük (6th millennium BC), with wall paintings of bulls, deer, leopards and hunters, and a view of a town with a twin-peaked volcano erupting in the background, perhaps the world's oldest landscape painting; bronze ceremonial standards, figurines of bulls and

stags, and stunning gold jewellery from the Hatti tombs of Alacahöyük (3rd millennium BC); Assyrian pottery, idols and cuneiform tablets from Kültepe (18th and 19th centuries BC); a pair of striking red-clay bulls from the Hittite capital of Hattuşaş (16th century BC); Neo-Hittite monumental sculpture and orthostat reliefs from Carchemish (9th century BC); a reconstruction of the Phrygian tomb of King Midas at Gordion, and of the façade of a Phrygian house (8th and 7th centuries BC); a remarkably ornate wooden table from Gordion; and the famous 'Lydian Treasure' of gold and silver vessels, figurines and pieces of jewellery (6th century BC). The collection is rounded off with an exhibit of beautiful gold jewellery and glass vessels from the Hellenistic, Roman and Byzantine periods.

*A*nkara's Museum of Anatolian Civilizations gives a fascinating insight into Turkey's pre-classical cultures.

ANGORA WOOL

The small, curly coated Angora goat originated in ancient times in the region around Ankara, from which it takes its name. It is famous for its smooth, lustrous, long-haired fleece, known in Turkish as *tiftik* and in English as mohair (derived from the Arabic *mukhayyar*, meaning 'goat's-hair fabric'). Angora cloth was produced exclusively in the Anatolia region for thousands of years and was Ankara's most important industry until the 19th century, when Angora goats were successfully bred in South Africa and the United States.

Ankara's **Ethnographic Museum** (*Etnografya Müzesi*) is on Atatürk Bulvarı, south of Ulus Meydanı. It contains a fascinating collection of Anatolian folk art and Ottoman crafts.

Atatürk Mausoleum (Anıt Kabir)

On a low hill to the southwest of the city centre stands a huge monument to a huge personality. Mustafa Kemal, later known as Atatürk (literally 'Father of the Turks'), al-

most single-handedly built the foundations of the modern Turkish Republic on the ruins of the Ottoman Empire. The massive mausoleum, its form inspired by classical temples, is approached along a processional avenue lined with rose beds and Hittite lions. Wide stairs lead up from a parade ground to a peristyle of square columns in honey-coloured stone, and a pair of huge bronze doors guarded by members of the armed forces. The vast interior of the mau-

soleum is faced in red and green marble with an ornately decorated wooden ceiling. At the far end a 40-tonne marble monolith marks Atatürk's tomb – his sarcophagus lies in an octagonal crypt beneath it.

Opposite the mausoleum is the **tomb of İsmet İnönü**, Atatürk's friend, prime minister and successor as president of the Republic. The galleries surrounding the parade ground house displays of Atatürk's cars, clothing, library and other personal effects.

The monumental tomb (Anit Kabir) of Kemal Atatürk, sits on a hill overlooking the city. The mausoleum is guarded by young soldiers, sailors and airmen – the changing of the guard is a popular photo-opportunity for visiting tourists.

Modern Ankara

The main artery of Ankara is Atatürk Bulvarı, which runs south from Ulus Meydanı for 6km (4 miles) to the suburb of Çankaya. On the way, it passes through the lively district of **Kızılay**, the modern shopping centre and hotel zone. A number of side streets here have been made into pedestrian precincts, lined with cafés, restaurants and bars.

Atatürk Bulvarı continues past the new **Grand National Assembly** building (*Türkiye Büyük Millet Meclisi*), seat of the Turkish Parliament, to the wealthy, residential neighbourhood of Çankaya. Here, the **Presidential Mansion** (*Cumhurbaşkanlığı Köşkü*) sits amid beautiful ornamental gardens. Within the grounds is the **Çankaya Atatürk Museum** (open Sundays and holidays only, 1.30 to 5.30pm; guided tours only, passport required). This mansion was presented to Atatürk in 1921 by the local *mufti,* and he lived there for the following 11 years as he oversaw the birth of the new republic. The rooms have been preserved as they were when Atatürk lived here, and include a games room for billiards and cards – the president was an enthusiastic player.

Excursions from Ankara

Hattuşaş (Boğazkale)

The site of the ancient capital city of the Hittite Empire lies about 180km (112 miles) to the east of Ankara, across a rolling agri-

cultural landscape enlivened by vast fields of sunflowers. Eight kilometres (50 miles) beyond the farming town of Sungurlu, a minor road on the right leads to the village of Boğazkale, with a few pensions, some restaurants, a carpet shop and a campsite. On the rocky hill above the village lie the excavated ruins of the city of **Hattuşaş**, the seat of power of the Hittite kings from the 17th to the 12th centuries BC.

A 5km (3-mile) road loops around the site, passing all the main features. First stop is the **Great Temple** (*Büyük Mabet*), whose massive stone foundations lie amid a complex of houses and storerooms. Steps mark the entrance to the temple precinct, a triple threshold of smooth stone with holes for the hinge posts of the vanished bronze doors (many of the huge stone blocks in the wall have holes which once held bronze locating pins). A paved street leads past a market area on the left, with huge *pithoi* (clay storage jars) buried in the ground, and the mysterious 'green stone' – a roughly cubic block of polished green rock, possibly from Egypt, whose purpose is unknown. The paved street turns right, left and right again to the entrance of the temple itself, another triple threshold of smooth stone. At the far end of the *cella* is a platform for a cult statue and a stone basin for ritual ablutions. The terrace below the temple is covered with *pithoi* and storerooms where archaeologists discovered thousands of clay tablets

Despite intensive investigation by archaeologists, the Hittite city of Hattuşaş still holds many mysteries. This green stone, in the Temple precinct, may have had a ritual purpose – we just don't know.

that helped scholars to decipher the written language of the Hittites, and to piece together the history of their empire.

Above the temple take the road's right-hand fork to the top of the hill and the city walls and gates. First is the **Lion Gate** (*Aslankapı*), flanked by two impressive stone lions, the delicately rendered hair on their manes still visible after 3,500 years. Further along is the **Sphinx Gate** (*Sfenkskapı*), notable for a 70m (230ft) long **tunnel** that runs through the wall beneath it. The tunnel, a corbelled vault of rough stone, probably had some ceremonial function. It leads to the foot of the massive, sloping city wall, a masterpiece of military engineering. If you turn left at the far end you will find stairs in a corner of the wall that lead back to the gate at the top; the two stone sphinxes that once guarded it are now in museums in Istanbul and Berlin. A third gate, the **King's Gate** (*Kralkapı*), has a plaster cast of a warrior god on its inner side (the original is in Ankara's museum); the outer portal is formed by two huge stone jambs that curve together at the top.

The road now heads downhill again to an area called **Nişantepe** (Marked Hill). To the left of the track is a rock outcrop bearing a weathered inscription in both Hittite and Egyptian hieroglyphs, possibly recording a treaty between the two kingdoms. Across the road is the recently excavated **King's Tomb** (*Kral Mezar*), a corbel-vaulted chamber bearing reliefs of the Hittite kings Shupiluliuma (on the back wall) and Tuthaliya IV (on the left wall near the front); the right wall is covered in hieroglyphics. Further down the road, on the right, is the **Great Castle** (*Büyükkale*), the fortified royal palace used by the Hittite kings in the 13th and 14th centuries BC. Many of the 25,000

The 'inner sanctum' of the Hittite temple at Yazılıkaya. The rock-cut recesses at the back once held cremations, and the walls are decorated with carvings of gods.

mountain gods) and his consort Hebat, the Queen of Heaven (standing on a panther); behind Hebat is their son Sharruma, also standing on a panther. Near the entrance is the figure of King Tuthaliya IV, carrying a standard with a winged sun-disk.

A passage on the right of the main chamber leads to a narrow defile beneath a pinnacle. Recesses cut into the rock at the far end contained evidence of cremations, suggesting that this was a royal burial place. On one wall is a well-preserved relief of 12 warrior gods in procession, holding scythe-like swords and wearing tall, pointed helmets. Opposite is a representation of the god Sharruma embracing King Tuthaliya with his left arm, and holding aloft a child with his right (possibly representing the soul of the dead king).

A half-hour drive from Hattuşaş is **Alacahöyük**, another important Hittite site. The Hittites took over this settlement from the earlier Hatti people around 2,000 BC; the extensive finds of bronze ceremonial standards and gold ornaments recovered from the Hatti tombs here are on display in the Museum of Anatolian Civilizations in Ankara, as are the superb 14th-century orthostat bas-reliefs from the later Hittite occupation.

The site itself offers less to see than Hattuşaş. The main features are the **Sphinx Gate**, with copies of the museum reliefs to either side. Those on the left show a king and queen offering libations to a god in the shape of a bull, followed by a procession

cuneiform tablets recovered from Hattuşaş were found here, including the famous Treaty of Kadesh, the oldest written peace treaty in the world, between King Hattusilis II and Rameses II of Egypt (now in the Museum of the Ancient Orient in Istanbul, see p.96).

The beautiful open-air temple of **Yazılıkaya** (Inscribed Cliff), the Hittites' principal religious centre, lies about 2km (1 mile) from Hattuşaş. The walls of this natural rock enclosure bear a number of reliefs depicting Hittite gods and kings, mostly dating from the 13th century BC. In the main chamber there are processions of gods on the side walls; at the back are representations of Teshub, the weather god (standing on the bowed heads of two of priests leading sacrificial goats, and a group of musicians and acrobats with a ladder. Beyond the gate are the foundations of various buildings, and the tombs of the Hatti kings, which yielded the bronze, silver and gold grave goods you can see in the museum in Ankara.

Gordion

Another ancient capital lies about 100km (60 miles) southwest of Ankara, near the town of Polatlı. Gordion was the capital city of the Phrygians, a mysterious people who dominated central Anatolia in the 8th and early 7th centuries BC. While their origins have been lost in the mists of time, it is thought that they migrated south through Thrace from the Danube region during the 13th and 12th centuries BC, and swept across central Anatolia, burning Hittite cities and building their own on the ashes.

The site of Gordion was occupied in Hittite times, but it became the Phrygian capital under King Gordios during the 8th century BC, and reached its height during the reign of his successor, the legendary King Midas (c. 725-696 BC). The main features of the site today are the acropolis mound and the burial tumuli of the Phrygian kings. On the **acropolis** you can see the remains of the city gate, and the excavated foundations of the Phrygian houses called *megarons* (rectangular rooms with a central hearth, entered through a vestibule). Over 100 burial mounds lie scattered over the surrounding plain. The largest is the **Great Tumulus** (*Büyük Hüyük*), over 50m (164ft) high and 300m (984ft) in diameter; experts disagree over whether this was the tomb of Midas or of Gordios. It was first opened in the early 1950s, when coal miners were brought from the Black Sea coast to dig a 60m (197ft) tunnel into the centre. There the

THE GORDIAN KNOT

The Phrygian kings Gordios and Midas are mentioned in the Greek stories of the Golden Touch (see box p.165) and the Gordian Knot. An oracle foretold that a man would arrive in an ox-cart at the gates of Gordion; he would become king and rule wisely over the Phrygians. Gordios, who was without heirs, seized on this prophecy, and when the peasant Midas rode into the city on his cart the king immediately adopted him as his son and successor. Gordios dedicated the ox-cart to Zeus and placed it in a temple on the acropolis hill.

The yoke of the wagon was bound to the shaft with a thong of cornel bark, tied in an elaborate knot that had no visible ends. A second oracle then declared that whoever could undo the knot would conquer all of Asia. The Gordian Knot remained intact until Alexander the Great arrived in Gordion in 333 BC. Unable to resist such a challenge, he made his way to the temple and studied the knot. Then, with a single stroke of his sword he solved the 400-year-old puzzle; the prophecy was, of course, fulfilled.

archaeologists found a wooden chamber, with the bones of a small, 60-year-old man lying on a wooden bench, surrounded by grave goods which included bronze cauldrons and exquisite, inlaid wooden furniture. The goods, and a reconstruction of the burial chamber, are on show in Ankara's Museum of Anatolian Civilizations.

Safranbolu

The town of **Safranbolu** lies about 210km (130 miles) north of Ankara, along the motorway toward Istanbul. Leave the motorway at Gerede, and follow signs for Karabük and Bartın. Ten kilometres (6 miles) beyond the grimy steel town of Karabuk, you will arrive in Safranbolu 'new town'; bear right at the roundabout

*The white stone walls
of the huge Cinci Hanı rise among
the timber town-houses of
Eski Safranbolu.*

(signposted 'Kastamonu'), and five more minutes will take you to the 'old town'.

Eski (Old) Safranbolu is a picture-postcard town set in a lovely river valley, one of the few surviving examples of an Ottoman town of the 18th and 19th centuries. The hillsides are covered in traditional, wooden-framed townhouses (*konaklar*), with mud-brick walls and cantilevered upper storeys, shuttered windows, wide eaves and red-tiled roofs. In the centre of town is the bazaar area (lively market on Saturday), with the massive **Cinci Hanı**, a huge Ottoman caravanserai that is being renovated and converted to a hotel. Across the way, a narrow cobbled lane (immediately left of the TC Ziraat Bankası) leads uphill to the *Kaymakam Evi,* the old Governor's Mansion. This has been restored as a **museum**, and offers a glimpse of daily 19th-century life in a well-off Ottoman household. The lane continues steeply up to a park at the top of the hill where you can enjoy a good view over the town.

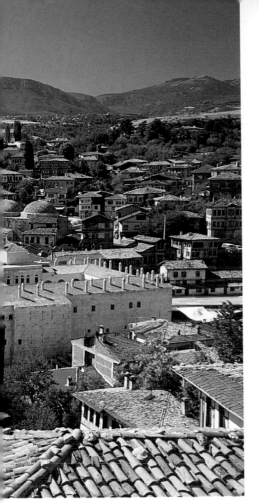

Amasya

Amasya, 340km (210 miles) northeast of Ankara, is one of the most scenic, most pleasant and most interesting towns in central Anatolia. Occupying a strategic position at a narrowing in the valley of the Yeşilırmak River, Amasya was the ancient capital of the Kingdom of Pontus, and the birthplace of the Greek geographer Strabo. In succeeding centuries it passed through the hands of the Romans, the Byzantines, the Seljuk Turks and the Mongols, before falling to the Ottomans, who lavished fine mosques and *medreses* upon it.

The town straggles along both sides of the river, tucked beneath the towering crag of the citadel. A delightful shady promenade runs along the south bank, with a leafy square lined with cafés, and a view of Ottoman *konaks* overhanging the water on the far side. But your gaze will inevitably be drawn to the **tombs of the Pontic kings**, cut into the sheer rock face above the town. To take a closer look, cross the footbridge by the tourist information booth and follow the signs for '*Kral Kaya Mezarları*' beneath the

---

THE KINGDOM OF PONTUS

In the wake of Alexander the Great, the independent Kingdom of Pontus was established in north-central Anatolia, with its capital at Amasya. It captured land along the Black Sea coast, and in 183 BC the capital was moved to Sinope (see p.300). The kingdom reached its zenith of power under Mithradates VI (*c.* 120-63 BC), whose expansionist ambitions brought him into conflict with the might of the Roman Empire. He declared war on Rome in 80 BC and met with initial success, driving the Roman armies back to the Aegean, and winning support from the Greek cities of Asia Minor. But the empire struck back, and in 66 BC Mithradates was roundly defeated and Pontus was absorbed into Rome. A few years later, while planning a new attack on Rome, his own troops deserted him. Having failed in an attempt to poison himself, the king ordered a Gallic mercenary to slay him. His body was entombed at the royal capital of Sinope.

Mithradates' son, Pharnaces II, rebelled once more against the Romans, but the legions of Julius Caesar crushed him in battle near the modern town of Zile (60km, or 36 miles south of Amasya) in 47 BC, a victory which Caesar reported phlegmatically to his mistress with the famous words, '*Veni, vidi, vici*' ('I came, I saw, I conquered').

This attractive Ottoman mansion overlooking the swirling waters of the Yeşilırmak (Green River) in Amasya is now open as a museum. On the cliffs beyond are two of the tombs of the Pontic kings.

BC, are empty and bear neither decoration nor inscription. The summit of the **citadel** can be reached by a difficult and dangerous path above the tombs; a much easier route is to take a taxi up the road that climbs the back of the hill. The cliff-top is littered with the ruins of an Ottoman fortress, abandoned in the 18th century, and provides an unforgettable view of the town.

Overlooking the river beneath the tombs you will find the **Hazeranlar Konağı**, a restored, two-storey Ottoman mansion, now opened as a museum. It has a cruciform central hall with a room set in each corner; the rooms have a long,

railway, and up a steep cobbled path through retaining walls to a terrace and café. This was once the site of the royal palace of Pontus, and later of Seljuk and Ottoman sultans (called *Kızlar Sarayı,* or 'Maidens' Palace'), but nothing remains save a ruined Ottoman *hamam* behind the café.

A group of three tombs lies above the café; two more can be reached via a path on the left which leads through a short tunnel and up a spectacular rock-cut staircase, complete with balustrade. The huge, arched recesses, which date from the 3rd century

---

STRABO

Strabo was an ancient Greek geographer and historian whose most famous work, *Geography*, is the only surviving text that describes all the lands and peoples known to the Greeks and Romans around the time of the birth of Christ. He was born in Amasya in 64 or 63 BC, the son of a prominent local family, and studied in Nyssa (see p.188) and Rome. Although he travelled widely, from Armenia and the Black Sea coast as far as Tuscany and Egypt, even sailing up the Nile as far as the borders of Ethiopia, most of his *Geography* draws on the works of earlier authors; he was especially interested in identifying the cities mentioned in Homer's *Iliad*. Strabo completed the *Geography* in AD 23, and died soon afterwards.

cushion-covered divan along one side, with colourful carpets on the floor and decorative alcoves above the hearth.

Back on the south bank, upstream from the footbridge, are the glistening domes of the **Mosque of Sultan Beyazıt II**, set in a beautiful garden with spreading plane trees and splashing fountains. This Amasya's largest mosque, was begun by the sultan and completed by his son in 1486. Wander through the grounds to the main street. A few hundred metres to the right is the **Gök Medrese Camii** (Mosque of the Sky-blue Seminary), a 13th-century Seljuk building which takes its name from the blue tiles that once covered the portal and pointed turret. In the opposite direction is Amasya's excellent **museum** (open 8.30am to noon, 1.30 to 5.30pm, closed Monday). On the ground floor are displayed the beautifully carved wooden doors from the Gök Medrese Camii (13th century) and the Mehmet Paşa Camii (15th century). Upstairs are Hittite and Urartian finds, including a bronze figurine of the weather god Teshub; Hellenistic, Roman and Byzantine pottery, jewellery and coins; and an ethnographic section with Ottoman costumes, weapons and household paraphernalia. In the garden are pieces of sculpture and sarcophagi, and a tomb containing five desiccated 'mummies' found beneath the Burmalı Minare Camii.

Heading back towards the town centre, you pass the crumbling grassy ruins of the **Taş Han**, a 17th-century caravanserai housing a few ironmongers' shops, and behind it the twisted spire of the 13th-century **Burmalı Minare Camii** (Mosque of the Spiral Minaret), with its uncharacteristically plain Seljuk portal. Down on the riverside beyond the statue of Atatürk are several more historic buildings: the **Tımarhane Medresesi** (Lunatic Asylum

Seminary), which was built as a mental hospital by the Mongol governors of Amasya in 1308-9; the **Mehmet Paşa Camii**, built in 1486 and now a girls' Koranic school; the **Beyazıt Paşa Camii**, an early Ottoman mosque of 1419 comparable to the Yeşil Camii in Bursa (see p.138); and the **Kapı Ağa Medresesi** (Seminary of the Chief White Eunuch) across the river, built in 1488 and still serving as a religious school.

Sivas

South of Amasya the highway follows the valley of the Yeşilırmak for 116km (72 miles) to **Tokat**. At a roundabout by the river you turn right and head uphill along the town's tree-lined main street, with the rocky prominence of the ancient citadel rising ahead. Tokat boasts many Seljuk and Ottoman buildings dating from the 12th to the 18th centuries, and makes a fascinating stopover for devotees of Islamic architecture. If you are pushed for time, take a look around the town's **museum**, housed in the restored 13th-century Gök Medrese, a low reddish-ochre building with an ornate Seljuk portal to the right of the main street. Alternatively, visit the **Latifoğlu Müze Evi**, a 19th-century wooden Ottoman mansion on the left-hand side at the far end of town.

Another two hours' driving takes you to **Sivas**, an ancient town that is famous for its rich heritage of medieval architecture. It was originally the Roman and Byzantine town of Sebasteia, but was renamed Sivas when it fell to the Danishmend Turks in the 11th century. It occupied an important position at the intersection of the north-south and east-west trade routes to Baghdad and Persia, and reached a peak of prosperity under the Seljuk Turks, who took the city in 1172.

The Mongols made vassals of the Seljuks following their victory at the Battle of Köse Dağ (between Sivas and Erzurum) in 1243, but the city continued to flourish; during the 13th century, Sivas was one of the most important cities in all Anatolia, with a population estimated at 150,000.

The city was sacked by Tamerlane in 1400, a blow from which it never recovered. It was a modest provincial capital under the Ottomans, but earned a lasting place in republican history when it hosted Atatürk's Second Nationalist Congress in 1919, an event that put the final nails in the coffin of the Ottoman Empire. The modern town is unremarkable, but its medieval heritage has left it with perhaps the finest collection of Seljuk architecture in the country.

In the centre of town is a pleasant, open main square with a fountain in the middle, called Konak Meydanı. Wander through the leafy park that lies opposite the town hall, where three of Sivas's Seljuk buildings can be found. On the left, opposite the tiny square Ottoman mosque called Kale Camii, is the **Bürücüye Medresesi**, a religious college built in 1271-2 by the Seljuk vezir Muzaffer Bürücirdi (his tomb lies in a chamber to the left of the entrance vestibule). The great portal is decorated with a delicate tracery of carved arabesques, surrounding the pointed niche characteristic of Seljuk Anatolia. The courtyard within contains a peaceful tea garden, while the surrounding chambers are draped with beautiful carpets and kilims.

At the bottom of the park rise the twin red-brick spires of the **Çifte Minare Medrese** (Seminary of the Twin Minarets), endowed by a Mongol vizier in 1271-2. Only the façade remains – the twin minarets crown an elaborate portal, with intricate arabesques and Arabic calligraphy surrounding an ogive arch

THE SELJUK MEDRESE

As the Seljuk Turks spread their influence throughout Anatolia, they brought with them the traditional Muslim buildings – mosques, minarets and mausoleums. They also introduced a new kind of building, the *medrese* (school). A *medrese* was usually paid for by a private citizen, and served as a college for the teaching of Islamic law. It thus had to provide accommodation for students and professors, and rooms for lecturing and study. The tomb of the benefactor was often built into the *medrese*.

supported on engaged columns with acanthus-leaf capitals, this in turn framing a scalloped niche. Opposite is the **Şifaiye Medresesi**, one of the city's oldest buildings, built in 1217-18 by the Seljuk

*S*ivas secured a place in Turkish history when it hosted
Atatürk's National Congress in 1919, but it also has a rich architectural
heritage – the Çifte Minare (left), and Bürücüye Medresesi (above).

Sultan Keykavus I, whose tomb lies inside. It was originally used as a hospital and medical school, but the courtyard and its surrounding chambers are now given over to a bazaar and tea garden. The portal is decorated with the heads of bulls and lions, symbolizing the moon and the sun.

At the far end of the park turn left along Cemal Gürsel Caddesi, where you will find the **Ulu Camii** (Great Mosque), the oldest mosque in Sivas. Built in 1197, it is a congregational mosque, a large prayer hall with a flat roof supported by a forest of 50 wooden pillars; the brick minaret, still bearing scraps of turquoise tiling, is 35m (115ft) tall. Beyond the mosque, turn right on Cumhuriyet Caddesi for a few blocks to reach the **Gök Medrese** (Sky-blue Seminary). With its twin minarets it resembles the Çifte Minare Medrese, but it is far more elaborately decorated; the portal is flanked by two ornamental panels, with Arabic inscriptions and motifs depicting the tree of life and eight-pointed stars. It was built in 1271 by Sahip Ata, a Seljuk grand vezir who funded similar buildings in Konya and Kayseri.

Divriği

Stuck in the middle of nowhere in the hills southeast of Sivas is the small iron-mining town of **Divriği**. It was once a Byzantine outpost, but later became the seat of a tiny Seljuk principality, the Mengüçek Emirate, in the 12th and 13th centuries. It has gained a place on the tourist map because of a fascinating Seljuk monument, the **Ulu Camii** (Great Mosque) built by the Emir Ahmet Shah in 1228-9. The mosque's richly decorated north and west portals are unique in Turkey, almost baroque in their exuberance. The gate surrounds are ornamented with fussy floral and geometric designs carved in very high relief, punctuated with the figures

of birds and human faces. (This is a very rare feature in Islamic art, as the depiction of living things was prohibited from the 8th century on. It was claimed that the representation of a living thing was an act of competition with God, for He alone can create something that is alive.) The interior of the mosque is, in contrast, very plain, with a vaulted roof supported by 16 columns, and an equally plain *mihrab*.

Attached to the mosque is the **Darüşşifa** (Sanatorium), founded by the wife of Ahmet Shah, which displays an equally idiosyncratic design. It contains an octagonal pool and a platform for musicians, so that the patients might be soothed by the sounds of tinkling water and soft music. The tombs of the emir and his father are in one of the rooms.

Kayseri

Whether you arrive from Ankara, Cappadocia or Sivas, the approach to Kayseri is dominated by the huge, snow-capped peak of Erciyes Dağı (3,916m; 12,850ft). The city sits at the foot of the mountain, about half-way along the ancient trade route between Konya and Sivas. Originally called Mazaca, it was renamed Caesarea in AD 17 when it was made the capital of the Roman province of Cappadocia. It was first captured by the Turks in 1067, but changed hands several times before becoming part of the Seljuk Sultanate of Rum in 1168. The following 75 years were Kayseri's golden age, and most of the city's monuments date from that period. It was sacked by the Mongols in 1243, and passed through the hands of several rival Seljuk dynasties before being finally absorbed into the Ottoman Empire in 1515. Modern **Kayseri** is famed for its goldsmiths and carpet sellers, and its natives have a reputation as shrewd businessmen – shopping in Kayseri's bazaar is the ultimate test of your bargaining skills!

All the Seljuk monuments lie within easy walking distance of the city centre, which is dominated by the grey battlements of the **Kale** (Fortress), rising along the south side of the main square. The crenellated walls,

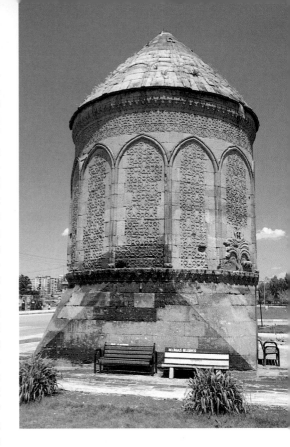

The form of Seljuk tombs, such as the Döner Kümbet in Kayseri, mimics in stone the shape of traditional funeral tents.

THE 'UZUN YOL'

The road from Konya to Aksaray, and on through Cappadocia to Kayseri, follows one of Turkey's oldest trade routes. In medieval times it linked Konya, the capital of the Sultanate of Rum, with the other important Seljuk cities of Kayseri and Sivas, and continued through Erzurum and Persia to the homeland of the Seljuk Turks in central Asia. Fortified *hans*, or caravanserais, were built along the road at intervals of one day's travel, to provide shelter and protection for the camel caravans. The single gate was barred at night against bandits, and the animals were fed and watered in the courtyard while the men made themselves comfortable in the rooms around the walls.

---

built in the early 13th century by the Seljuk Sultan Alaeddin Keykubad I, conceal an open-air bazaar. Keykubad was also responsible for the **Mahperi Hunat Hatun Medresesi**, which lies opposite the east end of the Kale, near the tourist information office. The seminary and its adjoining mosque were founded in 1237 by Mahperi, the wife of the sultan; her tomb is by the entrance. The ornate portal leads to an open courtyard flanked by two *eyvans*, which now house the city's Ethnographic Museum.

Across the wide open space of Cumhuriyet Meydanı, the **Sahibiye Medresesi** occupies a busy street corner. It dates from 1267-8, and was endowed by the Seljuk vezir Sahip Ata, who also funded the İnce Minareli Medrese in Konya (see p.288); it is currently used as a book market. Mimar Sinan Caddesi (Architect Sinan Street) runs along the side of leafy Atatürk Parkı, and is named for the great Ottoman architect who designed the **Kurşunlu Camii** (Mosque of Lead), whose shiny domes rise above the trees to the left. Facing it across another park to the right are the twin portals of the 12th-century **Çifte Medrese** (Double Seminary). The right-hand *medrese* housed one of the earliest medical schools in Anatolia; both buildings have been restored and now contain a fascinating museum explaining Seljuk medical practices. On the other side of Atatürk Parkı is Kayseri's **bazaar** district; its former importance as a trading centre is attested to by the presence of three *bedestens* (covered markets), ranging in origin from the 15th to the 19th centuries.

Kayseri is also noted for its Seljuk tombs. About 1km (½ mile) along the road leading towards Hisarcık and Erciyes is one of the best of these, the **Döner Kümbet** (Revolving Tomb), conspicuously located on the central reservation of the dual carriageway. Its squat bullet shape mimics in stone the traditional Turkish funeral tents of central Asia, right down to the guy ropes carved on to the conical roof. The tomb houses the remains of Shah Jehan Hatun, the daughter of Sultan Alaeddin Keykubad I, and dates from around 1275-6. Near by is Kayseri's **Archaeological Museum** (*Arkeoloji Müzesi*), whose collection includes finds from the Hittite sites of Kültepe and Göllüdağ, and Hellenistic and Roman sculpture from ancient Caesarea.

The snow-capped volcanic peak of Erciyes Dağı looms on the horizon. Its ancient eruptions covered the region with a carpet of ash, which has been eroded into the weird landscapes of Cappadocia.

Erciyes Dağı (Mount Argaeus)

The extinct volcano of **Erciyes Dağı**, the ancient Mount Argaeus, rears up to the south of Kayseri. The conical summit peak, almost 4,000m (13,000ft) high, is rarely free of snow. A road, rough and cobbled for most of its length, climbs up to the unlovely ski resort of Kayakevi at 2,200m (7,200ft), 28km (17½ miles) from the centre of Kayseri. In summer the mountain is a desolate landscape of cinder cones and lava flows, interspersed with grassy pastures; in winter it is a spectacular snowscape, offering some of the best skiing in the country.

Kültepe (Kanesh)

About 20km (13 miles) northeast of Kayseri, on the road to Sivas, archaeologists have unearthed the remains of the Hittite and Assyrian city of Kanesh, dating from the 3rd millennium BC. Kanesh was an important Assyrian trading colony, and the most valuable objects found here have been the thousands of cuneiform tablets that have provided a detailed picture of the economic life of the period. The site itself is a huge mound called **Kültepe** (Mound of Ashes), where excavations have exposed the mud-brick walls of houses, shops, storerooms, palaces and a market. A layer of vitrified bricks bears witness to the great fire that destroyed the city around 1900 BC; the site was later occupied by the Hittite city of Nisa.

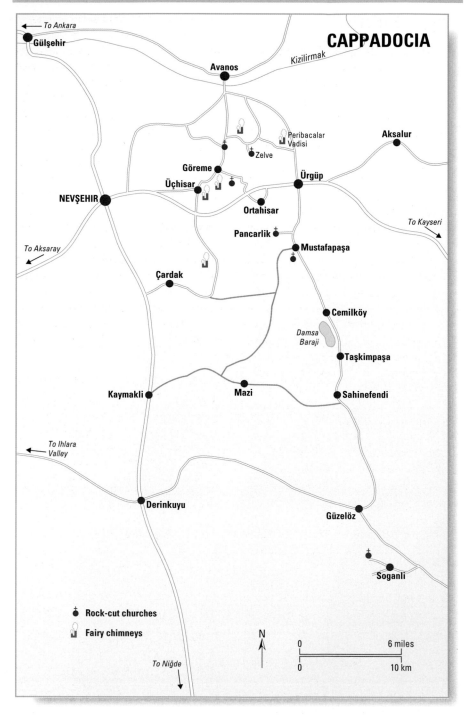

274

Cappadocia

The fantasy landscape of **Cappadocia** is probably the best-known tourist attraction in inland Turkey. Thousands of postcards, posters and guidebook photographs have attempted to capture the magic of its 'fairy chimneys' and fretted ravines, glowing gold, pink and green in the rays of the setting sun.

The origins of this outlandish landscape lie in the mountains of Erciyes, Melendiz and Hasan Dağı, which raise their conical summits to the east and south. Millions of years ago these were active volcanoes, their explosive eruptions spewing out vast clouds of debris that rained down on the Cappadocian Plateau, covering it in a thick carpet of volcanic ash called 'tuff'. Through time, the action of rain and river has eroded the soft tuff into strange fluted gullies and tortured pinnacles; in places a layer of more resistant rock has protected the tops of the pinnacles, creating the weird phallic pillars christened *peri bacalar* ('fairy chimneys') by the Turks. The presence of iron minerals in the tuffs has given them delicate tints – a soft desert pink, pale pastel green, and rust-tinged yellow – that emphasize the surreal effect of the bizarre landforms.

Tourist brochures often claim that the name Cappadocia means 'land of beautiful horses'. While the region was indeed famous for its fine steeds, the name actually comes from the ancient inhabitants of the region, the Katpatuka, which is Assyrian for 'at Tuka's side', though who or what 'Tuka' is, we don't know. In ancient times the region known as Cappadocia was much larger than today, extending from the Taurus Mountains to the Black Sea, and from the central plains to the valley of the Euphrates. From the 4th to the 1st centuries BC Cappadocia was an independent kingdom, often allied to Rome, and from AD 17 it was a Roman province with its capital at Caesarea (modern Kayseri). It was a nucleus of early Christianity, and the 4th-century 'Cappadocian Fathers' played a crucial role in the development of the Orthodox Church. The rock-cut churches and monasteries of the region are a treasure house of early Byzantine art, having largely escaped the ravages of the Iconoclastic Controversy (726-843) which resulted in the destruction of similar works elsewhere (see box).

With the arrival of raiding Arabs in the 7th century the population took to the hills, carving churches and dwelling places out of the soft rock, and even creating complete underground communities, as at Kaymaklı and Derinkuyu (see p.283). The Seljuk Turks took over in the

---

THE CAPPADOCIAN FATHERS

The Cappadocian Fathers – St Basil the Great (AD 329-79), the Bishop of Caesarea (Kayseri); his brother St Gregory of Nyssa; and Basil's friend and former fellow student, St Gregory of Nazianzus – played an important role in the early development of Christianity, defending the orthodox faith against the Arian heresy. They maintained belief in the doctrine of the Holy Trinity (God as 'three equal Persons', the Father, Son and Holy Spirit, 'in one substance'), as opposed to the Arian Creed, which denied the divinity of Christ and insisted on the essential 'oneness' of God. Although they faced severe opposition and persecution from the Roman Emperor Valens (who was an Arian), their beliefs eventually prevailed. Valens' successors, Gratian and Theodosius, took up the defence of orthodoxy, which was confirmed in the Nicene Creed issued by the Council of Constantinople in 381.

ST GEORGE IN CAPPADOCIA

St George was a popular subject for the Byzantine artists who decorated the churches of Cappadocia. He was a Christian martyr who lived sometime during the 3rd century, but little is known of his life or deeds. Legend tells that he was a knight from Cappadocia who rescued a princess from a terrible dragon; in gratitude, the maiden's father and his subjects converted to Christianity. He soon came to symbolize the triumph of good over evil, and his legend was brought back to England (where he was adopted as the patron saint), by knights returning from the crusades.

12th century, and were much more tolerant of Christianity, being far more interested in controlling the important trade routes that cut through the region. Their principal legacy is the string of impressive caravanserais that lines the ancient caravan route between the splendid cities of Kayseri and Konya. Cappadocia remained home to a considerable number of Greek Orthodox Christians right up until the 1920s, when they were moved to Greece as part of the post-War of Independence exchange of populations.

The region known as Cappadocia (*Kapadokya* in Turkish) today lies between Kayseri and Aksaray, extending

EARLY CHRISTIAN ART

Ironically, the earliest surviving image of Christ is a blasphemous graffito scratched on a wall in the House of the Imperial Pages in Rome. Apparently poking fun at a new convert to the faith, it shows a man looking at a crucified figure with an ass's head, above the words 'Alessameno worships God'. The early Christians themselves were very reluctant to create religious images, partly because they were a persecuted minority and did not want to draw attention to themselves, and partly because of religious doubts prompted by the words of the Second Commandment: 'You shall not make for yourself a graven image, or any likeness of anything that is in heaven above, or that is in the earth beneath, or that is in the water under the earth'. The earliest Christian images were coded symbols, such as the 'chi-rho' sign (the first two letters of Christ's name in Greek, X and P, superimposed) and the fish – the first letters of the Greek words for 'Jesus Christ Son of God Saviour' spell *ichthus*, the Greek word for fish.

Byzantine artists finally overcame their reluctance to paint the figure of Jesus around the 4th century, and began to decorate their churches with scenes from the life of Christ. In those days, when most of the population was illiterate, these narrative frescoes provided a sort of 'strip-cartoon' gospel accessible to all. They also promoted the idea of the church as the setting for Christ's life on earth, where the celestial and the terrestrial came together. An accepted form for the location of the various scenes soon evolved, with Christ Pantocrator gazing down from the central dome, and the apse coming to represent the cave of the nativity, with the Virgin and Child in the conch above, flanked by the archangels Michael and Gabriel.

The argument over the use of religious images flared up in the 8th and 9th centuries, when the Iconoclastic Controversy ripped through the Byzantine Empire. The use of icons (religious images) was officially banned in 730 – many works of art were destroyed or defaced, and the iconodules (venerators of icons) were severely persecuted by the iconoclasts (breakers of icons). The controversy raged until 843 when, on the first Sunday in Lent, it was finally declared that icons might be venerated but not worshipped – the day is still celebrated in the Eastern Church as the festival of the Triumph of Orthodoxy.

north to the Kızılırmak River and south to Niğde. The main tourist zone, however, is concentrated in a much smaller area, in a rough triangle bounded by Nevşehir, Ürgüp and Avanos, and centred on the village of Göreme. If you have your own vehicle, then Ürgüp makes the best 'base camp'; if you are backpacking or relying on public transport, head for Göreme.

Ürgüp

Ürgüp is the tourist capital of Cappadocia, a pleasant, lively town set in a valley beneath a crag riddled with rock-cut houses. Many of the best hotels and restaurants in the region are clustered in and around the town, and the **shopping** – for carpets, jewellery and antiques – is excellent. The citizens combine tourism with agriculture, tending the vineyards, orchards and vegetable gardens that surround the town. The rich volcanic soil and sunny climate make Cappadocia ideal for growing grapes, and each year, in the first week of June, Ürgüp hosts a **wine festival**. You can, however, sample Cappadocian wines at any time of year by visiting one of the six local wineries; the Turasan vineyard is reckoned to be one of the best.

Göreme

Unlike Ürgüp, which has managed to accommodate the influx of tourists without losing too much of its charm, the small town of **Göreme** is in danger of being swamped by new development. The old pensions are being ousted by new hotels and motels, and the family carpet sellers edged out by a modern shopping precinct crammed with the names of the big Istanbul carpet companies. The village is famous for its troglodyte ('cave-dweller') houses, hollowed into bizarre, cone-headed pillars of tuff, which cover the floor of the valley like a forest of giant, petrified toadstools.

More famous still is the nearby **Göreme Open-Air Museum** (open daily 8.30am to 7pm, 5pm in winter). This steep-sided little valley once housed a thriving monastic community, living and worshipping in houses and churches cut into the surrounding cliffs. The frescoes in these churches, which date from the 9th to the 11th centuries, are some of the finest in Cappadocia; those from the 11th century are true masterpieces of Byzantine art. Unfortunately, Göreme is the number one destination for tour coaches; the valley is overrun with guided groups practically from the moment the gates open, and you often have to queue to get into the churches. If you can, try to visit after 4.30pm, when things are much quieter. The best frescoes are in the so called 'columned churches', dating from the 11th century – Elmalı Kilise, Karanlık Kilise and Çarıklı Kilise. They are currently undergoing restoration, and some of them may be closed when you visit.

From the entrance, a path loops around the site. Keeping to the right, the first church you come to is the *Bazıl Kilise* (St Basil's Church), which you can safely miss; continue to the **Elmalı Kilise** (Apple Church). Like the other 'columned churches', this has an 'inscribed cross' floor plan, with four columns supporting a central dome, and three apses. The frescoes depict the usual Byzantine subjects of angels and saints, and scenes from the life of Christ – the Nativity, the Baptism, the Last Supper, the Crucifixion. The Baptism (to the right of the entrance) is particularly interesting, as it shows a pillar in the River Jordan (to the right of the figure of Christ) which was described by pilgrims returning from the Holy Land.

Around the corner is the **Barbara Kilise** (Church of St Barbara). In contrast to the Elmalı, the decoration here is very sparse – mostly geometric designs and imitation masonry done in red ochre. On the left is a fresco of St Barbara, facing across the church to the figure of Christ enthroned. Straight ahead are saints George and Theodore, and above them, between two crosses, is a crudely drawn insect-like creature which appears to have horns. No one knows what it is or what it symbolizes.

The **Yılanlı Kilise** (Snake Church) lies ahead at the top of the hill. It takes its name from the large fresco on the left showing saints George and Theodore, on horseback; St George, mounted on a white steed, is spearing the legendary dragon, which writhes beneath the horses' hooves. The two figures holding a wooden cross are Constantine, the first Roman emperor to convert to Christianity, and his mother. Opposite is the naked figure of St Onuphrius, a hermit who lived alone in the Egyptian desert for 60 years, his modesty preserved by a shrub. (Tour guides will probably recount a local belief that he was originally a beautiful young woman, who asked God to make her male so that she could escape the attentions of men.)

The path leads down to a terrace below the **Karanlık Kilise** (Dark Church), named for its lack of windows. It was part of a monastic complex, half of which has disappeared in ancient rockfalls. The centuries of darkness have preserved the bright colours of the frescoes, which are among the best in the region. Around the corner a metal staircase leads up to the entrance of the **Çarıklı Kilise** (Sandal Church), named after the foot-shaped imprint in the floor opposite the doorway. The frescoes here are bright and lively; note Christ Pantocrator surrounded by archangels (in the dome), and the Hospitality of Abraham (above the left-hand apse).

Outside of the museum area, across the road from the entrance (and sometimes locked) is the **Tokalı Kilise** (Church of the Buckle), with the most spectacular frescoes in Göreme. There are actually two churches – you enter into the Old Church, the rear part of which has been dug away to create the New Church. The frescoes in the New Church are magnificent, the figures more elegantly rendered than in the old, and outlined against a vivid blue background of lapis lazuli.

Üçhisar

South of Göreme is the village of **Üçhisar** (Three Castles), whose craggy citadel can be seen for miles around. As you get closer you will see that the tower of rock is riddled through and through with holes and tunnels, like a woodworm-infested tree stump. Conventional houses cluster around the rock dwellings, some of which are still inhabited. There are a number of pensions here, some of them in troglodyte houses. The top of the crag is the highest point in the district, and provides a magnificent view over the surrounding landscape, especially at sunset.

Zelve

Half-way along the road from Göreme to Avanos, a minor road on the right leads to the triple valley of **Zelve**, passing a forest of phallic pillars on the way – a favourite spot for photographers. Zelve was another

The valley of Zelve, late in the afternoon, is a good place to enjoy the subtle colours of the Cappadocian landscape – rusty yellow, pale green and rose pink.

monastic community, and the sides of the valleys are honeycombed with stairways, tunnels, storerooms, living quarters, pigeon houses and churches. The valleys were inhabited by Turks as recently as the 1950s, when the lack of services and increasing danger from rockfalls forced them to leave. There is a rock-cut mosque near the entrance to the valleys, and the Arabic word 'Allah' has been carved above the door of one of the churches.

Valley of the Fairy Chimneys (Peri Bacalar Vadisi)

If you continue past Zelve and turn right you will find yourself in a valley whose sides are covered in a spectacular forest of 'fairy chimneys'. At the top of the valley, to the left, is another favourite sunset-watching spot.

Avanos

The northern edge of the Cappadocian plateau is marked by the muddy, brick-red waters of the *Kızılırmak* (Red River), Turkey's longest river. Known in ancient times as the River Halys, it rises in the hills between Sivas and Erzincan, and flows southwest to Cappadocia before returning in a great loop north and northeast to reach the Black Sea between Samsun and Sinop.

The local red clay that gives the river its colour is used to make the **pottery** for which Avanos is famous. The streets

*T*he town of Avanos, on the northern edge of Cappadocia, is famous for its pottery. One of the local potters created this monument, which sits in the town square – on one side is a laughing tourist, complete with camera.

around the main square are lined with potteries where you can go in and watch the potters at work. The pots are thrown on ancient stone flywheels, powered by the potter's foot, before being fired in a coal furnace. The finished items range from traditional, unglazed earthenware bowls and urns to all kinds of glazed and coloured plates, vases and sculptures, including imitation İznik tiles.

Soğanlı

About 35km (22 miles) south of Ürgüp is the remote **Soğanlı Valley**, which was almost unknown a few years ago, but has now been discovered by tour companies trying to escape the crowds at Göreme. The primitive village of Soğanlı at the foot of the valley has built a café and handicrafts market to cash in on the tourist trade, and you can even make a tour of the rock-cut churches on one of the village donkeys.

On the way to Soğanlı you pass the **Pancarlık Valley**, where you can explore a number of interesting frescoed churches, and **Mustafapaşa**, formerly the Ottoman Greek village of Sinasos. The road continues along the floor of a cliff-lined valley, before climbing up beyond Şahinefendi to pop out on to the top of the plateau, with a view of snow-capped Erciyes shimmering away to the northeast. Then, just as suddenly, the road dives down another valley, like a rabbit bolting for its burrow; turn left at the bottom to reach Soğanlı.

The best churches are in the right fork of the valley. Walk along the road to the **Karabaş Kilise** (Church of the Black Head), which has the best frescoes. At the road end is the **Yilanlı Kilise** (Snake Church) and its neighbouring monastic complex. The frescoes in the church are disappointing, but take a look in the monastery, where you will find ovens,

The rock-cut churches of Cappadocia have been hollowed out of natural rock. Some have been adorned with elaborate frescoes; others, like this one that can be seen at Pancarlık, have simpler decoration.

Saklı Kilise (Hidden Church), which also has a secret room at the back and with the door still in place. The path continues over the shoulder of the ridge and descends back to the village.

Underground Cities

Perhaps even more remarkable than the cliff dwellings of Göreme and Zelve is the warren of underground cities that lies beneath the plateau to the south of Nevşehir. Here the land is flat, but it is underlain by the same soft beds of tuff that outcrop further north. Perhaps as long ago as the Hittite era, men began to burrow into the bedrock, seeking shelter and safety from invaders. Later inhabitants enlarged and extended the maze of tunnels, stairways and ventilation shafts, adding living quarters, animal pens, storerooms, latrines, wells, kitchens, wineries and churches, all hewn out of the solid rock. The largest of these cities had eight or nine levels extending 55m (180ft) underground, and could hold up to 30,000 people. In times of danger, the whole city could be sealed off with heavy 'millstone' doors rolled across the entrance tunnels. With their animals, stocks of grain and fodder, underground wells, and ventilation shafts cleverly disguised at the surface, they could hold out for weeks. Christian communities lived here in the 7th and 8th centuries, seeking refuge from Arab

storage cisterns for oil and water, and vats for crushing grapes. At the back of the main hall a narrow passage leads to a secret chamber, where the monks took refuge in time of danger. The entrance could be closed with the huge circular stone door which now lies on the floor.

Cross the stream and follow a path along the hillside, past a church with a tower hewn from the rock. Just past this, downhill to the left, is the aptly named raiders, but the ancient Greek soldier and historian Xenophon records underground cities here as long ago as 400 BC.

A number of these unusual subterranean settlements has been discovered, and two of the finest examples, at **Kaymaklı** and **Derinkuyu**, have been fitted with electric lighting and opened to the public. Both sites have a system of signs to guide you through the maze of tunnels – red arrows for the way in, blue for the way out. There are also guides for hire, who can explain in detail the various features you will see. The tunnels are often very narrow and low-roofed, with steep stairs – no place for the claustrophobic or the infirm.

Of the two sites, Derinkuyu is the larger and more interesting, with eight levels going down over 40m (130ft) below ground level; its 'millstone' security doors are very well preserved. Right at the bottom level there is a church with a cruciform floor plan, plus walk-through 'confessional' and a very deep well.

Niğde

The small provincial town of **Niğde** sits on the southern fringe of Cappadocia, its ruined Seljuk fortress guarding the old trade route from Kayseri through the Cilician Gates to the Mediterranean. There is little to see in the town, but 10km (6 miles) to the north is the beautiful rock-cut monastery of **Eski Gümüşler**. This fascinating site is unusual in that its fine 10th- and 11th-century frescoes have not been damaged by vandals.

The church and living quarters are cut into the vertical walls of a square **courtyard**, which you enter through a dark tunnel; there is a hole in the roof of the tunnel through which boiling oil could be poured onto attackers. The floor of the courtyard is pocked with cisterns for storing water, oil and wine, and with tomb chambers – in the far right is a recently discovered **grave** complete with skeleton. To the left are storerooms with more chambers for grain, oil and wine, and a 'safe room' which could be sealed off from the inside by a heavy 'millstone' door like those in

At Derinkuyu and Kaymaklı entire cities have been dug into the soft rock, complete with kitchens, wineries and churches. In times of trouble, the tunnels could be sealed by stone doors.

the underground city of Derinkuyu (see above). At the back are two mysterious tunnels disappearing into the darkness; the complex has not yet been fully excavated, and more levels wait to be discovered.

You enter the **church** through an arched door in the far wall of the courtyard. To the right is the nave, with a central dome supported on four columns decorated with geometric designs. The frescoes are splendid: Christ Pantocrator in the dome; a slender Madonna against a rich, dark blue background; and a lively Nativity which, in a nice touch, shows the ox and ass peering over the edge of the manger at the swaddled Jesus.

Ihlara Valley

At Gölçük, some 17km (10 miles) south of Derinkuyu, a road on the right heads through a landscape of grassy pastures, lush farmland and outcrops of brown rock towards Güzelyurt and Ihlara. To the south rises the dormant volcanic cone of Hasan Dağı (3,268m; 10,720ft), and its neighbour Melendiz Dağı. It last erupted within recorded history – Strabo describes it as being active during the 1st century AD, and a famous wall painting found at the neolithic site of Çatalhöyük, near Konya, shows a town with a twin-peaked volcano spewing smoke in the background.

The northern slopes of these volcanic peaks are drained by the Melendiz Suyu, which flows westwards to the great Salt Lake (Tuz Gölü) of central Anatolia. At Ihlara, near the foot of Hasan Dağı, the river has carved a spectacular **gorge**, which formed the focus of a Christian monastic community between the 6th and the 14th centuries. The tall, columnar cliffs of golden-brown rock were once riddled with 4,500 rock-cut houses and over 100 churches, but rock falls and river ero-

The lovely Ihlara Valley is lined with columnar cliffs, which contain a number of rock-cut churches. The wooded valley-floor provides pleasant riverside walks.

sion have carried many of them away. The **frescoes** in the remaining churches provide a valuable record of early Christian art. (A flashlight is necessary to see the frescoes properly.)

Quite apart from its historic and artistic interest, the **Ihlara Valley** is a beautiful and spectacular place, and well worth exploring for its own sake. The wooded valley floor is loud with bird song and croaking frogs, and the riverbank provides countless attractive picnic spots. Eagles soar above the crags, martins skim along the stream, and goldfinches, redstarts, nuthatches and hoopoes can be spotted. You can hike along the full length of the valley from Selime to Ihlara village, a distance of 16km (10 miles), or make a shorter loop walk from the Valley Restaurant. The restaurant is perched on top of the cliffs a few kilometres north of Ihlara village, and offers access to the valley floor via a flight of 383 steps.

The best churches are near the foot of the steps, where a wooden bridge crosses the river. Immediately on the right is the **Ağaçaltı Kilise** (Church Beneath the Tree), with bright, naively painted frescoes; on the dome is Christ ascending into heaven, surrounded by portraits of kings and prophets. Further upstream, on the near bank, are the Pürenli Seki Kilise and the Kokar Kilise. The most fascinating church in the valley, the **Yılanlı Kilise** (Church of the Snake), lies on the far side

of the stream – cross the bridge and turn left for 100m (110yd) to a flight of stairs leading to the entrance. The church gets its name from a fresco on the west wall depicting the suffering of souls in hell: in the centre is a large, three-headed serpent with a condemned soul in each mouth; to its left, Satan reaches towards the winged figure of St Michael, who weighs a soul in his scales; to its right, four female sinners are tormented by snakes.

Sultanhanı

At Aksaray, northwest of Ihlara, the road descends from the volcanic plateau of Cappadocia into the huge, mountain-fringed basin of central Anatolia. To the north lie the shimmering mirages of the Tuz Gölü (Salt Lake); to the west, a rolling expanse of wheat and pasture recedes to the horizon. The road from Aksaray to Konya follows the route of the Selçuk trade route known as the 'Uzun Yol' (see box p.271). About 40km (25 miles) from Aksaray you reach the village of Sultanhanı, which contains one of the best-preserved Selçuk caravanserais in the country.

The caravanserai (meaning 'caravan palace') was built in 1229, but has been much restored. The massive high walls and grand portal show the emphasis placed on security; travelling merchants were a prime target for bandits. The courtyard provided room for 300-400 crouching camels; the bales of merchandise were stored in the ground-floor rooms around the arcade, while the men were billeted in the upper rooms. A tiny prayer hall rests on four arches in the middle of the courtyard, raised above the noise and filth of the tethered livestock. In the bitter cold of the central Anatolian winter both men and animals could retreat into the cathedral-like hall beyond the courtyard.

Konya

Konya is the historic capital of the Sultanate of Rum, the Seljuk state that controlled most of Anatolia during the 12th and 13th centuries. At that time it was one of the most brilliant cities in the world, a famous centre of Islamic learning and culture, endowed by its rulers with many fine works of architecture. The philosopher Celaleddin Rumi, later known as Mevlana, arrived here in 1228 and founded the mystical Sufi order known to us as the 'Whirling Dervishes'. Mevlana's tomb and museum, and the city's fine legacy of Seljuk buildings are Konya's main attractions for visitors; allow at least a full day, preferably two, to enjoy them fully.

Konya is one of the oldest continually inhabited urban centres in the world. Excavations on **Alaeddin Tepesi**, the hill in the centre of the city, have revealed evidence of a settlement here since at least the 3rd millennium BC. According to a Phrygian legend, the city was the first to be revived after a great deluge destroyed humanity. Its ancient name, Iconium, is said to derive from the image (*eikon* in Greek) of Medusa with which Perseus defeated the natives before establishing a Greek city on this site. Iconium was incorporated into the Roman province of Galatia in 25 BC, and became capital of Lycaonia province in AD 372; St Paul visited the city on his missionary journeys between AD 47 and 53 (see box, p.241).

The hill of Alaeddin Tepesi, in the centre of Konya, has been inhabited for over 3,000 years. Today it is a wooded park, with pleasant outdoor terrace-cafés

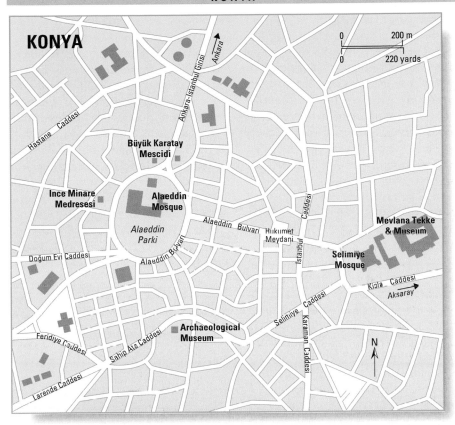

KONYA

0   200 m
0   220 yards

Ankara-İstanbul Gürsi

Ankara

Hastane Caddesi

Büyük Karatay Mescidi

İnce Minare Medresesi

Alaeddin Mosque

Alaeddin Parki

Alaeddin Bulvari

Hükümet Meydani

İstanbul

Caddesi

Mevlana Tekke & Museum

Selimiye Mosque

Doğum Evi Caddesi

Alaeddin Bulvari

Kişla Caddesi

Aksaray

Feridiye Caddesi

Sahip Ata Caddesi

Archaeological Museum

Selimiye Caddesi

Karaman Caddesi

N

Larende Caddesi

Seljuk Architecture

The Seljuks captured Iconium in the late 11th century, and changed its name to Konya. The ruling sultans built their palace on the slopes of the Alaeddin Tepesi, which today is occupied by a beautiful wooded park. Nothing remains of the palace except for a crumbling tower, now protected by a modern concrete canopy, but the city's principal mosque, the **Alaeddin Camii**, has survived, and is currently undergoing restoration. It was begun around 1150, and completed during the reign of Sultan Alaeddin Keykubad I (1219-36), whose tomb rests in an octagonal mausoleum at the rear of the mosque; beside it is a second, pyramid-roofed mausoleum holding the remains of the mosque's founder, Sultan Meshud I (1116-55,) and seven other Seljuk sultans. The prayer hall has a wooden roof supported by 42 marble columns capped with Roman and Byzantine capitals (these obviously taken from some earlier, unknown building), and a superb, delicately carved ebony *mimber*.

Across the street from the concrete canopy is the **Karatay Medrese** (1251), which houses the city's ceramics museum. Its ornate portal is decorated with Arabic inscriptions and an interlocking geometric design inlaid with blue and white marble. Inside, the dome is covered in ceramic tiles imitating the night sky. Following the street anticlockwise around Alaeddin Tepesi, you soon come to the even more elaborate portal of the **İnce Minareli Medrese** (Seminary of the Slender Minaret). Its baroque ornamentation resembles heavy draperies, with two ribbons of inscription descending from a gathered pelmet and twisting into a knot above the door. The large, rectilinear knot motifs to either side are similar to patterns that appear in local carpets. The building dates from the 1260s, and now houses a fine museum of stonemasonry and woodcarving. The minaret still retains its decoration of blue and orange tiles, and is topped with a lightning conductor; it was badly damaged by a lightning strike in 1901 and now stands to only half its original height.

On the south side of the hill, a right turn down Sırçalı Caddesi will lead to Sahip Ata Caddesi and Konya's **Archaeological Museum** (*Arkeoloji Müzesi*). Its small but interesting collection includes prehistoric and Hittite finds from nearby Çatalhöyük, Karahöyük and Canhasan, and a magnificent 3rd-century AD Roman sarcophagus depicting the Labours of Hercules.

The neolithic site of **Çatalhöyük**, which yielded many of the prehistoric treasures on view in Ankara's Museum of Anatolian Civilizations, lies about 60 km (38 miles) southeast of Konya, near the town of Çumra. It was excavated during the 1960s and revealed 13 levels of habitation, these ranging in age from 6800 to 5500 BC. It was a large community of mud-brick and timber houses, which were entered through a hole in the roof and decorated with wall paintings. Although the site is open to visitors, there is nothing to see except the huge settlement mound, covered in wildflowers, and the eroded remains of the archaeologists' trenches.

Mevlana Museum

Konya's main street, Alaeddin Caddesi, leads eastwards from Alaeddin Tepesi past hotels, carpet shops and restaurants to Konya's most important monument, the **Mevlana Museum**. Although it is called a museum, it is also one of the foremost Islamic shrines in Turkey, and so when

The green-tiled spire of Mevlana's tomb rises beyond the domes of the Selimiye Camii. It was here that the mystic sect called the Whirling Dervishes originated.

visiting you should dress and behave respectfully. It is housed in the *tekke* (lodge) that once accommodated the members of the dervish order – the fluted turquoise spire that sits above the tomb of Mevlana is a famous symbol of Konya.

The entrance leads into an attractive courtyard with an Ottoman *şadırvan* and colourful flower beds. Remove your shoes and enter the **mausoleum** (the door to the right of the fountain). The 65 tombs inside belong to the family, friends and followers of Mevlana. His own tomb is at the far end of the chamber, on the right behind an ornate silver screen. Mevlana's sarcophagus lies in front of his eldest son's, draped in richly embroidered silks. His father's tomb stands upright to the left, symbolizing the older man's respect for his son's learning. The tombs lie beneath an octagonal dome (the interior of the turquoise spire), richly decorated in red, green and gold, and adorned with verses from the Koran.

Opposite the tombs, to the left, is the **semahane**, the room where the dervishes used to perform their whirling dance, flanked by galleries for musicians and spectators. Musical instruments, clothing, ancient carpets, and other objects associated with the order are displayed here and in the small adjoining mosque. A case in the middle of the *semahane* contains the museum's most precious possession – a hair from the beard of the Prophet Muhammad. Other exhibits include the original illuminated *Mesnevi*, Arabic calligraphy and miniature Korans; one case displays six grains of rice, each of which bears a verse from the Koran inscribed in minute script.

Next door to the *tekke* is the **Selimiye Camii** (Mosque of Sultan Selim), built in 1567 by a student of Sinan. The interior is fairly unexceptional, except for the *mimber,* which mimics the spire on Mevlana's tomb.

Lake District
(Göller Bölgesi)

To the west of Konya lies Turkey's Lake District, a scenic region of blue lakes and snow-capped mountains, fragrant cedar woods and wildflower meadows. The area can easily be reached from either Konya or Antalya, and deserves at least a day or two of exploring. The large freshwater lakes of Beyşehir Gölü and Eğirdir Gölü are the most attractive; the town of Eğirdir has a number of pleasant waterfront hotels and pensions.

Beyşehir Gölü

At 45km (28 miles) long and 25km (15 miles) wide, **Beyşehir Gölü** is Turkey's third-largest lake (after Lake Van and Tuz Gölü), and is its largest body of fresh water (the other two are salt lakes). Although the mountains on its western shore rise to nearly 3,000m (10,000ft), the lake is only about 10m (33ft) deep. Its blue-green waters, teeming with carp and other fish, drain underground through a cave system in the southwestern corner.

The **town of Beyşehir** lies at the southeastern end of the lake, where the old routes from Konya to Antalya and Izmir diverge. The town's heyday was in the late 13th to early 14th centuries, when it was the seat of the Seljuk Emir Eşrefoğlu Seyfeddin Süleyman. The emir built Beyşehir's most important monument, the **Eşrefoğlu Camii**, in 1296-9. It is Turkey's best-surviving wooden Seljuk mosque; the flat roof is supported by a veritable forest of pine-log columns topped with ornately carved wooden capitals, and the *mimber* is an outstanding example of Seljuk woodcarving.

The road heads north along the east shore of the lake, through lush fields that are scarlet with wild poppies during

springtime. About 15km (9 miles) from Beyşehir a sign points the way to the **Eflatun Pınar** (Lilac Spring). At one side of a spring-fed pond stands a Hittite shrine dating from the 13th century BC. The altar-like structure is made of large stone blocks, and is carved with the figures of Hittite gods and winged sun-discs.

At the north end of the lake a poor road branches off towards the mountains and cedar forests of **Kızıldağ National Park** and goes down the west shore of the lake.

An ancient water lifting device stands idle on the shore of Beyşehir Gölü in Turkey's Lake District.

At the rarely visited village of Gölyaka (more easily reached by boat from Beyşehir) are the excavated ruins of the **Kubadabat Sarayı**, a summer palace built by the Seljuk Sultan Alaeddin Keykubad I in 1226. The palace is remarkable for the ceramic tiles found here, now on display in Konya's Karatay Medrese. Although Islam proscribes the depiction of living creatures, these tiles bear images of Seljuk princes and their consorts, animals, birds and mythical creatures.

Eğirdir Gölü

The **town of Eğirdir** (also spelt Eğridir) enjoys one of the most attractive settings of any inland town in Turkey. It sits on a neck of land surrounded by the emerald waters of Eğirdir Gölü, beneath the rocky 2,635m (8,645ft) peak of Davraz Dağ. Its easily defensible position means it has been inhabited since the earliest times. The Byzantines called it Akrotiri (Greek for 'peninsula') for obvious reasons, a name which was corrupted to Eğridir (meaning 'bent' or 'curved') when the town was captured by the Seljuk Turks in the early 13th century. During the 13th and 14th centuries it was the most important city in the region; the famous Arabic geographer Ibn Battuta described it as 'a great and populous city with fine bazaars and running streams, fruit trees and orchards' and 'a lake of sweet water'.

A causeway runs out to the tiny island of **Yeşilada**, where the town's most charming hotels and pensions are concentrated. Depending on which side of the island you choose to stay on (you can walk right around it in 15 minutes), you can have a room that enjoys a view of the sunset or the sunrise. At the far end is the ruined 12th-century Byzantine church of Ayios Stefanos, and a little harbour where you can rent rowing and motor boats.

Back on the mainland are a few remnants of Eğirdir's days of past glory. In the centre of the town is the 13th-century

Dündar Bey Medresesi, which now houses a shopping centre, and the **Hızır Bey Camii** (1308), with finely carved wooden doors and a roof supported by wooden columns. Overlooking the start of the Yeşilada causeway are the ruins of a Byzantine and Seljuk **fortress**, which is said to rest on foundations laid during the reign of King Croesus of Lydia in the 6th century BC.

İsparta and Around

İsparta is a pleasant modern town set high in the mountains southwest of Eğirdir. It was a Seljuk possession until 1381, when the ruling Hamidoğlu emir sold it to the Ottomans. The town is famous for two things: attar of roses, which is extracted from the petals of flowers grown in the huge rose gardens that surround the city; and İsparta carpets, which can be bought at the **Halı Saray** (Carpet Palace), a bazaar near the town hall.

In the mountains to the south of İsparta, above the village of Ağlasun, are the ruins of the ancient Pisidian city of **Sagalassos**. This is a very old settlement, inhabited since at least the 13th century BC. There are scattered ruins of a theatre, an *agora,* a couple of temples and some rock tombs, mostly dating from Roman times. But the main attraction of the site is its beautiful setting, with grand views of the surrounding mountains.

From Ağlasun a minor road twists through the hills to the highway just south of Burdur, where you will find the entrance to the **İnsuyu Cave** (*İnsuyu Mağarası*). A 600m (650yd) long subterranean walkway leads to the *Büyük Göl* (Great Lake), an eerie blue-green pool in the sump at the far end of the cave. Depending on rainfall, the lake can rise from the bottom of the sump up to the level of the viewing terrace.

Mevlana and the Whirling Dervishes of Konya

The Life and Work of Mevlana

Mevlana Celaleddin ar-Rumi was born in Balkh, Afghanistan, in 1207, the son of the respected teacher Bahaeddin Veled. Balkh was the capital of Khorasan, and a famous centre of Islamic learning, but in the early 13th century it was threatened with invasion by the Mongols. Fearing for their safety, Bahaeddin and his family formed a small caravan and set off towards Baghdad (his decision was timely – Balkh was completely destroyed by the hordes of Genghis Khan in 1220). They travelled around the Middle East for several years before arriving in Anatolia, where they finally settled in Karaman, to the south-east of Konya, in 1221 (the 'ar-Rumi' of Mevlana's name means 'the man from Anatolia'). Sultan Alaeddin Keykubad I, on learning that the famous Bahaeddin Veled was living near by, invited him to come and teach in Konya, which he did until his death in 1231.

Celaleddin, well trained in Islamic theology, took over his father's teaching post. He had read widely, including the works of the classical Greek authors, and was exposed to a wide range of world views by Konya's cosmopolitan population. He soon acquired a reputation as an accomplished scholar and an original and provocative thinker, and attracted a small band of devoted students. In 1244 he met a kindred spirit in the shape of Shems, a wandering Sufi from Tabriz in Persia – the pair became inseparable, and lost themselves in philosophical disputations for weeks at a time. Celaleddin abandoned his teaching, much to the chagrin of his jealous followers, who began to plot against Shems. However, the Persian dervish caught wind of these machinations and left town.

Celaleddin was distraught at losing his soul-mate, and searched frantically for him. He eventually tracked down Shems in Damascus, and begged him to return with him to Turkey. But back in Konya the plotting began again, and in 1247 Shems mysteriously disappeared, never to be seen again (he was probably murdered by a group of Celaleddin's disciples led by his youngest son). Heartbroken, Celaleddin completely immersed himself in music and poetry, seeking the spirit of his lost friend; he also explored the path offered by Sufism (a Sufi is an Islamic mystic who seeks the truth of divine love and knowledge through a personal union with God).

Inspired by his love for Shems, Celaleddin (now known as Mevlana – the name is Arabic for 'Our Master') expounded his personal philosophy in a great mystical poem, the *Masnavi* which ran to six volumes containing 26,000 couplets in Persian, and which has been described as 'an encyclopaedia of mystical thought in which everyone can find his own religious ideas'. For many Muslims this great work ranks second in importance only to the Koran and the Hadith (the sayings of the Prophet Muhammad). Mevlana's tolerance and compassion won him many followers, and he was held in great esteem by people of all faiths. He invited everyone to join him in seeking the way of enlightenment: 'Come, come again, whoever or whatever you may be, come! Heathen, fire-worshipper, idolater, come...Ours is not the portal of despair or misery...All who enter will receive a welcome here'. When he died on 17 December 1273, his funeral procession took a full day to pass through the city.

The Mevlana Museum at Konya is housed in the former tekke *of the Mevlevi Dervishes. It is an important place of pilgrimage.*

The Mevlevi Dervishes

After Mevlana's death, his band of followers – the Mevlevi Dervishes – led by his eldest son, continued to study and disseminate his teachings, based at their *tekke* (lodge) in Konya. The Mevlevi order spread rapidly through Anatolia, and found favour with the Ottoman sultans. *Tekkes* were established in towns and cities throughout the Ottoman Empire, even as far away as Egypt.

Over the centuries the Mevlevis and other Sufi orders, with their strong appeal to the common masses, attained a large degree of political power. In 1925, following the establishment of the secular Turkish Republic, Kemal Atatürk outlawed the mystical brotherhoods. In a speech to parliament he declared, 'Gentlemen, you and the whole nation must know, and know well, that the Republic of Turkey cannot be the land of sheikhs, dervishes, disciples and lay brothers...The heads of the brotherhoods will...at once close their lodges, and accept the fact that their disciples have at last come of age.'

The Mevlevi *tekke* in Konya was officially converted into a museum, but many people adhere to their old beliefs and treat it as a place of pilgrimage. Since 1954, the Mevlevis have been given special permission to perform the *sema* for tourist audiences. These performances take place in Konya for two weeks each December, to commemorate the anniversary of Mevlana's death.

The Sema

Although all dervish brotherhoods seek mystical experience, the different orders use different means for attaining a mystical state – music, dance, poetry, chanting. The Mevlevi order developed a ritual dance known as the *sema*, in which the dancers abandon themselves and seek a union with God. Their clothing has a

Pilgrims gather at Mevlana's tomb.

symbolic significance – the white robe represents their shrouds, the dark cloak their tombs, and the tall hat their tombstones. At the beginning of the dance they shed the cloaks, symbolizing their escape from the earthly tomb, and begin to spin. Each dancer revolves on his right foot, with his right hand raised palm-up towards heaven, his left palm-down; this shows his desire to act as a conduit, receiving God's blessing from above and passing it on to the world below. As they whirl, the dancers revolve around each other, representing the rotation of the heavenly bodies, and chant a ritual prayer, or *zikir* ('remembrance of God'), under their breath.

Pontus Euxinus – the Hospitable Sea

The Black Sea coast of Turkey offers a complete contrast to the shores of the Aegean and Mediterranean. These northern lands are cooler, wetter and greener. The ancients called the Black Sea the *Pontus*, and added the adjective *Euxinus* – hospitable – because of its clement weather. Today it is still a hospitable region, often overlooked by Western tourists. But for those who enjoy getting off the beaten track, it is well worth exploring. Trabzon is where most people head for, to see the area's two 'unmissable' sights – the frescoes of Ayasofya and the spectacular Sumela Monastery.

Mountains line the coast for most of its length, and are thickly wooded – the region accounts for a quarter of all Turkey's forested area. Not surprisingly, such a fertile zone is intensely cultivated. Most of the settlements are farming towns and villages, with different districts specializing in different crops – hazelnuts and cherries grow around Giresun and Ordu, tobacco at Samsun and Trabzon, and tea in the hills behind Rize. Industry is concentrated around the coal mines of Zonguldak in the west, and at the major ports of Trabzon and Samsun.

This is a region largely neglected by western tourists, who prefer the sun-drenched beaches of the south. Here the sea is cooler, the weather less dependable and the tourist services less well developed. But the prices are lower, the people are just as friendly and the scenery is often spectacular. Perhaps most importantly, the Black Sea coast offers the opportunity to see a completely different side of Turkey.

The coast west of İnebolu is still remote, served only by twisting, potholed roads that are occasionally closed by landslides – the trip from Amasra to Sinop is a major expedition. Driving from Ankara or Istanbul, the easiest place to get to is the port of Samsun.

The Black Sea coast is quieter and less developed than the Aegean and Mediterranean. It is a coast of mountains and forests, with rocky shores and historic harbours.

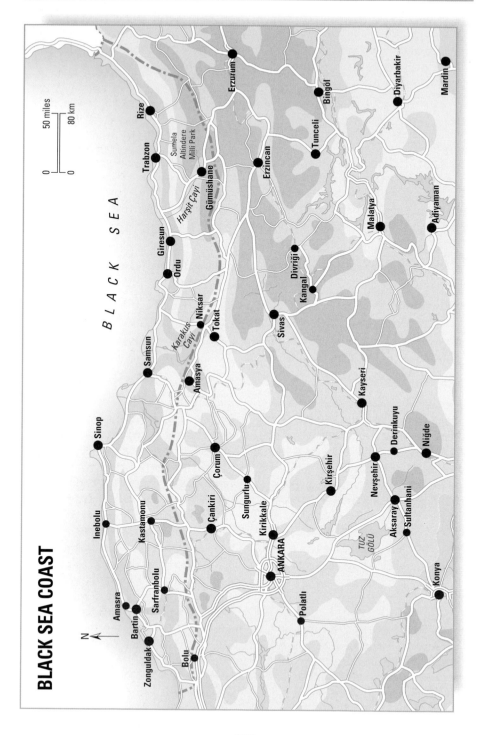

BLACK SEA COAST

N

50 miles
80 km
0

BLACK SEA

Sumela
Altindere
Milli Park

Harşit Çayi

Karakus Çayi

Erzurum
Bingöl
Diyarbakir
Mardin
Rize
Tunceli
Trabzon
Erzincan
Gümüşhane
Malatya
Adiyaman
Giresun
Ordu
Divriği
Kangal
Niksar
Tokat
Sivas
Samsun
Amasya
Kayseri
Sinop
Derinkuyu
Niğde
Çorum
Nevşehir
Kirşehir
Aksaray
Sultanhani
Çankiri
Sungurlu
Inebolu
Kastamonu
Kirikkale
ANKARA
TUZ GÖLÜ
Konya
Amasra
Safranbolu
Bartin
Polatli
Zonguldak
Bolu

298

West from Samsun

Samsun, with a population of 250,000, is the largest city on the Black Sea coast. It began life in the 7th century BC as Amisus, a colony founded by traders from Miletus (see p.180). It continued to flourish as a trading centre under the Romans, Byzantines and Turks, and today it is a major port and a centre for the region's tobacco industry. Kemal Atatürk stepped ashore here on 19 May 1919 to begin the organization of his nationalist movement, an event that marked the beginning of the Turkish War of Independence. It is commemorated by the 'First Step' monument on Atatürk Bulvarı. Apart from that, there is little to see in Samsun, and you will probably want to move on quickly.

Sinop

As it heads west from Samsun, the highway cuts through the countless acres of tobacco fields that cover the wide delta of the Kızılırmak, Turkey's longest river. Beyond, the headland of Sinop soon comes into view across the bay. The city of **Sinop** straddles a narrow isthmus linking the Boztepe Peninsula to the mainland. It was an important town in ancient times, having the only safe natural harbour on the Black Sea coast. It has long since been overtaken by Samsun, and today makes its living from fishing and tourism.

According to legend, the city was founded by the Amazons, who named it after their queen, Sinova. It became a

---

LIFE IN A BARREL

Sinop was the birthplace of Diogenes, the 4th-century BC founder of the Cynics, a philosophical sect that advocated self-sufficiency and the rejection of luxury. For Diogenes, this also meant the rejection of conventional ways of life. Exiled from Sinop, he moved to Athens, where he slept rough and begged for food. He saw the family unit as an 'unnatural' institution, which should be abandoned in favour of a 'state of nature' where men and women were promiscuous and children were looked after communally. Not surprisingly, many stories were told about him, most of them probably untrue. He was supposed to have lived in a barrel, where he was visited by Alexander the Great. When asked if there was anything the famous warrior could do for him, Diogenes replied, 'Yes: stand aside, you're blocking my light'. Another tale tells of him being asked to find an honest man; Diogenes searched in broad daylight carrying a lighted lantern.

THE BATTLE OF SINOP

On 24 November 1853, in the opening months of the Crimean War, a Russian flotilla spotted the masts of the main Ottoman fleet moored in the harbour at Sinop. The Russians returned to their base at Sebastopol, but six days later they came back in force and caught the Turkish ships unprepared. No less than 720 guns were trained on the trapped Ottoman fleet and the shore batteries beyond – all of the Turkish ships were destroyed except for one steam auxiliary under an English captain, which hastened to Istanbul with the bad news. The Battle of Sinop gave the British and French fleets an excuse to enter the Black Sea – to protect Ottoman shipping – and led to Britain and France declaring war on Russia in March 1854. Back in London, *The Times* had thundered, 'The English people are resolved that Russia shall not dictate conditions to Europe, or convert the Black Sea…into a Russian lake'.

prosperous trading colony, and in 183 BC was chosen as the capital of the Pontic kings (see box, p.265), who endowed it with massive walls, and many fine buildings and monuments. More recently, at the start of the Crimean War in 1853, Sinop was attacked by the Russian navy; the Ottoman fleet was destroyed, and much of the city laid waste (see box p.299).

Approaching Sinop today, the massive **fortifications**, rebuilt by the Byzantines and Seljuks, are still prominent. Down by the sea to the left of the road is the **Kumkapı** (Sand Gate), the old city gate; to

the right, the ancient walls house a modern prison, keeping people in instead of out. The main street, Sakarya Caddesi, is a narrow, shop-lined canyon leading to the main square, passing the 13th-century **Alaeddin Camii** on the way. To the left is the **museum**, which contains a collection of

The remains of the harbour fortifications at Sinop are crowded by the buildings of the town centre. The walls were badly damaged during the bombardment by the Russian fleet in 1853.

Long stretches of the Black Sea coast (as here, near Gerze) are lined with near-deserted sandy beaches. They are often quite difficult to reach, but for the determined explorer they offer the welcome opportunity to escape from the tourist crowds.

19th-century Greek Orthodox icons, a reminder that the region had a large population of Ottoman Greeks before the War of Independence. In the garden are a few pieces of sculpture and some fragments of columns and architrave from the Hellenistic **Temple of Serapis** that once stood here.

Downhill from the square is the waterfront, overlooked by a well-preserved

Sinop to Amasra

The coast to the west of Sinop is rather dull as far as İnebolu, an unattractive town with a huge shingle beach and a handful of hotels and restaurants. Beyond İnebolu the road deteriorates to a potholed, single-track switchback (allow at least four hours to drive the 170km, or (106 miles), from İnebolu to Amasra), but the scenery improves dramatically, with steep mountainsides dropping straight into the sea, tiny sandy coves, and a few small fishing harbours. There are attractive **beaches** at Kayan, Akbayır, Kapısuyu, Çakraz and Bozköy.

Amasra (ancient Amastris) is a sleepy little harbour town, tucked beneath the crumbling walls of a Byzantine fortress. There's not much to see, but it's a pleasant place to wander round before having lunch in one of the restaurants. A street of woodworkers' shops stretches across the neck of the fortified promontory that separates the modern harbour from the Roman one to the west. Above the Roman harbour, the fortress gate is plastered with the coats of arms of Genoese merchants, who occupied the town in the 14th and 15th centuries.

East from Samsun

The most attractive part of the Black Sea coast lies between Samsun and Trabzon. East of Samsun the highway crosses the marshy delta of the Yeşilırmak, a maze of overgrown channels and lagoons, to the beach resort of **Ünye**, where the real holiday coast begins. From here on, the road is lined with beaches, campsites, hotels, pensions and restaurants, aimed mainly at Turkish and eastern European tourists (which means that prices are usually fairly low). There is a long and beautiful curved

stretch of the city walls. Turn right before the tea gardens and go through the arch, where a sign points the way to the 'Entrance to the Tower'. Stairs lead up to the **ramparts** of one of the defensive towers, which offer a good view over the harbour with its serried ranks of fishing boats (the quayside along to the right has several good seafood restaurants).

beach backed by pine groves at **Çaka**, and another pleasant stretch of coast around **Perşembe**, with rock coves, fishing harbours and live-fish (*canlı balık*) restaurants. **Ordu** is another beach resort, with an attractive tree-lined promenade and waterfront park; a few kilometres to the east is the riverside meadow of **Turnasuyu**, with a beach of golden sand at the river's mouth.

Giresun

The houses of **Giresun** cluster picturesquely around a steep promontory topped by the ruins of a Byzantine fortress. Known to the Greeks as Pharnacia, and to the Romans as Cerasus, it was famous for its cherries. Although cherry orchards are still an important part of the local economy, hazelnuts (*fındık* in Turkish) have taken over as Giresun's chief product, exported by ship from the new harbour. Although there is not much to see in town, it is a very pleasant place to stay while you explore the nearby coast.

Apart from a number of fine restaurants, the main attraction in Giresun is the **Kalepark**, a delightful wooded park at the summit of the citadel crag. Shady walks meander around the ruined walls of the Byzantine castle, and there are picnic tables and a couple of tea gardens with good views over the town. Beside the main highway, east of the promontory, is a green-domed 19th-century Greek Orthodox church which now serves as the local **museum**.

Each year on 20 May Giresun holds an open-air **festival** at the mouth of the Aksu River a few kilometres east of town. The festival has its pagan roots way back in the mists of time, and is associated with the Anatolian mother goddess and the return of spring. The festivities begin at the river mouth, where the participants throw handfuls of pebbles (symbolizing last year's troubles) into the stream, before sailing out to

> ### CHERRY ROOTS
>
> In ancient times Giresun was known as Cerasus, and even then was famous for its cherries. The Romans introduced the fruit to Europe, and its Latin name *cerasum* (from the town of Cerasus) became the root for its name in most Western languages – cherry in English, *cérise* in French, *Kirsche* in German, *cereza* in Spanish, *ciliegia* in Italian – and in Turkish *(kiraz)* and Arabic *(krez)*.

island of **Giresun Adası**, which they circumnavigate three times anticlockwise. The ritual is accompanied by much eating, drinking and dancing. The island was sacred to the Amazons, and Jason and his Argonauts are supposed to have made a sacrifice there on their way to find the Golden Fleece. Today, there are only the scant ruins of a Byzantine monastery to be seen.

Trabzon (Trebizond)

Trabzon is a city of romantic associations. In ancient times it was the land of the Amazons, the legendary race of women warriors, and provided the first sight of the sea for Xenophon's exhausted army (see box). Tales of beautiful Trapezuntine princesses incarcerated by infidel tyrants inspired Cervantes to set Don Quixote on his famous quest for Dulcinea, and in her 1950s novel Rose Macaulay describes 'the towers of Trebizond shimmering on a far horizon in luminous enchantment'.

The city was probably founded in the 8th century BC by colonists from Sinope, and marked the eastern limit of Greek colonization on the Black Sea coast. It was built on a flat-topped acropolis hill that gave it its Greek name, *Trapezus* (meaning 'table'). (Down the centuries this has been rendered as 'Trebizond' in English, '*Trapezunt*' in German, '*Trébisonde*' in French, and most

THALASSA! THALASSA!

The Greek soldier and historian Xenophon, in his famous work *Anabasis* (*Expedition*), describes his experience as a mercenary in the army of King Cyrus of Persia. Following Cyrus' defeat in 401 BC, Xenophon led a force of exhausted Greek mercenaries (called the 'Ten Thousand') from Persia through the unknown and hostile territories of Kurdistan and Armenia to the Black Sea at Trabzon. In a memorable passage he relates how, nearing the top of a pass in the mountains, he heard a great clamour among the men at the front of his column, and rode forward expecting another hostile encounter. Instead he found them yelling *'Thalassa! Thalassa!'* ('The sea! The sea!'), '...and coming to the top, they embraced one another and their generals and captains, with tears in their eyes, and bringing together a great many stones...made a great cairn.'

recently, '*Trabzon*' in Turkish.) The city prospered under Roman rule, but achieved its zenith during the 13th and 14th centuries when it was the seat of the Comneni of Trebizond, an offshoot of the Byzantine Empire (see box). Under Ottoman rule, its governorship was often given to the son of the sultan to prepare him for the administration of the empire. Süleyman the Magnificent was born and raised here while his father, Selim II, was governor.

Modern Trabzon is a major city with a large commercial harbour, and little remains of its former air of romance. However, there are enough historic monuments to keep you busy for a day, and the city is the best jumping-off point for a visit to the unmissable Sumela Monastery in the mountains to the south. One of the first things you will notice are the signs in Russian that appear in shops and hotels all over town. Since the collapse of the Soviet Union, Trabzon has become a focus for small-time Russian traders. They cross the border from Georgia 175km (110 miles) to the east, sell their cheap merchandise to the Turks, and load up with consumer goods to sell back home. There is a huge **Russian Bazaar** (*Rus Pazarı*) beyond the highway tunnel at the east end of town. The city also attracts a large contingent of Russian prostitutes, something which should be borne in mind by budget travellers – many of the cheap hotels in Trabzon and the coastal towns to the east are brothels in everything but name.

THE EMPIRE OF TREBIZOND

Following the sack of Constantinople by the crusaders in 1204, two grandsons of the Byzantine emperor, Alexius and David Comnenus, managed to escape to Trebizond. There, with the help of their aunt, Queen Thamar of Georgia, they founded a small empire of their own that flourished for over 250 years. There were several reasons for the success of the Trapezuntine Empire. Its rulers formed extensive alliances through marriage with neighbouring powers (the Comneni princesses were famed for their beauty); also, its relative isolation meant that it was largely bypassed by the Seljuk and Mongol invasions. The empire accrued wealth through the export of locally produced silver, iron, cloth and wine, and creamed taxes from the trade that passed through its port – a branch of the Silk Road ran from Tabriz in Persia to Erzurum, and thence over the mountains to Trebizond, a safer alternative to the routes further south, which were threatened by marauding Mongols in the late 13th century. Although the empire was torn apart by factional disputes in the late 14th century, the Comneni Dynasty ruled longer than any other Byzantine family back in Constantinople. Trebizond was eventually annexed to the Ottoman Empire in 1461.

City Centre

Trabzon sprawls across a mountainside above the sea, and many of its historical monuments are inconveniently far away from the city centre. Unless you are prepared for a day's energetic walking, a taxi or organized tour is recommended. The focus of the modern city is the shady park of **Atatürk Alanı**, surrounded by banks, restaurants and travel agencies; there is a tourist information kiosk in one corner. To the northeast lies the old bastion of **Leontokastron**, built by Genoese to protect their traders. The highway now tunnels beneath it, and a private club occupies the summit, but there are pleasant tea gardens on the west side, a favourite haunt of young *Trabzonlus* in the evenings.

The centre of medieval Trabzon lies about a kilometre (½ mile) to the west, within the massive walls of the **Hisar** (fortress). On foot, you can reach the fortress along Uzun Yol (the street at the southwest corner of Atatürk Alanı), which leads to a deep ravine crossed by the Tabakhane Bridge. A 400m (440yd) detour leftwards up the hill before crossing the bridge takes you to the **church of St Eugenius**, the patron saint of the Empire of Trebizond. Eugenius was martyred by the Emperor Diocletian for protesting against the cult of Mithra at Trapezus. The church was built by Alexius Comnenus on the spot where the martyr's skull was allegedly found in the 13th century. It was converted to a mosque, the Yeni Cuma Camii, by Mehmet the Conqueror in 1461.

Tabakhane Bridge leads into the **Ortahisar** (Middle Fortress) district of the city, beneath the upper citadel, all that remains of the fabled 'Towers of Trebizond'. Here you will find the **cathedral of Panayia Chrysokephalos** (now the Ortahisar or Fatih Camii). This was originally the cathedral church of the empire of Trebizond, where the imperial coronations, weddings and funerals were held. The appellation *'Chrysokephalos'* (Greek for 'gold-headed') refers to the original copper dome, which was plated with gold. You can admire the fine architecture, but the imperial tombs are gone, and the decoration too – the frescoes have been plastered over, and the mosaic floor has disappeared beneath a thick layer of 20th-century concrete.

Church of Hagia Sophia (Ayasofya)

In order to view a Trapezuntine church in something resembling its original glory, you'll have to travel 3km (2 miles) west of Atatürk Alanı, to where the monastery **church of Hagia Sophia** sits on a grassy terrace overlooking the sea. Founded by the Emperor Manuel I (1238-63), the church has a cross-in-square floor plan, with a triple apse at the east end and porches on the three other sides. The weathered frieze above the entrance to the south porch portrays the story of Adam and Eve; the arch above is crowned by an eagle, the symbol of the Comneni Dynasty.

Inside, the central dome is supported on four columns whose capitals are decorated with a 'bunch of grapes' motif; the fresco of Christ Pantocrator in the dome is badly damaged. Better paintings survive in the apse, where the Virgin Mary is flanked by the archangels Michael and Gabriel, with the Ascension above. But the best frescoes are in the **narthex**, especially the cross-vault which is adorned with *trompe-l'oeil* seraphim and cherubim; at the south end are scenes showing the young Christ teaching in the temple, and the Marriage at Canaan; at the north end are Christ walking on the water, and also calming the storm. Take a look at the west porch (outside the narthex)

The best-preserved frescoes at Hagia Sophia are in the narthex. This one, at the south end, shows the Marriage Feast at Canaan, with the figure of Christ at the centre.

where the curious blend of styles that characterized Trapezuntine architecture is evident – the portal has Seljuk-style scalloped niches, and the columns have Seljuk-style capitals on top of Byzantine ones. The nearby bell-tower was added in 1427.

Atatürk Köşkü

Even further out of town, on a cool hillside 750m (2,500ft) above sea level, is the striking mansion where Atatürk stayed during his visits to Trabzon. It was built for a Greek banker, Constantine Kapayiannides, in 1903, and is set in a lovely wooded

garden. The rooms are simply furnished, apart from a billiard table in the main hall (Atatürk was an enthusiastic player); a wall map upstairs bears lines pencilled in by Atatürk when he was planning a response to a Kurdish revolt in 1937.

Sumela Monastery

South of Trabzon a road cuts through the Pontic Mountains, following the old trade route to Erzurum. At the village of Maçka, a road branches left (signposted Sumela/ Meryemana) up a side valley towards the Black Sea coast's most famous tourist

The Church of Hagia Sophia in Trabzon was founded by the Comneni Emperor Manuel I in the 13th century. The frieze above the south porch (visible here) bears a relief showing the story of Adam and Eve (following pages).

The famous monastery of Sumela clings precariously to a sheer cliff, high above a thickly wooded valley. It can be reached by climbing for 30-45 minutes up a steep, zig-zag mule track.

'Virgin of Blackness/Darkness', possibly a reference to an icon of the Virgin, painted in dark colours, around which the monastery was founded; another theory claims that the 'black' refers to the dark-coloured rock of the monastery cliff. According to the legend, the Athenian monks Barnabas and Sophranias came to Sumela in AD 385 after its sacred cave was revealed to them in a vision, and built a shrine around the icon of the Virgin, which was supposed to have been painted by St Luke. There may have been a monastery of sorts here from the 8th century; it was re-founded by the Emperor Alexius III Com-nenus of Trebizond (1349-90), and received many donations from the imperial coffers. Sumela was protected by the Ottoman sultans, who respected the miraculous powers of its icon, but it was during the 18th and 19th centuries that it reached its peak. The original ramshackle wooden cells were replaced by the masonry buildings you see today, and the approach path, stone stairs and an aqueduct were added. These luxuries were not for the benefit of the monks, but for the thousands of pilgrims who made the long trek to Sumela each year.

The monastery was abandoned in 1923, when Ottoman Greeks were expelled following the Turkish War of Independence. The buildings fell into ruin, and the frescoes were damaged by the elements and seriously defaced by graffiti. A restoration

attraction, 46km (29 miles) from the city centre. **Sumela Monastery** occupies a spectacular situation, clinging to a sheer cliff beneath a huge overhang, 300m (1,000ft) above the floor of a wild mountain valley. A tarmac road leads to a picnic area and restaurant beside the river, from where you must climb a steep switchback of a donkey track to the monastery; the climb takes 30 to 40 minutes.

The name Sumela is said to derive from the Greek *Panayia tou Melas*, meaning the project is currently under way, but the finished work makes the place look brand new, and rather detracts from the atmosphere. None the less, it is well worth making the climb, if only for the magnificent setting.

At the top of the path you climb a flight of stairs to the gate and descend to the courtyard on the far side, which is tucked beneath huge, bulging overhangs. To the right of the stairs are the **pilgrims quarters**, complete with original toilets – stone slabs with keyhole slots that discharged down the cliff face. On the left is the **Sacred Spring** (*Ayazma*), a well fed by drips from the overhanging rocks above. The original **church** is up the stairs ahead, built into a natural cave in the cliff, with a rock ceiling and an apse hollowed into the rock. Both the interior and exterior are covered in 18th- and 19th-century frescoes, many of them mutilated almost beyond recognition. In places, the painted plaster has flaked off to reveal 14th-century frescoes beneath.

East of Trabzon

To the east of Trabzon the mountains get wilder and the weather gets wetter – this is the rainiest corner of Turkey. There is little here to attract the tourist, unless you are planning a trek in the Kaçkar Mountains. This is tea country – the hillsides are carpeted with tea bushes, and the tall chimneys of tea-processing plants (Ofçaysan, Karçay, Zenginçay, Ofçaykoop and Çaykur) sprout from the towns.

The scenic valley of the Çamlıhemşin River cuts deep into Kaçkar Mountains, a region popular among trekkers and mountaineers.

Çamlıhemşin is reached via a road which leaves the coast between Pazar and Ardeşen, and climbs scenically alongside a foaming green river for 22km (14 miles). The road passes a good trout restaurant and a couple of ancient hump-backed bridges before reaching the town, which is squeezed into a narrow gap between the river and a steep cliff. There are a few hotels here if you want to spend the night, and some good restaurants on terraces cantilevered out over the river. The left fork of the road continues up to the spa town of Ayder, which is the jumping-off point for mountaineers and trekkers exploring the Kaçkar Mountains.

At the ugly industrial town of Hopa, 155km (97 miles) from Trabzon and 20km (13 miles) from the Georgian border, a road cuts inland across the mountains to Artvin, and then heads up the spectacular valley of the Çoruh River towards Erzurum (see p.313)

The Highest Peak, the Oldest City, the Biggest Lake – the East is a Land of Extremes

Eastern Turkey is a land apart. Compared with the rest of the country it is wild, remote and sparsely populated. It spans extremes of climate, from the baking plains around Şanlıurfa, where summer temperatures regularly top 40°C (104°F), to the 'Turkish Siberia' of Erzurum, where the mercury dips below freezing for 130 days of the year. In the east, you leave 'tourist Turkey' behind – here the distances are greater, the roads are poorer, and the hotels are fewer and less comfortable.

The eastern marches of Turkey have always been a battleground. The frontiers of empires and kingdoms have moved back and forth as the tides of invading armies have washed through. As long ago as the 2nd millennium BC the Hittites clashed with the Hurrians, as did the Assyrians with the Urartians; they in turn battled against invading Medes and Persians. Here the Romans and Byzantines struggled to maintain their eastern frontier against Seleucids, Parthians, Armenians and Arabs until they were overwhelmed by the Seljuk Turks, who scored a crushing defeat against the Byzantines at the Battle of Manzikert to the north of Lake Van in 1071. The Seljuks were then overrun by the Mongols, and the Ottomans policed their frontier against the Armenians, Georgians, Russians and Persians. Sadly, the region is still suffering from unrest, with continuing clashes between the Turkish army and Kurdish separatists (see A WARNING, p.315).

In the east of Turkey the influence of the Orient is more strongly felt. The Yakutiye Medresesi in Erzurum owes much to Persian designs.

Erzurum

Turkey's highest city spills across a sloping plain at the foot of the Palandöken mountains, basking beneath the big skies of eastern Anatolia. At 1,850m

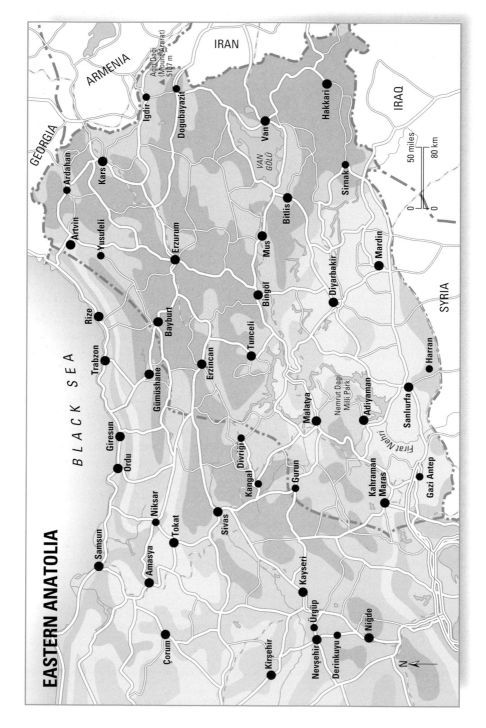

EASTERN ANATOLIA

A WARNING

Unfortunately, the terrorist activities of the PKK (Kurdistan Workers' Party) make travel to many parts of eastern Turkey hazardous. In 1993 and 1994 a number of western tourists were kidnapped while travelling in the east, and there has been serious fighting between the PKK and the Turkish security forces, especially in the area to the south and east of Diyarbakır, but also as far north as Tunceli and Bingöl, and in the Mount Ararat region. Until the situation changes, **Berlitz advises you not to travel in this region.**

The PKK's campaign has also affected western Turkey, with several bombs going off in Istanbul, Marmaris, Fethiye and Antalya. As of December 1994, the British Foreign Office and the US Department of State advise their nationals to avoid eastern Turkey except on essential business; they currently do not advise against travel in western Turkey. To find out the latest information on these matters, contact the Foreign Office Travel Advisory Unit in the UK, tel. (0171) 270 4129, or the Department of State Travel Advisory Service in the USA, tel. (202) 647 5225.

(6,000ft) above sea level, the spring air is cool and fresh, and the pastures of the high steppes are a vibrant green. Erzurum is only four hours' drive from the Black Sea coast, but it inhabits another world, of treeless plains and bare rocky mountains, parched in the summer and gripped by snow for four months of the year.

Erzurum sits on an ancient trade route between Anatolia and Iran, and has been occupied since Hittite times. In the 4th century AD it became the city of Theodosiopolis, a fortified outpost of the Byzantine Empire; raiding Arabs called it *Arz er-Rum* ('land of the Romans'). After the Battle of Manzikert in 1071, it was occupied by the Seljuks, and later sacked by the Mongols. Its fortunes revived under the Ottomans, who used it as a military staging post for their eastern campaigns, and as a commercial depot for goods travelling between Iran and the Black Sea ports. The Russians occupied Erzurum briefly in 1829, and again from February 1916 to March 1918; following their withdrawal Armenian forces massacred the population, a blow from which the city is still recovering. Today, Erzurum continues to combine its ancient roles of military outpost and trading centre, hosting a major army base, and sitting astride the only road and rail outlet from Iran into Europe.

Modern **Erzurum** is rather drab and featureless, but it hides enough historic monuments to keep you busy for a half day. Most are to be found along the main street, Cumhuriyet Caddesi. Beginning at the east end, beneath the crumbling Byzantine citadel, is the **Çifte Minareli Medrese** (Seminary of the Twin Minarets), thought to have been endowed in 1253 by the daughter of the Seljuk sultan Alaeddin Keykubad II; her sarcophagus and several inscriptions were carried off as war booty by the Russians in 1829. The elaborate façade and the two blue-tiled minarets are reminiscent of the Gök Medrese in Sivas (1271). The portal leads to a large, empty courtyard lined with students' cells, with the empty tomb of the sultan's daughter at the back.

Next door to the *medrese* is the **Ulu Camii** (Great Mosque), Erzurum's oldest mosque. A plain stone building with seven wide aisles, it was built by a local emir in 1179; at the centre of its forest of columns a scalloped skylight admits a shaft of sunshine. At the main intersection half-way along Cumhuriyet Caddesi is the **Lala Mustafa Paşa Camii**, a small Ottoman mosque with an unusual striped minaret, dating from 1562; the interior still bears bullet-marks from the 1916-18 Russian occupation. Beyond on the right is a small park containing the **Yakutiye Medresesi**, built by a Mongol emir in 1310. The portal and the interlacing geometric design on the minaret show strong Persian influence. On each side of the portal, which projects from the wall, is a carving of a palmette with two lions below and an eagle above.

Cumhuriyet Caddesi leads to a roundabout with a fountain in the middle; turn left here and walk uphill for ten minutes to find Erzurum's **museum**. The most interesting exhibits are the Hittite and Urartian objects in the first room – pottery with bird and deer motifs, gold jewellery and a bronze quiver. The ethnographic collection includes some fine carpets and kilims, Seljuk pottery and Ottoman clothes, including a hat decorated with hundreds of coins. A rather grisly exhibit records the massacre and mass burial of a local village by Armenian revolutionaries.

Mount Ararat (Ağrı Dağı)

The highest peak in Turkey stands like a sentinel at the far eastern edge of the country, guarding the borders with Armenia and Iran. The huge volcanic dome of **Mount Ararat** actually has two summits, 11km apart – Büyükağrı Dağı (Great Ararat: 5,137m; 16,850ft) and Küçükağrı Dağı (Little Ararat: 3,896m; 12,780ft) – which are permanently snow capped, and usually cloaked in cloud. Seen from the plains of Iğdır to the north, the mountain is a truly majestic sight.

Mount Ararat is, of course, best known as the place where Noah's Ark came to rest when the waters of the Flood receded. However, this commonly held belief is based on a questionable interpretation of the Book of Genesis, which says that the Ark came to rest 'upon the mountains of Ararat'. *Ararat* was the Hebrew word for Urartu, an ancient kingdom centred on Lake Van that flourished between the 9th

---

THE HUNT FOR NOAH'S ARK

There is a long tradition of hunting for evidence of Noah's Ark on the slopes of Mount Ararat. There was once a village on the northern slopes of the mountain, on the spot where Noah was supposed to have built an altar and planted the first vineyard after the flood waters had receded. An Armenian monastery here was dedicated to St Jacob, who had tried to reach the summit of Ararat in search of the Ark's remains. Sadly, the monastery and village, along with its 2,000 inhabitants, were wiped out by an earthquake and landslide in 1840.

More recently, a number of people claimed to have found fragments of wood belonging to the Ark, sparking off a flurry of Ark-hunting activity in the late 1970s and early 1980s. James Irwin, the former American astronaut, led five expeditions seeking to confirm the truth of the biblical story. Others were intrigued by an aerial photograph taken in the late 1950s that appeared to show a boat-shaped outline on the lower slopes of the mountain, at an altitude of about 1,525m (5,000ft). This was located and investigated extensively in the 1980s. Initial excitement centred around its shape and size – a narrow oval, pointed at both ends, and about 137m (450ft) long (Genesis tells us that Noah's Ark was 300 cubits in length, and a cubit was about 18in). While some still cling to the belief that this could be the Ark, most serious scientists have dismissed it as a freak geological formation. Further investigations will have to wait until the Turkish government reopens the area.

and 7th centuries BC. The Armenians believe that the Ark grounded on Süphan Dağı on the north shore of Lake Van, while Muslims claim that Cudi Dağı, near Cizre (on the Iraqi border), is the actual spot.

If you feel like following in the footsteps of those who have scoured the slopes of Ararat hunting for evidence of the Ark, think again. Ararat is currently off limits because of terrorist activity in the foothills. Even if it should be opened up to climbers again, you would have to apply for a trekking permit from the Turkish Embassy in your own country at least three months in advance, and go along as part of a guided expedition (the ascent takes five days for the round trip). Check out the current situation through a branch of the Turkish

The great cloud-capped peak of Mount Ararat stands guard over the eastern marches of Turkey.

Ministry of Tourism and Culture (see TOURIST INFORMATION OFFICES, p.14).

The town of **Doğubayazıt** lies at the foot of Mount Ararat to the south. It's a dusty truck stop on the overland route to Iran, and there's no reason to stop here unless you're on your way to climb Ararat, or to visit the romantic ruins of the **İşak Paşa Sarayı**, perched on a bluff 5km (3 miles) to the southeast. This unlikely fortress palace was built during the 18th century by İşak Paşa, a Kurdish emir who was governor of Doğubayazıt from 1769 to 1797. The self-contained complex included barracks, stables, an arsenal, a mosque, a *medrese,* storerooms, a bakery and kitchen, an audience chamber, bedrooms with fireplaces and baths, all arranged around two courtyards with magnificent portals. The architecture is a hotchpotch of Seljuk, Ottoman, Persian, Armenian and Georgian styles, and the whole looks rather like the film set for a Hollywood biblical epic. On the right-hand side of the inner courtyard are the ornately decorated tombs of İşak Paşa and his favourite wife.

Lake Van (Van Gölü)

Lake Van is an inland sea, big enough to swallow the county of Cornwall or the state of Rhode Island with room to spare – it covers 3,713 sq km (1,434 sq miles), and is 119km (74 miles) across at its widest point. It was formed when lava flows from the volcano of Nemrut Dağı on its northern shore (not to be confused with the better known Nemrut Dağı near Malatya) blocked the river valley at the west end. The lake has no outlet; its level is maintained by evaporation, and the resulting alkaline water is useless for drinking or irrigation. There is no animal life in the lake except for one species of fish (called *darek* in Turkish) that has adapted to the soda-rich environment.

Lake Van was formed when a larva flow blocked a river valley. The river had nowhere to go, resulting in the lake we see today. Beyond is the peak of Mount Ararat.

In ancient times the Lake Van region was ruled by the kingdom of Urartu, which flourished from the 9th to the 7th centuries BC. The Urartian capital city, Tushpa, lay on the east shore of the lake, near the modern city of Van. The **Rock of Van** (*Van*

Kalesi) is a long, narrow outcrop of limestone rising out of the plain between the city and the lake, sheer on its south side. The rock is capped by the crumbling ochre walls of the **Urartian citadel**, its eroded battlements looking for all the world like a giant termite mound (the walls and towers lower down the hill were added by the Seljuks and Ottomans). The **rock tombs** of the Urartian kings and several **cuneiform inscriptions** dating from the 8th century BC are carved into the cliffs below.

The ruined buildings to the south of the rock are the remains of Old Van, destroyed during the upheaval of World War I; only a couple of broken minarets still stand above the heaps of overgrown rubble. The new city to the east is bland and modern, but has a couple of good hotels. You may want to shop for Kurdish kilims, which are hard-wearing and attractive; though less expensive than they would be in Istanbul, they're still far from cheap. New Van's only real attraction is the **Van Museum** (open 8.30am to noon and 1.30 to 5.30pm, closed Monday), which houses a fine collection of Urartian gold jewellery, plus terracotta figurines and bronzes.

A required excursion for all visitors to Van is a day trip to **Ahtamar Adası**, a tiny island in the lake about 40km (25 miles) southwest of the city. (Boats ferry visitors out to the island from a quay a few kilometres west of the town of Gevaş.) Ahtamar is graced by the beautiful 10th-century **Church of the Holy Cross**, built between 915 and 921 by Gagik Artsruni, the ruler of the petty Armenian kingdom of Vaspurakan. It follows the typical Armenian pattern of a cross-shaped floor plan, topped by a 16-sided drum with a conical roof. But the church's chief glory is the magnificent **carvings** that adorn its exterior – mainly Old Testament scenes such as Adam and Eve, Jonah and the whale, David and Goliath, Abraham and Isaac, and Daniel in the lion's den, but also depictions of animals and mythical

THE ARMENIANS

The Armenians are an ancient race, who emerged in the region around Lake Van and north-eastern Turkey following the collapse of the kingdom of Urartu in the 7th century BC. They called themselves the 'Hayk', and appear to have moved into the area from the west; Herodotus links them to the Phrygians (see p.263). During the reign of Tigranes the Great (95-55 BC) Armenia consolidated its power in an alliance with Mithradates of Pontus (see box p.265) and briefly challenged the might of the Roman Empire.

Armenia was the first country to adopt Christianity as its official religion, in AD 300, after its king was converted by St Gregory the Illuminator. Another monk, the 5th-century St Mashtots, devised the Armenian alphabet, which is still in use today. Armenia then began to disintegrate into petty regional dynasties, the most dominant of which was the Bagratids of the north, who made their capital at Ani, near Kars.

Armenian culture, especially church architecture, flourished in the 9th and 10th centuries until Armenian territory was annexed by the Byzantines in the 11th century. Then came the invasions of the Seljuks and Mongols, whose depredations drove many Armenians south to found the medieval state of Little Armenia in Cilicia (see box p.244). In the succeeding centuries Armenia became an object of contention between the Ottomans and Persians, until Russia entered the picture in the 19th century, waging war on Turkey and stirring up nationalist feelings among the Armenian population.

In an attempt to stamp out any separatist movement, Sultan Abdül Mecit encouraged the persecution of the Armenian population, and many were massacred. During World War I, when the Russians, aided by Armenian revolutionaries, captured parts of eastern Turkey (including Erzurum and Van), the sultan ordered the mass deportation of about 1.75 million Ottoman Armenians to the deserts of Syria. At least 600,000 people died of starvation or were slaughtered, and many others fled into exile. After the war Armenia was incorporated into the Soviet Union. Today, much bad feeling still exists between Armenians and Turks.

creatures, and a portrait of King Gagik offering the church to God. There are also many inscriptions in Armenian.

Diyarbakır

The black battlements of **Diyarbakır** provide one of the finest surviving examples of medieval military architecture in Turkey. The city of Amida (as the Romans called it) was enlarged and fortified in AD 359 to serve as an outpost in the Roman campaigns against the Persians. In the succeeding centuries its possession was fiercely contested by the Byzantines and Persians, until it was captured by Arabs in 638. The invaders belonged to the Beni Bakr tribe, and renamed their new conquest *Diyar Bakr* ('district of the Bakr people'). The city changed hands among various Arab, Seljuk and Mongol dynasties before finally falling to the Ottoman sultan in 1516. Today it is an overwhelmingly Kurdish city, the unofficial 'capital' of Turkey's largest ethnic minority group, and home to many of the refugees who have fled the unrest in northern Iraq.

The **city walls** built by the Romans and Byzantines were expanded and restored by the Arabs, Seljuks and Ottomans. The massive ramparts of black basalt are 12m (39ft) high, 5m (16ft) thick, and 5.5km (3½ miles) long, and originally had 78 towers (72 are still standing). They enclose the old city of Diyarbakır, which still has an essentially Roman plan, with two main streets intersecting at right angles in the centre, and leading to gates at the four cardinal points of the compass. At the northeastern corner is the **citadel** (*İç Kale*), the oldest part of the city; it is a military zone, and off limits to the public. It is possible to ascend to the top of the walls at **Mardin Kapısı** (the southern gate) and follow them around the city in a clockwise direction, descending only at a few places where new roads have been cut through; there are interesting reliefs and inscriptions to examine. (There have been a few robberies on the walls in recent years, so don't venture there alone – go in the safety of an organized group.)

Apart from the city walls, there's not much reason to hang around in Diyarbakır. There are a number of historic mosques and an archaeological museum, but most of the city is drab and dusty. Its other claim to fame is its *karpuz* (watermelons), which are grown locally, and reach a prodigious size; 40-60kg (88-132lb) is not uncommon. In olden days, of course, they were even bigger. Local lore maintains that Diyarbakır watermelons once weighed 90-100kg (198-220lb) and had to be carried by camel. They were so big that a sword was needed to cut them up in the market. The city holds a watermelon festival each year in September.

Şanlıurfa

The dusty metropolis of Urfa (*Şanlı*, meaning 'glorious', was added only in 1983) lies baking at the edge of the Syrian desert. Local people claim that the prophet Abraham was born here about 3,000 years ago, and that he was living here when he was commanded by God to take his family to the land of Canaan.

Urfa is certainly an ancient city. The citadel was occupied around 3500 BC by the Hurri people, who named their town Orhoi. It was subsequently taken by the Hittites and Assyrians, before falling to Alexander the Great after his victory at Issus in 333 BC (see p.247). His successor

Seleucus (founder of Antioch) made it the capital of his Hellenistic empire and re-named it Edessa. In 132 BC it became in-dependent, and acted as a buffer state between the Romans and Persians. The city adopted Christianity around 150 AD, and was an important centre of the early Syrian Church. The Arabs took Edessa in 638 and held it until the 11th century, af-ter which it changed hands many times be-fore finally becoming a part of the Ottoman Empire in 1637, when its name was changed to Urfa.

At the centre of the city is the district called **Gölbaşı** (Lakeside), where Urfa's tourist sights are concentrated. Here you can feed the sacred carp in the **Pools of Abraham** (*Birket İbrahim*), with the graceful colonnade of the 17th-century Abdürrahman Camii mirrored in the still waters. According to local legend, the Assyrian King Nemrut commanded that the prophet Abraham be burned alive be-cause he had smashed the idols in the pa-gan temple. But when the executioners tried to carry out the sentence, the flames turned into pools of cool water and the glowing embers became gleaming carp. Today, it is against the law to catch the sa-cred fish; not that anyone would try, as it is said that those who catch or eat Urfa's carp are immediately struck blind.

Along Göl Caddesi, heading towards the Covered Bazaar, is the Mevlid-i Halil Camii, behind which is the entrance to the **Cave of Abraham** (*İbrahim Halilul-lah Dergâhı*), the reputed birthplace of the prophet. This is a place of pilgrimage for Muslims, who revere Abraham as a prophet, the first man to accept that there is only one God. Dress respectfully and remove your shoes before entering (there are separate entrances for men and women).

Urfa's other attractions include the colourful **Covered Bazaar** (*Kapalı Çarşı*), which offers a lively slice of oriental life; the massive **citadel** (*Kale*) above the pools, where you enter between a pair of Roman columns called the Throne of Nemrut; and the excellent **museum**.

Harran

A popular excursion from Şanlıurfa goes to the biblical town of Harran, about 50km (31 miles) to the south near the Syrian bor-der. Harran is one of the world's oldest continuously inhabited settlements – people have built their houses on this spot for over 6,000 years. Its best-known in-habitant was the prophet Abraham; as the Bible tells us in Genesis 11:31,

> And Terah took Abram his son, and Lot the son of Haran his son's son, and Sarai his daughter in law, his son Abram's wife; and they went forth with them from Ur of the Chaldees, to go into the land of Canaan; and they came unto Harran and dwelt there.

Harran was once an important crossroads on the ancient caravan routes of Mesopotamia, and a centre for the worship of Sin, the Assyrian moon god; the site of his temple is now occupied by a crusader castle. But the main reason for coming to Harran is to see its unusual **beehive houses**. These mud-brick domes are a very ancient form of dwelling, their form dictated by the region's lack of timber. Few of the villagers live in them any more, using them instead as storerooms and animal pens. (As you wander round the village you can expect to be followed by an escort of local children demanding sweets and money.)

Nemrut Dağı (Mount Nimrod)

The short-lived kingdom of Commagene declared its independence from the Seleucid Empire around 162 BC, and maintained a fragile existence by playing off the Romans against the Parthians until it was annexed by Rome in AD 17. But its king, Antiochus I (*c.* 69-34 BC), had an ego as big as the Roman Empire. He claimed descent from Darius of Persia and Alexander the Great, and considered himself an equal to the gods. Nemrut Dağı is a monument to his megalomania.

Antiochus chose the 2,150m (7,000ft) summit of Mount Nimrod as the site for a colossal mausoleum and temple dedicated to himself, from where he would fly to join his divine companions after his death. An inscription records his words:

I, the great King Antiochus, have ordered the construction of these temples, the ceremonial way, and the thrones of the gods, on a foundation which will never be demolished…I have done this to prove my faith in the gods. At the conclusion of my life I will enter my eternal rest here, and my spirit will ascend to join Zeus in heaven.

An enormous tumulus of fist-sized rocks is piled on the summit of the mountain. It is thought that the tomb of Antiochus lies at the bottom of it – you can see the marks of trial excavations made by archaeologists, but nothing has yet been found. At either end of the mound is a terrace with 10m (33ft) high limestone statues of the gods – Apollo, Tyche, Zeus and Hercules – with the king himself among them. The statues have long since been toppled from their thrones by earthquakes, but their weathered heads have been raised upright and now gaze sightlessly over the lost kingdom of Commagene. The scene brings to mind another ancient megalomaniac, the Egyptian king Rameses II, whose crumbling funerary temple inspired Shelley's poem *Ozymandias*. The words could well apply to Nemrut Dağı:

'My name is Ozymandias, king of
  kings:
Look on my works, ye Mighty, and
  despair!'
Nothing beside remains. Round the
  decay
Of that colossal wreck, boundless and
  bare,
The lone and level sands stretch far
  away.

Nemrut Dağı lies between Şanlıurfa and Malatya, near the town of Adıyaman; minibus tours to the summit can be arranged from any of these towns. It is traditional to arrive at the summit in time to watch the sun rise, although this means leaving Adıyaman at about 2am The uncharitable have suggested that this 'tradition' has more to do with the tour organizers wanting to maximize hotel profits in Adıyaman, and avoid overheating their ageing vehicles by making the long climb before the sun gets up.

The road is passable to ordinary vehicles, and there is nothing to stop you taking your own car up at any time you choose. But remember that the road will be closed by snow from October to May (at least); July and August are the best times to go. If you decide to make a dawn trip, take plenty of warm clothing – even in midsummer the summit temperature plummets at night, with an icy wind.

Beyond the Beach and the Ancient Cities – Shopping, Entertainment and Sport

When you've tired of exploring temples and theatres, but lying on the beach seems a little too lazy, then it's time to sharpen your bargaining skills and head for the bazaar. For those who find shopping too tame, Turkey's potential for adventure sports provides ample opportunity for excitement. And when the sun goes down, you can relax with a *rakı* while you plan your evening's entertainment.

Shopping

The markets and bazaars of Turkey offer some of the world's most interesting – and challenging – shopping opportunities. A huge variety of hand-made goods is available, much of it of very high quality – wool and silk carpets, kilims (flat-weave rugs), *cicims* (embroidered kilims), leather goods, pottery and ceramics, copper and brassware, and jewellery. There is also, of course, a lot

*I*t is impossible to visit Turkey without being invited into a carpet shop. Turkish carpets are not cheap, but they are beautiful and hard-wearing. This Aladdin's Cave is in Erzurum.

of poorer quality merchandise aimed specifically at the tourist market, especially in the big coastal resorts and in Cappadocia.

The principal shopping area in Istanbul is, of course, the Grand Bazaar, with over 4,000 shops crammed beneath its roof. Running downhill from here is Uzunçarşı Caddesi, lined with hardware shops, which leads to the Spice Bazaar, the best place to buy *lokum* (Turkish delight). The weekend flea-market in Beyazıt Square is an interesting place to browse, and there are bargains to be found among the bric-à-brac. Across from the square are the back streets of Laleli, the place to look for low-priced clothes. For more modern, upmarket shopping, you can join Istanbul's jet-set in the stylish boutiques of Nişantaşı and Teşvikiye, near Taksim Square, or head west to the Galleria shopping mall by the marina at Ataköy. For trendy craft shops, antiques and art galleries, take a stroll around Ortaköy on a Saturday or Sunday.

Shops are generally open from 9.30am to 7pm Monday to Saturday, closed 1 to 2pm, though many tourist shops stay open later and on Sundays. The Grand Bazaar is open 8am to 7pm Monday to Saturday. All Turkish towns have their own bazaars; among the most colourful and interesting are those in Bursa, Izmir, Kayseri, Safranbolu and Şanlıurfa.

Bargaining

In an economy where many products are handmade, each item has a different value depending on the quality of workmanship, and it shows. Bargaining is thus a way of determining an appropriate price, not simply a way for the shopkeeper to get more money from the buyer. To get the best price, though, you must get to know the market by browsing and asking the prices of comparable pieces.

When you find something you want to buy, ask the shopkeeper how much it costs, and then offer around half of what you're prepared to pay. The owner will feign amazement at such an insultingly low price, and discourse at length on the quality of the work, but will eventually suggest a lower price. You, of course, will plead poverty and suggest that you can buy the same thing more cheaply elsewhere, but end up making an offer slightly higher than your first. Ideally, you should have a partner who feigns impatience and tries to get you to leave. This good-natured banter will continue back and forth until you settle on a mutually acceptable price. If the item is expensive, say a carpet or a leather jacket, the process might involve several glasses of tea and a good half-hour of your time.

Two golden rules – never begin bargaining for something you do not genuinely intend to buy; and never mention a price that you are not prepared to pay.

In the resorts on the coast, many traders are aware that some tourists feel uncomfortable with bargaining, and will quote you their 'best price' straight away if you ask them to. This is the minimum they are prepared to accept, and you will probably be wasting your time if you try to force them any lower. Competition between shops is fierce, and many traders work on very narrow profit margins.

Antiques. It is illegal to take genuine antiques out of the country without an export licence. If you want to buy any object which might be considered a museum piece, you will have to obtain a certificate from the directorate of a local museum clearing it for export. Having said that, there are many interesting and attractive fake 'antiques' for sale in Istanbul, including swords and daggers, Ottoman coffee-making sets, jewellery, copper and brass tray tables with wooden stands, and so on. But even if your purchase only *looks* 'antique', it may still arouse suspicion at customs. Make sure the dealer gives you a *fatura* (invoice), stating the value of the piece, and when and where it was made.

Carpets and kilims. Turkish carpets are, of course, world famous for their beauty and durability, and are top of the shopping list for many visitors. Kilims are small rugs that are woven rather than knotted, and have no pile; a *cicim* is a kilim with embroidered decoration. All originated as floor and wall coverings for nomad dwellings – carpets as hard-wearing, insulated floor coverings, and kilims as covers and wall hangings. No two handmade carpets are identical. The traditional patterns and symbols are handed down from generation to generation and have great significance to the weaver, conferring good luck on the household, offering protection against the 'evil eye', or expressing the desire for a child. Ask the dealer to explain the symbols on any carpet you are thinking of buying.

The price of a carpet is affected by its age, rarity, quality of materials and dyes, and tightness of weave. The number of knots per square centimetre ranges from 20 to 30 for a coarse wool carpet, to 100 to 200 for the most expensive silk carpets, which can cost tens of thousands of pounds. Natural dyes look better and last longer than synthetics, but are more expensive. You can tell the difference by wetting a corner of a white handkerchief and rubbing the carpet. Synthetic dyes will stain the white material, while the smell of chlorine means that the carpet has been bleached to make it look older. Even if you are not an expert, asking a few pertinent questions will make the carpet seller less likely to fob you off with an inferior item.

Ceramics and pottery. The best ceramic tiles ever produced in Turkey came from the kilns of İznik, near Bursa, but these are now collector's items. Today, you will have to settle for the polychrome tiles, bowls, plates, vases and other items

One of the best places to shop for pottery is Avanos, where you can go into the workshops to watch the pots being thrown, glazed and decorated.

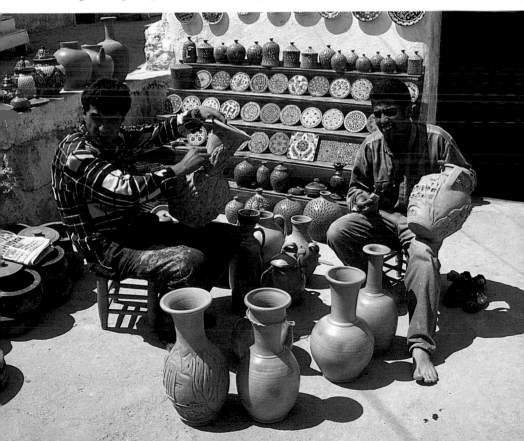

produced in Kütahya, which often copy the İznik designs and make attractive and relatively inexpensive souvenirs.

Copper and brassware. Gleaming, hand-beaten objects in copper and brass can be found in Istanbul in the shops around the Old Bedesten in the Grand Bazaar, and in Bakırcılar Caddesi (Coppersmiths' Street) behind Beyazıt Square. Braziers and shoeshine boxes, lamps, candlesticks, coffee-grinders, coffee-pots and samovars are among the many things available. The coppersmith will also be happy to make items to order, or to engrave your purchase. If you plan to use a copper item for boiling water or cooking, make sure that it is tinned on the inside as unlined copper can be slightly toxic.

Leather and suede. Istanbul's Grand Bazaar has many leather shops offering a huge selection of belts, purses, wallets, handbags, jackets, trousers and skirts. Prices and quality vary widely, but are generally about a half to two-thirds of what you would pay back home. While the leather is generally of good quality, some of the goods on offer in the popular tourist resorts suffer from poor stitching, so check the standard of craftsmanship carefully before buying. You can have clothes and shoes made to order at many shops, but good-quality work will take time.

Jewellery. The best place to shop for quality jewellery in Istanbul is the Old Bedesten in the Grand Bazaar; cheaper items can be found in the shops along nearby Kalpakcılar Başı Caddesi (the bazaar's main street). Gold is sold by weight, with a surcharge for workmanship (gold prices are posted daily in the bazaar); genuine sterling silver should carry a hallmark. There are many cheap imitations about, with fake stones and silver plating, so beware of rip-offs, especially in the coastal resorts.

Entertainment

A nargile is a traditional Turkish water-pipe. The tobacco smoke is drawn through water, making it cooler and mellower.

There is no shortage of evening entertainment in the main resorts of the Aegean and Mediterranean coasts; the bars and discos here stay open until the small hours, and the parties continue on the beach until dawn. Many hotels offer a weekly **folklore evening**, which provides the opportunity to see a number of traditional Turkish dances performed to live music, followed by the inevitable belly-dancer. The best entertainment is provided by the many local festivals that take place at different times throughout the country (see p.39).

Other items you might consider include **nargiles**, the famous 'hubble-bubble' pipes popular with old men in Turkish cafés; **meerschaum** pipes and figurines, produced in Eskişehir; luxurious Turkish **towels**, the best of which come from Bursa; colourful **Karagöz puppets**, made from dyed camel hide; traditional Turkish **musical instruments**, such as the mandolin-like *saz*, the *davul* (drum) and the *ney*, a dervish flute; and **lokum**, better known as Turkish delight, which comes in many flavours and can be found in the shops in and around Istanbul's Spice Bazaar.

M any hotels and tourist restaurants stage a weekly 'Folklore Evening' with traditional Turkish folk music and dancing.

Istanbul

Nightlife

Turkish-style supper clubs called *gazinos* offer an evening of folk music and belly-dancing, usually with dinner and drinks included. Organized tours usually include a night at a *gazino* as part of the package; otherwise you can book a table through your hotel or through a travel agent. Most of the clubs are in Taksim and on the European shore of the Bosphorus; one of the best known is at the top of the Galata Tower.

Western-style bars, discos and nightclubs can be found in the Taksim district, but be warned that the clubs in the side streets off İstiklal Caddesi are mostly rip-off joints where you will be charged an enormous bill for a round of drinks, and forcibly relieved of your wallet if you refuse to pay up. There are also good bars in Ataköy (southwest of the city), and in Ortaköy and Bebek on the Bosphorus, many of which have live music, either jazz, rock, or traditional.

Music and Cinema

The Atatürk Cultural Centre on Taksim Square offers a programme of opera, ballet and symphony concerts from October to May; during the Istanbul International Festival (mid-June to mid-July), the city hosts musicians and performers from all over the world. Jazz is popular in Istanbul, and in many bars and clubs live bands play at the weekends.

There are many cinemas in İstiklal Caddesi, and a multi-screen theatre at Çemberlitaş in the Old City, which show mainstream movies. Look for the word *orijinal* on the poster – this means that the film will be shown in its original language, with Turkish subtitles. Otherwise it will have been dubbed into Turkish.

Sound and Light Show

From June to September you can enjoy a free sound and light show at the Blue Mosque (the viewing benches are about half-way between the mosque and Hagia Sophia). The show, which begins each evening at 9pm, relates in melodramatic fashion the history of Istanbul, while coloured floodlights illuminate the spectacular architecture of the Blue Mosque. The commentary is in English, French, German and Turkish in rotation – check the notice by the benches for the date of the next performance in English.

Turkish Baths

No trip to Turkey would be complete without a visit to the *hamam*, or Turkish bath. There are a couple of historic baths in Istanbul which cater specifically to tourists, notably the 18th-century Çağaloğlu Hamamı in Sultanahmet, and the 16th-century Galatasaray Hamamı in Beyoğlu. There are *hamams* in most of the popular tourist resorts, too; some of the more expensive hotels have their own private baths. There are usually separate entrances for men (*erkek*) and women (*kadın*), but if there is only one chamber, then different times are set aside for men and women.

You leave your valuables in a locker at the desk, and get undressed in the changing room. Wearing a towel and bath-clogs you are shown to the steamy marble washroom, where buckets of hot water are poured over you before an attendant sets to work with a coarse glove, removing dirt and dead skin, and leaving you pink and glowing. You can also have a massage at this point if you like (for an additional fee). Afterwards you retire to the changing room for tea or a drink, feeling completely relaxed and brand new.

Sports

Turkey offers a wide range of opportunities for the more active holidaymaker. For more information on any of these sports, contact the Turkish Ministry of Tourism (see TOURIST INFORMATION OFFICES, p.14).

The Turkish coast makes a perfect summer playground for watersports' enthusiasts. This wind-surfing school is at Bitez, near Bodrum.

Watersports

Turkey's Aegean and Mediterranean coasts are a watersports paradise. All the standard beach sports can be enjoyed at the main resorts – windsurfing, water-skiing, parascending and jet-skiing – with equipment hire and instruction available for those who want it. There is a major windsurfing and dinghy-sailing school at Bitez, near Bodrum.

In Istanbul, pollution means that you will have to travel some distance from the city in order to enjoy clean water. The best beaches within easy reach of the city are the attractive Black Sea resorts of **Kilyos** and **Şile**. In summer, a bus leaves Üsküdar for Şile every hour from 9am for the two-hour journey. To get to Kilyos, take a ferry or bus to Sarıyer, where a taxi or *dolmuş* will take you the 12km (7 miles) to the coast. There are good swimming beaches on the **Princes' Islands** too, but they get extremely crowded at weekends. West of the city, there are beaches at Florya (20km; 12 miles), and further out at Silivri and Gümüşyaka (65km; 40 miles).

Much of Turkey's Aegean and Mediterranean coast is best explored by boat. You can choose between a gület cruise, where all the sailing is done for you, or a flotilla holiday, where you learn to sail your own yacht in company.

Sailing

The Turkish coast provides a superb cruising ground for yachts, with fascinating bays and inlets to explore, many of them inaccessible except by boat. Experienced sailors can charter a yacht from Bodrum, Marmaris or Antalya; beginners can book a flotilla holiday, where you sail in a group of several yachts under the supervision of an experienced lead crew, who take care of planning and navigation and are always on hand should you get into difficulties. If a yacht seems too much to handle, you can choose a dinghy sailing holiday instead. Full details are available through any travel agent.

Scuba-diving

Diving in Turkish waters is strictly controlled, because of government fears about the possible theft of antiquities from the sea bed. A number of companies offer dive trips and equipment hire for qualified divers, and courses of instruction for beginners; the main centres are Bodrum, Marmaris and Fethiye.

Skiing

You may not immediately think of Turkey as a winter sports destination, but its high mountains receive heavy snowfalls throughout the winter. There are several ski resorts right across the country, but the infrastructure is not too well developed as yet, although a number of ski-holiday companies in the UK are showing an increasing interest in Turkey.

Uludağ (1,800m; 5,900ft), above Bursa, is Turkey's largest ski resort, with a season lasting from December to March. A cable car (*teleferik*) links Bursa directly to the ski area; alternatively, you can drive 36km (22 miles) up a winding mountain road to the hotel zone. There are a dozen or so hotels, which are usually booked solid at weekends in winter; they can hire out equipment if needed. Each hotel has its own ski-tow – there is no comprehensive ski-pass system. The slopes are not very challenging, but there's enough to keep you interested for a few days.

The other major resorts are at Erciyes Dağı (Kayseri), Palandöken (Erzurum) and Saklıkent (Antalya). In springtime the latter resort offers the opportunity of skiing in the morning and sunbathing on the beach in the afternoon.

Hiking and Mountaineering

These sports are only just beginning to take off in Turkey, but the scope is enormous – Turkey is Europe's most mountainous country. At present, organized trekking is concentrated in two ranges: the Kaçkar Mountains between Erzurum and the Black Sea coast, and the Aladağlar range to the east of Niğde, near Cappadocia. An English mountaineering guidebook to the

Turkey has much to offer the casual walker as well as the more ambitious hiker. Many national parks and beauty spots such as Kurşunlu Şelalesi have easy, marked trails (overleaf).

latter area has recently been published. The spectacular Cilo-Sat range along the Iraqi border and Mount Ararat are currently off limits because of terrorist activity.

White-water Rafting

Another adventure sport that is being introduced is white-water rafting, which is being offered on the Çoruh River between Erzurum and Artvin in northeastern Turkey, and on the rather tamer Köprülü River east of Antalya.

Horse-riding

Cappadocia has always been famous for its fine horses, and there are now a number of stables around Ürgüp that offer guided, multi-day horseback tours of the region. They also rent out mounts for the day or half day.

Spectator Sports

Unique to Turkey is the national sport of **oiled wrestling** (*yağlı güreş*). An annual gathering is held in June at Kırkpınar, near Edirne, 230km (143 miles) northwest of Istanbul (see p.000). The competitors, wearing only a pair of leather breeches, coat themselves in olive oil, and perform a ceremonial procession before getting to grips with their slippery opponents.

An even more exotic spectacle is **camel wrestling** (*deve güreşi*), which can be seen in January at Selçuk, near Kuşadası. Camels are bad-tempered beasts, and when two moody males confront each other in the ring a sparring match ensues, in which they use their necks to try and throw each other off balance. They are separated before they can hurt each other, and the winner is decided by a panel of judges.

Horse-racing may seem rather tame by comparison. Race meetings are held regularly between April and December at the Veliefendi Hippodrome near Bakırköy, 15km (9 miles) west of Istanbul. In winter, the races move to Izmir.

Turkey's national passion, however, is **football**. The fortunes of the top teams – Galatasaray, Fenerbahçe and Beşiktaş from Istanbul, and Trabzonspor from the Black Sea coast, are followed eagerly on television screens in bars and coffee shops across the nation.

Many companies now offer adventure sports holidays in Turkey, involving mountain-biking, trekking, and river rafting, shown here at Köprülü Canyon.

The Right Place at the Right Price

Hotels

Finding a room in Istanbul is not usually a problem. However, if you want a room in a particular hotel you would be well advised to make a reservation, especially during the busy months of July and August. The main hotel areas are Laleli, Aksaray and Sultanahmet in the Old City, and around Taksim Square in Beyoğlu. Intense competition among the middle-range hotels in Laleli/Aksaray means that you can often bargain for a lower rate, especially if you plan to stay for more than two or three nights.

In other parts of the country there is a wide range of accommodation to choose from, ranging from village pensions to five-star luxury hotels. Most accommodation is inexpensive by European and North American standards, and usually of good quality, but in smaller towns and eastern Anatolia, facilities may be poorer.

Below is a list of hotels recommended by Berlitz; those outside of Istanbul have been chosen with the independent traveller in mind. If you find other places worth recommending we'd be pleased to hear from you.

As a basic guide we have used the symbols below to indicate prices for a double room with bath and including breakfast.

Remember that it is always worth asking for a lower rate, especially during low season or if you plan to stay for more than one night.

Key

I	below £25 ($35)
II	£25-50 ($35-75)
III	£50-80 ($75-120)
IIII	£80-130 ($120-200)
IIII+	over £130 ($200)

Istanbul

Stamboul (Old City)

Alzer III
At Meydanı 72
Sultanahmet
Tel. (212) 516 6262;
fax (212) 516 0000
Friendly, comfortable hotel in supremely convenient location across from Blue Mosque. Breakfast in sidewalk café, bowls of fresh cherries in your room. Noise from muezzin at dawn in front rooms. 21 rooms.

And III
Yerebatan Caddesi
Camii Sokak 46
Sultanahmet
Tel. (212) 512 0207;
fax (212) 512 3025
Unassuming hotel in backstreet opposite Yerebatan Sarayı. All rooms with private bath and satellite TV, most with good views. Rooftop restaurant has panoramic view of Hagia Sophia and Bosphorus. 45 rooms.

Ayasofya Pensions III
Soğukçeşme Sokak
Sultanahmet
Tel. (212) 513 3660,
fax (212) 513 3669
Beautifully restored wooden Ottoman houses in quiet backstreet right beside entrance to Topkapı Palace. Rooms have private bath, period furniture and Turkish carpets. You can eat in nearby Sarnıç Restaurant (see below). 61 rooms.

Grand Lord I-II
Mesipaşa Mahalles,
Azimkar Sokak 22/24
Laleli
Tel. (212) 518 6311;
fax (212) 518 6400
Good-value hotel in convenient location. Small but comfortable rooms with TV and private shower. Friendly and helpful staff. 42 rooms.

Kariye II-III
Kariye Camii Sokak 18
Edirnekapı
Tel. (212) 534 8414;
fax (212) 521 6631
Beautifully restored, pastel-green wooden mansion next door to the Byzantine mosaics of Kariye Museum. Garden restaurant and bar. Very peaceful location, about ten minutes' taxi ride from Sultanahmet. 27 rooms.

Küçük Ayasofya I-II
Şehit Mehmet Paşa Sokak 25
Sultanahmet
Tel. (212) 516 1988;
fax (212) 516 8356
Small, friendly hotel in restored

19th-century wooden house near Blue Mosque. All rooms have private shower and toilet, telephone and central heating. 14 rooms.

Merit Antique ||||
Ordu Caddesi 226
Laleli
Tel. (212) 513 9300; fax (212) 512 6390 (513 9340 for reservations)
Formerly the Ramada. Built in the 1920s, with four buildings around glass-roofed atriums. Attractive mix of original architecture and modern trimmings. Indoor pool, sauna and jacuzzi. 275 rooms.

Park |
Utangaç Sokak 26
Sultanahmet
Tel. (212) 517 6596;
fax (212) 518 9602
Modern rooms with private shower, good location downhill from Blue Mosque towards sea. Roof terrace with view of Sea of Marmara. 27 rooms.

President ||||
Tiyatro Caddesi 25
Beyazit
Tel. (212) 516 6980;
fax (212) 516 6999
Part of Best Western International chain. All rooms with private bath, satellite TV, minibar. Indoor swimming pool and sun-deck. 204 rooms.

Yeşil Ev ||||
Kabasakal Caddesi 5
Sultanahmet
Tel. (212) 517 6785;
fax (212) 517 6780
One of Istanbul's most famous and popular hotels, set in restored, four-storey wooden mansion behind Blue Mosque. Rooms have Ottoman brass beds and period furniture. Beautiful garden restaurant. 20 rooms.

Beyoğlu (New City)

Büyük Londra ||
Meşrutiyet Caddesi 117
Tepebaşı
Tel. (212) 293 1619;
fax (212) 245 0671
A fine old building uphill from the Pera Palas, and much cheaper. All rooms have private bath, many have balcony overlooking Golden Horn. Decorated in 19th-century Ottoman style. 54 rooms.

Dilson |||
Sıraselviler Caddesi 49
Taksim
Tel. (212) 252 9600;
fax (212) 249 7077
Attractive modern hotel near Taksim Square. All rooms have private bath, air-conditioning and satellite TV. 114 rooms.

Family House ||–|||
Gümüşsuyu Kutlu Sokak 53
Taksim
Tel. (212) 249 7351;
fax (212) 249 9667
An 'apart-hotel' with five apartments. Each has two bedrooms (1 double, 1 twin), living room, kitchen, bathroom and TV. Laundry and baby-sitting service. Ideal for families.

Istanbul Hilton ||||+
Cumhuriyet Caddesi
Harbiye
Tel. (212) 231 4650;
fax (212) 240 4165
Huge luxury hotel complex near Taksim Square with three swimming pools, tennis and squash courts. All rooms have private bath, satellite TV and air-conditioning. 500 rooms.

Pera Palas ||||
Meşrutiyet Caddesi 98/100
Tepebaşı
Tel. (212) 251 4560;
fax (212) 251 4089
City's oldest hotel, built 1892 for Orient Express passengers. Grandiose lobby and bar, beautifully renovated rooms with period atmosphere, all mod cons. Three restaurants, two patisseries. 145 rooms.

Richmond ||||
İstiklal Caddesi 445
Beyoğlu.
Tel. (212) 252 5460;
fax (212) 252 9707
Attractive hotel only five minutes' walk from Tünel top station. All rooms with private bath, satellite TV and air-conditioning. Pleasant Café Lebon next door. 101 rooms.

Star ||
İnönü Caddesi
Sağlık Sokak 11/13
Gümüşsuyu
Tel. (212) 293 1860;
fax (212) 251 7822
Rather drab looking on the outside. Rooms are small but comfortable,

with private shower. Good value for location off Taksim Square, and near Dolmabahçe Palace. 26 rooms.

Yeniğehir Palas ||–|||
Meşrutiyet Caddesi
Oteller Sokak 1/3
Tepebaşı
Tel. (212) 252 7160;
fax (212) 249 7507
Attractive, good-value hotel in central Beyoğlu location. All rooms have private bath, satellite TV and air-conditioning. 137 rooms.

Bosphorus/ Marmara

Bebek ||–|||
Cevdet Paşa Caddesi 113/115
Bebek
Tel. (212) 263 3000;
fax (212) 263 2636
A small, old-fashioned hotel in the middle of the lovely suburb of Bebek, about 10km (6 miles) from city centre. Back rooms enjoy fine view over the Bosphorus. 47 rooms.

Çırağan Palace ||||+
Çırağan Caddesi 84
Beşiktaş
Tel. (212) 258 3377;
fax (212) 259 6687
New luxury hotel in restored 19th-century Ottoman palace on the shores of the Bosphorus. Hotel complex includes health club, sauna, Turkish bath, shopping centre, indoor and outdoor pools. 324 rooms.

Epos ||
Istanbul Caddesi
Havlucular Sokak 3
Bakırköy
Tel. (212) 543 6254;
fax (212) 571 6437
Comfortable and welcoming hotel above coast road near Galleria. All rooms have private shower and air-conditioning. Only ten minutes by taxi from airport. 37 rooms.

Holiday Inn Istanbul ||||
Sahil Yolu
Ataköy
Tel. (212) 560 4110;
fax (212) 559 4905
Luxury hotel overlooking Ataköy Marina and Galleria shopping centre, only 8km (5 miles) from airport. Fitness centre, conference rooms. 170 rooms.

Thrace and Marmara

Bursa

Almira ||||
Ulubatlı Hasan Bulvarı 5
Tel. (224) 250 2020;
fax (224) 250 2038
Huge five-star hotel on main highway at foot of hill, popular with tour groups and convenient for tourists with their own car (garage parking). Full facilities, including rooftop swimming pool, Turkish bath, gym, squash court, casino and nightclub. 235 rooms.

Çelik Palas ||||
Çekirge Caddesi 59
Çekirge
Tel. (224) 233 3800;
fax (224) 236 1910
Bursa's most famous spa hotel, complete with hot spring baths and mineral water on tap in every room. All rooms have five-star facilities. The old wing of the hotel was a favourite retreat of Atatürk's. 173 rooms.

Dikmen |
Maksem Caddesi 7
Tel. (224) 224 1840;
fax (224) 224 1844
A pleasant budget hotel with a garden terrace café-bar, conveniently located in centre of town, near Ulu Camii. Rooms have private bathroom, TV and minibar. 60 rooms.

Aegean Region

Izmir

Baylan |
1299 Sokak No. 8
Basmane
Tel. (232) 483 1426;
fax (232) 483 1498
One of the best of Izmir's budget hotels, in a quiet backstreet only a few minutes' walk from the railway station. All rooms are simply but comfortably furnished, with private bathroom and TV. 33 rooms.

Karaca ||
Necatibey Bulvarı 1379
Sokak No. 55
Tel. (232) 489 1940;
fax (232) 483 1498
A modern and very comfortable hotel with helpful and friendly

staff. All rooms have private bath and air-conditioning, many have large balcony overlooking quiet, palm-lined street. Centrally located a few hundred metres from Cumhuriyet Meydanı, and about 10-15 minutes' walk from Old Bazaar. 73 rooms.

Pullman Etap Konak |||
Mithatpaşa Caddesi 128
Konak
Tel. (232) 289 1500;
fax (232) 289 1709
Four-star hotel overlooking Izmir's pedestrianized central square, convenient for the archaeological and ethnographic museums. Many rooms have fine sea views across the Gulf of Izmir. 76 rooms. (Not to be confused with its 'big brother', the Pullman Etap Izmir on Cumhuriyet Meydanı, which is bigger (168 rooms) and more expensive (||||). Tel. (232) 489 4090; fax (232) 489 4089.)

Selçuk (Ephesus)

Güven |
Atatürk Mahallesi 1002 Sokak
No. 9
Tel. (232) 892 6294;
fax (232) 892 4222
Pleasant budget hotel in town centre. All rooms have private bathrooms, balconies and air-conditioning. A few minutes' walk from museum, and only 3km (2 miles) from Ephesus. 44 rooms.

Hitit |||
Atatürk Caddesi 2
Tel. (232) 892 6007;
fax (232) 892 2490.
Modern, clean and comfortable, with private bathrooms, balconies, TV, air-conditioning and a large swimming pool. On the highway about 1km (½ miles) north of town; 4km (2½ miles) from site of Ephesus, 20km (12 miles) from Kuşadası and Pamucak beach. 96 rooms.

Bodrum

Karia Princess ||||
Canlıdere Sokak No. 15
Tel. (252) 316 8971;
fax (252) 316 8979
A luxury poolside hotel on the hillside above the western bay. All rooms have air-conditioning, satellite TV, balcony and minibar. 52 rooms.

Seçkin Konaklar |
Neyzen Tevfik Caddesi 246
Tel. (252) 316 1351;
fax (252) 316 3336
A delightful little hotel right at the far end of the western bay, near the marina. Rooms with private bathrooms are set in 'villa' blocks around a swimming pool. Friendly bar. 37 rooms, 14 apartments.

Seray |–||
Gümbet Beach
Tel. (252) 316 1969;
fax (252) 316 6739
Attractive family hotel, with balconied rooms (all with private bathroom) ranged around the swimming pool and children's play area. The beach (which has a windsurfing school) is a few minutes' walk away. 50 rooms.

Pamukkale

Kervansaray |
İnönü Caddesi
Pamukkale
Tel. (258) 272 2209
One of the best and most popular of the many inexpensive pensions in the village below the terraces. Double rooms with bathroom, rooftop restaurant, and swimming pool.

Pam |||
Karahayıt Köyü.
Tel. (258) 271 4140;
fax (258) 271 4097.
One of several new hotels to have sprung up a few kilometres to the north of Pamukkale, outside the national park area (the older hotels inside the park are scheduled for demolition as part of a policy to return the terraces to their natural condition.. All rooms have balcony, air-conditioning and private bathroom. 158 rooms.

Mediterranean Coast

Marmaris

Begonya |
Hacı Mustafa Sokak 71
Tel. (252) 412 4095
Inexpensive family-run hotel set in old village house behind gület harbour. Simply furnished rooms with shower/WC, and attractive garden. Closed November to March.

Knidos ▮▮▮
Datça Yolu
Hisarönü Mevkii Çabucak Köyü
Tel. (252) 466 6406;
fax (252) 466 6067
Large, brand-new luxury hotel on secluded private beach about 18km (11 miles) west of Marmaris on the road to Datça. Five-star facilities include watersports, tennis, scuba-diving and sauna. 277 rooms.

Yavuz ▮–▮▮
Atatürk Caddesi 10
Tel. (252) 412 2937;
fax (252) 412 4112
Friendly and comfortable hotel on the waterfront west of town centre, with rooms overlooking the bay. Private bathrooms, rooftop swimming pool, balconies. It has a sister hotel, the Yavuz 2, in İçmeler. 54 rooms.

Fethiye
Dedeoğlu ▮
İskele Meydanı
Tel. (252) 614 4010
Comfortable, good-value hotel on waterfront at far end of town. Rooms have private bathroom, TV and air-conditioning, and there is a swimming pool. 47 rooms.

Pırlanta ▮▮
1 Karagözler Mevkii
Tel. (252) 614 4959;
fax (252) 614 1686
The best hotel in town, set high on the hillside overlooking the marina. All rooms have balconies and private bathrooms, and many enjoy a fine view of the bay. 90 rooms.

Antalya
Sheraton Voyager ▮▮▮▮
100 Yıl Bulvarı
Tel. (242) 243 2432;
fax (242) 243 2462
Perhaps the best of Antalya's many five-star hotels, strikingly situated above the sea on the western edge of the city, but only a couple of km from the city centre. All the luxury you would expect, including 2 swimming pools, 4 tennis courts, watersports, sauna, Jacuzzi, and shopping mall. 409 rooms.

Tütav Türkevleri ▮▮
Mermerli Sokak No. 2
Kaleiçi
Tel. (242) 248 6591;
fax (242) 241 9419

A beautiful and atmospheric hotel set in three restored Ottoman houses tucked behind the city wall above the old harbour. Rooms have period decor and Turkish rugs, private bathrooms, and air-conditioning. 20 rooms.

Alanya
Bedesten ▮▮
İçkale
Tel (242) 512 1234;
fax (242) 513 7934
The best place to stay in town is this restored 12th-century caravanserai near the summit of the castle rock. The rooms are small but comfortable, arranged around the central courtyard; all have private bathrooms. There is a swimming pool, a bar and a dining terrace with spectacular views. 20 rooms.

Antakya
Büyük Antalya ▮▮
Atatürk Caddesi 8
Tel. (326) 213 5860;
fax (326) 213 5869
This good-value four-star establishment is Antakya's top hotel. It is conveniently located only a few minutes' walk from the museum. All rooms have private bathrooms, air-conditioning and TV. 72 rooms.

Central Anatolia

Ankara
Ankara Hilton ▮▮▮▮+
Tahran Caddesi 12
Kavaklıdere
Tel. (312) 468 2888;
fax (312) 468 0909
Five-star luxury in the embassy district on the city's south edge. Indoor swimming pool, Turkish bath, sauna and solarium. 324 rooms.

Best ▮▮▮
Atatürk Bulvarı 195
Tel. (312) 467 0880;
fax (312) 467 0885
Luxurious but reasonably priced hotel about 3km (2 miles) south of Ulus, an easy bus or taxi ride from all the main sights. All rooms with balcony, air-conditioning, satellite TV and minibar. 48 rooms.

Erşan ▮–▮▮
Meşrutiyet Caddesi 13
Kızılay
Tel. (312) 418 9875
Conveniently located in pleasant, modern Kızılay district, with many shops and restaurants near by. Rooms have private bathrooms and TV, but traffic noise can be a problem in rooms overlooking the street. There is limited parking. 64 rooms.

Karyağdı ▮
Sanayi Caddes
Kuruçeşme Sokağı 4
Opera Meydanı
Tel. (312) 310 2440;
fax (312) 312 6712.
Central, good-value accommodation close to Ulus and within 15 minutes walk of the Museum of Anatolian Civilizations. All rooms have private bathrooms, some have TV. There is limited parking. 40 rooms.

Konya
Balıkçılar ▮▮
Mevlana Karşısı No. 1
Tel. (332) 350 9470;
fax (332) 351 3259
Ideally situated in city centre, just across the street from the Mevlana Museum. All rooms have private bathroom, TV and air-conditioning. Fine view from rooftop terrace bar. 48 rooms.

Cappadocia
Alfina ▮
İstiklal Caddesi
Ürgüp Girişi No. 25
Ürgüp
Tel. (384) 341 4822;
fax (384) 341 2424
The rooms in this hotel are carved out of the soft volcanic rock, and have sunny terraces overlooking a courtyard. All rooms have a private shower and WC. 32 rooms.

Perissia ▮▮–▮▮▮
Kayseri Caddesi
PK 68
Ürgüp
Tel. (384) 341 2930;
fax (384) 341 4524
This large, modern, luxury hotel offers all mod cons, including satellite TV, heated swimming pool, tennis courts, rooftop bar and nightclub. 230 rooms.

Black Sea Coast

Sinop
Melia Kasim   I
Gazi Caddesi
Tel. (368) 261 4210
The best hotel in the town centre, set on the waterfront near the main square. All rooms have private bathrooms, some have TV; ask for one with a balcony overlooking the sea.

Giresun
Kit-Tur   I
Arifbey Caddesi 2
Tel. (454) 212 0245;
fax (454) 212 3034
This three-star hotel is the top address in town. All rooms have private bathrooms and TV, those at the front have views over the harbour. 50 rooms.

Trabzon
Usta   I–II
İskele Caddesi
Telegrafhane Sokağı 3
Tel. (462) 321 2195;
fax (462) 322 3793
The three-star Usta is just about the only decent hotel in central Trabzon. All rooms have private bathroom, some have TV. It is located in a quiet side street near Atatürk Alanı. 76 rooms.

Eastern Anatolia

Erzurum
Büyük Erzurum   I–II
Ali Ravi Caddesi No. 5
Tel. (442) 218 6528;
fax (442) 212 2898
The grand old man of Erzurum, now a little frayed around the edges, but still comfortable. All rooms have private bathrooms and balconies, some have TV. Good central location. 50 rooms.

Van
Büyük Urartu   II
Cumhuriyet Caddesi No. 60
Tel. (432) 212 0660;
fax (432) 212 1610
This pleasant, modern hotel is the best choice in central Van. All rooms have private bathroom and TV. 75 rooms.

Şanlıurfa
Harran   I–II
Atatürk Bulvar
Tel. (414) 313 4918; fax (414) 4743
A comfortable hotel situated in the modern city centre, just over a kilometre (½ mile) from the Cave of Abraham. Rooms have air-conditioning, TV and private bathroom, and there is an attractive terrace restaurant. 54 rooms.

Restaurants

Turkish cities and resorts offer a wide range of places where you can eat, from cheap *kebap* stalls to expensive hotel restaurants. However, many of the restaurants in the popular tourist areas suffer from overpriced, mediocre food; for better quality you will have to go up- – or even down- – market.

The inexpensive *kebapçıs* and *köftecis* in the back streets often serve up far tastier meals than the tourist traps, and at half the price. At the other end of the scale, you get what you pay for – exquisitely prepared Ottoman cuisine in the top hotel restaurants, or the freshest of seafood in one of the many waterfront restaurants along the shores of the Aegean and Mediterranean seas.

Chinese and Italian restaurants are growing in popularity in the big cities and coastal resorts, but the food will rarely be as good as the freshly prepared Turkish fare on offer in the neighbouring *kebapçı*.

Below is a list of restaurants recommended by Berlitz; if you find other places worth recommending we'd be pleased to hear from you. As a basic guide we have used the following symbols to give some idea of the price of a three-course meal for two, excluding drinks:

Key
I	below £15 ($20)
II	£15-30 ($20-45)
III	over £30 ($45)

Istanbul

Stamboul (Old City)
Havuzlu   I–II
Gani Çelebi Sokak 3
Kapalı Çarşı
Tel. (212) 527 3346
Enjoy traditional Turkish cuisine in the heart of the Grand Bazaar, at this popular, old-fashioned restaurant. Located next to the post office. Open for lunch only. Closed Sunday.

Lale   III
Merit Antique Hotel
Ordu Caddesi 226
Laleli
Tel. (212) 513 9300 ext 5054
Luxury restaurant serving top-quality Turkish cuisine. The hotel also contains an excellent Chinese restaurant, the Dynasty. Reservations recommended.

Ocakbaşı   II–III
President Hotel
Tiyatro Caddesi 25
Beyazit
Tel. (212) 516 6980
Smart restaurant offering international and Turkish cuisine. Buffet lunch noon to 3pm. In evening, Turkish folk music and belly-dancing. The hotel also has an English-style pub.

Pandeli's   II
Mısr Çarşısı 51
Eminönü
Tel. (212)522 5534
Istanbul favourite located above main entrance to the Spice Bazaar. Famed for its excellent food – fresh fish, grilled meats and Ottoman vegetable dishes. Open lunchtime only. Closed Sunday and holidays.

Pudding Shop   I
Divan Yolu 18
Sultanahmet
Famous backpackers' haunt of the 1960s and 1970s, still doing business. Turkish-style self-service cafeteria, with excellent puddings such as fırın sütlaç (baked rice pudding).

Rami   I–II
Utangaç Sokak
Sultanahmet
Tel. (212) 517 6593
Romantic, candle-lit restaurant set in restored wooden mansion on far side of Blue Mosque from Hippodrome. Seafood and Turkish dishes.

341

Sarnıç II
Soğukçeşme Sokak
Sultanahmet
Tel. (212) 512 4291
*Atmospheric restaurant set amid the
vaults and pillars of a 1,000-year-old
Byzantine cistern. A huge open
fireplace makes this a cosy dinner
spot during winter. International
menu with a few Turkish specialities.*

Yeşil Ev Hotel II
Kabasakal Caddesi 5
Sultanahmet
Tel. (212) 517 6785
*This fine old Ottoman mansion has a
restaurant set in its cool, shady
garden, with tables around a tinkling
fountain. Choice of traditional
Turkish or international dishes.*

Beyoğlu (New City)

Çatı II
İstiklal Caddesi
Orhan A. Apaydın Sokak 20/7
Beyoğlu
Tel. (212) 251 0000
*Pleasant rooftop restaurant (on 7th
floor) popular with locals.
Interesting menu of Turkish and
international dishes, including
unusual Ottoman desserts like
candied tomato with walnut. Closed
Sunday.*

Çiçek Pasajı I
İstiklal Caddesi
Galatasaray
*Not one restaurant, but several,
grouped together along this 19th-
century arcade. Popular with tourists
and locals; you can enjoy a full meal,
or just a snack of fried mussels and
chips washed down with a beer.*

Dört Mevsim II
İstiklal Caddesi 509
Tünel
Tel. (212) 245 8941
*Attractive little restaurant in
unassuming brick-fronted building
near Tünel top station. 19th-century
furnishings, fine Turkish and inter-
national cuisine. Specialities include
French onion soup, crêpes, desserts.*

Galata Kulesi II
Büyük Hendek Caddesi
Şişhane
Tel. (212) 245 1160
*Enjoy the fine views from this
restaurant set at the top of the
Galata Tower. Turkish, French and
international cuisine, with live
music in the evenings.*

Rejans II
Olivya Geçidi 15/17
Galatasaray
Tel. (212) 244 1610
*Famous restaurant founded in the
1930s by White Russians fleeing the
effects of the Russian Revolution.
Excellent menu includes classics
such as bortsch, beef Stroganoff and
chicken Kiev. Closed Sunday.*

Revan III
Sheraton Hotel
Taksim Parkı
Tel. (212) 231 2121
*Luxury rooftop restaurant special-
izing in Ottoman cuisine. If the
menu is too intimidating, you can
opt for the ten-course set dinner, at
a reasonable price.*

Bosphorus

Café Çamlıca II
Büyük Çamlıca Parkı
Ümraniye
Tel. (216) 335 3301
*Beautiful setting in hilltop park
above Üsküdar, highest point in
Istanbul, with view over Bosphorus
to Stamboul and southwest to snow-
capped Uludağ. Standard Turkish
fare.*

Kaptan II
Birinci Caddesi 53
Arnavutköy
Tel. (212) 265 8487
*Former fisherman's restaurant on
the shores of the strait, now a
popular eating place for local
students and ex-pats. Wide selection
of fresh fish straight out of the net.*

Körfez III
Körfez Caddesi 78
Kanlıca
Tel. (216) 413 4314
*Superlative seafood restaurant on the
Asian side of the Bosphorus. If you
call in advance, the owner's boat will
ferry you across the strait. The house
speciality is levrek tuzda (sea bass
baked in salt). Closed Monday.*

Tuğra III
Çırağan Palace Hotel
Çırağan Caddesi 84
Beşiktaş
Tel. (212) 258 3377
*One of the city's newest and most
luxurious restaurants, set in the
sumptuous surroundings of a
restored imperial palace. Diverse
menu of rich Ottoman cuisine.
Closed Monday.*

Urcan III
Ortaçeşme Caddesi 2/1
Sarıyer
Tel. (212) 242 1677
*Famous seafood restaurant, opened
in 1943, and patronized by the rich
and famous (Marlon Brando and
Burt Lancaster have dined here).
Choose your meal from the huge
selection of live fish, lobsters, crabs
and shellfish.*

Ziya III
Muallim Naci Caddesi 109/1
Ortaköy
Tel. (212) 261 6005
*Elegant bar and restaurant with
garden overlooking the Bosphorus;
live jazz in summer. French-
influenced menu; seafood
specialities.*

Thrace and Marmara

Bursa

Adanur Kebapçı I
Ünlü Caddesi
Heykel
Tel. (224) 221 6440
*Situated beyond Atatürk's statue at
east end of main street, this modest
restaurant serves Bursa's speciality,
İskender kebap. Wash it down with a
glass of şıra (grape juice).*

Aegean Region

Izmir

Çin Lokantası I–II
Necatibey Bulvarı 1379
Sokak 57/,
Alsancak
Tel. (232) 425 7357
*Set in a quiet back street next to the
Karaca Hotel (see p.339). The
name means simply 'Chinese
Restaurant', and the menu includes
a selection of popular Chinese
dishes. Good for a change, but
lacking authenticity.*

Deniz II
Izmir Palas Hotel
Vasif Çınar Bulvarı No. 2
Tel. (232) 422 0601/4572
*Elegant seafood restaurant much
frequented by Izmirli business
people at lunch. Waterfront location,
with outdoor tables in summer.*

Deux Mégots   II
Atatürk Caddesi 148/A
Tel. (232) 224 8686
This is an upmarket bistro on the waterfront to the south of Cumhuriyet Meydanı, a popular meeting place for wealthy young Izmirlis. It serves a cosmopolitan selection of light meals, snacks and sandwiches.

Mediterranean Coast

Antalya
Hisar   I–II
Kaleiçi
Tel. (242) 241 2198
An atmospheric restaurant, set in a series of vaulted chambers in the fortress walls above the old harbour, and serving traditional grilled meats, fish and mezes. Try to get one of the tables with a view over the harbour.

Yedi Mehmet   I
Konyaaltı Beac
Kenan Evren Bulvarı
Tel. (242) 241 1641
An excellent Turkish restaurant on the beach below the Archaeological Museum (see p.224); the perfect place to head after a morning of browsing through the museum displays. The menu is standard Turkish fare, but is fresh and appealing.

Antakya
Han   I
Saray Caddesi
Old Quarter
To find this restaurant, cross the bridge from the museum and head right along Hürriyet Caddesi. Go upstairs to the Aile Salonu (Family Room), a pleasant, shady courtyard. Excellent grills and mezes – try the şato piliç, a grilled patty of ground chicken, tomato, hot peppers and herbs, with melted cheese in the middle. Mint leaves and lemon slices are served on the side – an Arabic touch.

Central Anatolia

Ankara
Akman Boza ve Pasta Salonu   I
Atatürk Bulvarı 3
Ulus
An attractive lunch spot just south of the Atatürk statue in Ulus Meydanı, with outdoor tables set around a terrace garden in a courtyard. The menu includes pastries, sandwiches and light meals, plus the traditional drink called boza, *made from fermented millet.*

Boyacızade Konağı   II
Berrak Sokak No. 7/9
Hisar
Tel. (312) 310 2525
Set in a large, restored, 19th-century Ottoman mansion, with a garden terrace offering spectacular views of the city. The food is traditional Turkish cuisine, including Central Anatolian specialities such as mantı *(a kind of ravioli).*

Körfez   I
Bayındır Sokak 24
Kızılay
Tel. (312) 131 1459
An attractive and good-value restaurant with sidewalk terrace, serving kebaps, grilled meats, mezes and seafood accompanied by traditional unleavened bread, freshly baked. There are Black Sea specialities such as lagos güveç *(whitefish stew) and* hamsi *(fresh anchovies), and a good selection of wines.*

Vera   II
Ahmet Mihtat Efendi Sokağı 26/A
Çankaya
Tel. (312) 441 2399
Ankara's only Russian restaurant. Russian specialities such as bortsch *beef Stroganoff,* blinis *(pancakes) and caviar are served in a small dining room with attractive classical decor (outside tables in summer).*

Yeni Hamsiköy   I–II
Tunalı Hilmi Caddesi
Bestekar Sokak 13
Kavaklıdere
Tel. (312) 427 7576
This attractive terrace restaurant in the upmarket Kavaklıdere district specializes in cuisine from Turkey's Black Sea coast, especially fresh anchovies (hamsi) *and other seafood dishes.*

Konya
Sifa   I
Mevlana Caddesi No. 9/F
Tel. (332) 352 0519
A clean, bright and inexpensive restaurant offering Konya specialities such as fırın kebap *(roast mutton) and etli ekmek (a large, thin piece of* pide *bread topped with minced mutton and hot peppers).*

Black Sea Coast

Trabzon
Zindan   I–II
Atapark Zağanos Burcu
Tel. (462) 322 3259
A relatively new restaurant set in the Zağanos Tower, a bastion in the medieval walls of the old fortress. The menu is traditionally Turkish, with some Black Sea specialities such as hamsili omlet *(omelette with fresh anchovies).*

Eastern Anatolia

Erzurum
Güzelyurt   I
Cumhuriyet Caddesi
Tel. (442) 218 1514/9222
This is the best restaurant in town, established in 1928, with friendly black-jacketed waiters and heavy pink tablecloths. The speciality is mantarlı güveç, *a stew of tender lamb, mushrooms, sweet peppers, tomatoes, onions, garlic and black pepper served sizzling in a blackened clay dish, and drizzled with melting cheese. It is also one of the very few restaurants in town where you will be able to buy alcohol.*

Index

References to illustrations are in *italic*; those in **bold** refer to main entries; those with an asterisk refer to maps.

INDEX

Discover the world
with **BERLITZ**®

Australia
Britain
Brittany
California
Canada
Egypt
Europe
Florida
France
Germany
Greece
Ireland
Israel
Italy
Kenya
Loire Valley
New England
Normandy
Portugal
Prague
Pyrenees
Rome
Singapore
Spain
Switzerland
Turkey
Thailand
Tuscany

IN PREPARATION

Scandinavia

BERLITZ DISCOVER GUIDES do more than just map out the sights – they entice you to travel with lush full-colour photography, vivid descriptions and intelligent advice on how to plan and enjoy your holiday or travel experience. Covering the world's most popular destinations, these full-colour travel guides reveal the spirit and flavour of each country or region. Use *DISCOVER* as a travel planner or as a practical reference guide. You'll find sightseeing information and suggested leisure routes, extensive full-colour maps and town plans, local hotel and restaurant listings plus special essays highlighting interesting local features. Colourful historical and cultural background is complemented by practical details such as what to visit and where to stay, where to eat and how much you should expect to pay.

No matter where you're going, make the most of your trip:

DISCOVER the world with BERLITZ.